So you want to be a journalist?

ONE WEEK LOAN

So you want to be a journalist? is a practical hands-on guide to the world of journalism, particularly for the beginner. It contains step-by-step instructions on writing for the news media, as well as sound advice and suggestions on all facets of reporting. It covers the basic skills of:

- research and investigation
- interviewing
- writing news and feature material
- basic subediting and layout and design
- the essentials of grammar, spelling and punctuation
- relevant laws
- understanding and calculating data
- print, radio, television and online reporting
- ethical and professional behaviour.

The book demonstrates its points with many examples of fine writing and reporting in the very best traditions of journalism by some of the hundreds of students who have worked with the author over many years. It also shows what excellent work student reporters can produce, despite not having the resources of large news organisations behind them. It not only reveals how to do it, but also shows what can be achieved. *So you want to be a journalist?* is the book no student or novice journalist can afford to be without.

Bruce Grundy is Adjunct Professor in the School of Journalism and Communication at the University of Queensland. He has been a journalist for over 40 years, and has taught practical and theory courses in television, radio and print journalism since 1979.

So you want to be a
journalist?

Bruce Grundy

 **CAMBRIDGE**
UNIVERSITY PRESS

CAMBRIDGE UNIVERSITY PRESS
Cambridge, New York, Melbourne, Madrid, Cape Town, Singapore, São Paulo

Cambridge University Press
477 Williamstown Road, Port Melbourne, VIC 3207, Australia

Published in the United States of America by Cambridge University Press, New York

www.cambridge.org
Information on this title: www.cambridge.org/9780521690492

First published 2007

Printed in Australia by Ligare Book Printers

A catalogue record for this publication is available from the British Library

National Library of Australia Cataloguing in Publication data
    Grundy, Bruce.
    So you want to be a journalist?
    Bibliography.
    Includes index.
    ISBN-13   978-0-52169-049-2 paperback
    ISBN-10   0-52169-049-8 paperback
    1. Journalism.   I. Title.
070.4

ISBN-13   978-0-52169-049-2
ISBN-10   0-52169-049-8

Cover photo: © Stephen Cooper/Newspix
Cover design: Design by Committee

Contents

Acknowledgments

For more than 25 years I have had the chance to work with a host of talented young and not-so-young people who made my life at the University of Queensland one to be envied. To teach them whatever I could was a privilege, to learn from them humbling, to be inspired by them rewarding, and at times to be left beaming and rejoicing at the things they did and the stories they wrote was simply, as they would say, "awesome". There are too many to name, but they will know who they are. My grateful thanks to each one of them. And to think, semester after semester, group after group, we maintained a great team spirit as well – and even had fun! What more could one ask?

To the various members of staff with whom I worked at UQ, again too many to mention, my thanks for your contribution to the "cause" and for the contribution you made to my knowledge of journalism and therefore your contribution to this book. I can only hope the product matches the contributions you made to it.

There are many others who helped in all kinds of ways. Staff in many departments in the university, my various bosses for supporting our efforts to do some good journalism, journalists and editors in the business in various parts of the country and supporters of the papers we produced for more than a decade.

Some should be named – and probably deserve awards: Grant Dobinson, for effort beyond the call of duty in teaching me what I know about computers and how to make them do things; Bob Bottom and Evan Whitton, for the challenges and example they set through their journalism and their books and for the unfailing light they shed on the matter of what journalism is about; one who must remain unnamed for his encouragement to go on when there was no shortage of discouragement to do so; Mark Jones and his staff at Biggs and Biggs, who provided great support and equally great advice (for nothing, bless them) which kept the defamation writs at bay; and the guys on the floor and in the plate room at Rural Press who always managed to get the paper printed even if we messed up.

There are some of the team who will never be forgotten: Jason, for his remarkable reporting in the first year of the *Weekend Independent*; Paula, for what is still the most extraordinary example of sustained, quality and defiant journalism I have had the pleasure to be associated with as a teacher; Chris, who in an extraordinary effort sat at night for the equivalent of a week in a Datsun 120Y and kept a diary of how security firms were not fulfilling their contracts with the businesses that employed them; George, who among other things nailed a lie that the population had been fed for almost a decade; Susann, who not only chased some of our major stories but who made the Justice Project (justiceproject.net) possible; Alyssa, who also gave them hell, kept the Justice Project running and made me laugh whenever that was necessary; the wonderful Eleanor, without whom the *Independent Monthly* would almost certainly never have made deadline; and Henrik, who also volunteered his knowledge and time to assist the cause. And that's only a few. Extraordinary young people. How lucky I was.

Throughout much of the last 16 years there was Kevin Lindeberg, whose fight to see honesty, integrity and justice prevail was nothing short of monumental. He was an inspiration and a source of energy to pursue a story that is now recognised internationally as one of the great public administration scandals of the twentieth century: Australia's *J'Accuse*. Without his dogged determination I would not have had the raw material nor the drive to chase the story and help unravel as much of it as we have.

My long-suffering family has had to cope with this odyssey, and with the various publications I have edited and superintended. Who knows how many phone calls cornered so much of my time, and the wild goose chases I went on looking for people who did not even exist because the names I had been given were wrong, and the thousands of kilometres trying to find some victim of abuse at the hands of one of the Churches or the State. These trips and activities were vital to me. They meant I could still say I was a journalist and those in my classes could know that maybe I could justify standing up in front of them making noises about journalism. Brother Geof was always there, constantly encouraging, but most unhappy that I should write this book instead of the one about the odyssey. Merle and Melissa and Lindsay just put up with it, did whatever I asked and let me get on with the job. They missed out on who knows how many weekends and how many nights when deadlines came around, but did not complain. Without their consideration there would have been no *Weekend Independent* and no *Independent Monthly* and no *Inside Queensland*, and the stories of so many kids who suffered such appalling abuse would never have been told.

This book is dedicated to them, and to the students who worked with me side by side.

Finally, I wish to acknowledge the support, courtesy and help I received from everyone at Cambridge University Press. It was a pleasure to work with such professional and considerate people. Thanks in particular to Jill Henry, Kate Indigo and the absolutely amazing Helena Bond.

Introduction

This book does not contain everything one needs to know to be a journalist. No book could do that. It would have to contain everything there is to know about everything, and that is a tall order. But it is the kind of book I wish had been around when I was starting out. Back then there was precious little training. You sank or you swam. You found out what to do by listening and watching and reading what others did. Your eyes and ears told you what was good and what was bad. Sometimes you would be given some advice, but not much explanation.

In a way that kind of experience was, indeed, a good teacher. It made you think about what you were doing, about what was good and what was no good and why. It made you think about what made sense and what didn't, what was logical and what wasn't, what worked and what flopped. And in the end, it seems, I swam.

Then came another most useful experience. I started teaching what I had been doing for 20 years to those who were just starting out. The classroom was not a newsroom. The classroom was a university, so it was no good saying: Do it this way because I am the boss and if you don't do it this way you can find another job. Students wanted to know, quite correctly, why? Why do we have to do it this way – or that? Is there an explanation? Or is it just a convention? If it's a convention, why is it a convention? The "why" questions had to be answered.

The short answer to the "why" questions is, in fact, another question. Here it is – and it's worth remembering. Do you want to communicate with your audience or don't you? That is the explanation, in as few words as possible, behind all the suggestions made in this book. My suggestions do not necessarily match the style of every news outlet in the country. That is not possible because there are different rules in different newsrooms. But all my suggestions are based on the fundamental notion that everything you do as a reporter should be done to ensure the reader or listener or viewer gets the message, whatever it is, clearly and precisely without any need to struggle with your words. For that outcome, some discipline will be needed. Some rules even.

Young people, I have found, often have a problem accepting that things should be done in a certain way. They find it a nuisance, time-consuming, and constricting of their talents and creativity. All of which may be true. But on the bookshelf behind me as I write is a copy of a quite thick book (over 400 pages) that simply has the words "Style manual" printed large on its spine. In fact, the full title is *Style manual for authors, editors and printers* and while primarily "written with Commonwealth government publications in mind" (p. xi), it is widely used elsewhere. At one point the book says this:

> The purpose of writing is to convey to another person what is in the writer's mind. 'Good writing', therefore, is writing which does this effectively. Every organisation needs to encourage good writing for at least three reasons. Firstly, it is efficient: if what is in the writer's mind is conveyed effectively, time will not be wasted in sorting out misunderstandings. Secondly, it is economical: efficient communication saves both time and money. Thirdly, good writing gives a good impression of the organisation (p. 3).

If all of that is true for people who write memos and reports and position papers to be read by others who get paid to read them, how much more relevant are those words for the journalist whose readers are volunteers who have no obligation to read even a single word of what has been written?

Newspapers are a good example. People read newspapers for all kinds of reasons. People read bits of newspapers for all kinds of reasons. Sport, for example, and business. Some read the ads, some the comics. Some are keen on motoring, or fashion. And so on. Some read them for the news they contain. And some read them for stories about people and places and things that may have little to do with the news. Some don't read them at all.

Newspapers today are very conscious of the importance of all of the above. For the journalist this means, more than ever, that being a good reporter and meeting deadlines and being accurate and so on is not enough. Reporters have to be good writers too.

Newspapers are acutely aware that there are, in the main, two kinds of readers out there: those who are pressed for time and those who are not. The time poor and the time rich, if you like. Most days of the week, the first group is rushing. Work, school, kids, meals, dancing lessons, football training, homework, whatever. The second group is not. They have a little time; they are not so pressed. The time poor want to know what has happened in the world as quickly as possible. The time rich want that too, but they want more from a newspaper – a good read. They want something that is not just informative but also enjoyable.

This book will deal with writing for both groups of readers. And it will deal with the other things a journalist needs to know. Of that there is a great deal.

The library shelves are full of books that talk about what journalists and their news organisations do. This is not one of those books. This is a book about **how** to do it. This is a book for the student journalist, for someone starting out in the business, for someone who wants to be a journalist and wants to be shown the way. Whether the budding journalist will eventually get a job will be another matter. Much will depend on the individual. But he or she will know what to do. And, importantly, why.

The material in this book draws on the experiences of 45 years doing it and 25 years teaching it. In particular, I wish to record the contribution of thousands of young people who have sat in my classrooms or newsrooms and who, for over a dozen years, helped produce the material that made *The Weekend Independent* and *The Independent Monthly* newspapers at the University of Queensland such excellent publications. I have included examples of their work in the book as an encouragement to other young people.

One final point to consider. Journalism comes in many forms and fulfils many functions in our society. At the heart of the matter, though, is one central issue never to be forgotten – journalism is an essential ingredient in that complex and all too vulnerable social structure we call democracy. Unless we remember that, we are all in trouble.

PART 1

Getting started in journalism

Writing news for newspapers

Where to start?

It has become fashionable recently to claim that traditional news media forms   newspapers, radio and television – are finished, and that the new world is all about the internet. The currency this view has gained has even reached a stage where it is suggested that knowing how to report for traditional media is no longer relevant. Not only is reporting for the internet claimed to be the only relevant form of journalism, but it is also suggested that reporting for the internet requires its own special form of journalism.

It is all nonsense, of course. Although the internet is important and is having an impact on them, traditional media are not finished just yet.

Despite fierce competition from radio, television and the net, figures show that Australians actually pay for close to 22 million metropolitan, provincial, country, rural and ethnic newspapers each week. (Audit Bureau of Circulations report 2006). And while for some of them circulations are certainly down on what they used to be, these papers contain more pages than ever. As well, an untold number of free papers are given away each week and millions still watch the news on TV and listen to it on radio. The net is a challenge for all of them but from the point of view of journalism the forms in which material appears on the internet are those same forms that exist in traditional news media.

If you can't write a news story for a newspaper or for a radio or TV bulletin, you will not be able to write one for the internet. And if you can't report a story (get information, find sources, marshal facts, collect opinions, sift chaff from wheat, and so on) for a traditional media outlet, you will not be able to do so in the brave new world of the internet. What's more, the internet is overflowing with garbage. Anyone who can scratch together the funds to claim a domain name has a site, and then fills it with stuff which, in most cases, is of totally unknown reliability or credibility.

The real point about the internet is this: knowing how to turn out your stories in one form (print, radio or television) may have been enough in the past but it may not be enough in the future. The internet certainly demands a range of skills. However, everything in these pages will serve you well for a career in journalism – whether you work online, in print, radio or television.

Being able to write for newspapers is a good place to start. Indeed, it is the best place to start. Since I ended up in newspapers, having started in radio and then television, I feel well qualified to say so. The discipline involved in writing for newspapers will help you wherever you go. So don't skip the pages that deal with newspapers because you are only interested in radio or TV. That would be a serious mistake.

The inverted pyramid

Journalism textbooks refer to the style journalists use when writing what they call "hard" news stories as the "inverted pyramid" style. It is a reasonable description. They might have called it all kinds of other things that indicate a hierarchy of significance, or a tapering off of importance, but "inverted pyramid" has stuck, so that will do.

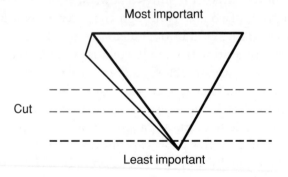

The inverted pyramid just means that what is new, what has just happened, what is most significant, what is most interesting, comes first. The least important comes last.

There are a number of reasons why the inverted pyramid became the accepted conventional style for writing news.

Reason 1: Putting the news first

The first and most obvious reason recognises the importance of the reader, particularly the busy reader, the time-poor reader, in the business of publishing news. The inverted pyramid puts the news – what has happened – at the beginning of the story. Busy readers can discover in a paragraph or two what has happened. If they are interested in the story, there is more to read. If not, at least they have the crux of the story and can move on to something else. The interested reader can go all the way to the end.

But there are other reasons why the inverted pyramid became conventional news style.

Reason 2: Wire services

It's not just that there are all kinds of readers out there with all kinds of interests who will have varying degrees of attachment to stories, but the wire services and news agencies that provide copy to all kinds of news outlets have all kinds of subscribers too – and they have different levels of interest in the stories as well.

Some may want every word, and splash all of them over the front page. Some may have no interest in a story whatsoever and ignore it completely. Others may use a couple of pars in a column of news briefs at the back of the paper, while some may run 15 or 20 centimetres on an early general news page.

Significantly, the inverted pyramid style covers all possibilities. The news is at the top; what has happened is at the beginning. After that, the story trails off. Those who want it all, take it all. The rest can cut it from the bottom up, taking 20 cm or 10, or maybe just the first two pars. The most important, the new, is at the top. So by cutting from the bottom, the most important is not lost. The way the story is written suits everyone.

> ### Pars explained
>
> The terms "paragraphs" and "sentences" are not ones you will encounter often in a newsroom. The term journalists use is "pars". A "par" is a sentence. So, if you are asked to write 20 pars on a story, write 20 sentences. Journalists also talk about "words" (as in "Give us a few more words", or "Do us 500 words"), or "centimetres", which means column centimetres. But you will seldom hear them talk about "paragraphs" or "sentences".

Reason 3: The production process

The inverted pyramid also became the conventional style for writing news because it suits the news production process.

A story is written and placed on a page. Then something happens that should be in the paper too. It may replace the first story completely, but if both should be in the paper, the first can be cut from the bottom without completely destroying it to make some space for the second story.

This can be done with minimal fuss. Both stories are in the paper, not as much of the first as originally planned, but never mind: the crucial bits of the story are still there. Because they were at the top of the story.

If the first story had **not** been written in the inverted pyramid style, cutting it from the bottom to shorten it, without rewriting it completely, may have produced nonsense. The news, the most important parts, may have been lost.

Cutting an inverted pyramid story from the bottom can be done in a trice. Rewriting a whole story takes somewhat longer. Here is a typical inverted pyramid news story. It could be cut anywhere, as indicated by the dotted lines.

High tech trial in fight against drugs, bombs and weapons

Australia's most advanced security scanner will be trialled at Brisbane International Airport early next year to help in the fight against the illegal importation of weapons, drugs and explosives.

- -

The neutron scanner, developed jointly by the Commonwealth Scientific and Industrial Research Organisation (CSIRO) and Customs, will replace existing X-ray scanners used to detect illegal explosives, drugs and weapons in air-freight containers.

- -

Customs spokesperson Amanda Palmer said the large containers currently had to be unpacked to allow their contents to be individually processed.

- -

The neutron scanner would allow the contents of an entire container to be identified in several minutes, Ms Palmer said.

- -

"There will be a huge upgrade in terms of the time it will take," she said.

- -

CSIRO spokesperson Meg Reeve said the technology had originally been developed to scan ore samples for the mining industry.

- -

Customs recognised its potential as a border protection tool and approached CSIRO to jointly develop the technology, Ms Reeve said.

- -

"X-ray scanners were able to pick up objects based only on their density and shape," she said.

- -

"Ours allows them to build a whole image of the scanned object."

Ms Reeve said construction had begun on the scanner at CSIRO's Lucas Heights facility in Sydney.

(M Chase, *The Independent Monthly*, May 2004, p. 3)

How to tell a (news) story

The difference between a story and a news story is quite simple. A story starts at the beginning and works its way to the end. A news story starts at the end and works its way back toward the beginning.

The following example is not an attempt to trivialise. It is an illustration that has helped countless students grasp the essential requirement of writing news – getting what is new, first. Here is the story. You may recognise it.

The beginning:

Once upon a time there were three bears – a father bear, a mother bear and a baby bear. They lived in a house in the woods. On the edge of the woods lived a little girl called Goldilocks. One day Goldilocks went for a walk in the woods.

The ending:

Goldilocks ran as fast as she could and reached the edge of the woods just in time. She never went into the woods alone again.

And here is how that same story would appear as a news story – an inverted pyramid story:

Girl escapes angry bears

A young Forest Glen girl escaped unharmed today when she was chased through the woods by three angry bears.

The girl, 10-year-old Goldi Locks, was resting at her Primrose Street home this afternoon recovering from her ordeal.

Ms Locks told reporters she had gone for a walk in the woods, but had become very tired and hungry.

She said she found a cottage in the woods and went to sleep in an upstairs bedroom.

Some time later she was wakened by three angry bears who began threatening her.

> She said she escaped by jumping out a first floor window.
>
> However, Ms Locks said, the bears had pursued her and she had just managed to reach the edge of the woods in time.
>
> "I will never go into the woods alone again," Ms Locks said.
>
> A spokesperson for the Forest Glen Wildlife Conservation Group said the bears were there first and people should treat wild animals with caution and respect.

The same structure applies to any inverted pyramid story. Get the news up front. As above. The reader, or a faraway subeditor, can cut such stories wherever he or she likes – after the second par, in the middle, wherever.

The whole point of the inverted pyramid is the recognition that news is principally about what has happened. That is what people want to know. How much they might want to know then becomes a matter of choice. But even the casual reader who scans just a bit of the story will know the basics of it. Those who read more will find out some, or all, of the detail as well.

The formula

There is a formula to writing a simple inverted pyramid news story. It's a checklist really. If you follow it, you should be able to write a publishable story immediately. The elements, the ingredients if you like, that you have to get right are these:

1. accuracy
2. no comment or opinions
3. the lead
4. sources
5. logic
6. background
7. attribution
8. tense
9. voice
10. punctuation
11. sentence length.

> In terms of "newswriting", or "writing news", the first six headings are about "the news", the remainder about "the writing".

1 Accuracy

Accuracy is clearly non-negotiable. Don't make things up, don't make wild guesses, don't rely on a fuzzy memory, spell correctly, get the names of people and places right, quote your sources accurately, not approximately. And so on. These are not just matters of professionalism. There can be serious legal consequences if you are careless about accuracy.

2 No comment or opinions

Until you have a recognised reputation or some expertise, no comment or opinions please. For the moment, your job is to report, not comment. Until you get the job of writing the leaders, editorials or opinion pieces for the paper, leave the pulpit and the soapbox at home.

It is important, legally, that comment be separated from reporting. That will be discussed in the chapter on the Law. So it's as well to realise that if you mix the two, there could be a legal issue to wrestle with.

If necessary make it clear that controversial views are not yours. It can be done very easily in print. Put quote marks around the words involved. It's a little harder in radio and television reporting, where quote marks effectively disappear, but this will be covered in chapter 2.

Back to the list above. Until it becomes second nature, check your stories against this list. If you have these elements right, your story should be publishable without anyone having to fix it, or fix much of it.

It may not have much flair, but let's get the basics right before we start worrying about flair.

3 The lead

Getting the lead to a story right is vital in writing news stories. The lead may be all some people will read. The lead may convince others to read on.

There are six essentials that need to be addressed (some to a greater or lesser degree) when writing a news story: five Ws and an H – **who**, **what**, **where**, **when**, **why** and **how**.

> Unless specifically referenced, examples in this section have been prepared for illustrative purposes only and do not represent actual events or refer to actual people.

But the most important of them is **what**. If the novice reporter remembers nothing else, this is the essential issue in writing leads, and thus news stories. What is it that has happened? What is happening? What is expected to happen? What was said? Here is an example:

> Pharmacies are being inundated with requests for bird flu vaccine and stocks are running low.   (J London, *The Independent Monthly*, October 2005, p. 1)

In fifteen words on a very important topic the reporter told her readers precisely **what** was happening in their community.

When you are covering an incident or an event (an accident, a fire, a football match), the **what** is obvious. It is what you saw in front of you. It is what happened. Or it is what other people saw, because they were there at the time and told you what took place. At a parade, a football match, a fire, a war – the **what** that has happened will not be hard to find. There may be a range of options, of course, because several things might have happened. As the reporter, you will have to choose. Making choices is what journalists do all the time. It is a very powerful position to be in. What you choose not to report, in effect, has not happened.

But the **what** is important in circumstances other than the event or incident.

Even in the case of someone giving a speech or a press conference, the essential issue will be: **what** was it that was said? That will be the lead. The issue is almost never that someone (the **who**) gave a speech, or the place where it was given (the **where**), or the day or time it was given (the **when**), or even the reason (the **why**) or the manner in which (the **how**) it was given – despite the importance of these things.

Certainly these other Ws and the H can make a lead, but not often. For example, your newspaper story could begin:

> The Prime Minister addressed a gathering of drought-weary farmers in Whereverville last night.

You would be reporting accurately, of course. But the farmers did not go all the way to town just to get a glimpse of the Prime Minister. They can see him on the television every other night. They went to town to tell him something, or to hear what he had to say. And that is what your news story has to reflect. **What** did they tell him? Or **what** did he say to them?

So, the issue is not the who, or the where, or the when (or the how or the why), because the important issue is what is missing from that sentence . . . the **what**. What was it the Prime Minister said in his address to those drought-weary farmers?

Thus, it is not just incident or event stories that demand the **what** lead. Even in the case of somebody saying something, it is **what** was said that is important – and that is the lead. So, the story becomes:

> An extra $200 million would be earmarked for drought relief, the Prime Minister told a gathering of worried farmers in Whereverville last night.

The questions to ask to find the **what**, and thus the lead are very simple:

1. What is it that has **happened**?
2. What is it that was **said**?
3. What happened that is **new**?
4. What happened, or what was said, that **may interest the reader**?

For example:

> The Forest Glen Conservation Society held its annual flower show yesterday.

This may well be true. And, in answer to question one, it certainly is what happened. But such a lead is hardly likely to attract much attention from readers who are not members of the society.

So, tell the reader something **interesting** that happened. Was the show a success/flop because of the drought/flood? Were entries a record? Did a visiting judge from somewhere say it was the best exhibition of some-things she had ever seen? How many attended? Who scooped the pool of awards? Who won Grand Champion? Or any number of other options that would almost certainly produce a more interesting **what** than the lead above.

Why be boring when you can be interesting? What has happened is fine, what is interesting about what has happened is best.

Of course, any number of things can happen when a newsworthy event occurs. Any number of **whats** if you like. But some will be more significant than others. In the end, you will have to decide which is the most significant, or interesting, or relevant to your readership. For example, here is an outline of a fictitious, but all too common news event:

1. Two vehicles collide head-on on the Hungerford Highway 12 km north of Palm Bluff.
2. One was a four-wheel-drive Overlander.
3. The other was an Orion sedan.
4. A family of four (man, woman and two children) returning from holiday was in the Overlander.
5. Three teenagers were in the Orion.
6. Ambulance and Fire and Rescue crews had to use heavy cutting equip-ment to release some of those involved from the wreckage.
7. All were taken to hospital.
8. Despite the efforts of ambulance officers, two of the teenagers died before they reached the hospital.

So now you have to write the story. What happened? You have to choose the **what**. You might decide:

> Two vehicles collided head-on on the Hungerford Highway, 12 kilometres north of Palm Bluff, yesterday.
>
> One of the vehicles, a four-wheel-drive, was carrying a family of four returning from holiday.
>
> Three teenagers were in the second vehicle, a small sedan.
>
> Ambulance and Fire and Rescue crews at the scene had to use heavy cutting equipment to free some of those involved from the wreckage.
>
> All were taken to the Western Region Base Hospital, but two of the teenagers died on the way.

That story certainly starts with a **what**. But is it the most significant **what**? Hardly.

The inverted pyramid structure says the most important goes first. Therefore, an inverted pyramid story would put the deaths of the two teenagers at the beginning of the story, not at the end. The other details would follow.

If the question is: "What is the lead?" The answer is: "**What** is the lead." The significance of the **what** cannot be overemphasised. For example, here are all the other ingredients of a news story, **minus** the **what**:

> A five-year-old boy (*who*) . . . bird flu (*how*), health officials (*who again*) in central Thailand (*where*) confirmed yesterday (*when*).

We have lots of important information, four Ws and an H, but the crucial bit, the **what**, is missing. Without it, all the important information makes no sense at all. The vital, missing bit could be: "is the latest victim of"; or "has died from"; or "is recovering from". Depending on which of these alternatives is the case, very different stories emerge.

The point is, without the **what**, the other Ws and the H do not make a news story. With the **what**, you have a story:

> A five-year-old boy has died from (*what*) bird flu, health officials in central Thailand confirmed yesterday.

The **what** is often a critical verb. Finding the really important verb can be the way to finding the lead. The critical verb in this case is "died". And that was the basis of the lead in this story. But the **what** might have been a critical noun as in:

> A five-year-old boy is the latest victim of bird flu, health officials in central Thailand confirmed yesterday.

Now here's another example. All the ingredients for a news story are present, except one:

> In Canberra (*where*) today (*when*) the Prime Minister (*who*) said he had acted in accordance with Australia's international treaty obligations (*how*) because the country's national interest demanded an immediate response (*why*).

This could never be the lead to a story. It might be a second par, but never a lead, even though all the other ingredients are present. The problem is that it does not contain the **what**: what it was that the PM had done.

So, when you sit down with your notebook or your tape recorder to write a story, don't worry about searching for the **who**, **when**, **where**, **why** or **how**. Search for the **what**. That is where your story will be. You will need some of the others, if not all of them, but the shape and content of the story will be determined by what you decide is the **what**.

Finding the lead

Finding the lead to your story will depend on two things: who you are writing for, and what you know when you file your story.

For example, let's say a group of journalists attends an incident or news event. It is possible, but unlikely, that the leads to their stories will all be the same. One of them works for a radio station and has to file immediately. Another is a TV news reporter, who has several hours to deadline and can do some checking with other sources and ask some interesting questions about what happened. A third writes for a national newspaper, a fourth for a metropolitan, a fifth for a local suburban, a sixth for an out-of-town provincial daily, a seventh for a business paper, an eighth for a wire service, and so on.

They all have different audiences, different readerships, and will write their stories with that reality in mind. And so they should. You must not forget who your readers are. The leads could all be different. So it is wrong to conclude that there is only one lead to a story. There may be, because the story is just so important. But there may be more than one. There usually is. You will have to choose.

How to choose? It can be hard to go past the obvious: what happened?

> Three members of one family died when their home in Whereverville burned down last night.

Struggling to find another angle to a story about three members of the one family perishing in a house fire may produce little reward. Indeed, the result may be downright silly:

> Fire crews took an hour to put out a fire which destroyed a home in Whereverville last night.
> Officers said the fire was so fierce they had no hope of rescuing three of the occupants trapped inside.

But it all depends. If you learned that the lives of the three had recently been threatened – or someone had acted with enormous bravery trying to save them – you might go with a different lead:

> A firefighter risked his life to save a woman trapped in a house fire in Whereverville last night.
> The woman's husband and two of her children perished in the blaze.

And if there are numerous choices, such as you might encounter covering 15 parallel sessions at a major international conference, different reporters may produce quite different leads and quite different stories and they could all be appropriate. By the same token it is quite possible that they will all seize on the very same address or paper – and produce similar stories – because what was said was so significant.

Nevertheless, it is hard to say that there is only one way to write a particular story. What can be said, however, is that there are many wrong ways. Some wrong ways include: not having the latest, or the most important, or the most interesting and significant, as the lead. For example:

> A man appeared in the Whereverville District Court today charged with the unlawful killing of his father.

Which is satisfactory – as long as the man did not enter a plea. If he did, the story should have read:

> A 25-year-old man pleaded not guilty in the Whereverville District Court today to a charge of having unlawfully killed his father.

The "plea" is more significant than the "appearance". (And while we are on the subject, there is no such word in English as "pled". It does not exist. The word is "pleaded".)

But if the man had pleaded guilty, this could still be the wrong lead, because the judge may well have sentenced him – and the story then should have read:

> A Whereverville man was sentenced to 10 years jail today for killing his father.

The sentence handed down by the judge is more important than the plea.

Angles

Journalists call the different "takes" on a story that one might choose to lead with, "angles".

"What angle are you taking?" is an expression frequently heard when journalists discuss a common story. Or a chief of staff might stipulate an "angle" when assigning a story to a reporter.

Different "angles" may or may not be obvious at the outset of a reporting assignment. But certainly different options usually open up as the minutes tick by and new developments related to a story occur or emerge. Here are some examples:

Angle 1 A 10-year-old girl escaped unharmed yesterday when she was chased through the woods by three savage bears.

Angle 2 The relieved mother of a 10-year-old girl who yesterday just managed to out-run three fierce bears has warned parents not to let their children play in the Taringa Woods.

Angle 3 Angry residents of Primrose Street have called on the state government to cull the bear population in the Taringa Woods.

Angle 4 Animal rights and conservation groups have sprung to the defence of a group of bears that chased a terrified girl through the Taringa Woods yesterday afternoon.

Angle 5 Police are investigating claims that a girl who was chased through the Taringa Woods yesterday afternoon by three angry bears had smashed some of their furniture and taken food from their kitchen without permission.

The newspaper reporter will have to choose which angle to go with because, more than likely, there will be only one story published. The radio reporter, with bulletins on the hour every hour and updates in between, might file several stories about a single event and cover various "angles".

For the reporter, getting the "angle" right is a matter of judgment. There is another word for it (two words actually): news sense.

There will be times when one angle will be as good as another. But not that many. For example, if, a week after strenuously defending its tough mandatory detention policy toward illegal immigrants, the government releases most of them, and you lead with "Good news for detainees" while everyone else goes with "Backflip over detainees", it might be obvious you missed something.

One good way to get your lead right is to know who your audience is. And another is to know what has already been in the news. Keeping up-to-date is essential for the journalist.

The summary lead

One of the best ways to write a lead (from the reader's point of view) is to write a summary lead – a lead that, in one sentence, summarises the whole story.

This is a lead that condenses the essence of the story into a single paragraph, and if the readers were to get nothing else, they would know the gist of what happened. For example:

> The world's population could explode in the next decade, an international expert said today.

Such a lead provides an overview of the story, and it also uses broad, general or generic terms and descriptors rather than specifics. The detail comes later. And note the **what** comes first:

> <u>The world's population could explode in the next decade</u>, an international expert said today.

It's not as effective to start with the **who**:

> <u>An international expert</u> said today the world's population could explode in the next decade.

You want your readers to get the point of the story first. Put the **what** first, not the **who**.

There are cases where the use of general descriptors is not appropriate, but one does have to use common sense. When the subject or the focus of your story is known to everyone, there is no point beating about the bush. Do not say: "A prominent member of a well-known European royal family has passed away" when what you should have said was: "The King is dead".

If the subject of your story is not well known to your readers, you should give them some idea of the standing of the person about whom you are reporting – some idea of the credibility of your source to make the statements he or she has made, before you announce their name. Hence, the summary lead and general descriptors are appropriate. They flag the crux of your story and provide some indication of the authority that can be attached to it. That is why you never start a story with a name unless that name is very well known. There is just no point. Even when the name is well known, the person's **position**, or **what the person is well known for**, should almost always come before the name.

Hence:

United States president, George W Bush . . .

Not:

George W Bush, United States president . . .

Having established the summary, the overview, the essence of the story, the **what** in a few words, you then provide the detail – the **who**, **when**, **where**, etc.:

The world's population could explode in the next decade, an international authority on disease control said yesterday.

World Watch executive director Margaret Morris said the number of people on the planet was likely to rise by 10 per cent by the year 2015.

So, you have the general summary as your lead. That, we hope, will hook the reader, and you have started to introduce the detail. In this case, as a matter of logic, the **who** . . . the expert who made this prediction.

Then comes the **where** and the **when**. In other words, what were the circumstances in which this statement was made? And to whom was it made? Your readers will want to know. So tell them:

Professor Morris was addressing the 21st World Congress of Town Planners and Demographers at the Trade and Convention Centre yesterday.

Now you have begun to flesh out the detail for your interested reader and to elaborate on your lead, to give the detail of what Professor Morris said. The casual reader who is not interested may have moved on, but at least he/she will have the crux of the story. For the interested reader you now provide more of the detail. What else did Professor Morris say? How did she support the claim she made?

Which introduces the issue of logic.

Getting the logic of a story right is where many budding reporters fall down. And we will deal with that shortly. Let us also be clear that it is not suggested that the summary lead is the only way to write a lead to a story. It is often the best way. But it is not the only way ... and it may not be the best way, depending on the story. We will deal with that later too.

Here is another summary lead. The crux of the story in one sentence:

> Another $200 million will be provided in drought relief assistance for Australia's farmers.

In terms of a lead, $200 million is certainly a significant **what**. But with this lead there is no source.

Here is the second par, which expands on the first and, importantly, provides the source for the lead. Logic says the readers will want to know who is responsible for committing the government to spending another $200 million!

> The Prime Minister told a meeting of several hundred farmers in Whereverville yesterday the money would be made available immediately.

Another possible lead to the story might have been:

> An extra $200 million dollars had been earmarked for drought relief, the Prime Minister told a meeting of several hundred worried farmers in Whereverville yesterday.

Both these leads are fine, providing in the first case that the logic of what must come next, identifying the source for the story, does comes next. What would be silly would be a story that went like this:

> Another $200 million will be provided in drought relief assistance for Australia's farmers.
> Much of the eastern states have had record low rainfalls for the last two years.

In this case the second par does not develop what was in the lead. If the information in the lead is so important that it starts the story, why is there nothing about it in the next par? The second par falls down on the basis of logic. It is not a logical development of the fact flow established by the lead. More on logic shortly.

There is another important point thrown up by the two good leads above – the issue of sourcing your story.

4 Sources

Stories that don't have sources, or stories that have sources who prefer not to be identified, or stories that are based on information from dubious or peripheral sources, or stories that quote partisan sources without acknowledging any other side/s to an issue, may not be stories at all. They might be the start of a story, but that is all. Of course, they might be more than that. It will depend.

The issue is credibility. What weight can be placed on a story when no one is prepared to be connected to it? Or if someone is happy to be named and quoted, does the person bring with them any real authority? Or if the source is on the record and recognised as a relevant contributor, is the story simply one-sided if that person is the only source quoted?

These are important questions that have to be considered ... because your credibility as a reporter, and the credibility of your publication, are at stake.

When writing a story you should identify the source, or at least one of the sources, as soon as you sensibly can. The reader will want to know. If you write a summary lead, the identity of your source can be indicated in general or generic terms:

> Rural industry leaders have called for more government action to halt the rising incidence of suicide in the bush.

The detail of who the "rural leaders" are and the facts and figures involved will follow.

What you should avoid is writing a story like this:

> Governments have to do more to address the serious problem of suicide in the bush.
>
> The latest figures show the number of people in rural communities to have taken their own lives has risen 14 per cent in the last 12 months.
>
> In all, a total of 42 deaths in country shires were attributed to suicide last year.
>
> However, there has been no expansion in the provision of psychiatric services in country areas since 2002.
>
> The alarming increase in the number of country people taking their own lives has been put down to the drought, declining returns for many farm commodities and high debt levels among primary producers.
>
> Rural producer representatives at a meeting in Canberra have called on governments to do more to address the problem.

This story contains almost 100 words before there is any mention of a source. But that is not all that is wrong. The first paragraph may well be a summary lead, but since it has no source, and the information in it cannot be regarded as common knowledge, the lead could be seen by the reader as comment or opinion expressed by the reporter writing the story. From time to time, in certain circumstances, reporters do get the chance to comment on the material in their stories. But these opinion pieces or columns are clearly identified.

And then there is the issue of the figures quoted in the story. They may well be accurate, but the reader is entitled to know whose figures they are. A reporter sounding knowledgable is not good enough. Readers deserve better. Those figures should have been sourced, not later, but at the time they appeared.

The story above was constructed purely as an illustration. But it is a good example of the kinds of stories budding reporters are inclined to write. And it is a bad story, for the reasons explained above.

If we take a good example used earlier:

> An extra $200 million would be earmarked for drought relief, the Prime Minister told a meeting of several hundred worried farmers in Whereverville yesterday.

The source (the Prime Minister) is in the lead. Another satisfactory version of the story may not identify the source until the second par:

> Another $200 million will be provided in drought relief assistance for Australia's farmers.
> The Prime Minister told a meeting of several hundred farmers in Whereverville yesterday the money would be made available immediately.

Of course, there may be stories and treatments where delaying the identity of a source may be appropriate – stories written outside the inverted pyramid style, for example. But for the most part you, the reporter, should remember that readers need to know where your story is coming from. And normally you need to make that very clear, very early in the story. Having to wait, or search, for a source to be identified is very frustrating for readers.

In general terms, reporters should observe the following:

- Unless information is widely accepted, or is common knowledge, it should be sourced (generically in the first instance perhaps, but then specifically).

- Material that is controversial, debatable, open to question or a matter of opinion, should always be sourced.
- Facts and figures (unless common knowledge) should be sourced.

How many sources?

There will be occasions when you write a story based on information from only one source. If there is only one person who has the information, or only one who is prepared to talk, there is not much else you can do but write the story based on a single source.

However, many, if not most, of the matters you will cover as a reporter are multi-faceted. There are different sides and opinions and shades of opinion to most things that go on in the world.

This is why single-source stories tend to set off some alarm bells in newsrooms. A single-source story may be a very thin story. Lazy perhaps and not necessarily very professional. Readers come with all manner of views and opinions and if they see theirs (or at least some other options) are not covered in a story, they may dismiss your work. There may be complaints about bias and lack of balance. And they may be justified.

So, just because you get a good story from someone does not mean that is all you should write. You should consider who the other stakeholders or interested parties might be. And you should go after them too.

What is more, if a source is critical of someone else, reporters have a professional, ethical and often legal obligation to seek a response from that person for inclusion in the same story. Contacting them (or making efforts to contact them) for a response after the story has appeared is not good enough. Giving people an opportunity to have a "right of reply" at the time a story critical of them is published is not only the decent thing to do, it may be particularly significant if the matter should go to court.

In the end, it will be the subeditors and the issue of space that will determine how much of your story gets in. But you will have provided those who have to make such decisions with a good story to work with, not a half-baked one.

And a final point. In chasing up other sources you may find that your original information was not quite right, somewhat misguided, or downright wrong. That kind of effort can save more than a little embarrassment. Or you might get an even better story, or at least a better angle. This is why single-source stories ring alarm bells in newsrooms.

An important message for the student or new reporter is this: an interesting story based on only one source, even if it fulfils the word count required, meets the deadline and contains no spelling or style errors, may still not be highly regarded by those to whom it is submitted. Journalism usually requires more effort than that.

But it is also acknowledged that there are plenty of circumstances where there may be only one source for a story.

Anonymous sources

There is a place for stories that carry no one's name, but not often. Usually it's when the public interest is so great, for instance, that it overrides the usual demand that stories be sourced. The editor, however, will need to be convinced.

No doubt Ben Bradlee at the *Washington Post* was reassured to know, as his paper pursued the Watergate scandal, that their "Deep Throat" source was the Deputy Director of the FBI. Apart from Bradlee and the two reporters Woodward and Bernstein, no one else knew – for 30 years. Which raises the other issue about anonymous sources. If their identity cannot be revealed, it must never be revealed, unless the source agrees. As happened, eventually, in the *Washington Post* case.

Remember, a journalist was jailed recently in the United States for not revealing the identity of a source to a court. Four journalists in Australia have also gone to jail in the last 20 years or so rather than identify a confidential source. Are you prepared to similarly protect your confidential sources? You must be.

The history of what has been done over the years to courageous individuals who "blew the whistle" on something is littered with stories of retribution, harassment, intimidation, and even violence that was then meted out to them for what they did. Little wonder not everyone is happy to go on the record. Little wonder that if they should talk to you "off the record" they would expect you to protect their anonymity.

Beware, though – there are plenty of people around who are happy to use the media to float a story or to push a barrow, if they can remain anonymous. Reporters have to be careful that they are not being used.

If you are not careful, you could become the unwilling victim of someone "flying a kite" . . . someone trying to test public reaction to an idea without being seen as responsible for it or connected to it in any way. Kite-flying is one of the favourite pastimes of politicians and those around them. You could be the vehicle they might want to use to "get a kite up" just to test public reaction to some scheme. If the reaction is bad, and if questioned on the matter, they might deny any knowledge of it and even suggest you got it all wrong. It would not be the first time a reporter has been accused of taking something out of context that wasn't taken out of context at all. Your opportunity to defend yourself will be quite limited too. Your credibility could be in question all because you chose to use an anonymous source. Beware.

Credible sources

Stories need to have credibility. Using a bit-player as the basis for a story will not pass unnoticed by your readers. They will feel badly done by and will scoff. If a minor figure is the best you can do, it would be better to look for another story.

Keen young reporters often write things like: *Mr Jones believed the matter could be settled quickly*. And I ask, how do you know Mr Jones believes that? And I am told by the reporter, because that's what he said. And then I say, that is what you should have written. Mr Jones may not believe it at all. But he might be happy for a keen young reporter to say so. Which means, don't write: *Mr Jones believed the matter could be settled quickly*. Write:

Mr Jones <u>said</u> he believed the matter could be settled quickly.

And do the same with "feels", "hopes", "intends", "wants" or any number of other possibilities.

Sources – avoid being captured

Don't be taken hostage by your sources. If you come to rely on them so much that you are in their debt, or they believe you are, you are in trouble. Sources have to know that you will write whatever has to be written and if they are involved in a negative way, that will be too bad.

So keep your distance.

And don't give your sources the right to check your stories. That has been a sackable offence in days gone by. Of course, check anything you need to, but do not fax or email your story to your source/s for approval. You are the journalist, not your sources. You make the decisions about what is newsworthy, not your sources. You are the professional, not your sources. If your doctor refers his/her diagnosis of your ailments to you for your opinion and approval, and defers to your judgment, you should change doctors. Apply the same rules to the stories you write.

There is more about sources in the chapter on the fundamentals of reporting.

On or off the record

It is essential that you understand what your news organisation means by terms such as "on the record", "off the record" and "background". It is also essential that the people you deal with understand what those things mean. If you and they have different understandings, you may publish something a source was not expecting to see and the source might accuse you of breaching a confidence.

For this reason some news organisations are wary of "off the record" material. Be sure you know your organisation's views before you make commitments to go "off the record". Here are some guidelines, but be sure to check:

- **On the record**: the source can be quoted and named.
- **Off the record**: what you have been told may be used but not attributed to your source . . . who must not be identified in any way.
- **Background**: for your information, to assist you, but may not be used.

5 Logic

It has been claimed that logic in a news story is a bit like beauty – in the eye of the beholder. But, if that should be your view, try telling a subeditor.

Logic, wherever it arises, is what makes sense. Logic is what follows from the premise, or the par, that has just been established or written. Logic is what follows sensibly from what is already known. Logic demands that you take your readers through your story bit by bit so that they don't have to scratch their heads trying to work out what your story is about or how to make sense of it. Logic in a news story can go wrong quite early. As early as the second par, in fact, as we have seen already:

> Another $200 million will be provided in drought relief assistance for Australia's farmers.
>
> Much of the eastern states have had record low rainfalls for the last two years.

Logic in a news story goes wrong at the second par if it doesn't expand on **the key point of** the lead. If it does not do that, either the second par is wrong or the lead is wrong.

Every par in a news story contains at least two elements (and possibly more), as most sentences do. In fact, most sentences have at least a subject, a verb and an object. They often have more.

However, the logic issue is: which of the elements in a par is to be developed in the par that follows? And which one in the par after that? Let's take an example – a simple one. It has just two elements (apart from the verb):

> Retailers (1) have reported record Christmas sales (2).

First of all, if that is the lead, one or other of those two elements – retailers, or record sales – must be developed in the next par. It is no good saying, for example:

> Retailers have reported record Christmas sales.
>   Shops will be open until midnight on Christmas Eve.

Here, neither of the elements in the first par is developed in the second. In fact, the second does not even mention either of the elements in the first. And that is a clear indication that something is wrong.

Every par in a news story, unless it begins with a qualification such as *however*, or *but*, or *meanwhile*, or the like, must be directly linkable to the par that precedes it. In other words, in any par (apart from the first obviously) there must be an element of the story that is recognisable (if not in same words, at least instantly recognisable) in the preceding par.

Unless there is a qualification, as described above, a succeeding paragraph containing elements that are not immediately recognisable in the par above is wrong. There is no logic to such a situation. The reader will be confused and will wonder what this new information has to do with what he or she has just read. You don't want to confuse readers; you want to communicate with them.

So, in the example above the second par has to contain either an expansion of what the retailers are saying, or some detail of the frenzy of the Christmas buying spree. Expanding on the first element of the story would go something like this:

> Retailers have reported record Christmas sales.
>   Retail Trades Association general secretary Norma Fleming said several department stores and major shopping centres had recorded December turnover figures well in excess of budget expectations.

Ms Fleming's remarks are a direct elaboration of the information contained in the summary lead. She represents "retailers", the word chosen to introduce the first par. The logic is clear.

But choosing to elaborate on the other ingredient in the lead does not produce such a logical outcome:

> Retailers have reported <u>record Christmas sales</u>.
>   Spending this year in several department stores and shopping centres had exceeded budget expectations, Retail Trades Association general secretary Norma Fleming said yesterday.

Thus, while the reporter in the second case may have embraced an element in the lead (which is vital) to develop as the second par, the choice was not a sound one.

If we decide that the retailers' claim is the lead to the story, the next par requires that the reader be told precisely who it was who made the claim, and what support there might be for such a claim. That is what logic means and demands. If the step-by-step logic of your story evades you, you will provide gainful employment for those who work on the subs desk. They will have to get it right.

If we look at our story about the angry bears, you will see every new bit of information is introduced by, or linked to, something we have already been told.

This story is the simplest of all examples, but what it illustrates is most significant in writing news. Readers should not have to go back through your story to work out what it is all about. It should be clear. New information should be introduced on the back of something they already know (unless you use a transition such as *but*, *however*, or *meanwhile*, to signal a change of direction). Just observe the arrows:

> A young Forest Glen girl escaped unharmed today when she was chased through the woods by three angry bears.
>
>   The girl, 10-year-old Goldi Locks, was resting at her Primrose Street home this afternoon recovering from her ordeal.
>
>   Ms Locks told reporters she had gone for a walk in the woods, but had begun to feel very tired and hungry.
>
>   She said she found a cottage in the woods and went to sleep in an upstairs bedroom.
>
>   Some time later she was wakened by three angry bears who began threatening her.
>
>   She said she escaped by jumping out a first floor window.
>
>   However, Ms Locks said, the bears had pursued her and she had just managed to reach the edge of the woods in time.
>
>   "I will never go into the woods alone again," Ms Locks said.

The arrows (above) and coded words (below) reveal how existing information introduces, or connects with, new information. Not one par in the story above stands unattached to the one preceding it. Or put another way, all succeeding pars contain an element of the story we have already met.

This is the logic of the story. The logic of how the facts flow, or what journalists call the "fact flow".

A young Forest Glen girl **escaped** unharmed today when she was chased through the *woods* by three angry **bears**.

The girl, 10-year-old Goldi Locks, was **resting** at her Primrose Street home this afternoon recovering from her ordeal.

Ms Locks told reporters she had gone for a walk in the *woods*, but had become very tired and hungry.

She said she found a cottage in the *woods* and went to sleep in an upstairs bedroom.

Some time later she was wakened by three angry **bears** who began threatening her.

She said she escaped by jumping out a first floor window.

However, Ms Locks said, the **bears** had pursued her and she had just managed to reach the edge of the woods in time.

"I will never go into the *woods* alone again," Ms Locks said.

6 Background

Not every story requires backgrounding. But many do. Reporters should not assume their audience will be as well informed about what has been going on as they are.

Background can be vital. Imagine if our fictitious story were to read:

A young Forest Glen girl escaped unharmed today when she was chased through the woods by three angry bears.

This is the second such incident in a week.

Background can be needed as early as the second par. Indeed, it can even be part of the lead:

In the second such incident in a week, a Forest Glen child has been chased through the woods by three angry bears.

Exactly where the background should appear will depend on the story. It will depend on how significant the background is. The more significant, the closer to the lead it should be.

Leaving background to the end can have a certain impact as a "closer" to the story – as it would in the case of our fictitious story above. But, since we are writing to the rules of the inverted pyramid, leaving the background to the end would mean that the matter was considered to be the least important part of the story. And thus, if the story were cut from the bottom, there would be no point blaming the subs for cutting out some vitally important information.

The message is clear. Background is important. Put it where its importance dictates it should be. Make sure the logic of the story is addressed so the reader is not confused. Make sure the connection with the main story is clear.

There can be a problem with background. Cutting a story with lots of essential background anywhere may not work. In this story it is the background that makes sense of the lead. The lead is new, and important, but without the background, who would understand that?

In a move believed to be without precedent in Australia, a federal parliamentary committee has called on Queensland authorities to charge former state Cabinet Ministers with a serious criminal offence.

Politicians and public servants should be treated by the law the same way as other people, the committee said.

The House of Representatives Legal and Constitutional Affairs Committee of Inquiry into Crime in the Community has recommended Queensland authorities treat public figures who destroyed evidence, including evidence of child abuse in 1990, in the same manner as occurred in the case of a citizen who committed a similar offence last year.

The citizen, a Baptist minister, guillotined a number of pages of the diary of a 15-year-old female parishioner in which she had recorded details of her molestation by a member of her church.

Despite the fact that the pages could be reconstructed, the minister was convicted earlier this year of destroying evidence and given a suspended prison sentence.

The Attorney-General, Mr Welford, has since appealed the sentence on the grounds that it was "manifestly inadequate".

The Crime in the Community inquiry noted, however, that the treatment of the Baptist minister contrasted markedly with that afforded members of the Goss Labor Cabinet and a group of senior public officials who recommended, ordered and carried out the complete destruction of a large number of documents and tape recordings in 1990.

The material was destroyed to prevent its being used in legal proceedings.

No action has ever been taken against those involved.

In its report into the shredding of the Heiner Inquiry documents and the related issue of abuse of children at the John Oxley Youth Detention Centre, the Crime in the Community inquiry said: ". . . there is sufficient evidence to conclude that the Labor Government, in deciding to shred the Heiner documents, has a case to answer under the Queensland Criminal Code Act (1899) for destroying evidence required in legal proceedings. It is open to conclude that the Government's actions – and possibly those of Government departments and agencies – were illegal, but equally importantly, immoral".

The committee said charges should be laid.

(The Independent Monthly, September 2004, p. 1)

7 Attribution

Almost all stories will contain a reference to someone saying something. Even a story you may have witnessed first-hand will probably contain comments from others. These comments will have to be attributed to their sources.

On radio and TV, it can be easy . . . just play an audio or video "grab" of the person actually speaking. In newspapers, however, it is more complex. The writer has to cue the reader with signs (punctuation marks) to indicate what he or she wrote and what someone else might have said. There are conventions to make this process work. Journalists and their readers understand them. Attribution is something else the reporter has to get right.

There is a logic to it as well.

A person's name is obviously important. But what is more important is the person's authority to make the comments he or she has made. The person's position, or title, or relationship to the story (an eyewitness or bystander perhaps, or an expert) is often more important than the name, even though the name is obviously important.

What all this means is quite simple. Unless someone is so well known that their title or position or status is common knowledge, put the title or position (and the organisation in which they hold that position or title) before their name when you introduce them to your readers. Thus:

(a) President (*position/title*) of the National Council of Trade Unions (NCTU) (*organisation*), Sean Burnett, (*name*) . . .

Or, more likely (unless the combination is too cumbersome):

(b) National Council of Trade Unions (NCTU) (*organisation*) president (*position/title*) Sean Burnett (*name*) . . .

Which of the above forms is preferred is a matter of what is known as House Style – the in-house rules that ensure consistency within a publication. House styles are explained in greater detail in the chapter on subbing. Version (b) above is the most common in newsrooms, except where the person's title becomes too long, convoluted or confusing. For example:

> Global Food and Beverage's South East Asian Regional Market Development Manager Ric Somebody . . .

This is something of a mouthful and would be better written as:

> The South East Asian regional marketing development manager for Global Food and Beverage, Ric Somebody, . . .

This is much easier to read and digest. Nevertheless, some newspapers do not change the form even when the title is long and convoluted, as in this example from a metropolitan paper:

> University of Queensland's Centre for Accident Research and Road Safety Queensland deputy director Jeremy Davey . . .

Two important points emerge from the examples (a) and (b) above. The first is that (b) is two words shorter than (a), and that saves seven character spaces, which is important. But that is not all.

The second point is, in the case of (a), the name is preceded and followed by commas. And the reason for that? The name is really more than a name. It involves an inferred qualifying clause (which we will cover in the section on grammar). What example (a) really says might have been written as:

> . . . president of the National Council of Trade Unions, [who is] or [whose name is], Sean Burnett, . . .

Thus the need for the comma before the name and the comma after it. One comma before or one after will not do.

If we use the attribution form illustrated in example (b), the organisation, and the individual's title in that organisation, become a descriptor, an adjective if you like (not an inferred adjectival clause) and the commas are not needed. That saves two more spaces. The form expressed in example (b) is not only clear and accurate, but it saves in all nine character spaces. In the world of newspapers, nine character spaces are significant.

What all of the above means is this:

- If your form of attribution places the **title** of the person you are quoting ahead of the name of the **organisation** the person represents, then you will need a comma **before** and **after** the name of the person – as in example (a).
- If your form of attribution places the name of the **organisation** before the person's **title**, you do not use commas before and after the person's name – as in example (b).

> **(a)** The director general of the Department of Education, Brian Fairweather, said the new regulations would come into force on Monday. (*with commas*)
>
> **(b)** Department of Education director general Brian Fairweather said the new regulations would come into force on Monday. (*no commas*)

The (b) form is the form preferred by many, if not most, house style guides – for the reasons explained above. This style even appears in newspapers whose style guides recommend the alternative (a) above.

(Note: In the National Council of Trade Unions example above, the initials of the organisation or its acronym are placed in brackets immediately after the name of the body. This allows the reporter to use the shortened form of the name from then on in the story if he or she should wish.)

Direct and indirect speech

The words of those whose comments or speeches appear in our stories can be reported in two ways – direct speech and indirect speech.

Direct speech, as the term suggests, reproduces the actual words uttered. Direct speech statements or remarks are reproduced verbatim and are enclosed within quotation marks:

> "If that is what the law says, the law is an ass," Mr Bumble said.

Indirect speech is reported speech that is summarised or paraphrased by the writer, without quotation marks, in either of the following ways:

> If that was what the law said, the law was an ass, Mr Bumble said.
> Mr Bumble said if that was what the law said, the law was an ass.

Or, to add emphasis to a statement made by a source, or to make it clear that the reporter had not given a more colourful summary of what was said than the speaker had intended, a partial quote may be used:

> Mr Bumble said if that was what the law said, the law was "an ass".

Reporters use both direct and indirect speech when writing their stories. There are good reasons for this. Direct speech presents the actual words spoken by the person being reported. But people often ramble, use poor grammar, or use unfamiliar terms or expressions. Summarising or paraphrasing what they say is essential in a news environment where space is limited.

But there is another important reason. A newspaper story that contains nothing but direct speech, or nothing but indirect speech, defies an important reality in the world of print journalism. The eye appreciates variety. Stories in which all the paragraphs look the same, either all quotes, or no quotes, can be visually off-putting. Stories that have a mixture of the two are more appealing to the eye. There is variety within the columns and the reader, subconsciously at least, appreciates that.

How best to use direct and indirect speech introduces a matter that will be addressed constantly throughout this book – the matter of communication. As a journalist you are in the communication business. You are attempting, every day, to communicate with your readers. But that is not all. You should be attempting to communicate with them **effectively** and **efficiently**.

The two are vital in your work and they are different. Communicating **effectively** means that the reader reads and comprehends exactly what you intended – not something you didn't intend. Communicating **efficiently** means the reader should not have to struggle to get the message you intended. It was clear. It was not just unambiguous, it was straightforward. Readers will not struggle with your work. Why should they? They do not buy your newspaper to embark on a mind-wrestle with the people who wrote the stories in it. They are busy. They want the news, thank you, not a jigsaw puzzle.

So, if you want to communicate effectively and efficiently with your readers, you will carefully consider how best to use direct and indirect speech.

If we take a hypothetical story, we can propose some alternatives. Only one of them will do the job best.

Option one
Communities in the north of the state have been warned to expect a severe storm season this summer.

"Tropical sea temperatures are the warmest they have been for a decade and that is a danger sign," Bureau of Meteorology senior forecaster Geoff Smith said yesterday.

"Cyclones are a distinct possibility too," Mr Smith said.

Option two
Communities in the north of the state have been warned to expect a severe storm season this summer.

Bureau of Meteorology senior forecaster Geoff Smith said yesterday: "Tropical sea temperatures are the warmest they have been for a decade and that is a danger sign."

"Cyclones are a distinct possibility too," Mr Smith said.

- -

Option three
Communities in the north of the state have been warned to expect a severe storm season this summer.

Bureau of Meteorology senior forecaster Geoff Smith said yesterday tropical sea temperatures were the warmest they had been for a decade and that was a danger sign.

"Cyclones are a distinct possibility too," Mr Smith said.

The third option is the sensible, effective and efficient one. Introduce your sources, your speakers, via indirect speech, not direct. Direct comes later.

In the case of option one, we get an important statement before we discover who said it. That is annoying for the reader. It is ineffective communication.

There are two problems with option two. Firstly, the quote comes in the middle of a paragraph, which is a less effective placement of it, in terms of communicating with the reader, and secondly, that form of attribution (nominating the speaker, then a colon, then a direct speech statement) is seldom used in newspapers.

Option three (organisation, title, name, indirect speech before direct) is the most effective and efficient way to introduce comments or statements from the sources you are quoting – unless there is some very special reason to use option two. As the story is developed, option three might look like this:

Communities in the north of the state have been warned to expect a severe storm season this summer.

Bureau of Meteorology senior forecaster Geoff Smith said yesterday tropical sea temperatures were the warmest they had been for a decade and that was a danger sign.

"Cyclones are a distinct possibility too," Mr Smith said.

"Sea temperatures off the coast of the United States have been very warm this year and they have had a terrible hurricane season," he said.

"We need to be ready in case it happens here."

Mr Smith said a 24-hour cyclone watch had been in place for a month and although there had been no alerts so far this season, no one should be complacent.

Examined more closely what we have is:

> Communities in the north of the state have been warned to expect a severe storm season this summer.
>
> Bureau of Meteorology (*organisation*) senior forecaster (*title*) Geoff Smith (*given name and family name*) said yesterday tropical sea temperatures were the warmest they had been for a decade and that was a danger sign. (*indirect quote*)
>
> "Cyclones are a distinct possibility too," (*direct quote*) Mr Smith (*honorific and surname*) said.
>
> "Sea temperatures off the coast of the United States have been very warm this year and they have had a terrible hurricane season," he (*pronoun*) said.
>
> "We need to be ready in case it happens here." (*no attribution*)
>
> Mr Smith (*honorific and surname*) said a 24-hour cyclone watch had been in place for a month and although there had been no alerts so far this season, no one should be complacent. (*indirect quote*)

The order established above is worth noting, because it is effective and efficient:

1. organisation, title, first name and surname followed by indirect quote first;
2. direct quote followed by the appropriate honorific (Mr/Ms/Dr/Prof) and surname with "said";
3. direct quote followed by personal pronoun (he/she) with "said";
4. direct quote, no attribution;
5. honorific and surname followed by indirect quote.

The use of "said"

There are some matters many novice reporters get wrong. So much so they are serious problems.

In all the stories that have appeared so far, and in all those that will appear, one thing will be clear and consistent. The verb "said" **always** comes **after** the name of the speaker or that person's appropriate personal pronoun. For example, as in the story above:

> Bureau of Meteorology senior forecaster Geoff Smith said yesterday tropical sea temperatures were the warmest they had been for a decade and that was a danger sign.
>
> "Cyclones are a distinct possibility too," Mr Smith said.
>
> "Sea temperatures off the coast of the United States have been very warm this year and they have had a terrible hurricane season," he said.

It may be normal in the world of literature to write:

> "Cyclones are a distinct possibility too," <u>said Mr Smith</u>.

But it is **not** a form that is used in journalism. You may find it in a newspaper now and again, but you will have to read thousands and thousands of stories to find the odd example.

The reporter just starting out should take note. Subeditors (or lecturers marking your assignments) may well be harsh on you if you ignore this advice. If you are not convinced, consider the following extract from a conversation:

> I saw Tom and Joanne on the way to work this morning. They had a good time at the party last night, <u>Tom said</u>.

Or, perhaps:

> I saw Tom and Joanne on the way to work this morning. <u>Tom said</u> they had a good time at the party last night.

What no one would ever say would be:

> I saw Tom and Joanne on the way to work this morning. They had a good time at the party last night, <u>said Tom</u>.

Because it is such a common literary form, the use of "said" before the name of the speaker seems to be ingrained in the minds of many young people. But it is not a form used in conversation. And thus it is not a form used in journalism.

And don't worry about repeating "said". Despite being counselled not to, reporters writing their first stories almost invariably scour their dictionaries and thesauruses looking for alternatives. Don't bother. The industry doesn't.

> **Remember** – "said" comes **after** the name of the speaker or the appropriate pronoun.

For the most part the industry simply uses "said". Full stop. Where it is **accurate and appropriate**, "claim" or a version of it (claims/claimed) may be used.

> For the most part, when writing conventional inverted pyramid news stories, all you need remember is: people **say** things (hence "said" in past tense), figures **show** things, committees **report** and **say** things, investigations **reveal** things.

So when you feel the urge to use something else, don't. Check this list for words you should **avoid**: stated; remarked; commented; asserted; suggested; and most others you can think of. Some of the alternatives introduce shades of meaning that should be avoided.

The use of "according to"

Some newsrooms object to the use of "according to" as a form of attribution. They say the words come with some baggage – an inference that the source of the words may not be reliable. They say "according to" suggests that the quote should be treated with some scepticism . . . and that such an outcome is unsatisfactory and should be avoided.

> According to (*but whether you believe it or not is up to you*) the Prime Minister, life was not meant to be easy.

Not everyone agrees. Others claim such an interpretation of "according to" is simply in the eye of the beholder . . . and muddleheaded. They argue that English words mean what they say, and "according to" means nothing more than what it says. Consequently you will find it used in some publications, but not in others.

The objection to "according to" is probably reasonable in the case of daily publications. They can say with appropriate accuracy and deference to topicality: *Life was not meant to be easy, the Prime Minister said yesterday*.

But following that style, a weekly might have to say: *Life was not meant to be easy, the Prime Minister said last week*. Or last month, perhaps, in the case of a monthly. That makes the news quite old.

Life was not meant to be easy, according to the Prime Minister, is accurate and gets around the timeliness issue.

For the new recruit in the newsroom, the suggestion is this: find out if "according to" is OK before writing it in your story.

No adverbs, please

Always remember you are writing a news story, not a novel. Don't confuse the two. Thus, having accepted the advice above, don't try to make your writing more colourful by puffing up your attribution with adverbs:

> "Everyone should come to the aid of the party," Mr Smith said <u>thoughtfully.</u>

This is an example of what **not** to write in a news story.

The list of adverbs to avoid is quite long: emphatically, quickly, carefully, ruefully, angrily, sympathetically, and so on. No modifying adverbs after "said" is a good rule. None before it either. They introduce judgments into your writing and put a "spin" on your words.

You may have the impression that Mr Smith was being "thoughtful". But he might have just been clever or disingenuous to give that impression. The reader doesn't need your opinion in a news story. Just report what was said.

On the other hand, try not to repeat to the point of boredom the words, or terms, or names you use in your stories (apart from "said"). Find alternatives. The **Australian Council of Trade Unions** becomes **ACTU** or **Australia's peak trade union body**. Instead of **the car**, you might say **the vehicle** or **the sedan**. An **aeroplane** is also an **aircraft** or a **jet**.

Repetition is not only boring, but it can be evidence of laziness or a poor vocabulary. So, at the risk of being boring, let me repeat that. Avoid repetition apart from "said".

8 The serious issue of tense

Stories can be written in the present tense, the past tense, the future tense – and more. Electronic media (which present regular updates) strive for immediacy and write as much as possible in the present tense. Newspapers recognise that they appear daily (usually early in the morning) and that much of what they report happened yesterday, or earlier, in the case of a weekly.

For example, a radio news bulletin might say:

> The government <u>is</u> (*present tense*) set to crack down on tax cheats.
> Federal Treasurer Peter Costello <u>says</u> (*present tense*) tax avoidance is (*present tense*) costing the country squillions of dollars a year.

On the other hand, a newspaper story might say:

> The government yesterday <u>warned</u> (*past tense*) tax cheats to expect a major crackdown on avoidance schemes.
> Federal Treasurer Peter Costello <u>told</u> (*past tense*) parliament tax avoidance <u>was</u> (*past tense*) costing the country squillions of dollars a year.

Or more likely, in an effort to give an impression of greater "immediacy", instead of using the past tense, the newspaper might use the present perfect tense (what might be called the "present past" tense . . . see the chapter on grammar). The story would then read:

> The government <u>has warned</u> (*present perfect tense*) tax cheats to expect a major crackdown on avoidance schemes.
>
> Federal Treasurer Peter Costello <u>told</u> (*past tense*) parliament tax avoidance <u>was</u> (*past tense*) costing the country squillions of dollars a year.

Of course, the present tense (*The government says it will crack down on tax cheats*), or the future (*The government will crack down on tax cheats*), could well appear in a newspaper story. Nevertheless, newspapers use the present perfect and past tenses much more than radio or television newsrooms, and any suggestion that newspaper stories should be written in the present tense whenever possible is simply not borne out by industry practice.

A trap for the unwary

You may have noticed something earlier during the discussion on the logic of using indirect speech before direct speech when writing a story. If not, have another look.

When we interviewed him, our source at the Bureau of Meteorology, senior forecaster Geoff Smith, said: "Tropical sea temperatures are the warmest they have been for a decade and that is a danger sign." If we had used that statement as a direct speech quote, with attribution, the statement might have appeared as:

> "Tropical sea temperatures are the warmest they have been for a decade and that is a danger sign," Bureau of Meteorology senior forecaster Geoff Smith said.

But, since it is more effective and efficient, and ultimately logical, to begin our report of what a source said with indirect speech we wrote:

> Bureau of Meteorology senior forecaster Geoff Smith said tropical sea temperatures <u>were</u> the warmest they <u>had</u> been for a decade and that <u>was</u> a danger sign.

Note the change of tense. This is something inexperienced reporters constantly get wrong.

"Said" (or any equivalent) is past tense and if you are quoting a source in indirect speech, and your principal verb is "said", all related verbs must also be in the past tense. In other words it is not only incorrect, but also nonsense, to write:

> Bureau of Meteorology senior forecaster Geoff Smith said tropical sea temperatures <u>are</u> the warmest they have been for a decade and that <u>is</u> a danger sign.

The only way the present tense verbs above could be used after "said", as written above, would be as direct speech, thus:

> Bureau of Meteorology senior forecaster Geoff Smith said: "Tropical sea temperatures are the warmest they have been for a decade and that is a danger sign."

And as I have already noted, that form of attribution is seldom used in newspaper stories. The point needs to be reinforced, since so many get it wrong so often. This is not negotiable. "Said" is past tense and all related verbs in indirect speech must also be past tense!

I have corrected this error thousands, probably umpteen thousands, of times. Spare a thought for the subeditors. They will not be pleased if you go on making this mistake.

It is not just the tense of the verb that changes. The person (see the chapter on grammar) of the pronouns also changes. "I" in direct speech becomes "he" or "she" in indirect speech. "We" becomes "they" in reported (indirect) speech.

> In indirect speech, the verb "said" (or an equivalent, such as "told") is past tense, and all related verbs must also be in past tense. In other words:
> - "The time **has** come," the walrus said (*direct*)
> - The time **had** come, the walrus said (*indirect*)
> - The walrus said the time **had** come (*indirect*).

> So, more examples:
> "<u>I</u> **will** be ready for them when they **come**," the general said. (*direct*)
> <u>He</u> **would** be ready for them when they **came**, the general said. (*indirect*)
> -
> "<u>We</u> **can** do the job if <u>we</u> **get** enough support," Rotary president Charlie Tomkins said. (*direct*)
> Rotary president Charlie Tomkins said <u>they</u> **could** do the job if <u>they</u> **got** enough support. (*indirect*)
> -
> "<u>We</u> **will** have to do it tomorrow," the teacher told the class. (*direct*)
> The teacher told the class <u>they</u> **would** have to do it tomorrow. (*indirect*)

Here is a guide to how to change direct speech into indirect:

Direct speech	Indirect speech
am/are/is	was/were
can	could
will	would
shall	should
may	might
was/were	had been
have been	had been
could	could have
would	would have
I/we	he/she/they
he/she	he/she
our/your	their/our/ours

Some adverbs too are changed when converting from direct to indirect speech.

> "I wish you were all **here**," Ms Thomas said. (*direct*)
> Ms Thomas said she wished they were all **there**. (*indirect*)
>
> -
>
> "It must be done **now** because tomorrow will be too late," the teacher said. (*direct*)
> The teacher said it had to be done **then** because tomorrow would be too late. (*indirect*)

9 Voice

Whenever possible, conventional inverted pyramid news stories should be written in the active voice (see the chapter on grammar).

A sentence in active voice places the actor before the action and before the receiver of the action. A sentence in passive voice has the receiver first and the actor last:

> Active: The car (*actor*) hit (*action*) a tree (*receiver*).
> Passive: A tree (*receiver*) was hit (*action*) by a car (*actor*).

A useful indicator of a passive voice sentence is the presence of the word "by". If it indicates that something has been influenced or affected "by" something else, you have a passive voice sentence.

There can be no blanket ban on passive voice, however. Be sensible.

> A man <u>was killed</u> (*passive*) when he <u>was struck</u> (*passive*) by a train at the French Street level crossing this morning.

This is clearly more appropriate than saying:

> A train <u>killed</u> (*active*) a man at the French Street level crossing this morning.

It is quite likely a combination of both voice forms would be used in a case such as this:

> A man <u>died</u> (*active*) when he <u>was struck</u> (*passive*) by a train at the French Street level crossing this morning.

In journalism, the general rule is: active voice is best. It is direct and straight-forward. Passive voice is backwards writing, much loved by academics for their journal articles and papers. In such publications you are just as likely to see: *Much of modern science has been substantially shaped by Einstein's work* (which is passive), as: *Einstein's work has substantially shaped much of modern science* (which is active). Journalism prefers the latter.

10 Punctuation

There are punctuation forms that are standard in the world of newspapers and while you may think that a little mark here and a little squiggle there may not be very important, if they are wrong, someone has to change them. People who have to change things that could easily have been correct at the outset tend to get annoyed. So it is important to get your punctuation right. You need to know your house style, but here are a few tips. You will find more in the chapter on spelling and punctuation.

Quotation marks

In the world of journalism, unlike the bureaucracy, direct speech is always enclosed by double quotation marks (" " – also known as inverted commas or quote marks).

The closing quote marks (") always go after the punctuation mark that indicates a stop or a pause. Unless you are using a partial quote (a few words or a phrase from a complete sentence), the quote marks enclose the verbatim words that were spoken, as well as the associated punctuation marks:

> "To be, or not to be," Hamlet said.
> "That is the question."
> --
> "To be, or not to be", Hamlet said.
> "That is the question".

Make sure the closing quote marks go **after** the comma in the first sentence, and **after** the full stop in the second. The same applies to question and exclamation marks:

> "Who will come to the aid of the party?" the Prime Minister asked.
> "Stop!" the policeman demanded.

Where consecutive sentences are quoted (a running quote), they are **not** separated by closing quote marks:

> "To be, or not to be," Hamlet said.
> "That is the question.
> "Whether 'tis nobler in the mind . . ."

A quote within a quote is enclosed in single quote marks:

> "I said quite distinctly, 'Put the gun down'," Detective Struthers told the court.

A partial quote in a sentence of indirect speech (to emphasise, for instance, that the words are those of the speaker and not the reporter) is enclosed in double quote marks:

> The minister said such a remark was "rubbish" and he would not comment on it any further.

If a partial quote comes at the end of a sentence, the closing quote marks fall **before** the full stop:

> The minister said the remark was "rubbish".

Hyphens

A hyphen (-) is not a dash. If you need to use a dash, be sure you know which one to use and where to use it. The en dash occupies the space of the letter "n" (–) while the em dash occupies the space of the letter "m" (—). House style will determine which one to use. The hyphen is not a substitute for either of the dashes. If you are using Word and you need to find the dashes, select Insert on the tool bar at the top of the screen, select Symbol, and then select the dash you want from the options available. There are many other symbols available there that you may need to use one day.

Don't forget to use hyphens when reporting people's ages: *A three-year-old girl, a 33-year-old man.* Notice how the different ages are treated. Spell out numbers one to nine, use figures thereafter (unless house style decrees otherwise).

Hyphens should be used in the case of compound adjectives (*a hit-and-run driver, a red-letter day*), but not in the case of compound adverbs (*poorly chosen words, badly needed supplies*). Why? See the chapter on grammar.

Commas

There is a trend in newspapers these days to use fewer commas. But this can come at a cost. The absence of a comma may lead to confusion:

> The bus had collided with a sedan and a police patrol car on its way to another accident was diverted to the scene.

A comma in the right place can ensure the reader has no need to go back and re-read the sentence to make sense of it:

> The bus had collided with a sedan, and a police patrol car on its way to another accident was diverted to the scene.

This example also puts paid to the suggestion that it is incorrect to put a comma before "and".

Ellipses

The ellipsis (. . .), which indicates that something has been left out, is comprised of three, not four or more, full stops, and there is a space before and after the group of three, as shown.

Colons

The colon appears in two main ways in news stories, but neither of them very often. The first involves that form of attribution in which the details of the speaker precede, rather than follow, a direct quote:

The Prime Minister told the House: "We will not be moved."

Colons are also used to introduce a list of items (see semicolons below).

Semicolons

This is a punctuation mark that causes arguments among journalists. The different views can be summarised like this:

- The semicolon is a valuable punctuation mark; it should be used more often.
- The semicolon is old-fashioned; don't bother with it.

In terms of its strength in marking a pause, the semicolon falls between the comma and the full stop. As a tool in the kitbag of someone wanting to communicate clearly with his or her readers, it is clearly valuable. But your newsroom may frown on it.

Where it can be of value is in separating items in a list. For example:

> The coach said he insisted on a rigorous training regime for his athletes, including: daily track work; pumping weights; running up and down stairs, hills and sand dunes; push-ups, sit-ups and floor exercises; swimming laps; and speed skipping.

The use of commas to separate the items in the above list would not be sufficient since some of the items already contain commas. More commas (instead of semicolons) would only produce confusion for the reader.

These examples deal with some of the important issues that arise with punctuation. There is further information in the chapter on spelling and punctuation. House style will settle other punctuation issues.

11 Sentence length

If you wish to communicate effectively and efficiently with your readers (or listeners or viewers), you will appreciate the importance of limiting the length of your sentences. Readers cannot digest long, convoluted or complex sentences. So the message is clear. Make friends with the full stop. As a rule of thumb it is always suggested that 25 words in a sentence is plenty.

Of course, any number of pars have been written, and lots more will be written, with more than 25 words in them. But the message is a good one. No one can digest large doses of information effectively and efficiently without a pause.

Be conscious of your sentence lengths.

And also be aware that in the case of news stories your newsroom may want you to write single-sentence pars. Have a look at a news page in the nearest newspaper and see how many pars you can find that have more than one sentence in them. Some papers will have multi-sentence pars; some will have single-sentence pars with the occasional double-sentence par.

Write tight

Keeping an eye on sentence length and making friends with the full stop are important. But the news writer has to "write tight" as well. This means not using big words when small ones will do, and not using three words when one will do. A sportsman "attempting to" break a record would be just as accurately "trying" to break a record. You have saved six characters and the reader is just as well informed.

House style guides normally have lists of superfluous constructions and overblown words that should be avoided. Check the style guide in your newsroom.

Checking your story

When you have finished your story, work through your checklist. The order is not important (the numbering follows the order in this book), but they all have to be checked. If all are ticked, the story is ready to be filed. If not, the story is not ready. (The only items that may not be ticked will be questions 4b and 4c, and questions 6a and 6b, and then only if they do not apply.)

Checklist

1. Is everything you have reported accurate? ☐
2. Is the story free of your comments and opinions? ☐
3. Is the news the lead to your story? ☐
   (**what** has happened, is happening, or will happen, or **what** is most important or **what** is most interesting or unusual or **what** was said) ☐
4a. Do you have, or did you try to get, enough appropriate sources? ☐
4b. Is a "right of reply" involved? ☐
4c. If so, did you try to get it? ☐
5. Has the story been developed logically? Can the reader follow it easily? ☐
6a. Is background required? ☐
6b. If so, has it been provided? ☐
7. Is the attribution arranged effectively? ☐
8a. Are the tenses right? All of them? ☐
8b. Is the rest of the grammar right? ☐
8c. Spelling correct? (particularly names) ☐
9. Active voice wherever possible? ☐
10. Punctuation? ☐
11. Sentence length? ☐
12. Are you prepared to see your name on it? ☐

There are other ways to write news stories. We will deal with them later. Reporters need to get the basics right, and the discipline involved in writing a news story within the constraints of the inverted pyramid has never hurt anyone. In fact, the discipline involved will help with any kind of writing. What you need now is practice and experience writing news, and exposure to good examples.

Sample news story

This inverted pyramid story is one of many published around a major issue that we started investigating in 1992. It is the original version of a story that was published on page 3 of the *Courier-Mail* on November 3, 2001.

Centre inmate, 14, pack raped

Bruce Grundy

A young Aboriginal woman has confirmed claims by several former staff members of a Brisbane youth detention centre that she was gang raped while being held in the centre as a 14-year-old in care.

The woman, now in her mid-20s, said she was gang raped twice on a supervised outing from the John Oxley Youth Detention Centre in the late 1980s.

Former members of staff at the centre have also claimed the matter was officially "swept under the carpet" and "quietly hushed up".

One former youth worker said if what had happened to the girl in question had happened to a white girl, " . . . there would have been Hell to pay".

The woman, who cannot be identified under Queensland law, said she had been taken on a bus trip with a group of Aboriginal and white male inmates to an isolated spot in the country. One staff member had accompanied the inmates some distance into the bush and had left her with the boys. The man had returned to the carpark and to the other staff members.

The woman said the boys had begun to demand sex and started arguing about who would "go through her" first. She said she told them to leave her alone but they had forced her on to a large rock and raped her.

The woman said what had happened to her on the first walk was repeated later in the day.

When contacted about the incident, one of those reported to have been in charge of the excursion said: "I'm not interested in talking about that."

The man, a Families Department public servant, then denied he was aware of the incident.

A woman who also supervised the excursion said she would prefer not to comment.

She said she knew "what was alleged to have gone on" although she had no direct knowledge of what had occurred.

"I know that the manager of the centre informed [the girl's] mother of the allegations, and she came in to the centre, and . . . we were just told that when the mother was told all the alleged offences were committed by indigenous youth, they dropped it . . . so that was it . . . that was the end of whatever it was . . . they did not proceed."

Former leading criminal lawyer and Director of Public Prosecutions at the time of the incident, Des Sturgess QC, said "unless the story was incredible" the outcome of the matter was not one for the mother to decide.

"That would be for the police to investigate and determine," Mr Sturgess said.

However, the girl's parents have strenuously denied ever being told of the incident. They said the first they had heard of the matter was when asked by this reporter why they had decided not to take any action over it.

Both have called for a full investigation.

The manager of the centre at the time did not respond to a request for an interview. However, he said anyone with allegations about the abuse of children at the centre should take them to the department, to the police or to the Criminal Justice Commission.

"I would encourage anyone with such allegations to do so," he said.

The assistant manager at the time also declined to discuss the matter.

"I have no comment to make," she said. "How did you know I was here?"

The woman currently works in the Department of Families.

The Courier-Mail has been told by former members of staff they had "no doubt" the matter of the gang rape had been raised with the aborted 1989 Heiner Inquiry into the John Oxley Centre.

Following the closing down of the inquiry the manager of the centre was paid over $27,000 for "entitlements" to which he was not entitled and required to sign a secrecy agreement.

Writing news for radio, television and the internet

While the "inverted pyramid" concept of delivering information to news audiences originated in the world of wire services and newspapers, it is nevertheless the fundamental basis for the writing and reporting of news in the other news media too – on radio, television and on the internet.

News consumers, wherever they may be, are usually time poor. They want the news quickly and concisely, without having to struggle to find out what is going on in the world. So, the principles of the "pyramid", or most of them, apply equally in the other media. There is the odd exception. One that may not apply in radio, for instance, is the demand that stories be written so they can be "cut from the bottom". Radio stories are usually so short that writing stories to be "cut from the bottom" is not a realistic approach. That said, most of the checklist items from the first chapter are just as important in radio, TV and online journalism as they are in print.

What has to be recognised in reporting and writing for any media outlet is the special circumstances that apply in each case. Acknowledging these circumstances and dealing with them effectively is the task of, and a challenge for, the reporter. Newspapers are about text and still images; radio is about sound; television is principally about sound and moving images, though it can also incorporate text and still images; the internet is about text, still images, sound and moving images. In this sense, the internet embraces all the elements of the other three media. Having dealt with writing for newspapers, let us look at the others.

Radio and television

If the things you must get right when writing newspaper copy apply because readers will not struggle with your stories, then they apply even more strongly to radio and television news. Unlike readers, listeners and viewers will not get the chance to struggle with your stories – they will hear and/or see them once only. They cannot "re-read" your stories.

But there is more. Not all listeners or viewers are just listening or viewing. Many of them will be doing other things. This places a great demand on you to write copy and produce stories that can be immediately understood on a once-only basis.

So, as with writing news for newspapers, the most important messages for radio and television journalists are: write with clarity; and write sense. The clear, simple, unambiguous expression of your information, supported by the logical development of the content from beginning to end, is essential in writing news for radio and television. Too much at once, too much that is unfamiliar or obscure, and too many holes or hurdles in the fact flow must be avoided.

There is always some other station for your audience to choose if listening to your stories, or watching them, becomes difficult. Even if your audience does not switch off literally, they may still "switch off". Remember, radio and television audiences are not necessarily made up of people who devote their full attention to what is being broadcast. They are usually doing something else. You may not have their full attention at the best of times. So you will need to be good at what you do.

There are some other considerations to be kept in mind. While the radio or television news audience may not be glued to your every word or picture, you can be sure that they will want to hear news. But given that you may only cover 10 or maybe 20 stories in a major bulletin, you will have no shortage of material from which to choose. There are more than 10 or 20 stories around at any one time. You can easily select stories to provide a news service that suits the audience you have, or the one you think you have.

The suggestion that comes across from electronic media when they say, "Here is the news" – that there is only one "news" out there – is far wide of the mark. There are all kinds of "news" out there. You will see this very clearly if you listen to or watch a number of different bulletins over a few days. Some stories will be common, lots will not. The common ones will sometimes have exactly the same content, but often they will cover very different details. There is no such thing as "**the** news". There are lots of "our news".

On radio and television there are separate programs that cover news-related stories – parallel to features and commentaries in a newspaper. A time-rich audience can tune in to those kinds of programs if they want. When listeners and viewers turn on the news, however, news is what they want to get. Consequently, the structure of the inverted pyramid applies as much in the world of radio and television – or online news – as it does in newspapers. The audience will want to know **what has happened** or **what was said** in exactly the same way that newspaper readers want to know these things. So the issue of getting the news at the head of the story is just as relevant in these environments as it is in newspapers.

But there are some differences between the two. To start with, radio and television news bulletins cannot include as much information as a newspaper can. In his book *Looking at Television News*, John Henningham graphically demonstrated the claim that the text involved in a major TV news bulletin would fit on a single page of a newspaper…with room to spare. He transcribed a bulletin, desktop-published the text into the font and point size used by a major national daily and set the result across the column width used by the paper. The TV transcript filled just five columns of one eight-column page. In other words, the amount of news you get in a major national TV news bulletin occupies five eighths of a broadsheet page.

Another major difference is that newspapers seldom have much competition from other newspapers. They may have competition from other media, but even in some of our bigger cities a major daily may not have a competitor to worry about. Provincial dailies may only have weekly rivals to consider. A suburban paper may not have any competition at all.

Radio and television stations are in a very different situation. There is no shortage of competition, particularly in the bigger centres. And the competition facing internet news publishers is all but infinite. This means different things for different media.

Because there are likely to be more of them, radio stations will almost certainly seek to capture a special group or segment of the audience and not worry about the rest. That is the way radio operates. So the journalist working in such an environment will keep his or her eye on the audience as well as on the news. Decisions will be framed accordingly. There may be a competitor trying to capture the same market…or not.

Television stations, on the other hand, may favour particular segments of the audience with their programming (lots of sport, particular sports, infotainment or lifestyle programs, quizzes, sitcoms, etc.), but in general they will all be chasing the biggest possible audience, not the biggest possible audience in a "demographic" or audience segment. Thus competition in general in television, or meeting the expectations of a selected "demographic" in radio, may well determine content and approach to story selection.

The medium involved will also be significant in determining content. Television involves pictures. Stories with powerful or compelling pictures will compete strenuously for space in a TV news bulletin over stories with no, or less compelling, pictures, regardless of how important or "worthy" these stories might be. Stories with good "sound grabs" may overwhelm "worthy" stories on radio just because there are no "sound grabs" to accompany the "worthy" ones. Space or a set time slot is not necessarily an issue online, but it will be necessary to put content into some sort of hierarchy, and this might well be influenced by available pictures, video or audio.

Radio and television stations are criticised because they often place stories they can tell well (through pictures or sound grabs) ahead of more important stories, and because they highlight the dramatic over the normal, and the physical over the philosophical. And they do. Their response is: tell the people. Tell the audience. Convince them that they should watch something else. We operate in a commercial and competitive environment, the stations say, and if we don't have an audience, there is no station. The media system that operates within a society is therefore very influential in determining content. In this context, it is impossible to say there is only one way to report and write news.

Another key difference between the media is that communication between reporter and audience in the world of radio and television is very different from that in the world of newspapers. This is a crucial factor to be understood by the reporter working in radio and television news. The reporter takes on a dimension that has no parallel in the print world.

Readers may become attached to the work of a newspaper journalist, but contact in the reporting environment is limited. Unless there is a photograph beside the byline on a newspaper story, and even then it is often so small as to be downright obscure, reader and reporter operate in different spheres. But radio or television reporters enter the private space of their listeners and viewers. Their voices are known, their faces are known. Here, then, is a situation that the reporter can use to advantage. Not everyone does, but the opportunity is there for wise reporters to add another layer to their work – a layer of professional performance that recognises the special circumstances that exist in the relationship between reporter and audience in radio and television.

This layer depends on **how to write** when the opportunity presents itself to produce more than a 10-word intro to a sound grab or a vision clip; it depends on **delivery** of what has been written; and it depends on the **presentation** of the other two.

When these three things have been brought together, radio or television reporters will be maximising the opportunities and advantages offered by the medium in which they work. But these are not things that will necessarily be mastered overnight. They may take months. They may take years. Some may never master them and their careers may lie elsewhere.

Writing

Writing a one-sentence intro to a 10-second sound grab of someone respond-ing to a question, or introducing another reporter, is no great challenge. The issues to be sorted out will be simple. Is it to be a "straight" (or conventional or formal) news lead, or an informal lead? That answer will depend on the story itself, on what kind of station is involved and on what kind of image the station sets out to present to its audience.

A formal intro:

> The Prime Minister leaves Washington tonight after a three-day official visit to the United States' capital. Our reporter in Washington, Laura Long filed this update.

Or, perhaps, depending on the station:

> After a hectic three days in the States, the PM heads for home. Here's Laura Long in Washington.

There is nothing very difficult about either of those introductions.

Already two points – a similarity and a difference – between the electronic news world and that of newspapers have emerged. The similarity is: the news comes first. The difference is: the use of the present tense.

Tense . . . and being there

Radio news in particular is "on the hour, every hour". Television news may not appear quite so frequently but there are regular updates throughout the day. The two trade in immediacy, reporting "as it happens", and being "the first with the latest". Even if it has happened and whatever it was is over and done with, the present tense still abounds.

Even if it is still to happen, the present tense is used. In the case above, the Prime Minister may well have left Washington, may be leaving as the bulletin goes to air, or may leave sometime later in the day, but the present tense covers all three possibilities. Significantly it also creates a sense of immediacy that will, the journalists hope, appeal to listeners or viewers – because they feel as though they are being informed about an event at the very instant it is happening, even if it actually has happened, or is yet to happen. "The Prime Minister leaves Washington tonight" covers all three possibilities and maintains the atmosphere of immediacy that is prized in radio and television.

If the radio or television story cannot be presented in the present tense, or it cannot be sustained in the present tense, there is always the present imperfect (or present continuous) or the present perfect (see the chapter on grammar). The present imperfect is a present tense form appropriate to an action that is not complete – one that is continuing, that is not "perfect". The present perfect is a combination present and past verb form appropriate to an action that is complete (perfect).

For example, a newspaper might say:

> "The Treasurer told (*past tense*) Parliament there could be some surprises in this year's budget."

While radio or television might say any of the following:

> "The Treasurer says (*present tense*) there could be some surprises in this year's budget."
> "The Treasurer is flagging (*present imperfect or present continuous*) some surprises in this year's budget."
> "The Treasurer has flagged (*present perfect*) some surprises in this year's budget."

In the case of an event that has already occurred, there is every likelihood that present tense forms cannot be sustained throughout a written story. Sooner or later the circumstances in which the story arose may have to be mentioned and the past tense will be involved. If, instead, the rest of the story were presented via an "actuality" grab (of the Treasurer speaking, for instance), the present tense could obviously be maintained.

Just because the electronic media prefer present tense forms over the past does not mean that rules can be broken. Once *said* or *told* or any similar past tense verb is used in indirect speech, related verbs must also be in the past tense form, as in:

> The Treasurer said the size of the budget surplus **would** (**not** *will*) allow for substantial tax cuts.

Just as first-person references in direct speech become third-person references in reported speech, reported or indirect speech requires past tense verb forms. If this is deemed unacceptable or undesirable, "actuality" grabs of direct speech are the only solution. Mixing tense forms in reported speech is not just undesirable, it is unacceptable.

Unlike their newspaper colleagues, radio and television reporters, and newsreaders too, have no access to punctuation marks. A newspaper reporter may happily write, for instance:

> The situation was "desperate" and the minister acted "as quickly as possible".

If this were read on air, as a radio reporter might, the quotation marks would vanish, and it would appear that the reporter was making judgments about the seriousness of the situation and, in addition, defending or supporting the actions of the minister:

> The situation was desperate and the minister acted as quickly as possible.

Making judgments is not the role of a reporter. Since there is no audible equivalent of the punctuation mark, attribution is the only solution. Either of these alternatives would work:

> The situation was considered desperate and the minister said she acted as quickly as possible.
> The minister said the situation was desperate and <u>that</u> she had acted as quickly as possible.

Here is a case where "that" is not redundant. It is necessary.

> The minister said the situation was desperate and she had acted as quickly as possible.

In this copy it would not be clear whether it was the minister or the reporter who was making the judgment about how quickly the minister had responded. And we do not want there to be any confusion.

Clarity

Once upon a time, radio and even television news consisted of stories written by journalists and read by newsreaders. There were no sound grabs in the radio bulletin, no interviews, no actuality. Stories were written and what people said was reported in indirect speech.

Times have changed. It is unusual these days to hear a complete story read by a newsreader. Today, radio news involves a one- or two-line intro followed by a short sound grab of some kind. This might be taken from an interview with a person involved in the story and followed perhaps by another line or couple of lines from the newsreader to introduce another player in the story, or to provide the other side of the story. These are known as "grabs" or "voice pieces" because the main story is carried by a range of voices. Or the sound grab might come from a reporter on the spot or in the newsroom. If this is the case, the reporter will need to have something to say, will need to be able to write and will need to be able to present the material so the listener can follow and understand the story. These are often called "straight pieces", and they are most important in television news too, although they are used as much to show the news crew being on the spot as to contribute anything to the story.

The essentials of writing have already been covered. The most important issue in writing is clarity. Will the listener be able to follow the story? Once you write more than a single-line introduction to a story, the clarity of what you write immediately becomes an issue. What you write has to make immediate sense. There are any number of impediments to that. If you use convoluted constructions, if the fact flow you set down is not clear and logical, if the story does not unfold bit by bit or step by step, if the relationship between the players in the story and the story is not obvious, if your sentences are too long, or if you try to get too much in, you will have made a hash of the story.

The need for clarity will determine the style in which the story is written. If the story is complex, or the chronology of events significant, the story structure will require the complexity to be unravelled or the chronology presented bit by bit. There will not be any room for a display of literary skill. Such stories will not be the time to show how good a writer you are. Just worry about writing clearly.

If the story is simple, so that clarity is not the only issue, the next task is to make the writing interesting. The approaches covered in the chapter on writing for the reader are just as valuable in the worlds of radio and television as they are in writing for newspapers.

Once you have written your piece, you have to consider the issues of delivery and presentation. The piece has to go to air, so it has to sound professional.

Delivery and presentation

Your delivery of what you have written as a piece of radio or television journalism is critical. This is what the listener will hear, or the viewer see and hear. How good it sounds, how convincing, how authoritative, how clearly it can be followed, do not just depend on the words you wrote. These things will also depend on how you deliver them. They will depend on how well you understand the medium in which you are working and the environment in which your work will be seen or heard. You will need to be conscious of the pace of your delivery, of "light and shade" in your delivery, of the importance of timing, and pausing, and of rise and fall in your voice. You will need to be aware of the dangers of racing through your words, or of sounding monotonous, or mono-tone-ous, or dull, or rambling.

The issue of delivering your copy well has to be considered right from the start – at the writing stage. Choosing your words carefully and recognising the rules of clarity are essential. But how you put those words on a page so that you can read them well is also vitally important. In other words, if you write with the delivery – how you will sound – in mind, you will be halfway to sounding very good.

As you write you will be getting your words right, but you also need to keep the next step in mind – recording or speaking those words. Your punctuation will be vital at this stage. And there are only two punctuation marks to worry about – the full stop and the dash. The full stop means a major pause, the dash means all the other pauses, the comma, the colon, and the semicolon. The dash is better than these because it separates the words more distinctly on the page (more space between the words) and thus it presents the sense of your writing more clearly to you when you read it. And when you do come to read it, that will be important.

Use two hyphens, or figure out how to make your word processor produce proper dashes (ens or ems). One hyphen presents too small a space between words, and you might appropriately have a hyphen at the end of a line anyway – you don't want to confuse a hyphen linking the two parts of a compound word with a pause. All of this means your major pauses will be full stops, and your pauses – for effect, for pace, for light and shade – will be dashes or double hyphens.

The point of all this is quite simple. You do not want to sound as if you are reading your story to your listener, nor delivering a lecture, nor a sermon. You want to sound as if you are talking to your listener, albeit with presence and authority and dignity. The two hyphens, or the dash, will help you do this and do it better than with the usual punctuation marks.

Simply take the paragraph above and try reading it:

> The point of all this is quite simple. You do not want to sound as if you are reading your story to your listener, nor delivering a lecture, nor a sermon. You want to sound as if you are talking to your listener, albeit with presence and authority and dignity. The two hyphens, or the dash, will help you do this and do it better than with the usual punctuation marks.

Now write it my way. Your copy will look like this:

> The point of all this is quite simple. You do not want to sound as if you are reading your story to your listener -- nor delivering a lecture -- nor a sermon. You want to sound as if you are talking to your listener -- albeit with presence -- and authority -- and dignity. The two hyphens -- or the dash -- will help you do this -- and do it better than with the usual punctuation marks.

Now, if you read this version, I suggest you will sound much better.

There is something else you might want to do before starting the recorder – put in some mini-pauses. Like this:

> The point of all this/ is quite simple. You do not want/ to sound/ as if you are reading your story to your listener -- nor delivering a lecture -- nor a sermon. You want to sound/ as if you are talking to your listener -- albeit with presence -- and authority -- and dignity. The two hyphens -- or the dash -- will help you do this -- and do it better/ than with the usual punctuation marks.

The full stop, the dash and the forward slash will help you get the pace, the timing, the pauses and the "light and shade" in your delivery right.

Finally, at least in the early days, you might want to add one more aid. Underlining significant words may help get the emphasis right. Underlining does not have to mean heavy emphasis. It may mean just a little, and it will not be long before you will not need the underlining at all. Your final copy might look something like this:

> The point of all this/ is quite simple. You do not want to sound/ as if you are <u>reading</u> your story to your listener -- nor delivering a lecture -- nor a <u>sermon</u>. You want to sound/ as if you are <u>talking</u> to your listener -- albeit with presence -- and authority -- and dignity. The two hyphens -- or the dash -- will help you do this -- and do it <u>better</u>/ than with the <u>usual</u> punctuation marks.

The delivery may now sound better, but do you sound professional? Do you have a drawl? Do you speak through your nose, or slur your words together? Do you clip your words short? Do you say "In May . . ." clipped short, or "In Mayyyy . . ." where the vowel sound is drawn out that little bit? How are your vowels, anyway? Is it "The rain in Spain . . ." or "The rhine in Spine . . ."? And so on.

You will not learn to use your voice well by just reading a book on how to do it. You will need to get a recorder, and read a piece of copy and listen back to it, over and over. You will also need to listen to good broadcasters, and listen very closely. You may well need someone to guide you. You have to put in some effort because if you don't sound professional, no one will take your copy seriously. While you are on air, they will spend the time discussing how awful you sound.

Dos and don'ts for radio and television

There are writing conventions you should observe when reporting for radio and television, just as there are in newspapers. Here are some of them, and the reasons why there are conventions.

Remember the inverted pyramid

Listeners or viewers who tune in to news programs want to know what the news is. Don't spend forever getting to the point. And the what, who, when, where and why are just as important here as they are in newspapers. They are the things news is about.

It is claimed from time to time that the inverted pyramid structure has no place in broadcast news. The claim goes on to assert that every word in broadcast news is as important as every other word, therefore the inverted pyramid has nothing to do with radio and television newswriting. The claim is silly. It defies logic. All news stories, print, radio, TV, or whatever, have to be written in some kind of order. They must have some kind of structure. Something has to come first, something next, something in the middle and something at the end. If every word or sentence was as important as any other, and the inverted pyramid did not apply, you should be able to start a story at the end and read backwards. Or alternate the pars. Or pick any one of them as your lead.

Such propositions are nonsense. Broadcast news stories conform to an inverted pyramid structure as much as news stories do in print, whether the reporters or those who write books about broadcast newswriting agree or not.

Choose a strong lead

The summary lead is even more valuable in electronic news because you hold back the detail until the audience is listening or watching. Then you give the detail.

The style preferred by some broadcast newsrooms is to take a chatty approach to the news. Leads are soft rather than hard. This means the writer finds an indirect route to the news instead of getting straight to it:

"A fool and his money are soon parted, seems to be the lesson a bank robber learned on the Peninsula this afternoon.

An off-duty security guard walking past the local bank just on closing time saw someone inside holding a revolver to the head of a female bank teller.

The man waited behind a pillar at the front of the bank for the robber to emerge.

When he did the security guard also emerged, king-hit the robber twice, disarmed him and sat on him until police arrived."

A hard lead would be:

"Police charge a man with robbery with violence following a bungled bank hold-up on the Peninsula this afternoon".

There are said to be other kinds of leads – delayed leads, question leads, quote leads, and so on. These are just soft leads given fancy names. And some of them seldom appear. Starting a broadcast news story with a quote read by a newsreader is silly. An "actuality" quote may be different, but don't start with the newsreader reading a quote. The listener will wonder what could possibly be going on. Starting with a question is usually equally silly. A question lead will probably provoke a sarcastic, negative or "smart" response from the listener, and that is the last thing a news bulletin needs.

Don't start a story with figures or a name

These are likely to be important details in the context of the story, if not critical details, and if a listener doing other things misses them, the point of the whole story may be lost. The idea of a lead is to attract the listener, but you have to ensure they are tuned in before you provide such significant information. Don't assume they are tuned in from the start.

Round out figures . . . in words, not numbers

Don't write "$245,376" in your copy, or "almost $250,000". Write "almost 250 thousand dollars". And if the figure was $255,376, write "more than 250 thousand dollars", not "over 250 thousand dollars". In the same way, "3,588,970" becomes "more than 3.5 million", or "more than 3 point 5 million", or "more than 3 and a half million", depending on house style.

If it is important, indicate emphasis for the newsreader

"He began his career in <u>politics</u> in 1935." (Meaning: he had two careers, one in movies and one in politics. His political career started in 1935.) Unless you wanted to say: "He began his career in politics in <u>1935</u>" (not 1945 as most observers have incorrectly claimed).

Clarify pronunciation of names

Pronunciation is vitally important in maintaining credibility in radio and television reporting, just as spelling, grammar and punctuation are in newspaper reporting.

Names of people and places litter the news and many of them do not follow standard English pronunciation conventions. Some will be completely new, and just as likely, very awkward. Newsreaders and reporters should not be left to guess how to pronounce such names. There is nothing more likely to produce a scornful reaction from listeners than a name or word incorrectly pronounced in a news bulletin. And a response such as "If they can't get that right, what can they get right?" is likely to follow.

The answer is obvious, of course. The writer should provide an accurate phonetic spelling of the word immediately after it appears in the story, and at least until the newsreader becomes familiar with the word, on every occasion it appears in the story. It is unreasonable to expect a reader to scan earlier paragraphs looking for the phonetic pronunciation when the word appears again.

Some newsrooms have a set house style for presenting phonetic pronunciation while others rely on the writer to use well-known alternatives to express the sound of the syllables. An established house style is a good idea, because it reduces the scope for error. The style has to cover all the alternatives for each of the various vowel sounds (as many as six in the case of "e") and for each of those consonants that have hard or soft alternatives.

Without phonetic assistance would you know how to pronounce the name of a small country town called Kairi? There is an almost 100 per cent chance you would get it wrong. The pronunciation is KEER-Eye, or KEER-EYE, depending on the way the house style represents emphasis. In a news story the phonetic spelling should appear in brackets immediately after the name.

Such things are important. Over the years they may have grown used to it, but there was a time when the residents of Kairi (KEER-EYE) would fume every time a newsreader mispronounced the name of their hometown as KEYE-REE.

What would you do if you were reading a story – sight unseen – that covered something serious happening at Ebbw Vale? If you thought the writer had really meant Webb Vale, you would be wrong. And how would you go with a story about a person whose surname was Zvirgzdins? Or a story about a product containing cyanocobalamin? The case for including phonetic spelling in your stories rests.

Don't mimic the pictures

In television it is essential, unless there is something complicated on the screen, not to echo the pictures. Telling a viewer what he or she can quite plainly see is certainly boring, but worse, it's very lazy. It means the reporter has not done enough (or any) research, didn't get sufficient material when the story was shot, or didn't ask enough questions of the talent. The story then is thin, wafer thin, and the viewer will be able to tell. Narration or voice-over has to contain relevant but additional information, above and beyond what can be seen on the screen.

Checking your story

If you have to write a news story as a "straight piece", without a video or audio grab, you may have about 10 or 12 lines in which to do it. That is not a big ask. But it is easily botched unless you pay heed to each of the points above. As you'd expect, many points are similar to those made for newspapers, and the differences have been discussed above.

Checklist

1. Have you bitten off more than you can deal with adequately in so few words? Do your words complement any pictures (rather than describing them)? ☐
2. Is everything you have reported accurate? Is it clear? Is the story free of your comments and opinions? ☐
3. Have you used an inverted pyramid structure? ☐
4. Have you chosen an appropriate lead for the story and audience? No figures or names to open the story. ☐
5. Has the story been developed logically from beginning to end? Are there holes in the story? Can the reader follow it easily by ear? ☐
6. Have you explained who the sources are and why they are in the story? Have you explained any necessary background? Are you sure this will be clear to listeners? ☐
7. Are the tenses right? What about the rest of the grammar? ☐
8. How's your sentence length? Once you get to 20 words start looking for a full stop or a major pause of some kind. ☐
9. Active voice wherever possible? ☐
10. Have you written it so it can be read well? Pace, timing, pauses and emphasis indicated? Pronunciation of names clarified? ☐

The internet and online journalism

So much has been said about the wonders of the internet that in some people's minds it has taken on a presence akin to that of some omnipotent God. Figures of unimaginable proportions tumble out. Millions upon millions log on every day. No, silly, that was last week. Now it is every hour. Tomorrow, presumably, it will be every minute. Millions and millions have blogs or are into producing or accessing podcasts. Untold millions at least have sites where they can tell an enraptured world of their recent holiday to Somewhere and upload pics of the children smiling at the mobile phone camera to prove it. The internet is changing the entire world if not the universe as we know it, folks, and you had best get on board lest it simply steamroll you into oblivion.

There is a need for a reality check. A few reality checks really.

The internet is not a new medium, in the way that radio was when it first unshackled audiences from the confined space of printed text and still images and gave them sound. Nor is it a new medium like television, which offered not just sound but moving pictures as well. The internet has not brought those kinds of advances in audience experience. It just delivers what the others do: text, still images, sound and moving pictures. All at once if you like.

The difference is, unlike print, radio and television, the digital advances involved with the internet mean we can all participate in the delivery process. And we do. It is all so exciting.

But even the excitement is not new. When Marconi demonstrated in 1896 that he could send messages downstairs, across the garden and then over the horizon, and took his black box to London, the authorities saw its potential to support the vast empire that Britain had created (not to mention its military forces) and they welcomed him and his radio gizmo. The genie, however, got out of the bottle and the day of "ham radio" had arrived, and the hams sent da-da-dit-dit Morse code messages to each other all over the place. They loved it.

Within just nine years of Marconi's first tentative upstairs/downstairs experiments, the government of Australia (which was only a few years old itself) legislated to control the new-fangled airwaves lest their use get out of hand. "Ham radio" had taken off.

Reginald Aubrey Fessenden only made it worse when he superimposed the voice of a woman singing on a carrier frequency and scared the daylights out of those who heard it in their earphones instead of the little da-da-dits-dits they were used to. Broadcasting was born.

Today we might call them bloggers, but then they were called "hams" and by the time of World War I, there were so many of them playing with their weird wireless set contraptions they had to be banned in the interests of the war effort. When the war was over they all rushed back into their radio shacks and backrooms, and others followed. There were so many of them there was anarchy in the ether. Sound familiar? So, governments stepped in, asserted their right to control a limited public resource (the electronic spectrum) and licensed the use of the radio airwaves. The "hams" were put in a box and only the big outfits got to play. If ham radio had not been contained in the 1920s we would have had an "internet" experience 80 years ago.

But that is not the only back-to-the-future comparison we can make between radio and the internet today. There was the global experience, the irrelevance of national borders back then too.

Perhaps, because of the internet you don't listen to the radio any more. But if you do, you will know that at night you can pick up many more radio stations, and from all kinds of faraway places, than you can during the day. That is because the ionosphere, which acts as a giant reflector of radio waves around the planet, is somewhat dispersed by radiation from the sun during the day. At night it intensifies (no sun) and reflects radio waves back to earth. The existence of the ionosphere means that smarties can actually bounce short wavelength radio waves off the ionosphere in hops all round the globe. And lob them even into places that don't want them. It was, and still is, called short-wave broadcasting. It's what they do at Radio Australia, the BBC World Service, Deutsche Welle (the Voice of Germany), Radio Nederland, Voice of

America, and the like. Millions of people, all over the globe, have tuned in over the years to these signals and messages. A global mass medium that has been in operation for at least 70 years.

So while it's true that in this new and exciting world of global internet journalism you need to be culturally aware, and geographically aware, and politically aware, and so on, because the whole world might be listening, reading or watching, there's nothing new about that. That was new in the 1930s. It has been standard operating practice since then at Radio Australia, BBC World Service, Deutsche Welle and the like.

When the internet first emerged in the early 1990s, we accessed it via a program called Mosaic. Mosaic, you ask? Never heard of it. True. It has gone. What technological gadgetry will there be in another 15 years time?

Anyone forecasting the death of the existing media because of the existence of what we know today as the internet is a very brave person. It could happen, of course. The number of players able to access the available advertising revenue may grow and disperse the revenue so much that the costs of doing journalism may not be supported by the income it can generate. However, there have been victims of that imbalance (income vs outlays) in the world of journalism in Australia since at least the 1820s. Within a couple of years of a free press starting in this country, some of the players folded. It has been going on ever since. It is altogether premature to predict the death of the media as we know them today because of the growth of the internet, and likewise premature to predict the death of journalism.

There is one certainty. The need for journalism, good journalism, will not vanish. The need will be as great as it has ever been. Bloggers will not be the solution.

Furthermore, the Chairman of the Australian Competition and Consumer Commission (a body which keeps an eye on the matter of monopoly) told a Senate hearing into proposed new media ownership legislation: "We think the internet is simply a distribution channel. It hasn't shown any significant signs at this point in time of providing a greater diversity of credible information news and commentary" (*The Australian* September 28, 2006, p. 6).

So what have all the millions and squillions of bloggers and private pod-casters been up to for the last decade? Whatever it is, it has not been a major contribution to credible journalism.

Another reality check, for those just starting out. If you decide to spend your life in newspapers and magazines, you can ignore this whole chapter. If you decide radio or television is your thing, you can ignore this section of this chapter. But if you decide to go online, or if it seems that you may someday change direction in your career (which you probably will) and go on line you will not be able to ignore anything that has been written in this book so far. And, I would suggest, nothing in the rest of the book either.

The online environment embraces text, still images, sound and moving pictures . . . environments we already know as newspapers, radio and television. If you can do journalism for them, you can do it for the internet . . . with some adjustments to account for the audience being connected via a computer screen rather than a page of paper or a radio or television set. The fundamentals don't change. The internet is not something so different you can forget the others. But don't take just my word for it.

Stephen Quinn is probably the most widely published writer and academic on the subject of the internet and journalism in Australia. In his latest book (with co-author Vincent F. Filak) *Convergent journalism* Quinn notes some truisms. He says staff from a group of high-profile journalism schools in the United States were interviewed about their views on "convergence". Opinions differed except for one thing: " . . . that an emphasis on journalistic writing mechanics, journalistic style and English grammar were key to all good journalism programs". He went on to say: "Reporting comes first. To make your writing sing, you'll need to do some strong reporting before you do anything else."

And he also clearly identified the importance of the "inverted pyramid" in dealing with the "immediacy-based approach" required of journalism on the World Wide Web. "News writers are required to answer the who, what, where, when, how and why very early in the story, leaving the fine details and background for later. On the Web is no different. In fact," the authors say, "it's more important [on the Web] to produce compact and to-the-point stories". This is hardly surprising. People who go to the internet for news want to find it without fuss. The inverted pyramid meets this need.

Dos and don'ts for online reporting

The deadline is now

Every time someone clicks on your site you are on deadline. So you are always on deadline. But how old is your copy? When did you update a story or drop it. Do you tell the reader when your story was uplinked or updated? Or do you leave them in the dark because the stuff may be hours or days old?

While the net is a hobby and lots of fun for everyone, people may not care that you don't reveal the age of your stories, but as users become more and more selective, they will want to know, and you will have to respond. They are not going to bother with a source that is x hours old when someone else has the story up to date.

Rewrite your stories

If you don't care about your audience, or if you want to insult them, just uplink your stories exactly as they appeared in the newspaper they were originally written for, or the radio or TV bulletin. But if you are concerned about your audience on the net you will rejig the stories. Probably quite substantially. Why? There are three key reasons.

1. You may need a new headline.

   The one in the paper looked good, but it ran across the whole page, or it didn't, and the chances that the same headline will work across a portion of a computer screen, jostled by all kinds of other competing messages, is unlikely. The headline, or the link to the story, has to be good. People chasing news don't have all day.

2. The lead will have to be good.

   Thank goodness for the old inverted pyramid. If the one that was used in the newspaper or radio or TV bulletin worked well, it might be fine. But if it was tagged to some well-understood local or even national peculiarity, it will have to go. The question is, do you care about your audience? Your audience may be just down the street. Or it may be an expat in Rome. But it might be someone in Lebanon or Bolivia or China who has never heard of Fosters or XXXX.

3. Explain your copy; background your copy.

   Do what the short-wave broadcasters do, and have been doing for years. Names and titles and positions, place names, geography, political realities and much more have to be explained to a foreign audience. This takes room and time. But the alternative is confusion in your audience. It is no good saying the Head of CSIRO has supported calls for Australia to sign the Kyoto Accord. If that is what you are putting on the internet, you might as well not bother. Outside Australia, who knows what the CSIRO is? And even if you spell out the name, you will still have to say what it does.

Near enough's not good enough

Watch your accuracy. If your work is being read around the globe and not just in your own little patch, being near enough will not be good enough. If you should call a visiting dignitary from another country a Prime Minister when he is, in fact, a President, or someone a Head of State when he isn't, you will have made a fool of yourself and your organisation.

Now that you are playing on the internet, you are playing in the big league. Are you up to it? Do you check your facts or just take a stab? The issue at stake is credibility, once again.

How do you look?

Design of your site is vital. Just as a newspaper page can be off-putting or attractive, so can a website. The desire to get as many links as possible on a page, plus some copy and a couple of images, just to show everyone how much stuff you have has to be contained.

A site that is visually confusing, with links that are poorly written and take the reader where he or she did not want to go, is self-defeating.

Good design, good headlines, good links, not too much clutter. That will be a good start . . .

When was yesterday?

Time references in a world that is (thankfully) slowly spinning round and round need to be addressed. In so many cases on the internet they are not. Stories glibly talk about "today" or "yesterday" and may be updated or not. (And how would we know?) But for the reader in Edinburgh, or Nairobi, or Rio de Janeiro these are meaningless words. Dates and times can help. How many sites do you see with a link to an international clock or a time converter?

The basics apply

Just because there is a lot of anarchy out there, do not assume the internet is a free-for-all where anything goes. It is not. Your newswriting skills and your reporting skills will be as important here as they are in any newspaper or radio or TV station. The law even applies. Particularly the law of defamation. The internet may have its share of anarchy, but leave that for the cowboys in the blogosphere. Journalism requires discipline. Even on the internet.

Present tense

As in radio and television, on the internet you want to give the impression that you are up with the latest. So use present and present continuous tenses as much as you can, before acknowledging the past.

Writing stories for the reader

News organisations want more from their reporters than just an ability to write news stories. They want people who can also write **well** – to satisfy those who want more from their news outlet than just the news. Which means they want good writers. They want reporters who can write for the time-rich reader, not just for the news junkie. And writing a story for the reader is a very different challenge from writing a story within the constraints of the inverted pyramid.

In case you should think otherwise, writing for the reader is not just about writing feature articles. It is also about writing news.

Some time ago the Australian Prime Minister's cat was in serious trouble. There was a wonderful photograph of the villain, plus John and Janette Howard at home in Kirribilli House. Every newspaper at the time ran the picture and a story. Most of the stories were variations on the inverted-pyramid formula. But Christopher Niesche of the *Australian* wrote his front page news story way, way outside the pyramid. It started like this:

A prime ministerial list of things to do: Meet NZ PM, discuss defence agreements. Explain new position on reconciliation. Shift to new stance on population policy. Keep the cat away from the ducks.

What?

This is how the story unfolds.

> **December:** Ducks mysteriously disappearing around PM's harbourside house for some months.
>
> **Suspect:** Howard family cat Honeycomb. Described as white and ginger, elderly.

That is most certainly **not** a conventional inverted-pyramid lead. The story ended like this:

> **March 3:** PM's wife Janette gives okay for ducks' return. PM assures cat will be locked in at night.
>
> Official line from PM's office: "The Howards are keen to ensure wildlife in the grounds of Kirribilli House is protected."
>
> **March 7:** Ducks due home.
> There are a million stories in the harbour city. This has been one of them.

It was a splendid photograph, of course (and photographs are responsible for getting lots of stories into newspapers), but there is little doubt that everyone who bought that edition of the *Australian* would have read that story. And they would have read it all.

So what is this matter of writing outside the pyramid all about?

An out-of-the-pyramid rationale

The world of journalism, obviously, is full of stories. But behind the obvious, behind the public world of journalism, of tabloid or broadsheet pages, of voices through the ether or pictures on the six o'clock news, there is another world of journalism. The flipside.

And it too is full of stories. These are the stories of what went on, or how, or why, or when, behind the stories that appeared in print or on the six o'clock news.

These are stories of great reporters and mere mortals; of fearless reporters and foolish; of hard, determined slog and Tattslotto luck; stories of amazing adventures and flukes – some true, some half-true and some . . . well, who knows? Stories to make your hair curl or your sides split.

These are the in-house stories; stories about the business and what it is like to be in it. There is a moral to many, if not most of them. Free advice, if you like.

Take, for instance, the story of the far-off correspondent discussing the demands of an urgent assignment with an equally far-off chief of staff: "I don't have time for a thousand words," the correspondent complains. "I'm too busy. I'll do you two thousand instead."

The moral of this story is clear. And worth remembering. And a good place to start when talking about writing outside the pyramid. For good writing in a news story or a feature is no slap-dash matter.

The big problem, of course, is time – time not only to do a good job of getting the information, which can be hard enough, but time to write well. Time is always the enemy in journalism and, sadly, the pressure of the deadline can elevate the slap-dash.

That is why the pyramid is so convenient. It is a recipe. You just follow the pyramid, the formula, and, hey presto . . . if a reporter, through some intellectual misadventure, doesn't know what has to be done, the subs do – and can straighten the whole thing out in a trice.

The formula means that the show is always on the road, and when things get busy, thanks to the inverted pyramid formula stories can be written, even in a flying hurry, and still be ready in time.

There is pressure and stress, of course. But thrashing out a few pars, or quite a few, is not a problem once you know the formula, the recipe for the pyramid. Get the news up the front and work your way down from there.

The pyramid is important. You need it to be able to produce a newspaper every day. The trouble is, there is so much "hard" news style in newspapers. The pyramid is everywhere.

So what if you were to take the pyramid, that security blanket, away from your newswriting? What would you get then?

You might get excitement at being let off the leash. You might get fear instead – about what others, your colleagues, your friends, even your readers, might think of your efforts.

With no recipe, no formula, no inverted pyramid you will have to get out of your comfort zone. Now you might have to really start writing!

But what if it was fun? And what if your audience liked it? What if you were good at it? It could be an exciting journey.

A small step for journalism. A giant leap for you.

Non-pyramid news

Once you escape the inverted pyramid, the rules change. We are not necessarily talking about feature stories here. We are also talking about news stories. Even news stories that end up on page one. Here are some random leads from a collection that appeared on page one and page three of the *Sydney Morning Herald*.

Marian Wilkinson on the front page of the paper (October 25, 2001):

> Behind the wire mesh, the kangaroo mobs and a stray emu stared aimlessly about the bushland of the old defence site at St Marys, unaware that John Howard had signed them up to campaign for his favourite MP, Jackie Kelly.

Or Kirsty Needham on page three (March 1, 2003):

> Popcorn tubs and oversized cola dwarf the infant as her parents, having parked the all-terrain pram at the door, juggle rattles, cloths and fluoro-fluffy toys – and look for a seat.

Or Scott Rochfort on page three, branded as "News" in the folio line at the top (October 26, 2001):

> Dorothy Mathias didn't want to quack like a duck and act like a teapot when she arrived at Lewisham Public School yesterday morning.

Remember, now that we are not talking about the inverted pyramid, we are not talking about rules or conventions any more. There are none. You are off the leash as it were. How many conventional inverted pyramid rules are broken in the lead immediately above?

And you cannot look to me, or anyone else, for the recipe to replace the pyramid. There is no recipe. There is just good writing.

Do you have something to say?

It helps, if you want to write well, if you have something to write about. That's common sense.

It is not all that hard to fill up space with waffle, and plenty do, for there is no shortage of waffle around. Each week forests fall for it. *Media Watch* did a whole program on the subject once. It was embarrassing. Column after column of drivel produced by writers whose ideas were much more limited than their self-confidence, or arrogance, and confined principally to trivial events in the fascinating lives of their pets and children.

It's not that those subjects are duds, since children and pets and families can make excellent copy. It's not that we aren't interested either. It's just that the writers miss the point. The point is: why be so dull?

Don't we ever learn? Tom Wolfe's critique of writers we are all familiar with appeared in his book *The new journalism* in 1975 – more than 30 years ago!

> They usually start out full of juice, sounding like terrific boulevardiers and raconteurs, retailing in print all the marvellous mots and anecdotes they have been dribbling away over lunch for the past few years. After eight or ten weeks, however, they start to dry up. You can see the poor bastards floundering and gasping. They're dying of thirst. They're out of material. They start writing about funny things that happened around the house the other day, homey one-liners that the Better Half or the Avon lady got off, or some fascinating book or article that started them thinking, or else something they saw on TV. Thank God for TV! Without television shows to cannibalize, half of these people would be lost, utterly catatonic. Pretty soon you can almost see it, the tubercular blue of the 23-inch screen, radiating from their prose. Anytime you see a columnist trying to squeeze material out of his house, articles, books, or the television set, you've got a starving soul on your hands . . . You should send him a basket . . .

One of the best ways to good writing is to get something good to write about. Common sense – as above.

Except that is not always possible. Stories don't all come with bells and whistles. **You** have to make up the leeway. You have to put in some effort. And the best way to start, and to get something to write about, and not be dull, is to use, not just your common sense, but your common senses. Look, listen, touch, sniff, taste, etc.

But don't just look: see. Don't just listen: hear. Don't just touch: feel.

In the main, journalists are not encouraged to do these things. There is no room in the traditional news story for them. Indeed, such things are likely to be seen as self-indulgent. No time, no space for that kind of thing. And so we either get out of the habit of using our senses, or, more likely, we never had the habit in the first place.

To start with, we interview most of the people we deal with over the phone. We never see them. Wouldn't know them if we fell over them. Their verbal responses to our questions, except perhaps for some trembling (?), or angry, or guarded signals we detect in their voice, are all we get – and all we want. For what we want is answers, and we have shorthand books and pencils ready to make sure we get them down.

If we do go outside the office for a face-to-face encounter, the plot is still the same. Questions and answers dutifully recorded. All accurate to a fault. And nothing else. Why bother? They'd chop it out, anyway.

But the time has come, editors are saying, to speak of other things. The things that are all around the subjects of your stories. The sights, the sounds, the sensations, the smells, the lot.

This may involve a new reporting experience for some, and possibly many, in the newsroom.

It will involve making notes in the shorthand book about the things that are there in front of you, the things you see, the person doing the talking, his/her expressions, mannerisms, clothes, the room, the decor, people who interrupt. And the things you hear (as well as the answers to your questions). The things that strike you as odd and things that strike you as not. Interesting things. Little things. Big things. Maybe the weather. His shoes. Her brooch. Who knows?

In *Reporting in Australia*, Sally White says John Lahey of the *Age* had "one instruction for young reporters wanting to write soft news: worship detail. He advises keeping a notebook in which to jot down all kinds of arcane information that may come in handy later."

It's trite, but you need to use your common senses. And you need to appreciate the vital importance of detail. When reporting outside the pyramid you need to see the world through the telephoto lens, not the normal 130 degree lens we use all the time. Now you have to use the close-up lens. That way you might get some interesting detail.

Then you could have something to write about. Something outside the pyramid.

The "gripping" quality of what was known as (but wasn't really) the "new journalism", Tom Wolfe says, was gained through the use of just four devices:

> resorting as little as possible to sheer historical narrative . . . recording dialogue in full . . . the so-called 'third-person point of view' . . . [and, most importantly] . . . the recording of everyday gestures, habits, manners, customs, styles of furniture, clothing decoration, styles of travelling, eating, keeping house, modes of behaving toward children, servants, superiors, inferiors, peers, plus the various looks, glances, poses, styles of walking, and other symbolic details that might exist within a scene . . .

Wolfe leaves no doubt about the importance of detail: "the recording of such detail is not mere embroidery in prose. It lies as close to the centre of the power of realism as any other device in literature. It is the very essence of the 'absorbing' power of Balzac, for instance." (pp. 46–47)

Structures and tools

Outside the inverted pyramid there is no formula or recipe. Now there are only some things you need to keep in mind – structures and tools.

Structures

The structure of a story written outside the pyramid is very different. It looks something like this:

Beginning	Middle	End

A beginning, a middle and an end . . . and they are all important.

As well, this kind of story has a spine, or at least a thread, that runs through it from beginning to end. Which means you can't always do with this kind of story what you can with an inverted pyramid. You can't cut it wherever you like from the bottom:

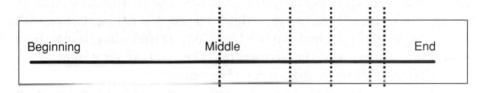

If you cut this kind of story from the bottom, you destroy it:

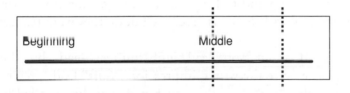

There is another feature of the structure of an out-of-the-pyramid story that should always be considered – linking the end back to the beginning:

Beginning	Middle	End

The best stories are complete units. The beginning makes sense because of the end. The end makes sense because of the beginning.

The earnest reporter will take some care with the first and last paragraphs, Evan Whitton says in *Amazing Scenes* (p. 8), "They may be all anyone reads." And that is often what happens. The beginning gets them in, the ending makes the journey worthwhile.

Get the beginning right

Many years in radio and television taught me a couple of things. One is that the most important was to get the start of the story right. Not just the pictures at the start, or the sound, but the script as well.

This applies in writing for any medium. **Get the beginning right**. Although you don't have to get it right immediately. There's a saying in the business that is excellent advice at this point: "Don't get it right, get it written. Then get it right."

You must understand when writing for the reader that your first finished piece is only a draft. You have to come back to it when it is done and fix all the things that need fixing. Including the lead.

Nevertheless, spend a bit of time when you have collected your material, working out a good beginning. There may be a thousand possibilities, but you don't have forever to choose. Sometimes you struggle to see one. But you have to make your choice sooner rather than later and go with it. Get started. You can always come back and get it right. The clock is ticking. Get on with the job. Seeking inspiration from "on high", or just the ceiling, is okay for a while. But you have to get the piece written. Then you can get it right.

So what is it that might make a good beginning?

A good beginning – lead, intro, whatever – is one that will get the reader in. That is it. The key. You have to capture your reader.

There are costs, however. You may have to use some valuable space to entice your readers in and to keep them reading. This is something newsrooms have to deal with. Space is precious, but do they want readers or don't they?

Textbooks talk about "soft" leads and "indirect" leads, but they are not good terms. They give the wrong impression. "Soft" leads aren't. They are hard – because they have to get the reader in, just as the so-called "hard" lead is meant to, and there is nothing soft or easy about writing them. They are much more difficult.

There are some drawbacks to writing outside the pyramid. After all, the pyramid is the most economical form of writing there is (in terms of space used). And we are most concerned about space, because there is never enough of it. But how many normal news stories, pyramid style, do you ever read to the end – apart from your own, of course?

The answer is: not many. Why not? Because unless you have a personal interest in the subject at hand, there is often very little in these stories to keep you reading.

Writing outside the pyramid attacks that problem. You keep them reading until the very end. First though, and foremost, you have to get them in.

Here are some suggestions, "off the rack" as it were, since there is nothing new in them: surprise; shock; contrast; the unexpected; humour; pathos; intrigue. Which is what most news is, anyway.

Examples

One way to get the reader in is not to reveal your hand too soon. Get them committed. If they know from the outset what the story is about, and the subject doesn't interest them, they will move on. You don't want that. So . . .

> Unless specifically referenced, examples in this section have been prepared for illustrative purposes only and do not represent actual events or refer to actual people.

Intriguing . . .

Not everyone has a sideboard at home groaning with sporting trophies. But it happens.

Not everyone has a gold medal at home for winning a marathon. But that happens too.

Only a few have both.

And not many could claim, when they collected their gold medal, that five kids back home were bursting with pride because of what their mum had done.

The unexpected . . .

Frank looked a million dollars. Dressed to kill as they say. Not a hair out of place and all very stylish. His mini skirt a fashionable navy and not too short.

Contrast, contradiction . . .

In the north there was water, water everywhere. Cattle, in their hundreds, were drowning in it. Out in the Warrego, Dave and Paula were carting the stuff to save theirs from dying of thirst.

The abnormal, out-of-the-ordinary, or aberrant . . .

Barry Simms is looking forward to the Goods and Services Tax.

Looking forward to the GST?

Where have you been, Barry?

But it's true. He can hardly wait. When the 33 per cent sales tax comes off everything in his shop, Barry expects to make a motza. He sells perfumes, home-grown perfumes.

The oblique, enigmatic, mysterious . . .

The voice on the answering machine was matter of fact and certainly mature. His message was brief. He would like to help, but, sorry, he said, he was illiterate. Couldn't read the letter. End of message. He didn't leave his name.

And keep in mind there are plenty of other skills in the newsroom that can add a great deal, not just to your story, but to your lead. As in this case:

> You would not describe David as tall. Far from it. Five foot six probably (no use talking centimetres – David is 59 and his generation is not into metrics). But, despite some evidence of spreading around the midriff, you can see David is solid. Shortish but solid – the perfect build for a Rugby League hooker you might say, the perfect Number 12. (*The Weekend Independent* Dec 1997, p. 1)

By itself it may seem an odd lead to a story. But it appeared under a bold headline across the top of the page that said: "The 'orphan' and the monsters of Neerkol" and in the middle of the page, without a caption, an illustration of a boy with a cross in the background behind him. There is a tear on the boy's cheek.

The reader knows from the other clues on the page that there is something coming in such a story.

There are various kinds of beginnings but two stand out: the one that goes at the story from "the jump" – the "hair trigger" lead, if you like – and the one that suspends the point of the story for a while, sometimes for almost the whole of the story. That might seem silly, but it's not. It can work.

The suspended lead

The suspended lead heightens intrigue, or suspense, and certainly interest. It delays for a few pars revealing what the story is really about. The suspended lead "sucks the reader in". What is this all about? Where is this story taking me? And when the answer emerges, it's too late; the reader is hooked and carries on to the end.

> Dreads and tattoos; boardies and tanned upper-bodies; everything is moving to the rhythm of bongo-drums echoing between the colourful bungalow-style houses.
>
> The sun is baking on the boulevard; the sidewalks are crowded with sweaty back-packers, slow moving hippie-survivors and noisy sales people. New Age-stores, hip surf shops and hostel-workers are all trying to wheel in a non-suspecting tourist.
>
> But still, I think I feel it; the laid-back mood hiding underneath all the hype.
>
> There are no traffic lights, no high-rise and no McDonald's. There's a special feel to it, a "vibe" if you like; people are smiling; it's Byron Bay, man.
>
> (K Heide Paus "Byron for Beginners")

The writing in the suspended lead has to be good, of course, but that is a given, for everything written for the reader has to be good writing. Just suspending the crunch for a few pars will not capture a reader unless the bait is well set and appetising, and the timing, the revelation of what the story is about, has to be right as well. A half-hearted attempt at a suspended lead, one that does not build up sufficient intrigue or suspense, is a flop. One that goes on too long is also a flop. Just as in comedy, timing is crucial.

In writing, as in other things, if it works, do it. If it doesn't, don't; do something else. The reader will not forgive you for not making your beginning convincing just because you were short of space. You should have done something else. Your beginning will have gone off half-cocked and, in turn, the reader will have gone off to find something more satisfying.

The suspended lead comes at a price – which has to be weighed against the value of the intrigue or suspense created. The price is the extra words it takes before you reveal what your story is about. It is a matter of space. Can you afford the extra pars required to produce the intrigue, suspense or interest before you reveal your hand? If not, you will have to go at it "from the jump" – straight to the point. A "hair-trigger" lead:

> Edwin can do with some privacy so we've changed his name. But he is real. Indigenous. 28 years old. Bright white Nikes, baggy pants – dressed to rap. He never really knew his parents. His grandmother in New South Wales brought him up, together with his younger brother, Shane. Shane is crippled. Shane calls him "The Man". Their grandmother is dead. Previous criminal history includes violence and time inside. This time it's break and enter. And resisting arrest.
>
> (Z Ellerman "Murrii Court")

For its extraordinary power to capture the reader, one of my favourite leads is the one Howard Kohn and David Weir chose to start their story about the mystery of what had happened to Patty Hearst. The young heiress of the wealthy Hearst newspaper family had been kidnapped for a ransom and had then joined the ranks of her anarchist kidnappers in a crime spree. In one episode she had been captured on a security camera toting a machine gun. Later there had been a shoot-out, but "Tania" had not been captured, nor had she died. Eventually *Rolling Stone* got the scoop on the Hearst story and this is how it began:

> Patty Hearst and Emily Harris waited on a grimy Los Angeles street, fighting their emotions as they listened to a radio rebroadcasting the sounds of their friends dying.
>   On a nearby corner Bill Harris dickered over the price of a battered old car.

The image of two young women listening "to a radio rebroadcasting the sounds of their friends dying" is about as powerful as it gets. The story was the scoop of the decade and not just in the United States. If you get the chance, read it all. You will find it reprinted in *The best of Rolling Stone: 25 years of journalism on the edge*.

The end

The inverted pyramid disregards the end. The end is wherever – wherever someone says the story has to be cut; wherever you run out of space. That is the whole idea of the inverted pyramid. (If your ending to a **conventional** inverted pyramid story is important, you had better discuss its importance with the subs. Someone might cut it out.)

But now the end of your story is most important. It makes the story whole, it produces an entity, a unit, a finished product, a result that is complete in all respects. You want to create a memorable end to your story. Don't let your endings trail off in typical pyramid style. Work on them. Do they link to the beginning? Have you thought about that?

This approach means not just that your finished story is an identifiable, clearly obvious unit, a whole, but that it makes sense; that there is a logic to what you have done, a logic to the choice of your beginning (because the ending makes the logic of that choice clear – it wraps up the story). If you don't tie your ending to your beginning, there is a danger your story will just fade away. For the reader it will be unsatisfying and frustrating and your story will be flat or unconvincing. These are grave risks for any writer to take. The prudent news or feature writer who chooses not to tie the ending to the beginning will always carefully consider his or her reasons for not doing so. There could be a heavy price to be paid for not undertaking this exercise.

Even a simple footnote, in brackets perhaps, at the end of a story can be a powerful tool for the writer. For example, see "Sin, Sweat and Sorrow" at the end of this chapter.

The advice holds good not just in news stories, or features. In her piece on *Shattered Glass* (the movie about the fall from grace of former US ace reporter

Stephen Glass), Georgina Robinson (*The Independent Monthly*, February 2004) made the linkage. Her beginning:

> The Morgan poll in 2000 ranked the public's opinion of newspaper journalists second-last out of a list of 27 occupations, smack bang in the middle of real estate agents and car salespersons (who came in last!).

And her ending:

> It [the story of Stephen Glass] is an unsettling demonstration of just how it happens that journalists end up being thought of with the same wafty regard as the friendly fellows down at Clive's Quality Clapped-Out Cars.

There is a motive behind using such an unsettling illustration in a book such as this. It provides an opportunity to stress the moral of the Stephen Glass story, namely, "Don't make things up!".

The middle

The middle should take care of itself. Although it does have to be good. If not, nobody will get through to discover the brilliance of your ending.

The problem with the middle is it needs to be good for a lot longer. Unlike the lead or the end, the middle is usually more than one or two pars. But it tends to be straightforward if you know what the beginning is and what the end is. The essential ingredients are good writing, good words, good pictures. Choose them carefully. Read them. Assess them. Change them. Keep the reader reading.

Evan Whitton tells more than the odd good story about journalism and what being in the business is all about. He attributes much of the wisdom he encountered along the way (a route that took him to five Walkleys and a Journalist of the Year) to "Solly" (Stanley Cecil) Chandler, former managing-director of the *Daily Express* and editor of the Melbourne *Truth*.

Some of Solly's wisdom (via Evan Whitton in *Amazing scenes*, p. 22) is worth another run: "Wordsworth is the patron saint of journalists. The words, my dear boy, must sing." Some may wish to argue about the identity of who should be journalism's patron saint, but who can disagree with the message?

"First and last, we must interest the reader," Solly maintained. There is no better way to interest the reader than to use words well. And, according to Solly, there was a practical point to it all.

"If you look after the reader, everything else – the circulation, the advertising, the revenue – will fall into place," he said (p. 23).

Amen.

To help understand what makes good reading, here are some tools.

Develop your own style

Don't reproduce someone else's style – develop your own. If there are a million stories in the harbour city, there could be a million ways to tell them. There is no one way. There are many right ways. The right way is the one that keeps the readers reading and when they have finished, wishing there was more. And they go back to the top to see whose name is there on the byline. Yours?

We are talking about style now, your style, not an industry convention. Style is many things. Style is like personality. It is you. Style is like quality. It is good.

- Style is about the words you use – which ones and in what order.
- Style is about your use of imagery – the pictures you paint; the pictures we can see in our heads or feel in our hearts; pictures we can relate to. Word pictures are critical.
- Style is also about presentation and delivery – it is pace, and cadence, and flow, and surprise.
- Style is about taking your reader prisoner. There is a great deal to cover.

If you mix flour and water you get dough. Or sludge. It's muck, really. If you add yeast, it puffs up and you get fluffy sludge. Or fluffy muck. But when you add something you cannot see – some heat energy – you turn the sludge into bread. Inviting, palatable, enjoyable, tasty bread.

Style is what comes from the energy you put into your writing. Style is the heat. No heat, no bread. Just sludge.

The analogy doesn't end there. If you take the bread out of the oven too soon it will sink – not enough heat. And if you don't put it back in the oven, but serve it up, you will find it left on the plate. Bread that is half-baked is really unappetising.

Writing is just like that.

Observe, observe, observe

The first rule of writing outside the pyramid is "observe". The second is "observe" and the third is "observe".

There are three reasons for this advice. The first has been mentioned already. **Detail**. To reinforce what has already been said (Evan Whitton in *Amazing scenes* again, p. 17):

> Sol was always on about details. I said to him once: 'You mean the significant details?'
> The corkscrew mind replied: 'No, the insignificant details'.
> I'm sure he was right: they're all anyone ever remembers.

Detail in your stories gets to the readers. They can feel you took the job seriously. You noted such wonderfully interesting things, such little things.

You don't have to fill your story with detail, but peppering it with details works wonders for your writing.

The second reason you need to observe, observe, observe can be summed up in a few words – Don't just tell us, **show** us. If you haven't observed, you will not be able to show us. How to show, rather than tell, will be dealt with separately a little later in this chapter.

There is a third form of observation the writer should pursue and that is to observe what others write. In other words, **read, read, read**.

To know what good writing is, you have to know what good writing is. You cannot know that unless you read. And without any further instruction, osmosis may do the trick for you. It may seep into your brain from the back of your eyes.

If you were to read nothing else, I would suggest *The best of Rolling Stone: 25 years of journalism on the edge* (Doubleday, 1993), including "Post-Orbital Remorse", Tom Wolfe; "Malignant Giant", Howard Kohn; "Tania's World", Howard Kohn and David Weir; "Fear and Loathing in Las Vegas", Hunter S. Thompson; and *The Penguin Book of Columnists* (Viking, 1997). You can take your pick of some splendid writers, but if you thought William Randolph Hearst was just a large rich guy with heavy jowls and a big house (I trust you have seen *Citizen Kane . . .*), then be sure to read *The Lemmings* (1940) column he wrote for his papers. If a media tycoon can do it, what is holding you back?

Write vividly

Choose your words

The strength and the appeal of your writing will depend on the power of the words you use and the pictures you paint in your readers' heads. Nouns and verbs are strong words in your armoury. Pick the right ones. Don't rely on tired or clichéd adjectives and adverbs to give feeble nouns and verbs a kick along. Find a better word or combination of words. This is why a good vocabulary, or a good thesaurus, is important.

Draw on the formula for writing inverted-pyramid stories. Active voice is still almost always best. Active verbs are strong verbs. On the other hand, now there are no rules. It is what works that matters.

Blowing up a weak noun or verb with a weak adjective or adverb will not do. Indeed, strong nouns and verbs may not need adjectives or adverbs at all to help them on their way. If adjectives or adverbs are used, they have to be strong too.

> Then began a time of <u>yellow</u> wedges of pumpkin, <u>burnt black</u> and <u>bitter</u> at the edges; mashed potato with <u>glassy</u> lumps; meat <u>aproned with gristle</u> in grey gravy; <u>warm</u>, <u>wet</u>, flatulent cabbage; <u>beds that wet themselves in the morning</u>; and <u>an entirely new sensation called loneliness.</u>

Anyone who has ever been to boarding school, or was at one at the time Bryce Courtenay describes in *The power of one*, (p. 1) knows that he has captured the scene precisely.

And Les Carlyon, in *Gallipoli* (p. 3):

> The shepherd owns a stick, too rough to be called a crook, and three <u>yellow</u> dogs with <u>pitiless</u> eyes.

As with the pyramid, beware descriptive and defining clauses. Adjectival or adverbial clauses can be traps – not **are** traps, but **can be** traps – for two reasons. Depending on the construction of your sentence they can put too much space, or distance or time, call it what you like, between the subject of your sentence and the object or complement of it. Too many words between the start of a sentence and the end can lose the reader.

And remember the second reason: we almost never use such clauses when we speak.

Create imagery

If the first, second and third laws of writing for the reader are observe, observe and observe, the fourth, fifth and sixth laws are imagery, imagery, imagery.

Sooner or later, writing for your readers means "writing pictures", pictures they can see, or feel, probably quite complex pictures, all crafted out of words. The issue is: "Don't tell us, show us!"

> It's a violent memoir of days gone past, with flags and canisters strewn across the floor. Music touches your ears from time to time, <u>just next to where the hair is standing up</u> . . .
>
> . . . Anti-American sentiment and Australian pride abound. Vivid imagery paints the walls in blood red, agent orange and army green.
>
> (Melissa Macafee "Vietnam Voices")
>
> -
>
> For many, <u>this weekly gathering is a shedding of the skin</u>. A means of slipping out of an ordinary existence and into another more enlightened world, albeit transitory and fleeting. (Susan Drum "The Choir")

When you can find no single word, nor even one supported by the best adjective or adverb you can think of to adequately describe what you are wanting to say, try imagery. Paint a picture.

For example, depending on the circumstances, instead of *the muddy water rushing through the streets*, it might have *swept* through the streets, or *sluiced* through them, or *tumbled* through them; or it might even have *bulldozed* through them. There may be better descriptions. It all depends on what you see in your head. Try to reproduce that picture in words.

Paint your pictures in oils, not watercolours. Watercolours are great, of course. But watercolour writing can be flat. What we need are pictures that are built up on the page – so we can see them. Sometimes a few words will paint a picture, but more often than not you will need several brushstrokes to produce a picture we can clearly see.

A blur, a fuzzy image, will leave the reader bored. Build up the picture. Don't tell us, show us. Some examples:

> If you've never had a shower or even an unexpected drenching in icy-cold water, it's not too hard to believe that maybe this is death. I had my eyes tightly shut but the hail of water was remorseless, a thousand pricks at a time drilling into my skin.
> (Bryce Courtenay, *The power of one*, p. 4).
>
> -
>
> Fish are for sale in panniers on the docks; they flop and send up frantic bubbles and skinny cats with the hearts of thieves crouch near a bollard, waiting for someone to get careless.   (Les Carlyon, *Gallipoli*, p. 6).

The task of the poet, Robert Gray told Margaret Throsby in one of her morning interviews on ABC Classic FM, is to say in words what cannot be said in words. And that is the challenge for those who want to write for the reader. You don't have a camera, but you have to show the reader. You don't have a picture and you cannot offer sounds or spoken words, but your reader has to feel as well as see. All you have is printed words. You have to find the best ones.

There are words you should get to know: **like**; **as**; **as if**; **as though** . . . They are "paintbrush" words. When you use them, you compare what you are describing with something the reader already knows. You can paint vivid, immediately recognisable pictures with them . . . if you couple them with the right words, of course.

Les Carlyon (in *Gallipoli*) knows the value of these words:

> The other ewes mill around the car, hoofs clicking like castanets on the bitumen (p. 3).
> -
> The tortoises are out grazing today, poking their heads from under black-and-khaki helmets, as though they have been outfitted by an army surplus store and are shy about their new clothes (p. 4).

Create images using similes rather than metaphors:
- **Simile**: a figure of speech directly suggesting a resemblance.
- **Metaphor**: a figure of speech in which a term or phrase is applied to something to which it is not literally applicable, in order to suggest a resemblance.

These definitions from the *Macquarie Dictionary* sum up the difference and explain why the first works well in journalistic writing and the second not nearly as well.

Similes compare what is being described by the writer with something the reader already knows and therefore they paint clear, unambiguous pictures. In *The Man from Snowy River*, Paterson wrote that the old man was there, "with his hair as white as snow". A simile.

Metaphors, on the other hand, are oblique rather than direct descriptors. You might call a swindler "a rat", or someone who had battled adversity a "Briton", but, physically, they might resemble neither. Thus, beware the metaphor.

Pace

Your story must have appropriate pace, which really means it must not drag. This is another reason the inverted pyramid is such a great device. If your story starts to drag, someone cuts it off. Another story can be slotted in to fill the space created. But cutting off an out-of-the-pyramid story will probably destroy it. If you are writing 500 words, or 1000 or 2000, you are in charge of your space, and you will have to use it well.

Padding will not do. You have to keep the reader reading. If the story starts to drag, your reader will move on. In ten pars this will not be an issue, but if you are doing a major piece there are a couple of useful devices that can be employed to maintain the pace and keep the reader interested.

Subplots

These are what make a good TV program. There are three or four stories running at once, all linked in some way.

Three or four may be too many for your story, but just one parallel plot, issue or divertissement can add intrigue and interest to your writing.

Introducing a subplot needs to be done carefully lest you confuse the reader. Typographic devices are there to be used, so use them. The drop cap (a large, bold capital letter) often makes the transition to a subplot obvious. Readers are aware of the use of such devices.

Rise and fall

It's not just changing the scene (subplots) that can be important. Changing the speed of the story may be important too.

Changing pace is a good idea: backing the story off for a bit, then hitting the accelerator again. A change of pace can add interest and intrigue to your story – if you have the space, that is. And sometimes you do. You need to con-sider these devices if you want your reader to stay with you for a major feature.

How many such pieces have you started to read and soon dropped off because the writing has been so pedestrian, so dull? Just another news story – only three times, or ten times, as long.

Punctuation

Everyone knows they have to make friends with the full stop. But try some other devices – the dash, the colon, the semicolon. They are supposed to indicate pauses of different strengths. Depending on your style, they might work. It doesn't bother me that I break almost all the rules. I do it deliberately for all kinds of effects.

For example, in the piece "Sin, Sweat and Sorrow", that appears at the end of this chapter, I might have written:

> When the sun beats down on Rocky, the city bakes. Tuesday, December 2, 1997 is a baking day. The second day of summer and first day of committal proceedings in the local magistrates court into matters alleged against a local man – multiple charges of indecent dealing with boys, numerous charges of indecent dealing with girls, rape, attempted rape, assault, assault occasioning bodily harm, carnal knowledge against the order of nature, and so on, seventy charges in all.

But instead, quite deliberately, I wrote something else:

> When the sun beats down on Rocky, the city bakes. Tuesday, December 2, 1997 is a baking day. The second day of summer and first day of committal proceedings in the local magistrates court into matters alleged against a local man. Multiple charges of indecent dealing with boys. Numerous charges of indecent dealing with girls. Rape. Attempted rape. Assault. Assault occasioning bodily harm. Carnal knowledge against the order of nature. And so on. Seventy charges in all.

The paragraph immediately above is a much more powerful use of words. It breaks the usual rules, of course; there are no verbs in those final sentences. A couple contain only a single word. But the full stop followed by the capital forces the reader to pause over the words, whereas the comma allows the reader to rush on without stopping. The difference in effect is dramatic.

I wouldn't recommend it, but Tom Wolfe knew the value of punctuation, so much so that he made up his own. He was boiled in vitriol for it, of course, but didn't flinch:

> I found a great many pieces of punctuation and typography lying around dormant when I came along – and I must say I had a good time using them . . . I found that things like exclamation points, italics, and abrupt shifts (dashes) and syncopations (dots) helped to give the illusion of not only a person talking but of a person thinking . . .   (*The new journalism*, p. 35–36)

Punctuation is a tool you can use to great effect. Use it. Wisely.

Sentence length

Vary your delivery. It works in cricket and it works in writing. Too many long sentences are just as bad as too many short ones. How many is too many? Who can tell? It depends on the topic. A story about being caught in the middle of a cyclone might be best with lots of short sentences. One about going back home, where you spent a carefree childhood, might have very few.

But, as a general rule, variety adds spice to your writing as well as to your life.

Sentence structure

If you want something to make an impact on the reader, put it first or last in the sentence, not in the middle. Last will have more impact than first.

But remember, your writing has to flow easily to the eye. Concentrating on which word to use at the end of each sentence is not likely to produce the best result. It is something to keep in the back of your mind, not in the front of it.

Humour

Not everyone is a comic. Writing humorous copy does not come easily to all. And half-successful attempts are not acceptable. They are an embarrassment. So, if it is not one of your talents, try something else. But if you can write with a sharp or witty edge, do it. There won't be much else like it on the page, or in the paper for that matter.

What makes people laugh? Or smile? Some of the elements of humour you may wish to exploit include: championing the preposterous and the outlandish; recounting another's (not too serious) misfortune; juxtaposing the unremarkable with the remarkable or the absurd; elevating the inconsequential; presenting as the reality that which everyone knows to be the opposite; satire; sarcasm; or irony.

One of the funniest pieces I ever read in a newspaper was a Phillip Adams contribution in the *Age* many years ago. Actually, he wrote only a few pars – witty though they were. The rest of the piece was supplied by the Census people. Two hundred and thirty- (or maybe fifty- or was it eighty-) seven different ways law-abiding citizens filling in their census forms had spelled, or had attempted to spell, their avowed religious inclination – presbytereum, or was it prespitern, or maybe prybiterian, or some other amazing concoction, etc., etc. Anything but presbyter . . . presbit . . . press . . . silly word, anyway.

So, maybe humour is hiding just around the corner. If so, seek it out. The readers will love you.

Dialogue

This is the device that most sets "new journalism" apart from the traditional pyramid approach. It is a very powerful device. But you will need lots of time – and plenty of tape. There isn't much "writing" involved if most of your copy is quotes. But when someone says something powerful, don't turn it into indirect speech. Otherwise, by comparison, the result could be a serious flop.

No licence to kill

And, above all, remember that writing outside the pyramid is not a licence to kill. Do not forget the demands of accuracy. Or the law. Or ethics.

Just because you are off the leash, you do not make up things. You do not create for the sake of effect. The words may be clever, but if they are fake, then you are not writing journalism, you are writing fiction. A novel perhaps. But not journalism.

This is where the criticism of "new journalism" emerges. And the criticism must be carefully heeded. We are reporters, not novelists. We write what we see and what we hear and what we are told. Not what we might have been told or what it would be good if we had been told.

One of the dangers, for example, lies in the "new journalism" technique of reporting in the first person what you were told by a second person. If you write what you were told accurately, fine. But if you start to lace your copy with feelings and thoughts the subject of your story "had" at the time, based on what you think the person **might have had at the time**, despite how likely or reasonable those thoughts and feelings might seem, you have crossed the boundary. You are no longer a reporter. You are into fiction. Indeed, you are a fiction writer.

One of the most powerful stories I have ever read as a teacher concerned a first-person piece by a young woman who attended the funeral of a friend killed in a car accident. The young woman had been driving the car in which her friend had died. Because of the circumstances, the police were at the funeral too.

I was greatly moved by the power of the story. The torment in the young woman's mind as she watched the victim's distressed family arrive. The sight of the coffin in the church. Her loneliness. Her remorse. Her regret. How others looked at her. Or how she felt they looked at her. The policeman sitting behind the sobbing family. And so on. Powerful stuff.

I was very concerned for the student who had written the story and contacted her as soon as I could find her to offer support and to make sure she was okay. Oh no, she said, that was a friend of mine. I was there with her and saw what happened.

She was a little surprised when I said the story had to be rewritten. Despite what she might have seen, and heard, she could not be that person. Perhaps if she had later interviewed the unfortunate woman, she might have come close to reporting. But that had not happened. What she wrote might have been accurate. But, equally, it might not.

In recent years, journalism in the United States has been rocked by some embarrassing scandals. One journalist won a Pulitzer Prize for a piece on a little kid who was a heroin addict. Unfortunately, it was later discovered, he didn't exist. He was a compilation, a sort of jigsaw-puzzle figure, created from bits and pieces of individuals the writer had known or heard about. The Pulitzer Prize had to be given back. A *New York Times* reporter was making quite a reputation for himself until it was revealed he was also making up the stories. Anyone can produce great stories by simply making them up. Don't.

For the reporter, writing stories for the reader **does not mean inventing stories for the reader**. Accuracy, honesty and integrity must not get left behind for the sake of a few clever words. There is a vast gulf between writing well and just beating up a story.

Beware the dangers

There are dangers in writing for the reader. Here are some warning signs to alert you to the most common ones.

The struggle

Unless you are exceptionally gifted, the right words may not flow off the keyboard in torrents. They may trickle out. Some lucky people may be able to write outside the pyramid with one hand tied behind their back, but the rest of us may have to struggle a bit – or a lot – with both hands.

It's no good if the pictures are out of focus, if the words are flat and dull. No good at all. You have to struggle with such pictures. Go back. Erase, change, add, and do it again if you have to. It's no good if it gets better three pars down. The reader won't make it three pars down.

You will have to wrestle with the problem pars. You will need other words, new words, or different words, but certainly better words. You may struggle to find them. You may struggle to put them in the right order. But you had better struggle. Give up and your reader will too.

Overwriting

You can try too hard. Your copy might be forced, flowery, overly flamboyant, or otherwise unconvincing. So don't try too hard. Big words are not the same as good words. Little words are almost always better. So "over the top" is not the way to go. There are dangers out beyond the pyramid – keep an eye out for them.

Fortunately someone is bound to tell you if you don't see them yourself. Probably something like, "What is this stuff!" Or, "What has got into you? We're not running this pap." Something subtle, I suspect.

Clichés

It hardly needs to be said that one should avoid clichés – unless there is a good case for using them. Clichés are obviously overdone (that's why they are clichés), indicate laziness on the part of the writer, and may even cause the reader to gag.

Sometimes, but only sometimes, there is a place for them, probably to make a humorous or satirical point. Beyond those circumstances, the use of clichés will simply diminish the quality of your work.

Generalisations and qualifications

Imprecise generalisations and qualifications discount the impact of your writing. And that is not what you want. "Hardly", "roughly", "generally", "almost" and the like do not paint a clear picture. They are fuzzy words. Lazy words. The good writer has to be precise.

The clock

Writing inside the inverted pyramid structure becomes second nature. Just reproduce the formula. Done. Outside the pyramid there is no formula. And so the writer must seek inspiration. What if inspiration is hard to find?

Well, one thing is certain. The clock will not stop ticking. They stop the clock in football matches and basketball games. But so far this has not happened in journalism. You can't go on forever looking for inspiration – for the perfect lead that will have the readers gasping. You have to hit the keyboard. When the clock is no longer ticking but racing, and the deadline no longer approaching but already at your next-door neighbour's desk, and there is no formula, you will find out what kind of a writer you really are.

Helpers

It's a good idea to have a shelf full of useful helpers at hand. A thesaurus, a book of quotes; and science, politics, geography, history dictionaries are highly recommended. You can use them for a specific story, or you can glance through them for general knowledge. General knowledge will always be a great ally for writers, including journalists.

Editing

Writing inside the pyramid means your stories are (unless you are a very bad writer or reporter) easily subedited. If you didn't get it right when you submitted your story, a subeditor will fix it.

But poor writing outside the pyramid is not so easily fixed. How does someone else know what words really deal with what you are trying to say? How does someone else see the pictures you are trying to paint? Or the feelings you are trying to convey?

They can't, of course. Indeed, the task is usually impossible. If your feature needs fixing, then it will probably be spiked. Discarded. No one else can really say what should have been said.

You have to be your own sub. First of all, when you have written it, put the article away for a while. A couple of days, if that is possible. Then get it out again. And go through it, carefully and critically.

William Blundell, in his excellent book on feature writing, refers to a good rule of thumb in the business of writing well. Final article equals draft minus 10 per cent. He gives some excellent examples of how it is done (pp. 218–221). Significantly, he uses his own work to explain. And the reason is obvious. The best person to get your work right is you.

Summary

Nothing that appears above is new. Nothing. Each of the points, all, some, most or many, can be found in a million good pieces of writing that are out there in newspaper land, pieces crafted by talented, or clever, or just hardworking souls who wanted to say something others would take the time to read.

And if Randolph Hearst knew the value of a good beginning, a good ending, the full stop, short sentences, word pictures, and the like, to write a powerful and compelling piece, what about us? Surely we can do as well.

Just one final thing. Writing a bit out of the pyramid will not do. The same old stuff with a few frills here and a few frills there will not be "writing for the reader". It will be the same old stuff – with a few frills here and a few frills there.

Sample stories for readers

What follows are some examples of writing outside the pyramid and writing for the reader. The first is a news feature.

Murrii Court

by Zoe Ellerman

(Journalism assignment published in *Writing for the reader*)

Edwin can do with some privacy so we've changed his name. But he is real. Indigenous. 28 years old. Bright white Nikes, baggy pants – dressed to rap. He never really knew his parents. His grandmother in New South Wales brought him up, together with his younger brother, Shane. Shane is crippled. Shane calls him "The Man". Their grandmother is dead. Previous criminal history includes violence and time inside. This time it's break and enter. And resisting arrest.

Yet today Edwin is told he is lucky, very lucky. And, perhaps for the first time, he is.

Edwin is the first offender to appear before the new Murrii Court, held today in Brisbane at the Roma Street Magistrates Court.

A court is like a horse. It can smell your fear. It can throw you with one prancing step, or one strange phrase. And this is true for all of us – from the fat cats to the street rats – facing a court is always a rough ride. But for Indigenous people this is doubly true. Fear. Fear of the law, of police, of court, of prison, has attached itself to Indigenous Australia like a limp body hanging from a shoelace, in a stinking, fetid cell.

Murrii Court is a new attempt to present an outstretched hand on the long arm of the law. Indigenous people pleading guilty to offences usually dealt with by a magistrate alone, can now be sentenced by Murrii Court. Murrii Court hopes to turn up the volume on Indigenous voices and spotlight Indigenous faces.

Today the defence and prosecution outline the facts of Edwin's offending. They both tell a story that crisscrosses over a garden bed of anger, grief and loss. Life's sores succoured on the teat of a Bundy bottle. It was pumped up, indignant, rum-soaked anger that night that jemmied open a window with a screwdriver and fought the cops when they tried to cuff him.

Edwin gets a chance to speak. He hasn't got too much to say. His memory of that night is blank from the booze.

"Like my solicitor said, I was on the drink that day, I was out of control cause of the grog."

His anger is impotent now. Soaked up and drained away by the beige walls and the navy lawyers' suits. Or is it the levelling shame of facing his people that quietens him?

Shane also gets a chance to speak up for his brother.

"I've been there since The Man got out of prison, he's doin' alright, gettin' on the right track and that, it's just always the grog, it's the alcohol and the emotion."

An elder sits together with the magistrate, not up on high, but at eyeballing level. He gets a chance to offer the wisdom of his people – people of the oldest surviving culture on earth.

But this is no ancient tribal law to be meted out to the young man from suburban Brisbane. The elder merely notes alcohol is a curse on his people. And that he sees sorrow in Edwin's eyes.

Edwin's lucky day. His luck is threefold. He now has fulltime work at an abattoir. Shane needs his help to change his colostomy bag and dress weeping sores inflicted by his mechanical chair. And he is Indigenous.

Life is looking up.

Although his people make up 2.5 per cent of the population they make up 25 per cent of those in prison. Edwin is not going back to prison today. Murrii Court gives him one last chance.

The next two pieces, both features on "a place", have been included because they were written by people whose first language was not English. If they can write so well in our language, what about the rest of us?

"I Saw the Red Roses"

by Olav Naess

(Journalism assignment published in *Writing for the reader*)

The left-side gunner hangs out the window, watching for landmarks and makes sure we don't crash into one of the other helicopters. He holds up three fingers. I nod, turn and shout; "Three minutes to landing." I do not think anyone can hear me.

The sharp turn around the mountain wall makes the buckle on my chest press the flak jacket tight.

Sarajevo opens under us. Like a river between the Bosnian mountains, it stretches out of sight.

The clouds above us are white and grey. Through the holes in the clouds, the sun sends streams of concentrated light. It is a flight through a cathedral.

My mission was, as part of a company of Norwegian soldiers in 1997, to provide security for the NATO headquarters near Sarajevo Airport.

The buildings that surround the airport look as if they have taken the blast wave from an atomic bomb. A metre of jumbled bricks is all that is left of what was once a home.

The front line ran through here for much of the war.

This city was strangled by siege for 1395 days. Now it gasps for air, swallows hard, coughs and strokes its bruised throat while tears trickle from its eyes, hurt and shocked, yet relieved to be alive.

The road in from the airport to the city is nicknamed "Snipers' Alley". Grey communist blocks of houses are followed by modern buildings; shot in hatred and burned by fire.

Traffic is old trams, camouflage-painted armed personnel carriers, cars from a 70's Tito factory, and Mercedes stolen in Germany last week.

"'Snipers' Alley" melts into the city centre. Red roses appear.

The main street is intact but marked by the bullets that missed a body.

In the new cafes, youth flirt and talk, while NATO soldiers with assault rifles enjoy their coffee and the warm spring.

Within a few hundred metres there are houses of worship representing all three religions in Bosnia.

The minarets and church roofs can be seen from the top of the burnt-out Olympic stadium.

The old cemetery has given its every inch; then flooded the fields by the stadium with white wooden crosses.

The once green fields that surround the burnt Olympic stadium from 1984 are now white as snow with wooden crosses.

Crosses like snowflakes, look the same, yet are unique.

In the evening the city's teens meet at the combined bar and pool place across the river from the library where hundreds of years were turned to heat in minutes. You can hardly see the pool table for the smoke, or hear the pool deck balls for the music.

A wave of people washes through the room from the entrance and the bar.

The last ones to make it to the floor are foreign peacekeepers who have never been shot at before.

The latest turf war among the city's mobster gangs damaged only window glass and the wall over the bar.

Sarajevo's youth get up from the floor, straighten their clothes, pick up a pool cue again and buy another can of beer.

In Sarajevo a red rose is not made of fragile petals, nor does it sting the finger. Here a rose is made with paint and stings the soul.

Every rose in the pavement is a grenade that struck and killed. A footprint to remind us of those who died to keep this city alive.

Byron for Beginners

by Katharina Heide Paus

(Journalism assignment published in *Writing for the reader*)

Dreads and tattoos; boardies and tanned upper-bodies; everything is moving to the rhythm of bongo-drums echoing between the colourful bungalow-style houses. The sun is baking on the boulevard; the sidewalks are crowded with sweaty back-packers, slow moving hippie-survivors and noisy sales people. New Age-stores, hip surf shops and hostel-workers are all trying to wheel in a non-suspecting tourist. But still, I think I feel it: the laid-back mood hiding underneath all the hype. There are no traffic lights, no high rise and no McDonald's. There's a special feel to it, a "vibe" if you like; people are smiling: It's Byron Bay, man.

My feet make a funny "whoop-whoop" sound as I stumble through the powdery sand. "Are you ready? Are you psyched?" Helene, my surf instructor, is all tanned muscles and white smile. Psyched? You bet. Ready? Not so very. The board is too broad and my arm is too short. It's slipping; I have to hold on with both hands or the wind carries it away. I'm wrestling my way down to the shore, trying not to trip on the ankle-strap. The wetsuit is warm and sticky; I'm officially exhausted before I even reach the water. I feel nothing like the cool surfers who are jogging slow-mo Baywatch-style with their little boards tucked neatly under one arm. The waves are huge and deadly; roaring tough-guys ready to punch me down just to let me know I'm on enemy territory. As if I didn't know! But I won't let them win, it's show no fear and dive in.

The paddling is a mystery to me; every new wave throws me off the board and leaves me gasping for air. Finally I'm outside the breaking point, sitting on my board just waiting for the right wave to catch. There it comes, nice and smooth. I throw myself onto the board and paddle like my life depends on it. "Whoosh," Helene had said, "wait for the whoosh and then get up." Yes, I can feel it; a huge force whooshing me forward grabs the back of my board. I get up: "Yeah!" And before I know what's hit me I'm tumbling around in a giant washing machine. There is no up and no down; my whole world is a whirlwind of water. After what I'm sure is close to an eternity under water I hear Helene's laughing voice through the thunder of the waves: "Wipeout!"

We're sitting on the beach having some lunch and everything tastes like saltwater. The sun is glittering on the endless waves of the Pacific. I'm utterly, thoroughly happy. The waves aren't tough-guys anymore; they're playful buddies calling my name. I'm sunburnt; I've got three-four litres of saltwater in my belly and muscles I didn't know I had are aching. But I'm invincible; I'm cool; I've tackled the Great Pacific! As far as the eye can see the ocean is in motion. Every sugarcoated frothing peak is waving: see you tomorrow.

The white leather seats are cool against my battered thighs as I'm slowly sipping a white-chocolate martini. The sleek interior of the bar is enveloping me and I'm drifting on a white cushion of mellowness. The soothing ocean-breeze filtered through palm trees and spring flowers brushes my sunburnt face. She's crashing down on the chair in front of me. The age is impossible to tell; the sun and ocean engraved on her face: I'm guessing 50. She's tanned and draped in purple caftans, the bangles on her wrists seem to make her dizzy. She talks of times long passed; what Byron used to be like. When it was a sanctuary for love, peace and happiness. Now it's all newcomers, drifters and hype. I'm slightly blushing behind designer-shades; I'm one of them, the newcomers. Can't really blame her concern, though. An estimated 300,000 tourists a year and only around 30,000 inhabitants is a draft. She carries with her the scent of incense and late 60's: the true smell of Byron Bay. But, she admits, the innocence of the hippie-generation is long gone, too. Most of her friends from back then are either battling a heroin or an alcohol addiction. The evidence sits on almost every corner of the small town, asking for change. I politely refuse the "spliff" she offers: I've got an early date with the sunrise tomorrow.

I'm up with the pre-dawn birds; I drive up the curvy road and reach the lighthouse just before the sky turns pink. I'm freezing and my eyes feel like they're still filled with sand. There's just one other car there; three guys in hooded jumpers. They're quietly staring at the horizon, so am I. A halo of beauty glances over the tip of the ocean; here they come: the first rays of sun to reach Australia this Wednesday morning. It's incredible, it looks like a giant cliché and it's gorgeous.

As I'm packing up my car to head back to Brisbane, a bearded guy carrying a surfboard asks me: "Are you coming or leaving?" I confirm my departure and he looks at me with true pity in his eyes as he says: "You poor thing! Byron Bay, man, Byron Bay is life!" If it's life, it's a surreal one, and unfortunately reality is calling me back from that strange little town. Byron Bay, barely balancing on the border between laidback dream state and real-life busyness.

Finally, there's hardly a moment goes by these days without another revelation of child abuse and paedophilia somewhere in the country. The courts are full of such cases and some legal firms are groaning under the workload.

But it wasn't always so. Just a few years back, a very few years back, there was nothing in the news about such matters. Nothing at all. The victims kept their counsel and their secrets. But little by little the stories, like this one, emerged. It is included to illustrate a range of things: pace, subplots, detail, punctuation, sentence length, and so on.

There is another point. The piece might be subtitled "Nothing happened today – or yesterday". It was an important piece because it had a message. The message is: when something important has to be written, it has to be written – even if you're not allowed to be there!

Sin, Sweat and Sorrow

by Bruce Grundy

(Inside Queensland: vol. 1, 1998)
Rockhampton, population 65,000, the unauthorised capital of central Queensland, 650 kilometres north of the state capital Brisbane, sits only a matter of metres north of the Tropic of Capricorn. The city almost escaped being in the tropics. A few kilometres south and it would have. But such was not to be. Climatically Rockhampton is firmly within what geographers call "the torrid zone" and over the years it has managed to get itself a reputation as a torridly tropical city – a reputation that even really tropical cities a thousand miles nearer the equator don't have – and would not want.

The three S's – "sin, sweat and sorrow" are what Anthony Trollope said best described the place. He was also responsible for passing into legend the story about the Rockhamptonite who died and went to Hell. The first night he was there, Trollope asserted, he was yelling for blankets.

"Rocky" is known the length and breadth of the Australian continent for two things – one, the statues of bulls (some rudely emasculated by wags or puritans), that line its arterial streets, and the other, the power of its summer heat.

It is not just that the city sits all but astride the tropic. It also sits on the spot where the early settlers could ford the river barring their access to the lands that lay to the north. The city grew up on the river at the point where it could be most easily crossed. The problem, climatically, has been that this point is about 40 kilometres from the coast. And just to ensure complete failure for any sneaky sea breeze that might attempt the trip, Rocky sits tucked in behind the perfect windbreak – the Berserkers – the Berserker Range. When the sun beats down on Rocky, there is nowhere to hide. The city bakes.

Tuesday, December 2, 1997 is a baking day. The second day of summer and first day of committal proceedings in the local magistrates court into matters alleged against a local man. Multiple charges of indecent dealing with boys. Numerous charges of indecent dealing with girls. Rape. Attempted rape. Assault. Assault occasioning bodily harm. Carnal knowledge against the order of nature. And so on. Seventy charges in all.

The magistrates court's front doors once opened on to the mall that used to be East Street. But renovations are in full swing to create a new court complex for Rockhampton. A temporary entrance has been created down the side of the old building next to where the new one will be one day. A wall of silver metal sheeting has been erected along most of the boundary line between the old court and the construction site next door – but not along all of the boundary line. Just where it is needed most, the wall was forgotten.

Instead a sumo-sized Kato swivelling crane is parked hard against the lattice walls of the covered public space outside Courtroom 2. This is the place where visitors and lawyers and offenders gather to organise themselves for the day's proceedings. Heavy diesel fumes and the powerful roar of the crane's big engine pass unhindered through the latticework walls to mingle with the next-door neighbours – the visitors, lawyers and offenders attending Rockhampton's magistrates courts. No fear of conversations being eavesdropped here today. Diesel fume asphyxiation may be a problem – but secrets in this place will be absolutely safe. At times a shout would likely not be heard.

Apart from the roar of the crane, electric saws saw and grinders grind. Heavy planks thump where they are dropped. Hammers thud on timber and clang on pipes. There are shouts from time to time and regular smashing noises as the flotsam and jetsam of construction, propelled off the third-floor level of the new court complex, arrives in the waste bin positioned on the ground below.

The hard planks of the benches that line the lattice walls of the public enclosure are half-filled with the morning's parade of Rockhampton's overnight problems – all awaiting their turn in Courtroom 1. Some display handcuffs on wrists clasped beneath bowed heads. Thongs and bare feet, dark skins and light, young and old. Legal Aid and duty solicitors hurry from client to client and to and fro. The scene is probably being replayed in a hundred courthouses across the country. It is just another day.

Or is it?

Courtroom 2 is shut. As 10 o'clock approaches the media arrive. They have notebooks and know each other and are the only ones talking freely. They check the court lists and note the case mentioned for Courtroom 2. One fresh-faced young man has WIN embroidered on his shirt and another young man in tow – to lug his TV camera. Two also-young women, un-embroidered, clutch shorthand books.

The door to Courtroom 2 swings open. A large young policeman sporting a belt any draught horse would be proud to wear as a girth, and adorned with pouches of all shapes and sizes, emerges. He dangles a couple of sheets of paper at a respectable distance in front of him. A very large spider is clinging to the leading edge of the leading sheet. The spider goes into the bin. Spider stories then engage the policeman, a colleague (with an equally impressive belt and array of pouches) and the media for the next hour and a half.

From time to time the police prosecutor appears in the lattice space for a cigarette. He too is young. His uniform is crisp and pressed, his hair close-cropped. His neatness seems quite out of place, contrasting starkly with that of most other occupants here. Except for one thing. Everyone smokes. Offenders and their supporters, the media, lawyers, police. The prosecutor. There is tension here. For whatever reason, everybody today is having his day, or maybe, another day, in court. Nervous energy is running free and a cigarette the only available antidote.

There is another who also looks out of place. Young, again, and slight – not a gram, let alone a kilogram, of extra weight – sandy hair to the shoulders, and tanned. You can tell because there are no sleeves to conceal bronzed arms and shoulders. A triathlete perhaps? As others lounge and loll about, this slender figure seems to have much to do. Black shoes, black stockings, black business dress and scarf. Plain but very stylish. Unlike her outfit the wearer is more than a little busy. In this door, out that one, a few words here, a few there, off again, back again, gone again. She must surely be lost – such is her incongruity in these surroundings. A rose among the thorns. Probably works for a stockbroker – if they have them in Rockhampton.

Above the grubby paved floor of the lattice space the skylights in the ceiling are doing an excellent job. Light from the now late-morning blazing Rockhampton sun glares in providing more than adequate illumination for the Legal Aid lawyers as they consult their now-thinning collection of clients and fill in appropriate forms. On the back of the light, the heat surges through the skylights. A few metres away the Kato crane roars up to full throttle, swivels a load of something up to the top floor of the skeleton taking shape next door, sighs back to idling speed, and roars into life again. And again. And again.

By now all the spider stories have been told. The two policemen with their pistols, handcuffs, pocket knives, torches, and whatever else they carry in their armoury of pouches, have gone. The media have by now sought space on the hard wooden benches and the early vigour of their conversation has dulled. They seem resigned to a long wait. And the heat marches on. The weatherman is going for 38 degrees.

The prosecutor appears for another cigarette and the WIN reporter asks a question on behalf of those still remaining.

"They're on their way," the prosecutor replies.

The minutes tick by.

At last a tall man in a dark suit, a short man in a lighter suit, a tall woman (young again) and a man in mid-blue trousers, blue figured shirt with sleeves rolled down and a pale blue tie that was all the rage in the fifties appear and head straight on in to Courtroom 2. The media follow.

Inside it is cooler, thankfully, and somehow the heavy doors and the vertical blinds over the windows keep the noise of the crane and the builders at bay. The room is just big enough for the magistrate's bench, a bench for the court staff and recording gear, a bench for the prosecutor and defence team, a witness box, a small dock and seats for maybe a dozen members of the public.

The furniture occupies the room – but hardly inspires a sense of awe. There is no crest behind the magistrate's chair. No lion, nor unicorn, nor "*Dieu et mon droit*" in sight. The walls are bare. No symbols. No flag. And no solid oak here. Fake maple perhaps. Chipboard laminated and spotted with the dark brown plastic blobs that hide the screws that hold it all together. A microphone for each of the actors. A screen behind the magistrate's chair and two screens next to the witness stand. Of such is the face of justice, Rockhampton, Queensland, 1997.

All rise as the magistrate arrives. Quite a young man (as would now be expected) in a black gown. Softly spoken, he begins proceedings.

The prosecutor announces his name as does the recently arrived man in the dark suit who represents the defendant. He apologises for being late.

The magistrate inquires if the prosecution intends amending charges 10 to 18. Papers and folders are flicked through and ruffled as prosecution and defence search out the relevant documents.

"April the thirty-first is not a date known to law, Sergeant," His Worship advises the prosecutor.

More flicking and ruffling.

Sorry, the prosecutor says, the date should be April 30. The defence does not object. Exhibits are then called and the busy young woman in the black business dress carries each forward in turn for the magistrate to stamp and number.

Statements, documents, sketch plans drawn by witnesses, aerial photographs, photograph albums, newspaper cuttings, 40 exhibits in all.

The prosecutor calls his first witness. The busy young woman in black. A constable in the Queensland Police Service.

She explains the detail of her investigation and identifies the man with the pale blue tie as the subject of the inquiries she has conducted. No further questions, Your Worship. The barrister then has some straightforward questions on the detail of her investigations, and that done she is stood down.

The prosecutor next advises His Worship that he had expected proceedings to this point to have taken a good deal longer and indicates it will take five or 10 minutes to get his first witness to the court.

Exercising caution, His Worship adjourns for 10.

Some of those involved venture out into the heat and the fumes. The media stay put. They had two hours of that earlier in the day.

Then the door opens and the prosecutor returns.

"This court is now closed," he advises all and sundry.

No submissions, no application, just a simple statement. The media file out and vanish. The door to Courtroom 2 closes. What is to happen inside that room over the next two days is only for those in the room to know.

Witnesses arrive one by one, men first. All are obviously tense and stressed, apparently dreading what lies ahead. Nerves have clearly taken hold of the pits of their stomachs. After 30 or 40 years they are about to relive some of the experiences of their childhoods. Once inside that door they will be interrogated on what happened to them in the minutest detail. Their faces, some pale, some drawn, some furrowed, tell they are already suffering what they are about to encounter.

The door closes. Whatever it is has begun.

Outside the lattice space is deserted save for its sad noticeboard and even sadder notices (which may not have had a real reader in years), a Coke machine and two rubbish bins with plastic liners spilling out from under battered lids. For most, the business of the day is over. But not in Courtroom 2.

Minutes dawdle by. The mercury and the carpenters press on.

At last the sumo crane falls silent. Construction workers must eat. The court too adjourns for lunch.

Outside, the fumes have gone – but the sun, glaring relentlessly down on the city, has not. The weatherman has done it again. Spot on – 38.

At 2.15 pm the hearing resumes. Justice Department staff usher the next witness through the lattice space, and the doors of Courtroom 2 swing shut again. The second witness, tall, well-built, jeans, figured shirt, sneakers, is also very tense.

Next-door the crane roars back into life spreading its fumes and noise through the latticework again. An hour later the doors open, the witness is chaperoned away, some of the actors file out for a few minutes break and a quick puff and another witness is ushered in. This time another man, slight frame, heavy beard, longish hair, dark trousers and shoes, white tee-shirt. The doors close for another hour.

When he reappears the court is adjourned for the day.

For the rest the tension remains. They will have yet another night to relive their memories. So what is new. They have lived those memories every day of their lives. This time there is one saving grace. At least they have company. There are others here who know – and they all gain strength aware that someone understands, that someone believes. Even if it is only one of them. Tomorrow will be the women's day. It is clear the men are going first.

Wednesday December 3, 1997, arrives. Outside Courtroom 2 there is a repeat of the day before. The line-up of offenders, the lawyers, the policemen, downcast eyes, some handcuffs, the media, the unrelenting heat, the crane and the fumes. A woman, pale as death, has her wrist in a sling. She offers comfort and support to her partner. Drug charges, the media advise. Heroin and cocaine.

This time there are no delays. One by one the witnesses appear. A youngish looking man, fair-skinned, cropped hair, shirt, trousers, shoes, tattoos. Like yesterday one could cut the tension with a knife. Each new witness grimly disappears through the door to reappear about an hour later.

A sun-tanned man, slightly built, baseball cap, heavy dark glasses, blue trousers, dark-coloured shirt is ushered in. A tiny older woman is by his side. His mother possibly. Her face is streaked by tears.

When he reappears it is clear he is distressed. The Justice Department staff lead the way to the witness room at the end of the corridor. A Victims of Crime volunteer, smartly dressed and motherly, offers comfort and support. The scene is repeated again and again. Just the names and faces change.

Finally it is the women's turn. A striking figure, tall with long hair and pearls standing out against a black business dress, black stockings, black shoes, demands attention. She is clearly tense and on the edge of her nerves.

Finally the time has come. She follows the slight figure of the police investigator into the court.

The interrogation begins.

Outside a policeman in plain clothes, Justice Department officers and the lady from Victims of Crime hover around. Sometimes in the witness room, sometimes on the mobile phone. Aware but unaware of what is happening inside the walls of Courtroom 2.

After an hour, the woman in black suddenly appears through a side door. She is very angry and upset. The police investigator is by her side. The Victims of Crime lady and the Justice Department woman rush down the corridor. She sits by the Coke machine, her voice raised above the noise next-door. He's only doing his job, she is told. She is not the one on trial here, she says. The prosecutor appears. There is to be a short adjournment. The strain on the woman's face is stark. She has clearly had more than enough of whatever is going on inside. The other women offer comforting words and little by little composure returns. Just in time. The adjournment is up. The hearing is about to resume. Prosecutor, barrister, solicitor and defendant head back into court. The woman in black stands and follows them in. Behind her the police investigator closes the door. The committal hearing of a man for alleged crimes against the woman, as a child, amongst others, resumes. Outside the crane roars on. And the sun beats down. As if nothing had happened.

At 1.30 pm it is over. The court adjourns until 2.30pm. Her evidence for the time being is behind her. Of course, this is only a committal. A trial may be yet to come.

A woman in a smart light-blue tailored skirt and white long-sleeved blouse is next. She too demands attention. Tense and trying to be calm but betrayed by nerves.

The man against whom she will testify returns from lunch and there he is, standing just over there.

Confronted, there is recognition. Words pass to a friend.

She is whisked away to a witness room and a few minutes later begins her walk down the short corridor to Courtroom 2. It is time to tell her story. An hour later she is back in the witness room. It is done.

But indeed it is not. There is a need to examine more witnesses and the hearing is adjourned for almost four months.

One by one the actors file out. The police investigator is still busy. The defence team collects its files and cases, and leaves. The prosecutor adjusts his broad-brimmed hat to protect his two-blade scalp from the ravages of the sun, and leaves through the opposite doorway.

A friend gives the woman in the light-blue skirt a hug. There are tears close to the surface – too close. She retreats to the witness room and to the women from Victims of Crime and Department of Justice. They vanish through a side door. Everyone has gone.

The lattice space is empty.

Except for the fumes from the sumo crane.

Maybe if there is to be a trial the new courthouse will be ready.

(On March 30, 1998, a Rockhampton man was committed to stand trial on 69 counts.)

The fundamentals of reporting

Being able to write a story is one thing. But if you have nothing to write about, it's not a very useful skill. Having something to write about is the first thing a reporter needs. Only then can you start writing. Getting stories, getting information, is the crux of the business.

Reporters need some personality traits and some skills. If the particular personality traits required are missing, they will have to be developed. For example, some people are very shy. They prefer to blend into the background. They are uncomfortable meeting new people, and are really uncomfortable about ringing anyone they don't know on the telephone. And so on. These are not ideal personality characteristics for a journalist. They will have to be overcome. Reporters don't need to be extroverts, but they do need to have, or at least be able to feign, some confidence.

There is more to journalism than reporting other people's lies

Some people have the wrong idea about reporting. You see it a lot on TV. And particularly in the coverage of parliament. The reporter gets a few words from the government, a few from the opposition and that's it; story done, back to the office for the pay slip. (I saw it last night, and turned the TV off in disgust.)

irst fundamental. Journalists need to know much more about
...on, and its background, than just the "tennis match" in front
...side serves up something, the other side returns, the first does
...s the second, and so on, deuce, advantage, deuce, etc. Reporting
...s important. A few reporters see that as all their job involves.
...ough, is more than that.

...involves finding out and reporting much more than the fore-
...ckhand return, forehand lob going on in front of them. What
is going on in the dressing room? Behind the scenes? In the shadows? Who are
the other players? The other stakeholders? Who is pulling; who is pushing?
Who is paying; who isn't? And so on.

Journalism is an essential part of democracy

That is why journalism is so important. Journalism is referred to as "the
fourth estate". The term, and its significance, should be clearly understood.

Historically, Western societies have their roots in British traditions in which
the three "estates" of the realm made up the democratic constituency – those
"estates" were, the lords spiritual, the lords temporal and the commons, or, if
you like, the clergy, the nobles, and the commoners. The British parliament,
for example, to this day acknowledges that past. It consists of a House of
Lords and a House of Commons.

Then along came the invention of printing, and in the 1700s an explosion
in the number of newspapers on the streets. Some of these newspapers began
reporting parliament and politics and commenting on them (despite it being
illegal at first). Thus arose in the political mix, to the fury of some, the influential "fourth estate": the press. The role of the press to act as a watchdog
"fourth estate" is now recognised (although continually threatened) as an
essential ingredient in the structure of democracy. And the extent to which
the press fulfils, or is allowed to fulfil, that role is further recognised as a
barometer of the strength of democracy in a given society.

The starting-out journalist needs to appreciate these things – that there is
more to journalism than looking good on TV.

The case for journalism has seldom been better put than it was by two
lawyers in Queensland some years ago. They had been asked by the government of the day to investigate a serious matter that had been raised by the
media (in particular by the *Weekend Independent*). This is what they said:

> The investigation which we have conducted serves to underscore, once again,
> the importance of the media in our community, as a "watchdog" in respect of
> improper conduct by governments and public authorities. The importance of

this function of the media, especially in a State where the Parliament does not include a "house of review", has received much comment in recent years, particularly in the context of the Fitzgerald Inquiry.

The role of journalists in such matters is often a difficult one. Lacking any compulsive powers apart from those which exist under Freedom of Information legislation, the first problem which they frequently encounter is to secure relevant information from public functionaries who are often extremely reluctant to extend their cooperation. Based on such limited information as they are able to acquire, they must attempt, as best they can, to identify whether any wrong-doing has been committed, often without the benefit of legal training or qualified legal assistance, running the risk of actions for defamation if the conclusions which they reach are ultimately held to be unsustainable.

Report to
THE HONOURABLE THE PREMIER OF QUEENSLAND
and
THE QUEENSLAND CABINET

of

AN INVESTIGATION INTO ALLEGATIONS by MR KEVIN LINDEBERG

and

ALLEGATIONS by MR GORDON HARRIS and MR JOHN REYNOLDS

Morris Howard Report

Theirs is the often difficult function of attempting to express quite complex issues in a way which is comprehensible to the readers of daily newspapers, and to the viewers of current affairs television programmes. Seldom do journalists have the luxury of publishing detailed reports, in which the evidence can be carefully weighed and examined; they must attempt to distil the issues to a degree of brevity which accords with the very limited attention span of their readers or viewers. Driven by perfectly legitimate commercial concerns on the part of their editors and proprietors, they do not have the opportunity to express their views in the kind of considered and qualified language which they may feel is appropriate given the limited information which is available to them: they must, at least to some extent, be driven by the public's desire for sensationalism.

And, most of all, they face the daunting task of maintaining public interest in issues of genuine public concern, whilst the great majority of readers and viewers soon tire of one story and await eagerly the next scandal to emerge.

When one considers all of the constraints under which journalists operate, one must readily acknowledge the extraordinary success achieved by a small number of journalists, in discovering many of the facts relevant to the matters which are the subject of our investigation, in identifying the possible areas of wrong-doing which those facts reveal, in compiling reports which summarise those facts with an acceptable level of accuracy, and – most importantly – in maintaining public interest and concern over issues which powerful forces in the community would have preferred to see covered-up.

Accordingly, we pay particular tribute to the standards of investigative journalism which have maintained the issues which are the subject of our investigation in the public spotlight.   ("Morris Howard Report", p. 16)

There is not a great deal more that needs to be said. The two barristers covered it very well. Theirs are remarks that should be "taken on board" – and not forgotten!

You can't know too much

Broad general knowledge is a help anywhere. It is of particular help in journalism. The broader your knowledge, the better.

Good specialist knowledge is fine too, and if you have any, you are better armed than the reporter who doesn't have it.

Bill Nye, a century and a quarter ago, neatly summed up the need for knowledge in a column he wrote in his *Laramie Boomerang*. He was responding to a suggestion that perhaps it would be desirable to start a journalism school in the United States. In his column Nye outlined his idea of a curriculum for such a school. He may have had his tongue firmly in his cheek, but the words nevertheless were wise. After outlining what the first 50 years of the course should involve, he concluded:

> The closing ten years of the regular course might be profitably used in acquiring a practical knowledge of cutting cord wood, baking beans, making shirts, lecturing, turning double handsprings, preaching the gospel, learning how to make a good adhesive paste that will not sour in hot weather, learning the art of scissors grinding, punctuation, capitalization, prosody, plain sewing, music, dancing, sculpting, etiquette, how to win the affections of the opposite sex, the ten commandments, every man his own teacher on the violin, croquet, rules of the prize ring, parlor magic, civil engineering, decorative art, calsomining, bicycling, baseball, hydraulics, botany, poker, calisthenics, high-low jack, international law, faro, rhetoric, fifteen-ball pool, drawing and painting, mule skinning, vocal music, horsemanship, plastering, bull whacking, etc., etc., etc.
>
> At the age of ninety-five the student will have lost that wild, reckless and impulsive style so common among younger and less experienced journalists. He will emerge from the school with a light heart and a knowledge-box loaded up to the muzzle with the most useful information.
>
> (in *The Penguin book of columnists*, p. 3)

As has been said somewhere, many a true word is spoken in jest.

The ink never washes off the page

Simply putting something on the public record is one of the greatest contributions a journalist can make to the better running of his or her community. Therefore even the smallest newspaper can make a difference. And for this reason alone I hope that newspapers will last forever, despite the closures of the last 30 years and stagnant circulations affecting many papers today.

The message is, report it. Just the act of getting it in the paper may give the place a good shake-up.

Keep shaking the bush

It is a big news story that lasts more than four days. And it is true that most newsrooms think the public gets sick of stories after four days. But if you are dealing with something big, your chances of getting to the bottom of it in four days are next to nil. On the other hand, whenever you "shake the bush", or persist in following up a story, something usually "falls out". And you have a lead for the next episode. Keep shaking the bush.

It took five years of shaking the bush to uncover what had been going on in a institution where strange things had happened involving rape of children in custody. It took several more years of shaking the bush to reveal that what the public had been told by the government of the day about a particular pack rape incident (see p. 120) was simply untrue. And they knew it was untrue.

Check your maths

If something doesn't add up, you have a mathematical problem. If two things don't add up, you probably have a story. If three things don't add up, it's almost certainly a story.

A 21-year-old committed suicide in jail. Thing number one. Why would he do that? A reporter discovered he had been transferred from another prison half a state away. Why did they do that? Two things. Very odd. She then discovered the young prisoner had been wired (fitted with a tape recorder) to catch those involved in trafficking drugs in the jail from which he had been transferred. Three things.

But drug rackets in jails? How could this be? Over the months that followed, the reporter produced a major series of stories about prisoners being bashed, even killed, because of their drug debts, and banks and TABs being robbed to settle other prisoners' debts, and mothers and fathers of prisoners working at two and three jobs to pay for their sons' drug habits in jail, and staff being involved in the trade. Finally, a new government established a Royal Commission-style investigation and everything the reporter had written was found to be spot-on true.

The headline on the front page when the first big story ran, screamed **"Drugs in jail"** – in red! The purists were appalled. You don't use coloured headlines! But you don't get a story like that one every day either. The matter of drugs in jails might be well known today, but that was the story that raised the problem of drugs in the state's prisons for the first time. It should also be recorded that some people were not happy about the story being reported fortnight after fortnight and the reporter was subjected to some serious encouragement to desist. They threatened her life. She never flinched. Her work was not only excellent reporting, it was inspirational.

Don't believe everything you hear, but don't disbelieve it either

An inclination to say "That couldn't be right", or to be dismissive, or arrogant, has cost more than the occasional reporter a good story. Some things that sound far-fetched are. But some aren't.

Back in 1974 a reporter was told, six months before it happened, that the Opposition planned to have the Senate, where the government did not have a majority, "block supply" (cut off money) to the Whitlam government. The reporter, being very knowledgable, was able to dismiss the suggestion and inform his source that under the Constitution the Senate did not have the power to amend or reject a money bill.

By the time it happened (the Senate didn't reject or amend the legislation, it simply refused to vote on it) everyone knew, and the reporter missed an extraordinary story.

Whitlam called a double dissolution of both Houses to resolve the matter. He won the resultant election narrowly. The following year the same thing happened. This time he declined to dissolve the parliament, and the Governor-General stepped in. The rest, as they say, is history. Whitlam was dismissed in November 1975. People might have scoffed, but it would have been a really good story in January 1974, almost two years before the crunch!

Assumptions are necessary but dangerous

Be careful about making assumptions, such as: they won't talk to us; he would never do that; no one is that crazy; etc. Wrong. They might talk to you, and they might do that, and they might be that crazy. Check it out instead.

By Boxing Day morning 1975, everyone knew that something terrible had happened in Darwin. Everyone also knew that the city was cut off to normal communications. All the phones were out.

A reporter sitting in Melbourne, on the other side of the continent, knew there was a story that had to be told, but how do you tell it from Melbourne when all the phones are out? And everyone knew all the phones were out. It was crazy, but the reporter picked up the phone . . . and dialled the ABC's Darwin newsroom. Instead of an "out of order" tone he heard the familiar "brrrp brrrp" that one hears when the phone at the other end is ringing. He grabbed a tape recorder, plugged it in, and just let it ring. In Darwin, ABC journalist Mike Hayes was surveying the devastation in his newsroom. A phone somewhere in the rubble of the newsroom started ringing. He picked his way through the mess and answered it.

There have been arguments about who got the first story out of Darwin after Cyclone Tracy but that reporter in Melbourne was certainly one of the first. (It transpired later that while almost all phone connections in the city were cut, a small number survived the fury of the cyclone. The line to the ABC newsroom was one of them). The reporter and Mike Hayes repeated their phone call exercise for some time and the stories of what happened in

Darwin, as relayed by Mike Hayes over that phone connection, went round the world.

You will have to make judgments and assumptions, otherwise you will be paralysed. But they can be dangerous. Weigh them, watch them, question them.

Thinking vertically is fine; so is thinking laterally

The obvious is always obvious. Clearly. Everyone will see the obvious. Except that different things are obvious to different people. But why not think of something else? Think sideways. Maybe there's a better story there.

You've searched high and low for Ms Brown and there's no sign of her. Perhaps it's not Brown at all . . . but Browne. Or Braun. A reporter was once told the person who would be able to give him the full story on what he was looking for was a certain Mr X, and the name of the man was spelled out for the reporter's benefit. The reporter scoured the city, but could not locate him. Weeks went by. Nothing. Time was passing and he was getting absolutely nowhere. In an act of desperation he called up all his notes. He went through every sentence and all the names he had gleaned over the years on that story one by one. There was one name at the very end of the exercise he concluded that had a certain similarity to the one he had been given, but it wasn't spelled the way he had been told and surely it could not be pronounced that way . . . surely. But it was. And that was the breakthrough that broke the dam wall on a story of rape (several), abuse of children in care (lots) and cover-up and lies (heaps, and at the highest levels). After four and a half years, the story is still being unravelled. Thanks to the man with the name that wasn't.

It must be said not all stories turn out like that. A reporter was also told that a man by the name of Winchester would know a lot about something the reporter was chasing. And he was given a first name as well. Every Winchester in the country with that first name was contacted. Every one. The reporter knocked on many of their doors. None of them had the slightest idea what he was on about. Very disappointing. But hardly surprising really, because one day the hapless reporter discovered the man's name was nothing like Winchester. The countless, fruitless hours he had wasted chasing people with the wrong name had turned out to be nothing more than countless, fruitless hours. And no amount of lateral thinking would have produced the right name. It was nothing like Winchester.

What if you were trying to contact a certain Mr Commonname? His other names are, let's say, John Oswald Edward. You check the telephone directory and search for an entry for *Commonname JOE*. If you saw one that read

Commonname Joe, would you spot it as your man? Or if the name was just John Oswald Commonname would an entry, *Commonname Jo*, leap out at you? Probably not. But if not you might miss your big story. Keep thinking sideways whenever you confront a problem.

People who register to vote have to nominate their address. But can they spell? If the electoral roll says a person lives in Kehoe Street in a certain town, but there is no Kehoe Street in that town, do you assume the voter has registered a false address? You could be right. But is there a Keogh Street in that town? There is. And in that particular instance, that was where the person a certain reporter was looking for lived. He was helpful too, up to a point.

Another story. A journalist was looking for a woman who had been the source of a major story five years earlier. She had moved. A search of the records showed there was a person with her surname and initial living in a city more than a thousand kilometres away. Unfortunately this person was not listed in the online phone directory. This meant it was not possible to call to see if it was her. So instead of her name, the journalist searched for "Jones" in the same area. Up came a hit. Five doors from where the woman might be living was someone called "Jones". Would they be good enough to take a message? It was worth a try. If you should do this and there is no "Jones" in the street, try "Smith". You might as well.

So, when you are getting nowhere, try thinking sideways. It may not help, but after all it is probably the only option left. And thinking sideways has often produced the answer.

Luck is good, but effort is more reliable

Some people talk about "investigative journalism" – as if there are two kinds of journalism, ordinary journalism that ordinary journalists do, and investigative journalism that "special" journalists do. There aren't two kinds at all. There is just journalism. Some of it takes longer, consumes more shoe leather, petrol, time and patience than the rest, but that is the only difference. It is effort (and using your brains) that produces the kind of stories that are sometimes said to be the product of investigative journalism.

One of the more extraordinary examples of effort, and of a reporter using his brains, that I witnessed while working with students on the *Weekend Independent* illustrates the point.

Two of Australia's major security companies had been prosecuted for collusion over pricing. A student wondered what kind of service the security industry was providing its customers. For example, were clients justified in having a good night's rest while leaving the safety of their businesses, their stock and premises, in the hands of security companies during the dark hours? Were the security companies doing what they said they would?

The reporter found they were not. The clients were being short-changed.

His front page story was a typical inverted pyramid piece. But, in typical inverted-pyramid style, it did not say what it took to produce the information it contained. That was on page two.

What page two revealed was amazing. A journalism student, who had to do a story for assessment, had spent what amounted to **one whole week, at night**, sitting in his little Datsun 120Y, watching the security industry at work. Or more accurately, the security industry not at work. It was a fine story. No luck involved (apart from being questioned only once by the police); just effort, tremendous effort.

A few words on effort from Evan Whitton to finish.

The way of the reporter is hard. He's out there, tireless feet crunching in the gravel and never a kind word from anyone (*Amazing scenes*, p. 132).

There is a lot of "tireless feet" involved. And not nearly as much luck.

Contacts are vital . . . in their place

By "contacts" I mean those people you might regularly contact for comment on stories. There is no doubt that having good contacts is very valuable. But don't get captured by your contacts. And stay away from having crooks in your kitbag.

Having a contact who is also a good mate can become a serious problem. If you want to do the business well, do it well. Keep contacts at a professional arm's length.

Once you get into people's debt, you are in trouble. Or more accurately, we are in trouble, because your reporting may not be what we think it is.

And watch out for your ego. When being seen in the company of important people becomes important to you, you are in trouble. We are in trouble. When you get asked by prominent people for your advice, and you start to realise how important you must be, you are in more trouble. We are in more trouble. Don't be trapped by your contacts. The fourth estate depends on your independence.

On a purely practical note, make records of your contacts' details and keep them up to date. Contact books can become messy as addresses and phone numbers change, and they can be lost. Computer records are fine as long as you have a separate copy and keep both up to date. Having the information on an organiser allows you to carry it when you are away from the office, and to back it up on the computer. But whatever method you use, you must have a reliable "contact book" system. One that is not accessible to others is best. Some of your contacts at least will expect that their existence, and certainly their address and phone numbers, will not be known to anyone else. Don't leave your contact book lying around, or the file open on your computer screen.

Your contacts must be able to trust you. If not, your contact list will be small. But you have to make it clear that you are running the stories, not them. If they do the wrong thing that is their fault, not yours.

There is no such thing as a free lunch

Depending on the kind of stories you are writing or the "round" you are covering (sport, politics, entertainment, the arts, local government, etc.) you may receive "gifts" from people. It happens in journalism. Indeed it happens a lot in journalism. And people will say, "That doesn't influence what I write." Like the policeman who says it's okay to get a free feed from some establishment because it's good for the establishment to have policemen on the premises.

Getting gifts may not happen in too many occupations, but that is simply a reminder that journalism isn't like some other occupations. It will usually be clear who the gift has come from. There isn't much point sending a gift if the receiver doesn't know who sent it.

Accepting the gift, whatever it might be, is not a good idea. Send it back. You will make a very powerful statement to the giver about what kind of person you are. Sending gifts to journalists is a well-known public relations ploy. It is best not to go there. It is better to be a returner than a receiver.

Policing is an occupation where "gifts" or "freebies" are not unknown and accepting them, officially at least, is frowned on. A former senior policeman told me he gave his troops specific instructions never to accept such kind donations. If they had a meal at a restaurant, he instructed, and found at the end that the kind host had advised the staff there was no charge, they were to call the person who served them and loudly proclaim for the benefit of other patrons what excellent service he or she had provided and hand over the price of the meal as a tip. That usually caused a bit of consternation in the mind of the proprietor.

"Freebies" abound in some of the rounds you may cover. Gifts have a hidden price-tag. Keep your dealings out in the open.

Know your technology

The reporter who knows how to do whatever is required is a useful reporter, because, like the mails, the story has to get through. A huge story sitting in a laptop in the middle of nowhere is not a story at all. It won't be until it lands in the office back at base. Do you know anything about computers, or computer packages, audio recorders or cameras? Telephones? Links?

A reporter on assignment overseas was trying to file a radio story via the tape recorder he had connected to the telephone in his hotel room. But, instead of his story, all the people back home were getting was a terrible buzzing noise. He unravelled the length of light insulated copper cable he carried with him (for this purpose) and connected his equipment to the outlet of the shower in his room. Fortunately the hotel was a few years old and its plumbing was metal. Earthing the equipment got rid of the buzzing noise and the story got through.

Knowing your technology can be useful in just getting the story, let alone getting it out. Technology these days is wonderful.

A journalist needed to find a source who had been the subject of a major story more than a year earlier. But by then the source had moved. Unfortunately, the reporter who had done the story, and who it was hoped might know the person's whereabouts, had also moved. The word was put out. Did anyone know where the reporter was these days? A message came back, from, of all places, Alaska! Try such and such, it said. The reporter was found. He was working on a newspaper somewhere in Europe and he phoned in. Did he remember the address of the source for that story, the journalist in far-off Australia asked? Well, no, the reporter said. After all, it was more than a year ago. However, he remembered the suburb and the house, he said. But there were a lot of houses in that suburb; could he describe where the house was exactly and what it looked like? The conversation went on. All-too-sketchy details emerged. But while he talked, the reporter in Europe called up Google Earth, zoomed in on the city back in Australia, and then the suburb, put a "bookmark" on the house in question, did a "screen grab" of the page and emailed it back to the journalist. By the time the conversation was over the journalist in Australia had a clear picture of the street and the house sitting on his computer screen.

Could you do that?

Ask others to ask questions

Sometimes, people can be less than frank with you. They may put a "spin" on an answer, they may delay answering, or they may not answer at all. As a reporter you cannot make anyone answer your questions. It may be telling if they do not answer you. It may even be embarrassing, but there is no compulsion on anyone to answer your questions.

However, there are some circumstances where people are supposed to answer questions, and one where they are expected to tell the truth – Question Time, or Questions on Notice, in parliament. Members of parliament will sometimes ask questions that you believe should be asked. These can be asked of a Minister during Question Time or via a Question on Notice. While a question asked during Question Time may produce more heat than light, a Question on Notice requires an answer and the answer may be useful. Of course, there is a hurdle that has to be cleared. There needs to be a Member who sees the need for a question to be asked. How this hurdle can be overcome I will leave to your imagination.

Where the hurdle has been overcome, I can report that some mighty interesting information has come to light. And there I will leave the matter with you. If parliament really **is** a bastion against tyranny, why not use it?

Putting it all together

These fundamental skills of journalism all work together. **How** can best be demonstrated through an example.

Some things weren't adding up, and I started asking questions about the destruction of documents related to a youth detention centre. In 1995 I started seriously investigating this institution and constantly published stories about it. After "shaking the bush" for several years I was eventually told in 2001 about the pack rape of a girl who had been held in custody in the centre around the time of the document shredding. She had been taken somewhere with a group of boys and left without supervision and had been raped. Despite my informants not being able to recall her name, by wearing out a lot of shoe leather, I found her.

She agreed to speak with me and then to try to find the place where she was taken. She had been just 14 at the time and did not really know where the place was . . . not even at the time of the rape. But she described it quite clearly and agreed to look for it with me. I assumed that clarifying any of the facts, including the location, would help me find out what had really happened.

I did some research on the area, and we started where I thought the most likely place would be. We searched all day but nothing matched her descriptions. Late in the afternoon she said something like "No, it's much further away. I have been here, but this is not the place." So we went through what she remembered once again. At one point, almost as an aside, she said it might have been X, an out-of-town suburb, but when we abandoned our search for the day we had achieved nothing and she could add nothing to what she had already told me. We agreed to try again the following day.

I happened to know this part of the state reasonably well. Because of what she had told me, the suburb X she had mentioned in her aside did not really fit the description of the terrain where she said she had been taken. But I knew there was a place a little more than an hour's drive away that sounded something like X. The next day we set off, not for X, but for the place that sounded like X.

We arrived in a small country town. Apart from asking the locals if they could nominate a spot where someone might commit rape, what to do? We chose the obvious. Most country towns these days have a locality map for the benefit of tourists, and this town was no exception. We found the map and noted where picnic spots and national parks were located. There were quite a few. So armed with this little bit of information we set off. We would visit each of them in turn, starting with the closest and working out from there.

We were looking for a carpark in the bush and in particular, a large flat rock.

I wrote two stories about that day. One was a conventional "inverted pyramid" news story, which the *Courier-Mail* ran on page 3, the other was a first-person piece for readers, which unusually they ran in the same edition, on page 14. The inverted pyramid story was reproduced at the end of chapter 1. Here is the first-person piece.

The Search for Kate

by Bruce Grundy

It had just been a hunch – pretty much a stab in the dark – and it had turned up trumps. The odyssey had been worth it. Against goodness knows what odds I had found what I had been searching for – no golden fleece, just a large flat rock, in not quite the middle of nowhere, but almost.

This was no ordinary slab of sandstone or whatever; this rock had witnessed a wretched crime and I was taking the young woman next to me, step by step, through what had happened to her here.

At first she had been excited.

"This is it. This is the place. I know it. I know it. No doubt," she had said.

At the start her words had flowed freely as we talked it through.

Where were you? Who else was here? Where were they standing? What were their names? Where were those who were supposed to be in charge?

But as the questions continued and the crunch they were leading to approached, her words began to slow. Slight pauses followed questions. Answers were harder now. Her voice began to tremble. Just that little bit. And much softer. Then tears filled her eyes and streaked her cheeks. Her answers now were sobs. But she kept going. Until the questions stopped.

"I have to go now," she had said through her tears, and crying she set off back down the path we had come to reach this place.

Twenty paces maybe and she sank to the grass beside the track and vomited until there was nothing left to lose.

She stood up and set off down the track again back towards the car park. Another ten paces and again she slumped to the grass and retched and retched – but there was nothing to bring up.

"I'm coming," I called out. "And I'm behind you."

She had asked me when we had first begun our search for this place not to walk behind her. Please. Please stay in front of me, she had said. I said I understood and wouldn't walk behind her. But now I was behind her.

I kept talking as I reached her so she would know where I was and not be startled. I put a hand, just a touch, on her shoulder (she had made it clear she did not like men touching her) and gave her my handkerchief to wipe her lips. I said I was sorry for what they had done to her here, and I said I was sorry that those who were supposed to look after her that day had not done their jobs. I said I hoped there would be justice for her in the end and that she might get the rest of her life back now.

But it was clear she wanted to be alone. I said I was going back to get some pictures – which is the sort of thing journalists do that puts other people off them. She stood up and set off down the track once more. No more vomiting this time. There was nothing left to vomit.

I took the pictures of where we had just been and walked back to the car park. She was sitting at one of the rough bush tables there with her mother, somewhere in her thoughts, head bowed, hair covering her face. Crumpled. Almost doubled up as if she had been winded. Again I said something inadequate about being sorry. But I knew my words were little comfort.

Then, as journalists do, I asked the rotten question. Would she go back with me where we had just been and go through it all again – so I could record it, absolutely accurately? I said some day I feared some bastard would say she had made it all up, that she had never been to that place, that it didn't even exist and nor did she probably. Someone would try to confuse her and get her to say she had never been pack raped on the rock we had been looking for, and had just found – never been pack raped there or anywhere else for that matter.

It took lots of courage but she said she thought that was a good idea and she did as I asked. We went through it all again.

The place was just as she had described it to me the second time we had met. On day one she had said nothing. Even on day two she had been very cautious and hesitant – telling some strange guy, in this case a strange white guy, what had been done to you was not something a woman would enjoy. She was really searching in her memory to call up the detail of what had happened. I did not give her any hints. I wanted to know from her if her story, and what I had been told by others, matched. Indeed they did match – and more. She remembered where the sun had been – shining through the treetops on her face; the geography and the topography and the vegetation of the place; and who was there. And then she even agreed to go with this strange white guy to try to find the spot again. A crazy idea really – a rock – one rock somewhere in the whole of South East Queensland! A rock in a few million hectares of bush and farms, and national parks, and mountains, valleys, ranges, etc. Crazy. But she agreed.

She had described the place again when I had taken her to where I thought it might have been but where it wasn't. No, Bwuce, she had said, (her "r" sounds always lost out to the "w" when she spoke). No. It's much further away. And the rocks aren't right. And the trees aren't right. And this isn't right and that isn't right either. I'm sorry but it is further out in the country somewhere.

Somewhere.

Perhaps there is a journalist's god because we finally found the place – the place where she had been raped all those years ago – as a 14-year-old in the care of the State. And it was just as she said it would be. The trees, the sun, the rock. The lot.

The place we were looking for was close to a hundred kilometres from where we had first looked.

Shortly after, the young woman submitted Freedom of Information applications to various State agencies. Nothing happened for months. Then one day, "out of the blue", a bundle of documents, and a bombshell, arrived. The documents did not deal with the place we had found at all. What they revealed was that the young woman had been the victim of an earlier pack rape excursion into an even more isolated and dreadful part of the south east Queensland wilderness. She had managed, as many women in that situation do, to block the incident out of her memory.

It took until 2001 to uncover the pack rape story. But then several more rape stories tumbled out. As a result of these investigations, what happened to the girl in the story reproduced above was featured in an episode of *Australian Story* in May 2004. Her story (and those of two others) also featured on the national *7.30 Report* in May 2006. Keep shaking that bush.

Of course, it could be said that it was luck, rather than persistence and lateral thinking that had allowed us to find that single slab of rock in the whole of south east Queensland. And there is some truth in that. But you can make your own luck, and lateral thinking (if they didn't take the girl where I was told they took her, where might they have gone instead?) is part of it. Practise the fundamentals of journalism and you will be able to play your role as a member of the "fourth estate".

PART 2

Writing skills

Grammar

Any attempt to raise the issue of problems surrounding grammar, spelling and punctuation usually causes students' eyes to glaze over. They are topics that are seen to be either boring or no longer important in today's world. Or, it is claimed, "everyone knows that stuff". The truth is, not only are they interesting, they are also important, and not "everyone knows that stuff" at all. There are examples of poor grammar and incorrect spelling and punctuation appearing in the news media every day and these are matters that are central to the issue of a journalist's credibility.

If you cannot spell, punctuate and use grammar correctly, those who can will laugh at you – and your publication. They will cut out your gaffes from the paper and email them to their friends with rude comments and ridicule you in the pub. Examples abound. The past tense of the verb "to sneak" is "sneaked", not "snuck". A person sentenced to capital punishment is "hanged" not "hung". Never, in the entire history of our legal system, has anyone "pled" his or her innocence; there is no such word. Indeed, if you do not know the difference between a gerund or verbal noun and a present participle and which requires a personal and which a possessive pronoun, what you write will either mean something other than what you meant to write, or it will cause your readers to sneer. Or both.

If you don't know the difference between a common and a proper noun, you will have problems with your spelling. Being unaware of the difference between a compound adjective and compound adverb will almost certainly produce some interesting, but incorrect, punctuation and/or spelling.

And while there are times when it is acceptable, even sensible, to split an infinitive, there are other times when it grates on your readers and detracts from your reputation as a writer. Do you know what splitting an infinitive means?

Radio and television reporters desperately write their stories, or as much of them as they can, in the present tense. For the most part, newspaper reporters rely on the past and the present perfect. Who knows the difference? Does it matter? It depends on how you feel about your credibility.

A newspaper wrote a glowing obituary about an internationally famous man it described in very large type as a "genious". A feature story appeared about a writer whose latest book *The Accidental Tourist* had just won some serious acclaim. Except that his book was actually titled *The Accidental Terrorist*.

For our purposes, grammar is about the use of words – the way we use words to speak, to write, to communicate. And if we fail to communicate professionally, we fail dismally. So grammar is important.

Grammar is also about the way we put words together (syntax). And it is about relationships between words.

Since our language is changing and evolving, the "rules" of grammar change too – as we accommodate new forms and structures, and even accept what was once unacceptable.

Grammar is complex. What follows is not a complete course in English grammar, spelling and punctuation. This chapter covers the most relevant issues involving the parts of speech (nouns, pronouns, verbs, adjectives, adverbs, prepositions, conjunctions and exclamations) as well as matters related to the construction of phrases, clauses and sentences, and the significance of case and mood in writing grammatically correct material. This will be enough to get you started, and may even convince you that you should know about these things.

Why should you care?

Problems emerge in many ways, some of them very simple ways, and some people claim that they are nothing to worry about really. Surely only an old fuddy-duddy, or pedant, would take exception to such trivial matters. But this is not so. If you wish to communicate accurately with your readers you have to get even the little things right.

For instance, some people liberally sprinkle their copy with capital letters. The theory seems to be this: if a word, usually a thing, is important, make it look important. Hit the shift key and start it with an upper-case letter.

But such a view reveals a misunderstanding of the role of capitals in our language. First letter capitals (except at the start of a sentence) establish the difference between proper nouns and common nouns. They are not there just for variety.

The difference between the two is critical. Writing *earth* when you should have written *Earth*, or *mercury* when it should have been *Mercury*, or *the church* instead of *the Church* will, unfortunately, say a great deal about you. More pub jokes at your expense.

Before we go any further, two things have to be acknowledged. The first is that our language is constantly evolving and what was once unheard of may now be commonplace. By the same token, what was once acceptable may no longer be, and no doubt there will be further shifts in this regard in the future.

The second point, unfortunately, is that in the context of analysing grammar and grammatical constructions it is not possible to place different kinds of words in convenient little boxes. Nouns are not always nouns, for instance. In a different context the same word may be a verb, or an adjective, or a verbal noun . . . or something else entirely.

For example in the sentence, *That boy told me that the snake was that big and I know that is not true*, the word *that* is first an adjective, then a conjunction, then an adverb and lastly a pronoun. A *box* is one thing (a noun). To *box* (to fight) is another (a verb). And used in the context of a *box* office it is an adjective.

Which means we have to know what these things are. So what are nouns and how should they be used?

Nouns

Nouns are the names we give to things. If you can see something, hear it, feel it or think about it as a concept, it will be a noun. Thus *river*, *rose*, *cat*, *mountains*, *music*, *love*, *faith*, *hope* and *death*, for example, are all nouns – common nouns. But capitalised, as in the *Murray River*, *Rose* (e.g. Hancock), *Faith* (e.g. Bandler) and *Hope* (e.g. Lange) are not generic things but specific names and they are referred to as proper nouns.

Dictionaries may not always use the upper-case first letter to differentiate the proper noun, which means the writer will need to know what the correct use of the word demands. Is it *east* or *East*? It will depend on whether the writer is talking about one of the points of the compass or a direction, or the Orient. And *mother* as in someone's mum is not the same as *Mother*, a senior figure in an order of nuns. What happened in *the state* this week is one thing, whereas a person who objects to the actions of the government would be directing his anger at *the State*. You might write about *Cyclone Tracy* being a particularly severe *cyclone*, but if you used the word *Cyclone* by itself with a capital "C", you might be using the brand name of a type of fencing wire.

House style may determine the correct usage of proper nouns in your organisation, and the subs may help too, so if you are unsure, look it up or ask.

First letter capitals

Other uses of upper-case or capital letters to begin a word include:
* days of the week and months of the year
* religions and religious festivals – *Buddhism*, *Easter*
* honorifics, titles and honours – *Maj-Gen*, *Sir*, *OAM*, etc. (note that in most newspapers today *Mr*, *Mrs*, *Ms* and *Dr* do not take a following full stop)
* the names of people (including nicknames)
* names of places and entities (companies, trade unions, sporting clubs, etc.)
* languages – French, Chinese, Indonesian, etc.
* abbreviations of names – UN, GPO, WHO, etc.
* brand names – Esky not esky
* trains, planes and ships – the Orient Express, the Queen Mary, etc.

Titles of books and movies, which always used to take initial capitals, excluding any conjunctions, articles and prepositions (*The House of Representatives Report into Crime in the Community*) are now a matter for house style, with many preferring capitals only for the first word and any proper nouns (*The House of Representatives report into crime in the community*).

If an object or inanimate thing is personified, or given the status of a being, it should be regarded as a proper noun (*Oh Death, where is thy sting?*).

These are things you must get right. Until you know, check.

Number

In grammar, nouns that refer to single things, or groups of things, are described as having "number" – singular for one, plural for more than one. Usually the plural is obtained by adding *s* to the singular. One *cat* (singular), two *cats* (plural). But not always. One *man*, but two *men*. And sometimes the singular is also the plural. One *deer*, two *deer*. And sometimes the plural is obtained by adding *es* to the singular. *The hen was sitting on her perch* becomes *The hens were sitting on their perches*. But should you be talking about fish, you would refer to a single fish as *a perch*, or to a bag full as *a dozen perch*.

This is all quite straightforward. But the matter of number becomes very significant for the writer because it is not just nouns that have number. Verbs have number too. And grammar demands that the number of a verb agree with its related noun (or pronoun) subject. This is where some people go wrong. Before discussing that we will need to deal with verbs in general. We will cover the issue of "subject/verb agreement" later.

Gender

In English there are few gender-specific words and in these days of non-discriminatory language, very few indeed. We no longer have policemen and firemen; we have police officers and fire fighters. Spokesmen have vanished under the weight of spokespersons and chairmen have been replaced by chairs. We no longer have actresses, although we still have princes and princesses. And some media outlets would surely collapse without them. But gender-specific suffixes (such as -ess) being added to a masculine noun to make it feminine are no longer a matter of much concern in English. Today's reporter needs to know the newsroom's views on the use of non-sexist, non-discriminatory language. There will be a policy on it.

Sentences

A sentence is a collection or group of words that express a complete thought. Sometimes, as in the case of a command, a sentence can be a single word. Normally a sentence will contain a subject, a verb and a predicate. It will start with a capital letter and end with a full stop, question or exclamation mark. Most importantly, a sentence is a group of words that as an entity can stand alone as making sense. Occasionally a single word may constitute a sentence.

> The sun (*subject*) sets (*verb*) in the west (*predicate*).

Sentences are usually about doing or being and thus normally contain three important ingredients – the subject of the doing or being, the action involved, and the object of the action.

Thus, in the example above the subject of the action is the sun, the action is the setting, and the object of the setting is the west.

> The sun (*subject*) sets (*verb*) in the west (*object*).
> The cat (*subject*) sat (*verb*) on the mat (*object*).

If we wrote instead, *The cat sat on the mat in the doorway*, we would have introduced another element into our sentence, the indirect object.

> The cat (*subject*) sat (*verb*) on the mat (*object*) in the doorway (*indirect object*).

Knowing what the subject of a sentence is and what the object is will become quite important as we delve deeper into the matter of grammar and the correct use of words.

Of course a sentence might not have an object. If we were to write, *The cat sat still*, we would have written such a sentence. In this case there is no object, but we still have a complete, sensible thought, so we have a sentence. In this case we describe the elements of the sentence as:

> The cat (*subject*) sat (*verb*) still (*complement*).

The difference between these two sentences introduces something important about verbs.

In the case of the first example, *The cat sat on the mat*, we can see that the action indicated by the verb has passed from the subject to the object. The mat has been the object of an action (the verb) undertaken by the subject of the sentence (the cat). Where the action passes between the subject of a sentence and the object we say the verb is **transitive** (from the Latin prefix, *trans*, meaning "across").

In the second case, *The cat sat still*, no action passes from the subject to anything (since there is no object) and we say the verb is **intransitive**.

Verbs

The word or words in a sentence which establish action or being are verbs. Except in rare cases, every sentence has a verb. The rare exceptions are exclamations or questions. For example, *Rubbish!*, or *No way!* or *Who?* where the verb and its subject or object are inferred.

What the examples above are really saying is perhaps:

> That is **rubbish!**
> There is **no way** that is correct!
> **Who** said that?

Tense

Actions that go on around us are time-related. They may be happening now, (the present), or have already happened (the past), or perhaps are yet to happen (the future). The action words we use, verbs, reflect these realities. Some establish an action as happening in the present, some in the past and some in the future.

> The sun sets in the west. (*present*)
> The sun set in the west. (*past*)
> The sun will set in the west. (*future*)

The time-related nature of verbs is referred to as the "tense" of a verb, and the simple tenses are present, past and future.

But our language is more complicated than that. What if we were to write: *The sun is setting in the west*, or, *The sun has set in the west*, or, *The sun will be setting in the west*?

We are still dealing with the present, the past and the future, but our verbs are now more complex. They are no longer single words, but comprise two words or a string of words. We refer to these as "compound verbs", and they introduce us to some matters that cause more than a few problems for the unaware or the unwary reporter and writer.

Compound verbs

Compound verbs have two parts. They are made up of a form of the principal verb, the one that establishes whatever the action is that is going on, and a form of either the verb "to be" or the verb "to have".

If we were to say *I walk* we would be using a simple present tense verb. But if we said *I am walking*, we would be using a compound verb, made of a form of the principal verb *to walk* (in this case *walking*) and an auxiliary verb (in this case *am*, which is a present tense form of the verb *to be*.

The simple tense forms of the verb *to be* are:

> am (*present*), as in **I am**
> was (*past*), as in **I was**
> will *or* shall (*future*), as in **I will** or **I shall**

If we said *I was walking* we would be using a compound verb, but this time it involves the past tense of the verb *to be* (*was*) and a present tense form to the verb *to walk*, i.e. *walking*. This verb form is referred to as a present participle.

I will be walking involves a compound verb that includes the future tense of the verb *to be* (*will be*) and the present participle of the verb *to walk* (*walking*).

Compound verbs do not always include forms of the verb *to be*. The other auxiliary verb that we use to form compound verbs is the verb *have* or *to have*.

And so we get *I have walked* and *I had walked*. We even use the two auxiliaries, as in *I have been walking*, *I had been walking* and *I will have been walking*. (These compound verb forms are sometimes called verb phrases, but we won't get into phrases just yet.)

The past tense form of the verb *to walk* is *walked* (today I *walk* . . . yesterday I *walked*) and in the case of the past compound verb form, we say *I have walked* or *I had walked*. In this case, the form of the principal verb (*walked*) is a past participle. Past participles are often, but not always, formed by the addition of *ed* to the principal verb (*wanted*, *wished*, *pursued*, *punished*, etc.). But the past participle of the verb *to see* is not *seeed* nor is *doed* the past participle of the verb *to do*. In the same manner, present participles can usually be distinguished, but not always, by their *ing* endings (*seeing*, *doing*, *wanting*, *wishing*, etc.). But *sing*, *thing* and *bring* are not present participles.

Nevertheless, it is important to know these verb forms, as they are very important in journalism. We have already briefly encountered the significance of the past participle in our discussion on tenses in the section on the inverted pyramid, so we will deal with that matter first.

Being "perfect" . . . or "imperfect"

Participles and compound verb forms have to be given some attention because their use is important in journalism.

For example, if we should say *I walked*, we are saying that the act of walking is over. Thus *walked* is past tense. And if we should say *I have walked*, we are also saying that the walking is finished; that the action is complete, that it is over, or as the grammarians say, perfect. But *have* is present tense (today I have something). Thus *have walked* is an example of what is called a present perfect tense.

If, on the other hand we should say *I am walking*, we are saying that the act of walking is going on at the time of speaking; that the act is continuing at that time. Grammarians recognise this situation as imperfect or continuous and the tense of *I am walking* can be described a present imperfect or present continuous.

I had walked is past perfect, *I will be walking* is future continuous, and so on.

The one that is most useful for newspaper reporters and commonly appears in their copy is the present perfect. The Government *has said* it will do something; police *have arrested* someone; floodwaters *have inundated* some place, and so on. The present perfect tense is important in some journalism contexts (particularly newspapers) because while it recognises that what is being reported has happened (by using the past tense of the principal verb), it gives the action a flavour of immediacy and currency by using the present tense form of the auxiliary verb. In other words, instead of writing "the government said" (past tense), the newspaper reporter would probably write "the government has said" (present perfect).

Problems with participles

Starting a sentence (such as this one) with a participle can lead to problems for some writers. By the time the end of the sentence is reached the poor participle is left without a subject. An unattached participle is a sorry grammatical sight. Here are four examples.

> Realising the way ahead was blocked, there was no point going on.
> Realising the way ahead was blocked, it was pointless pressing on.
> Realising the way ahead was blocked, the decision was made to turn back.
> Realising the way ahead was blocked, pressing on was not an option.

In none of the cases does the participle "realising" have a subject. The writer has made a serious mistake. There are two options to fix the problem. They both involve giving the participle a subject, as in:

> Realising the way ahead was blocked, the search party (*subject*) decided not to press on.
> The search party (*subject*), realising the way ahead was blocked, decided not to press on.

The other solution would be to use a conjunction instead of the participle. This result is also grammatically correct.

> Because the way ahead was blocked, there was no point going on.

Using unattached or hanging participles is a very common mistake. Here are some examples:

> Knowing (*present participle*) she wanted to be a lawyer, a good education was essential.
> Looking (*present participle*) out the window, the sun was shining brightly.

In neither case does the participle leading the sentences above have a subject (nor a principal verb). They should. For example:

> Knowing (*present participle*) she wanted to be a lawyer, Jane (*subject*) realised (*principal verb*) a good education was essential.
>
> Looking (*present participle*) out the window, he (*subject*) saw (*principal verb*) the sun was shining brightly.

The problem does not arise only with present participles (those which end with "ing"). Past participles get some writers into trouble too. For example:

> Battered and bruised (*past participle*), the fight was lost.
> Battered and bruised (*past participle*), it was clear the fight was lost.

Both are grammatically incorrect for the same reason that the earlier cases involving the present participle are incorrect. In neither sentence above does the past participle have a subject. What the writer meant to say, or should have said, was:

> Battered and bruised (*past participle*), he (*subject*) knew (*principal verb*) the fight was lost.

So, beware the hanging or unattached participle. Not only may your readers scoff, but also your communication will be unclear and quite possibly inaccurate.

Verbs, number and subject–verb agreement

We already know that nouns have "number", singular or plural. Verbs do too.
  The number of a verb depends on the number of its subject. A singular subject takes a singular verb. A plural subject takes a plural verb.

> One dog barks (*singular*)
> Two dogs bark (*plural*)

The rules of grammar say that the number of a verb must agree with the number of its subject. Nothing would seem to be more simple. Yet this is probably the area of grammar that produces more mistakes in the news media than any other. For example:

> . . . the police's pedophile taskforce have charged a 38-year-old man . . .

The subject of the sentence is *taskforce*, which is singular and therefore must take a singular verb. *Have* is plural (two people *have* something, but one person *has* something). The sentence should have read:

> . . . the police's pedophile <u>taskforce</u> (*singular*) <u>has</u> (*singular*) charged a 38-year-old man . . .

The only way to know what the number of a verb should be is to know what the subject of the verb is, and what number that subject is.

   Which of the following is correct?

> **(a)** She was one of the most gracious women who has ever lived.
> *or*
> **(b)** She was one of the most gracious women who have ever lived.

The answer, of course, is (b). There are various ways of arriving at the correct answer. With the grammatical tools currently at our disposal we would need to rearrange the sentence to reach the right conclusion and say:

> Of all the women who have/has ever lived, she was one of the most gracious.

Or we might substitute *to* for *who* and thus produce:

> She was one of the most gracious women to have/has ever lived.

The correct answer again is quite clear.

   With a higher level of grammatical understanding we might note that *who have/has ever lived* is an adjectival clause qualifying the noun *women*; *women* is plural; so the verb must be plural, and that means the verb must be *have lived*. But mistakes with subject/verb agreement abound. A colleague collects them.

   Conjunctions (linking words) can also cause problems.

> One of the boys <u>and</u> six of the girls <u>were</u> taken to hospital.

But:

> One of the boys <u>with</u> six of the girls <u>was</u> taken to hospital.

And joining two or more nouns and/or pronouns produces a compound subject which requires a plural verb, but *with*, *as well as*, and *in addition to*, linking a singular subject to other nouns and/or pronouns take singular verbs.

Each and none

Phrases containing a plural noun or pronoun that separate the subject of a sentence from its verb cause problems, and most particularly when that subject is **each**, as in:

> **(a)** Each of the boys make excellent coffee.
> *or*
> **(b)** Each of the boys makes excellent coffee.

Each is singular and therefore (b) is correct.
   None, a contracted form of "no one", is also singular.

> Despite the efforts of paramedics, no one was saved.

But which of these alternatives would you expect to see?

> Despite the efforts of paramedics, none was saved.
> *or*
> Despite the efforts of paramedics, none were saved.

Common usage is an issue.
   Even more problems arise with number when we have to deal with pronouns, which we will do shortly. Back to verbs.

The infinitive . . . to split or not to split

We have noted that verbs may be transitive or intransitive. But there are also other ways of looking at the verbs we use in our language and some of them are important to writers.
   Some verb forms can stand alone without an object and still make sense. Some cannot. Verbs that have a subject (and can stand alone) are called finite verbs. For example:

> The cat <u>wants</u> (*finite verb*) to sit on the mat.

We know that *wants* is a finite verb because it has a subject and it could stand alone – *The cat wants*.

Finite verbs have a subject, even an inferred subject. The command *Go* could be a sentence, even if it is only one word. The verb has an inferred subject, *(You) go*, needs no object, and is therefore a finite verb.

However, some verb forms do not have a subject and cannot stand alone. If we take the example *I want to go to town*, *want* is a finite verb because it has a subject (*I*) but *to go* does not, and it could not stand alone. We could not say, for example, *I to go to town*. In such a case the verb form is called in-finite or non-finite: *to go* is an "infinitive" verb form.

Now, if we were to say *I want to immediately go to town* we have inserted a word between the two parts of the infinitive. We have split our infinitive. And splitting an infinitive needs to be considered carefully.

We have all heard the line from Star Trek:

> To boldly go where no man has gone before . . .

and no one, as far as I know, has objected. But if you were to write *I want to immediately go to town* (instead of *I want to go to town immediately*) you might get some objection.

Splitting infinitives raises some issues apart from whether it is acceptable grammar. It can introduce shades of meaning into what you are trying to say. And making sure the readers know exactly what you are trying to say is vital if you want to communicate with them precisely.

If we take the sentence, *He failed to understand*, and wish to express the point more forcefully, we might say any of the following three sentences:

> He completely failed to understand.
> He failed to understand completely.
> He failed to completely understand.

But they do not deliver the same meaning.

> He completely failed to understand *means* there was a total lack of understanding on his part.
> He failed to understand completely *means* he understood at least some of whatever it was.
> He failed to completely understand *means* he understood most, but not quite all of whatever it was.

There is a big difference in meaning between the first of the three and the last. Thus to suggest that splitting the infinitive is always a grammatical sin, is silly.

Nevertheless, *occasionally you may need to split an infinitive*, or, indeed, you may need *to split an infinitive occasionally*, but it is to be hoped that you will never need *to occasionally split an infinitive*.

Pronouns

"Pro" is a prefix meaning "for", "in favour of" or "on behalf of", as in "pro-Labor", for instance. A "pro-noun" then is a word that acts on behalf of a noun.

Instead of saying: *John gave John's book to Mary and I want Mary to give John's book back to John*, we say, via pronouns: *John gave his book to Mary and I want her to give him back his book*.

In the last sentence above we have two kinds of pronouns – personal pronouns (*he, she, him* and *her*) and possessive pronouns (*his* and *her*). Not knowing the difference between them can make for some serious failures in communication – because you may send a completely wrong message.

Personal pronouns stand instead of names of individuals and things; possessive pronouns stand instead of their ownership of something.

The two are not necessarily interchangeable. The problem arises if writers do not know the difference between a present participle, for instance, and a verbal noun or gerund.

At the beginning of this chapter it was pointed out that words do not come with just one specific label. In different contexts the same word can mean different things and be different parts of speech.

Take the word *calling* for example. In the sentence *I am calling you*, *calling* is a present participle (of the verb *to call*). If you talk about *a calling card*, *calling* is an adjective describing a kind of card. In *an honest calling*, *calling* is a thing, a noun if you like, or more accurately, considering its verb connection, a "verbal noun" or a "gerund". As a writer, knowing whether you are dealing with a verbal noun or a participle is important and may keep you out of trouble.

Participles (verbs) take the personal pronoun while gerunds (verbal nouns) take the possessive pronoun. To get them wrong is to convey very different messages to the reader.

The difference can be seen in these examples:

It was a thrill to watch <u>him dancing</u> *means* it was thrilling because he is normally too shy to dance, or because he had been on crutches for the last six months.

> It was a thrill to watch <u>his dancing</u> *means* it was thrilling because his style and performance were so good.

In the first case, *dancing* is a participle and in the second *dancing* is a verbal noun. As you can see, they produce quite different meanings.

For the same reason, these two similar-looking sentences are not at all the same in meaning:

> I object to <u>him</u> (*personal pronoun*) <u>calling</u> (participle) me a liar *suggests* that the speaker may not mind if others call him a liar.
> I object to <u>his</u> (*possessive pronoun*) <u>calling</u> (verbal noun) me a liar *suggests* that the speaker objects to being called a liar by anyone.

The trouble with "its"

It's a very serious problem

There are some other things about personal and possessive pronouns we need to clear up, as revealed in the table below.

Person	Singular	Possessive	Plural	Possessive
First (person speaking)	I, me	me, mine	we, us	our, ours
Second (person spoken to)	you	your	you	your, yours
Third (person spoken about)	he, she, it	his, her, hers, its	they, them	their, theirs

This table shows that **none** of the possessive pronouns that end in "s", including *its*, takes an apostrophe.

The incorrect use of the apostrophe in the case of *its* or *it's* is probably the most common mistake made in the English language. Why this should be so is baffling.

Its (indicating ownership) is a possessive pronoun and possessive pronouns do not use apostrophes. (Well, there's an exception: the third-person impersonal pronoun *one* takes an apostrophe and an *s* to become possessive (*one's*) but it's still a handy rule to remember.)

On the other hand, *it's* (a contraction of the two words *it is*) does use an apostrophe, **not to indicate possession**, but to indicate that the two words (*it is*) have been contracted into one, and a letter from the original has been left out of the new word.

So *its* means something belongs to *it*, and *it's* is a shortened form of *it is*. What could be simpler? No doubt the poor old apostrophe will go on being abused on a daily basis. But it is hard to understand why.

A case for knowing about "case"

Take a close look at the pronouns below.

Person	Singular	Plural
First	**I**, me	**we**, us
Second	**you**	**you**
Third	**he**, **she**, him, her, **it**	**they**, them

You will notice something that is most important in grammar. The pronouns that have been set in bold type can only be used as the **subject** of an action, while those set in normal type can only be used as the **object** of an action.

We may say: *I saw him*, or, *He hit me*, or, *She told us*.

But we do not say: *Me saw he*, or, *Her hit they*, or, *Them gave we*.

In other words, some personal pronouns can be the subject of a sentence and some the object or indirect object of a sentence (in a situation grammarians describe as being "governed by" a verb or preposition). For example:

He <u>gave me</u> the book. or He gave the book <u>to me</u>.

So, in sentences or phrases, some pronouns can be subjects but not objects and some can be objects but not subjects. Some, *you* and *it*, can be either.

This rule is described as a form of "case".

There are various kinds of "case" and the precise number (and names they are given) varies depending on which authority you consult or which school of grammar you belong to. Nevertheless three are particularly relevant to us and the names I use for them are: "nominative" (which some call "subjective"), "objective", and "possessive".

That is not an exhaustive list, but I intend to deal only with those matters related to case that need to be raised. Similarly, there are a host of pronouns apart from the "personal" and "possessive" we have dealt with (relative, indefinite, intensive, demonstrative, interrogative, reflexive, distributive and reciprocal, for example) which I have not covered. For a complete course in English grammar you'll have to buy another book.

Nouns and pronouns that are the **subject** of a verb are in **nominative** case, those that are the **object** of a verb or preposition are in **objective** case, and those defining **ownership** are in **possessive** case.

In certain constructions *who*, *whom* and *whose* are described as relative pronouns or interrogative pronouns. *Who* is nominative (can be used as the subject of a verb), *whom* is objective (used in conjunction with, or governed by, a verb or preposition) and *whose* is possessive.

Now for the problems . . . and the conflict between strict grammar and colloquial usage.

The question is, which of the following is correct?

> **(a)** Who should I give this book to?
> *or*
> **(b)** To whom should I give this book?

If we were to analyse these sentences we would say: the subject is *I*, the verb, which is compound, is *should give*, the object is *this book*. This is true of both sentences. In the first sentence the indirect object is *to who*. In the second sentence, the indirect object is *to whom*. The grammatically correct answer to the question is therefore clear. Sentence (b) is correct. *To who* is not a grammatically correct construction. *Who* is nominative case and cannot be used as the object of a preposition. Thus the objective case pronoun *whom* has to be used instead.

Another way to consider the question is to rearrange the sentence.

> **(a)** I should give this book <u>to who</u>?
> *or*
> **(b)** I should give this book <u>to whom</u>?

I hope you can see that the first rearrangement is wrong.

Of course, the problem is that usage is changing, so that (a) is common usage, while (b) is still considered correct usage. Which to use has become a question of house style, one for the newsroom to answer. But usage sometimes overwhelms the dictates of grammar.

Let's take another example.

> **(a)** <u>This</u> (*subject*) <u>is</u> (*verb*) a <u>person</u> (*object*) <u>whom</u> (*indirect object*) we should all admire.
> *or*
> **(b)** <u>This</u> (*subject*) <u>is</u> (*verb*) a <u>person</u> (*object*) <u>who</u> (*indirect object*) we should all admire.

We know that *who* is nominative, not objective, and therefore it cannot be the object or indirect object of a sentence. The correct answer therefore is (a).

Of course we might have solved the problem by avoiding the issue, writing:

> This is a person we should all admire.

And, still on the subject of pronouns and case, while we might say *Tom and I gave Jack a present*, would we say *Jack gave Tom and I a present*? No, because *I* is nominative, and in this sentence *I* is part of the object, *Tom and I*, which is nonsense. We need the objective case pronoun not the nominative, and the objective is *me*. Thus, *Jack gave Tom and me a present* is correct.

A quick way to reach the right answer is to treat the proper noun (*Tom*) and the pronoun (*I*) separately. *Jack gave Tom a present* and *Jack gave me a present*, which means *Jack gave Tom and me a present* is the correct answer.

Adjectives

Adjectives are words that describe, define or qualify nouns and sometimes pronouns. For example: *the silly season, a daily paper, poor me, the cat, that animal*.

There are many kinds of adjectives, including:

- proper adjectives derived from a proper noun and requiring a capital letter, *the New South Wales government*
- qualitative or descriptive adjectives revealing an attribute or quality, *a fetching smile*
- quantitative adjectives indicating quantity or how much, *in my father's house there are many mansions*
- adjectives of number revealing specific numerical detail, *Snow White and the seven dwarfs*
- demonstrative adjectives revealing particularity, *put those toys away*.

In other circumstances, many adjectives, including some of those above, would not be adjectives at all, but other parts of speech. *New South Wales*, for instance, would be a proper noun, *fetching* a present participle (as in *bringing*), and so on. In the case of *It is **his** book*, *his* is a possessive adjective. But if we said *It is **his***, *his* is a possessive pronoun.

Our use of adjectives is very interesting. Through a process of socialisation or shared language learning, we use adjectives describing a particular thing in an accepted or fixed order. For example, we say, *You great big beautiful doll*. We don't say, *You beautiful big great doll*. And we never say, *You young cheeky pup*, or, *You old silly fool*. Professor Charles Darling has categorised this conventional use of adjectives into "The Royal Order of Adjectives". A most interesting order it is too.

There are some issues concerning adjectives that we must consider. The correct spelling, including hyphenation, of compound adjectives is one of them.

Compound adjectives

Compound adjectives are those that come in two or more parts – *a **five-star** hotel*, *a **double-barrelled** shotgun*, *a **still-born** baby*, *a **green-eyed** monster*. The hyphen is important. *A green eyed monster*, or *a still born baby*, or *a tall story teller*, or *a long felt want* present pictures in the mind of the reader that are somewhat different from their hyphenated versions.

But the hyphen is not always used when spelling compound adjectives. The problem arises most often when the compound adjective involves an adverb (see later section) ending in *-ly* and a past participle. In this case there is no hyphen. The unwary often hyphenate constructions such as:

His easily recognised features would need to be disguised.

But in cases where an adverb ending in *-ly* is used to form a compound adjective, there is no likelihood of any confusion being created in the mind of the reader. While there is a great deal of difference between *a tall story teller* and *a tall-story teller*, there can be no confusion if we say *easily recognised* or *easily-recognised*. In such a case there is no need for the hyphen, so we do not use it.

Compound adjectives sometimes involve *-ly* adverbs and words other than the past participle. They still don't need a hyphen. *A closely knit group* is an example, although the expression probably derives from the participle *knitted*. And remember, not all past participles end in *-ed*, so don't necessarily use that as a signal to drop the hyphen from compound adjectives. Take *a finely woven cloth*, for example. *Woven* as in *I have woven*, is a participle. A *seriously hurt victim* of a car accident is another example of a compound adjective formed by an *-ly* adverb and a word that is not obviously a participle, but is.

Adverbs that do not end in *-ly* may take the hyphen to form a compound adjective. The reason is obvious. *A fast-moving script* suggests a roller coaster plot, while a *fast moving script* might have pace, but it is emotionally charged (i.e. emotionally *moving*) at the same time.

Comparative adjectives

Adjectives of degree are described as positive (*the **big** pineapple*), comparative (*a **bigger** pineapple*) and superlative (*the **biggest** pineapple*). The comparative is often formed, as in the case above, by adding *-er* to the positive, and the superlative is often formed by adding *-est*. As in most things there are exceptions, of course – *good, better, best* and *bad, worse, worst* for instance.

In words of more than two syllables, the comparative adjective is usually formed by the addition of the word *more* to the positive, and the superlative is formed by the addition of *most*. For example: *competent, more competent, most competent* (not competenter, or competentest). There are many others that have to be treated similarly, such as *peculiar, cheerful, critical*, etc. But there are exceptions. *Heavy, easy, silly, funny* take *-er* and *-est* to form the comparative and superlative, as in *heavier, heaviest, easier, easiest, sillier, silliest* and *funnier, funniest*.

Some adjectives are intrinsically superlative and cannot be further expanded. They are referred to as "absolute" adjectives because they cannot be modified or qualified in any way. So be careful about trying to do so. Some people make the attempt, but the results are unsatisfactory.

Unique is an absolute adjective. It means something is one of a kind. So *rather unique, really unique, somewhat unique* and even *very unique* are nonsense constructions. The footballer who said the State of Origin series in which the rival teams had won one match each could not be *more perfectly balanced*, was clearly correct. If something is *perfect* it is hard to see how it could possibly be *more perfect*. But then footballers and grammar may not necessarily be well acquainted.

Adverbs

As adjectives describe or qualify nouns, adverbs describe or modify verbs and adjectives or other adverbs.

> The cat sat quietly on the mat.

The adverb *quietly* tells how the cat was sitting, so *quietly* is an adverb modifying the verb *sat*.

> The cat sat very quietly on the mat.

In this case *very* describes how *quietly* the cat was sitting. *Very* is an adverb modifying another adverb: *quietly*.

> The extremely lazy cat sat on the mat.

Extremely describes how lazy the cat was. It is an adverb modifying the adjective *lazy*.

Significantly in journalism, adverbs tell us how, when and where – two of the five "w"s and the "h". And just as we saw in the case of adjectives, there are various kinds of adverbs. Adverbs of time (*now, soon, then, daily*, etc.), adverbs of place (*there, here*), adverbs of manner (*boldly, quietly, dangerously, stupidly*, etc.).

Many of the adverbs of manner are the *-ly* adverbs – except, of course, that not all words ending in *-ly* are adverbs. *Silly* is an adjective and *folly* is a noun. Nevertheless many adverbs are formed by adding *-ly* to an adjective, as in *careful, carefully, dangerous, dangerously*. If the adjective already ends in *y*, we change that to an *i* and add *ly* as in *angry, angrily*. If it ends in a double *l* we just add *y* (*full, fully*), and with most of those that end with *ic* we add *ally* (*historic, historically, enthusiastic, enthusiastically*), although there are exceptions (*public, publicly*).

We have adverbs of degree (how much), *almost, very, quite, rather, partly*, etc.; adverbs of number (how often), *once, twice, thrice*; interrogative adverbs (that introduce questions of time, place, manner, reason), *how, where, when, why*; conjunctive adverbs (that modify and join), *so, for, because*, etc., and the list goes on.

Comparative adverbs

As with adjectives, forming comparatives by the addition of *-er* and *-est* is satisfactory when the adverb has only one syllable. But many adverbs have at least two (since an *-ly* syllable is often added to an adjective to form an adverb in the first place). *He spoke **passionately**, she spoke **more passionately**, the visitor spoke **most passionately**. But this is not always the case. For example, we would say, She spoke **slowly**, and, He spoke **more slowly**, but would we say, The visitor spoke **most slowly**?* Hardly. We would say, *The visitor spoke **even more slowly**.*

Prepositions

Prepositions are linking words, and thus perform a most important role in our language. To say *I am lost* means one thing, but to say, using a preposition as a linking word, *I am lost for words*, is quite another. *I am dying* reveals a most serious situation for the speaker. But, via the use of a linking preposition, *I am dying for a drink* becomes a little less concerning.

Prepositions abound in the language. Here are a few:

> about, above, across, against, along, around, at, before, behind, below, beneath, beyond, by, down, during, except, for, from, in, into, near, of, off, on, over, round, since, through, to, towards, under, until, up, upon, with, within, without . . .

While they may look innocuous enough, the right ones have to be used in the right places. If not, the writer's mistaken word becomes a subject for scoffing and sneering.

The most common mistake seen in the case of prepositions is probably *different to*. The correct construction is *different from*. But there are many pitfalls in the landscape inhabited by prepositions. *I was pleased when the captain compared my performance* **with** *Sir Donald Bradman's*, but ... *flattered when he compared me* **to** *Sir Donald*. We *compare with* (examine differences and similarities) but *compare to* (consider as in a category).

Prepositions ending sentences

There has long been a taboo on ending sentences with prepositions. The reason is that, because prepositions are linking words, their use presupposes an object following the preposition (a word, phrase or clause). However, this abuse of grammar is something up with which you should not put.

Perhaps this is a matter you were aware of.

And paid particular attention to.

Not ending a sentence with a preposition is certainly highly desirable – providing this does not produce writing that is stilted and obscure. Common usage is the best guide because we are in the business of communicating. To write in a way that the reader finds difficult or pretentious, that pays no attention to the way people speak, makes no sense.

And many verb constructions we use involve the use of the preposition in a compound form. For example, *back off, back up, pull up, pull over, go away, clear off, dig in*, etc., and many of these phrasal verbs are used at the end of sentences.

> Get your hands <u>up</u>.   It is time to move <u>on</u>.   There was nothing more to say so I hung <u>up</u>.   Please go <u>on</u>.   The tyre burst so I pulled <u>over</u>.

In such cases the preposition may be referred to as a "particle" and the construction as a "phrasal verb" (not to be confused with a "verbal phrase" (such as in the sentence *I* **have been going** *to the movies regularly*, in which three verb forms, *have*, *been* and *going*, are combined)).

To conclude that in a case such as *I told him to* **hang up** we are using a preposition at the end of a sentence, is incorrect. We are using a phrasal verb, a compound verb if you like. The verb is formed by two words, one of which in another context might be a preposition. Consequently, to use such an example to say it is acceptable to end a sentence with a preposition is to misunderstand what a preposition is. For example, to say that "A preposition is not a word to end a sentence with" is good advice but bad grammar. "With" in this case is not part of a phrasal verb, so that excuse will not do. As a result, "A preposition is not a word **with which** to end a sentence" is the grammatically correct construction. It might be better to say, however, "Prepositions should not be used at the end of sentences".

But if there is no alternative, or if the alternative sounds forced or pretentious, use a preposition at the end of a sentence, and be prepared to defend your decision.

Conjunctions

Conjunctions are linking words too. Indeed, they are joining words. They join words, phrases and clauses.

> **You** <u>and</u> **I** are one.

The conjunction *and* is joining two words: *you* and *I*.

> **At the going down of the sun** <u>and</u> **in the morning** we shall remember them.

The conjunction *and* is joining two phrases.

> **There was movement at the station** <u>for</u> **the word had passed around** <u>that</u> **the colt from old Regret had got away . . .**

The conjunction *for*, meaning *because* is joining two clauses: *there was movement at the station* and *the word had passed around*. The conjunction *that* is joining two clauses: *for the word had passed around* and *the colt from old Regret had got away*.

There are few grammatical issues concerning conjunctions that the journalist need consider. The ones that have to be dealt with will be covered under the sections on clauses and the section on punctuation.

The most important issue is, do you need to use them at all? Might not two sentences be better? They often are.

Exclamations

Exclamations are words that constitute utterances or clauses within themselves, not necessarily with grammatical connection. Exclamations, then, may have no grammatical connection to other words or constructions within a sentence. They may be sentences on their own.

> Stop!
> No.
> <u>Alas</u>, poor Yorick. I knew him, Horatio.

Exclamations may require exclamation marks to be placed after them, but otherwise they present no traps for the reporter.

The mood you are in

In this and in earlier chapters we have dealt with tense, voice, and case but there is another matter connected with verbs that has to be covered. This is the grammatical issue of "mood". Being able to recognise the mood involved in a construction may be valuable for the writer.

If we take the verb *to be* for example, and consider its tense and person forms, we may say, in the present tense singular *I am sick*, the past singular *I was sick*, the present plural *they are sick* and the past plural *they were sick*.

But we would surely never say *I were sick*. The trouble is we do. We have just encountered what grammarians refer to as "mood".

There are various ways to describe how verbs convey the sense of a sentence, or "mood" and these have different names (depending on your grammarian – they also disagree on how many "moods" there are).

The "indicative" mood refers to the manner in which verbs are used to convey facts and information. The "imperative" mood refers to the manner in which verbs are used to convey commands. The "subjunctive" mood refers to the manner in which verbs are used to convey the hypothetical. Use of the indicative and imperative are generally unproblematic; it is the subjunctive that can cause problems.

To take a simple case, we might say, in "indicative" mood, *I am a rich man* or *I was a rich man*. But if we were to raise the hypothetical and use the "subjunctive mood", would we say *If I was a rich man*?, or would we say *If I were a rich man?* Usage is changing, so it's possible that you might say either.

But if we put the hypothetical another way and said, *Were I a rich man, I would* . . . it becomes clearer. We would never say *Was I a rich man, I would* . . .

Thus in the subjunctive, *I were* and *Were I* are correct.

The subjunctive mood is worth remembering. Mistakes are made when it is not used correctly.

So much for the words that comprise the parts of speech. Now to the constructions we use when we put groups of words together.

Phrases

A phrase is "a sequence of two or more words arranged in a grammatical construction and acting as a unit in the sentence". But there is an additional important point that distinguishes the phrase from other grammatical constructions: the phrase does not contain a verb.

> On top of Old Smokey, all covered with snow . . .
> The boy stood on the burning deck . . .
> There was movement at the station . . .
> At the going down of the sun and in the morning, we shall remember them.

In each of the cases above, the phrases are introduced by prepositions, and introducing phrases is one of the major functions of the preposition.

But phrases are not always introduced by prepositions.

> Hearing a suspicious noise downstairs, I sent the dog to investigate.
> All the king's horses and all the king's men . . .

Hearing is not a preposition, although in such a case a preposition is inferred, as in *Upon hearing a suspicious noise . . . All* is a pronoun. The *of* as in *all of* has been dropped.

Kinds of phrases

> You will find a pot of gold at the end of the rainbow.

Of gold is adjectival, describing the noun *pot*; *at the end* is adverbial, modifying the verb *find* (describing where you will find); and *of the rainbow* is adjectival, describing the noun *end*.

Fortunately, phrases present few problems providing the writer takes a little care. The main thing to look out for is that careless placement of a phrase might give rise to a meaning other than the one you intended.

*The watchmaker fixed the clock **with only one hand*** produces an interesting ambiguity that might amuse some readers.

Beware starting a lead to an inverted pyramid story with a phrase, although there is no blanket ban on it. Phrases can delay getting to the point of the news:

> In full riot gear, police sealed off the centre of the city.
> -
> Police *in full riot gear* sealed off the centre of the city.

Get straight to the point in an inverted pyramid story.

Phrases that start leads can also be downright confusing:

> With just moments to spare before it collapsed, firefighters rescued a man from a blazing furniture factory this morning.

The grammar is bad and the sense obscure. It should read:

> Firefighters rescued a man from a blazing furniture factory this morning just moments before the building collapsed.

And now an acceptable use of a phrase to introduce a lead. In this case the phrase provides essential background, as in:

> Despite widespread protests, the government's new citizenship laws have been passed by parliament.

Reversing the order of the elements in the lead would not only fail to accurately represent the chronology and context in which the events occurred but also tends to link the protests to the parliament rather than to the passage of the legislation.

> The government's new citizenship laws have been passed by parliament, despite widespread protests.

But the essential issue with phrases is, they do not contain a verb.

Clauses

A clause is a sequence of words arranged in a grammatical construction and containing a finite verb (and therefore a subject and predicate). A clause may form a simple sentence on its own or be part of a compound or complex sentence structure.

> Nancy kicked the ball over the road.

Clauses in a sentence may be capable of standing alone. In the case above, the clause *Nancy kicked the ball* could be a sentence on its own. *Over the road*, a phrase, could not stand alone and make any sense.

Sentences may consist of more than one clause. In such a case, there will be a main clause (capable of standing alone), and other clauses (subordinate clauses) that describe or define or explain nouns or the verb in the main or other clauses.

> Nancy, <u>who was only six</u>, kicked the ball over the road <u>that ran by the river.</u>

The two underlined clauses above are adjectival. The first qualifies (describes) Nancy, and the second describes the road. Because they cannot stand alone, both depending on the main clause, *Nancy kicked the ball*, to make sense, they are called subordinate clauses. *Nancy kicked the ball* is referred to as the principal clause because it can stand alone. The principal clause will be the focus of a sentence.

> <u>When it came her way</u>, Nancy kicked the ball over the road.

In this sentence, the subordinate clause is described as adverbial since it describes, or explains, or modifies the verb *kicked*. It tells **when** the ball was kicked.

Subordinate clauses are described by the function they perform in relation to the principal clause — whether they act as an extended adjective or as an extended adverb.

If you are writing an inverted pyramid story, avoid starting your lead with a clause.

> <u>Whenever he felt like it</u>, shop assistant Fred Bloggs took money from his employer's till, the District Court was told yesterday.
>
> --
>
> Shop assistant Fred Bloggs took money from his employer's till <u>whenever he felt like it</u>, the District Court was told yesterday.

The trouble with "that" and "which"

Consider the following sentences:

> The cat that Isobel loved ran away.
> The cat, which Isobel loved, ran away

We are looking at two very different situations. In the first, of all the cats Isobel had, the one she loved ran away. In the second, Isobel's much loved cat ran away. In the first sentence, the subordinate clause *that she loved* **defines** one particular cat out of a number of cats. In the second case, the subordinate clause *which she loved* **describes** a particular cat.

The conjunction *that* introduces a defining clause and does not take a comma before or after, while the conjunction *which* introduces a describing clause and requires two commas, one at the start of the clause and one after.

Sometimes the conjunction *that* introducing a defining clause can be dropped. *The cat that he loved ran away* can be written perfectly clearly as *The cat he loved ran away*.

But the defining clause conjunction cannot always be dropped.

> The plane that did not return from the mission was a Spitfire.

All the other aircraft involved made it back. The one that didn't was a Spitfire.

And, as discussed above, that construction is quite different from saying:

> The plane, which did not return from the mission, was a Spitfire.

In this case a single, or particular, plane took off but did not return. It was a Spitfire.

Because they can change the meaning so much, you will need to pay particular attention to defining and non-defining clauses in your writing.

Sentences and paragraphs

The issue that arises with sentences and paragraphs in journalism is likely to be important for the newcomer. In journalism, stories are frequently – indeed mostly – written using single-sentence paragraphs. In earlier days, when newspapers were produced in "hot metal" each sentence of a story was typed on a single small sheet of paper, and thus the term "par" meant a single sentence, not a collection of sentences. That meaning of the word persists. A "par" may be a sentence, not necessarily several sentences strung together in a block to embrace a particular thought or matter.

Have a look at your nearest newspaper. How many paragraphs with more than one sentence can you find? In the first five pages of the one I received today there were only four paragraphs of more than one sentence. All the rest, scores of them, were single-sentence pars. The four with more than one sentence were two-sentence pars. The second was quite short. There were no three-sentence pars.

Spelling and punctuation

Like grammar, correct spelling and punctuation are necessary if you want to communicate with your reader. Some argue that these things are becoming more fluid and that journalists can move with the times; others argue that all writers, journalists included, should be "guardians" of standards. I argue that journalists should take the trouble to write clear, engaging text, to ensure that readers will read their work . . . and understand it.

Spelling

Now we have reached a minefield. Transgressions abound in the media. In some cases there are handy rules to help the poor speller. But in almost all cases there are exceptions to the rules. Then there are those words that sound the same but are spelled very differently and mean very different things. Use one in the wrong context and your readers will be scratching their heads over your meaning, laughing, or sneering. Do you want any of these reactions?

The right word in the right place

What follows is simply a list of examples to prove the point that you have to know how to spell, or if you are not a good speller, that you have to know your weakness. In such a case you will need to have a good dictionary close by if you want to keep your reputation as a credible writer intact. The list is not exhaustive. It is illustrative only. There are many more examples that might be included, but I hope that the point can be succinctly made – not maid.

> aural (*of the ear*)   oral (*of the mouth; spoken*)
> The explosion left her with a serious **aural** impairment.
> While her written tests were not very good, her **oral** work was excellent.

"Oral examinations" are interesting. They are sometimes conducted in schools and universities instead of written examinations. Candidates answer questions verbally. Dentists also conduct "oral examinations" in which the person being examined is encouraged not to speak at all – since doing so would severely hamper the dentist's capacity to have a close look at the patient's teeth and gums. And, of course, an "aural" test would not be conducted by a dentist, but rather by an audiologist.

> baited (*set as a lure*)   bated (*withheld; restrained*)
> The hook was **baited**; Dad cast the line and we waited with **bated** breath.
> -
> breach (*hole*)   breech (*loading point of a gun*)
> Once more unto the **breach** dear friends or fill up the hole with our English dead . . .
> Its **breech** was jammed and our only gun was useless.
> -
> born (*created*)   borne (*carried*)
> He may not have been **born** a hero, but a hero he was and he was **borne** aloft by the crowd.
> -
> **cannon** (*weapon; billiards shot; ricochet*)   **canon** (*religious title; fundamental principle; musical composition*)
> The service was conducted by a visiting cleric – a **canon** of the Church. For the devout, it was the most sacred **canon** in their faith.
> Pachelbel's **Canon** in D is one of the most haunting compositions in the classical music repertoire.

Imagine if you got it wrong!

It seems hard to imagine a *centurion* (a class of Roman soldier) being confused with a *centenarian* (someone 100 years old), but a newspaper did run a story about a local lady turning 100 and described her as a *centurion*. The woman's reaction is unknown.

Here are some more examples of pairs of words that sound or look similar but have important differences in spelling and meaning.

accept (*receive*) except (*leave out*); advice (*the noun*) advise (*the verb*); aid (*help*) aide (*helper*); altar (*shrine*) alter (*change*); annex (*the verb, to take*) annexe (*the noun, an addition*); ascent (*act of climbing*) assent (*give approval*); bail out (*to pay for one's release*) bale out (*to jump; to remove water*) bail up (*to hold up for robbery*); balmy (*beautiful*) barmy (*crazy*); caddie (*golf term*) caddy (*box or tin, especially for keeping tea*); check (*ensure*) cheque (*for payment of money*); complement (*that which completes or perfects*) compliment (*praise*); chord (*combination of notes*) cord (*rope*); council (*group with authority*) counsel (*offer advice; lawyer*); curb (*limit*) kerb (*roadway edge*); current (*flowing water/electricity; topical*) currant (*type of dried grape*); dependant (*the noun, someone who relies on another for support*) dependent (*adjective, dependent upon*); desert (*barren landscape; abandon – for added confusion, this second usage is pronounced the same as the next spelling*) dessert (*sweet; pudding*); draft (*conscript; preliminary writing or drawing, subject to revision; a bill of exchange; to sketch*) draught (*breeze; a drink; to pull; boat's displacement; beer on tap*); discrete (*distinct*) discreet (*careful*); dying (*approaching death*) dyeing (*changing colour*); ensure (*make certain*) insure (*protect against*); faze (*unsettle*) phase (*time period; electrical current*); formally (*officially*) formerly (*pertaining to the past*); grill (*to sear*) grille (*grating*); grisly (*macabre*) grizzly (*gnarled; bad tempered; a kind of bear*); hanger (*for clothes*) hangar (*for aeroplanes*); horde (*multitude*) hoard (*secret collection; to accumulate*); lead (*metal, present tense verb*) led (*past tense verb*); licence (*the noun*) license (*the verb*); loath (*reluctant*) loathe (*despise*); metal (*basic element*) mettle (*spirit*); metre (*unit of measurement; rhythmic pattern of poetry or music*) meter (*instrument that measures*); net (*knotted material*) nett (*less deductions*); plum (*fruit*) plumb (*to measure depth or the vertical*); practice (*the noun*) practise (*the verb*); principal (*most important; chief*) principle (*an accepted standard*); racket (*noise; an organised illegal activity*) racquet (*sporting implement*); raze (*destroy*) raise (*lift*); reek (*smell*) wreak (*to inflict*); review (*reconsider, critique*) revue (*theatrical performance*); sewage (*waste material*) sewerage (*infrastructure for moving sewage*); sight (*scene; capacity to see*) site (*location*); stationary (*not moving*) stationery (*office supplies*); storey (*the distinct levels or floors of a building*) story (*tale*); swat (*hit*) swot (*study*); tea (*drink*) tee (*golf term*); toe (*of the foot*) tow (*to pull*); tire (*become weary*) tyre (*rubber casing for wheel*); visit (*calling upon or being called upon*) visitation (*a paranormal experience*); way (*route*) weigh (*in motion; to measure*); whisky (*no "e" used for Scotch or brands made in Scotland*) whiskey (*with an "e" used for Irish, American and other varieties*); won't (*will not*) wont (*accustomed to*) want (*desire or require*) . . .

This is not a comprehensive list by any means. It covers some of the well-known problem cases. I could have gone on and on.

Troublesome word pairs

There are some words that cause real problems for many writers. One is *its* or *it's*, which has already been mentioned. Another is *affect* or *effect*.

Some books on writing and grammar will tell you there is a very simple solution to using them correctly. They tell you that *affect* is a verb and *effect* is a noun and if you use them accordingly, that's it. But there is more to it than that. *Effect* can be a verb too. And *affect* has two quite different and distinct meanings. For instance:

> The rain will <u>affect</u> the sugar crop.
> She <u>affects</u> an air of confidence in her work.

Affect can mean "to influence" or "to create an illusion".
  Now *effect*:

> The rain will have an <u>effect</u> on the sugar crop. (*noun*)
> He used his fists to great <u>effect</u>. (*noun*)
> He used his position to <u>effect</u> some major changes in people's thinking. (*verb*)

Getting the right word in the right place is important.

> <u>She thought being married might affect her employment</u> *means* she thought she might be fired.
> <u>She thought being married might effect her employment</u> *means* she thought being married might get her a job.

Another example of the wrong word used in the wrong place is *lay*.

> Police called on the man <u>to lay</u> on the ground.
> The injured woman was found <u>laying</u> on a blanket.

In the context in which someone is reclining, the infinitive form of the verb is *to lie*, not *to lay*, and therefore the present participle is *lying* not *laying*.

> Police called on the man <u>to lie</u> on the ground.
> The injured woman was found <u>lying</u> on a blanket.

One may *lay* a table or an egg (in colloquial usage, even another person) but to *lay down* would require an extraordinary biological transformation.

The dangers of spell checkers

Do not rely on spelling or grammar checkers. Even the most common and popular ones cannot detect silly errors, so there is no point in having any faith in them.

Most grammar checkers are best avoided entirely, as they are likely to introduce errors into your work.

Spell checkers will help with some things, but they won't save you from writing nonsense such as the following:

> I sore it was along cue, sew I went on a head.

The serious point about the sentence above is this: the spell checker in the program being used to write this book saw nothing wrong with any of the spellings in that sentence, even though I was attempting to write:

> I saw it was a long queue, so I went on ahead.

And even when I did something quite silly, the spell/grammar checker failed to notice.

> I sore it was quiet along cue, sew I went on a head.

The so-called "rules" of spelling

There are a number of "rules" that are supposed to help the struggling speller, but they are not worth considering. Most have exceptions, and if they do not work all the time, they are useless. Here is an example. You may have heard the one about "*i* before *e*, except after *c*", and it works well in many cases, *relief* and *receive*, for instance. But what about *eight, weight, height, sleigh, sleight, neighbour, leisure, vein* and *skein* to mention a few. So the rule was refined to accommodate only those words where the *ie* or *ei* combination was sounded as *ee*. However, that doesn't work either – *seize, weir, weird*, for example.

There are other so-called rules, but most have exceptions and some are so complicated they are impossible to remember. So we will move on.

Punctuation

As with grammar, sighs of exasperation and groans often meet the very mention of the word "punctuation". Not more pedantry, surely! But punctuation is not pedantry. Punctuation is vital for the writer. Punctuation provides important cues for the reader; cues that are signposts and signals so the reader can see exactly what it is you are saying, how you are saying it, and how you want it to be understood.

Punctuation marks enable you to flag to the reader precisely how your copy should be read. Punctuation marks refine and enhance communication. Without them we would all be lost. At a most basic level, the comma – for instance – is a mark on the page that separates bits of information from other bits so the reader does not have to struggle to make sense of a jumble of words. In addition, the comma allows the reader a chance to pause momentarily to take in what has been said. It also allows the writer to indicate that some description or expansion of what has just been said is coming. And so on. These are important cues. There is a further point. Without punctuation, writing would not just be unintelligible, it would also be lifeless. Punctuation allows the writer to add emphasis, nuance, and pace to his or her work. These are important qualities. Punctuation is important.

Full stops

The full stop indicates the end of a sentence; the end of a complete expression of thought or information. The capital letter immediately after the full stop clearly marks the start of a new sentence. Full stops do not present any problems for the writer. They might look insignificant, but they are wonderful little dots on a page and there is one piece of good advice for the journalist that might be offered at this stage. Here it is. Make friends with the full stop.

Commas

Commas are quite another matter. Ignored or incorrectly used they can be a serious problem. Their absence, in particular, can produce very misleading material and introduce some serious misunderstandings or ambiguities.

For example, the following two sentences have quite different meanings – just because of a single comma.

> We heard the boys and their horses were on their way back to the house *means* we were told that all the boys and their horses were on their way home.
> We heard the boys, and their horses were on their way back to the house *means* we could hear the boys somewhere and we saw their horses approaching.

There are some in the business of journalism who try to use as few commas as they can. "Get rid of the comma," they cry. But they do so at their peril, for the comma helps make sense of what is written on a page. To leave the commas out fails to recognise that writers are in the business of communicating with people. Why should readers struggle or be left confused when they read the newspaper? It doesn't make sense.

Commas do a variety of things. They indicate a short pause and are used: to define separate parts of a sentence, *"The time has come," the walrus said, "to speak of many things"*; or to make a sentence understandable to the eye. Instead of trying to read, *When it rains it rains pennies from heaven* or *Roses are red violets are blue*, we read, *When it rains, it rains pennies from heaven*, and, *Roses are red, violets are blue*. Much easier, thanks to the comma.

Commas are also used to separate a succession of adjectives and adverbs within a sentence where *and* could sensibly separate them. *It was a long, boring, uneventful flight*, or, *She was desperately, wretchedly, inconsolably sad*. Where *and* does not fit sensibly between the adjectives or adverbs, commas are not used. *She was a little old Greek lady*.

Commas are used before and after a "describing" clause. The describing clause, which we covered earlier, can be introduced by *which, who, when* or *where*, and is separated by commas.

> The teacher, who was new in town, was very lonely.
> In spring, when the snow has thawed, the valleys burst into life.

Commas are also used following an adverbial clause beginning a sentence, such as, *When the flood receded, the snakes came out*. Clauses indicating time (as distinct from those indicating cause or condition) introduced by *while* take a comma after them: *While the guns were firing, we kept our heads well down*. But not in the case of clauses indicating cause or condition, *Since the guns were firing we kept our heads well down*.

Commas are also used either before, before and after, or after a conjunction that establishes an elaboration, qualification, or contradiction.

> However, there was no going back.
> There was, however, no going back.
> It was a tough decision, but it had to be made.

Claims that you should not start a sentence with *and* or *but* are nonsense. And sometimes it can be the best choice.

Some writers have problems with *however*. They use it in the middle of a sentence with a single comma or without any commas. Sadly, having marked a million essays and stories, I know just how common this mistake is. *He said it was time everyone came to the aid of the party, however in the end very few came*. This is not a legitimate construction in English grammar. You need two sentences and one comma, or two commas, as in:

> He said it was time everyone came to the aid of the party. However, in the end, very few came.
> He said it was time everyone came to the aid of the party. In the end, however, very few came.

There are some myths about commas that crop up from time to time. One says you do not use a comma before *and*. Sometimes that is true. When commas are used to separate items in a list, no comma is needed before the *and* preceding the final item. *We needed tea, sugar, flour and salt.* But commas **are** used to define independent or separate parts of a sentence connected by a conjunction such as *and*.

> We could see both the boys and the girls were safe *means* we could see that not only the boys but also the girls were safe.
> We could see both the boys, and the girls were safe *means* we could see the two boys, and we also knew the girls were safe, although we couldn't see them.

The reader cannot be left wondering. Leaving out a comma to save some space can be quite silly.

Commas are also used to separate what might be called parenthetic expressions. Given that you would never use a single bracket to enclose such an explanatory phrase, you do not use a single comma to do the same job.

> Toby's father, the local policeman, was very angry.
> -
> Toby's father (the local policeman) was very angry.

Finally, commas are used if they are needed to make it clear to the reader what you are saying. Clauses that have different subjects are a case in point. Without a comma after "tree", in the sentence, *The car crashed into a tree and a man who had been standing on the footpath called the police,* the reader could be quite confused. Three commas might be necessary. *The car crashed into a tree, and a man, who had been standing on the footpath, called the police.*

Colons

The colon is used to introduce a list or a set of options separated by semicolons, to introduce a passage of direct speech and to introduce words that amplify, summarise or contrast with the preceding text.

The colon is rarely seen in newswriting, but should not be overlooked.

> The menu included: roast lamb, turkey, beef and duck; mushroom, Caesar, Greek and garden salads; and a selection of wines.

Punctuated in this way, the composition of the menu is quite clear. On the other hand, the form usually adopted by newsrooms, to ignore the colon and separate items in a list with the usual comma, can produce confusion. Unless there is some tinkering with the list, our example reveals the problem.

> The menu included roast lamb, turkey, beef and duck, mushroom, Caesar, Greek and garden salads, and a selection of wines.

Using commas alone is not enough. For a moment it appears that guests may have a choice of roast mushroom or roast Caesar. Without the colon and semicolon, an extra word is needed.

> The menu included roast lamb, turkey, beef and duck plus mushroom, Caesar, Greek and garden salads and a selection of wines.

Variations of this kind of treatment are normal in newswriting.

The other use of the colon does appear in newswriting from time to time. It can add emphasis to quoted speech.

> Summing up, the judge said: "This was a most terrible crime."
> The instructions were clear: "Place your hand on the top of the cap and pull the ring down."

Those new to newswriting, despite contrary advice, tend to use this form of expression, colon followed by quote, constantly. Those who are not new seldom use it.

Some newcomers even produce *The instructions were clear, "Place your hand on the top of the cap and pull the ring down."* In such a case, the comma is not a substitute for the colon.

Semicolons

Semicolons are used to mark a pause or provide emphasis stronger than that of the comma but less than that of the full stop. They are used in this way between clauses that could stand alone grammatically as complete sentences, but which are drawn together by their meaning.

> It is unfortunate that the semicolon is so seldom used; it can be a great help.

As discussed above, semicolons are also used to separate the contents of a list introduced by a colon.

> The following are essential: excellent grammar, spelling and punctuation; good communication skills; punctuality; and an ability to get along with people.

Dashes

The dash marks a pause for an explanation, summary or afterthought. *All good men should come to the aid of the party – and bad ones should too, for that matter.*

Be sure you know which dash, the en dash (width of an "n"), or the em dash (width of an "m"), your newsroom uses. It's a matter of house style. Here they are:

> It was the winter of their discontent – and they were feeling its bitter chill.
> (*the en dash*)
> It was the winter of their discontent — and they were feeling its bitter chill.
> (*the em dash*)

Two dashes are used to embrace an aside.

> He said – and I had to agree – that we were in serious trouble.

Whichever dash you are using it should have a space before and after.

Hyphens

The hyphen indicates a connection between words or a separation within a word. Hyphens are used in many ways. Firstly, to separate a prefix from its root when its use places two vowels together that need to be sounded, as in *pre-eminent* or *pre-existing*. Without the hyphen, the words would appear as *preeminent* or *preexisting*. Usage, however, now allows for *cooperate* and *coordinate* without the hyphen.

A hyphen is also used where its absence would create confusion among readers by distorting the meaning intended – *pro-testing*, which means "in favour of testing", is not the same as *protesting*, "objecting to something".

The hyphen is also used to link two or more words to form a compound word – often an adjective. *The junior teams played their first round games last weekend,* would have been better written as: *The junior teams played their first-round games last weekend.* What *round games* might be is a mystery. But everyone knows what *first-round games* are. Indeed, the hyphenated and non-hyphenated can mean entirely different things, as in:

> The <u>three-quarters</u> (*position*) played only <u>three quarters</u> (*of the match*).

Ages too are hyphenated – a *33-year-old woman,* or a *three-year-old.* Where two or more hyphenated (compound) words are used sequentially, all hyphens are retained, even if a portion of one or more of the compound words is omitted or deleted. For example, *The first-, second- and third-grade teams will all be playing on Saturday,* not, *The first, second and third-grade teams will all be playing on Saturday,* which is nonsense.

Remember, as mentioned in the section on adjectives, compound adjectives comprising an adverb ending in *-ly* and a past participle do not take a hyphen.

> His <u>easily recognised</u> features would need to be disguised.

But when the compound adjective is formed by an adverb that does not end in *-ly* and a present or past participle, the compound adjective is hyphenated:

> Her <u>well-established</u> reputation for generosity prevailed.
> The <u>fast-flowing</u> current swept him away

But wait, there is more. If such a compound is even more carefully expressed, or modified, by the addition of another adverb, the hyphen is dropped from the original: *The very fast flowing current swept him away.* And when comparatives or superlatives are used with participles to form compound adjectives, hyphens are not used, as in, *Scientists claimed it was a <u>faster growing</u> variety* (no hyphen) and *The <u>more accessible</u> items sold quickly.* The exception is when the lack of a hyphen creates confusion or changes the meaning:

> The Blues need <u>more experienced</u> players *means* they have some experienced players, but not enough
> The Blues need <u>more-experienced</u> players *means* the whole team lacks experience.

There is even more: *Her well-established reputation for generosity prevailed,* but, *Her reputation for generosity was well established.* The adjective is hyphenated, the complement is not.

Parentheses (round brackets) and square brackets

Round brackets enclose explanatory or supplementary information written by you, or, in the case of a quote, provided by the original author:

> This was a time (winter) when evenings arrived early.
> His mother (Lady Mavis Chilcott) would not have approved.

Square brackets enclose material added by a subsequent writer or editor to make the authorship of the material clear, or to indicate that the material added was not the work of the original writer, as in:

> In his letter Mr Jenkins said he "had poured [sic] for weeks over the report".

The square brackets make it clear it was Mr Jenkins who was the poor speller (the word should be "pored") and not the author of the article.

In the case of,

> His mother [Lady Mavis Chilcott] would not have approved.

the square brackets make it clear the additional explanatory material, *Lady Mavis Chilcott*, was inserted by someone other than the original writer.

Apostrophes

We are now heading into territory that can be controversial. The solution is to check your house style. For the moment, however, we will cover safe ground.

The apostrophe indicates possession or ownership, or that something has been omitted. In the first case, the apostrophe indicates the possessive case (possession or ownership) of singular and plural nouns. When a word ends in a letter other than *s* (regardless of whether it is singular or plural), add *'s*.

> The dog's bone; the people's choice; the women's movement.

When a word ends in the letters *s*, *es* or *ies*, add the apostrophe *after the last letter (s)*:

> Three dogs' bones; several tomatoes' stems; ten babies' rattles; Jesus' disciples; for goodness' sake.

But a word of caution: as we shall see, the above is not always the case.

When a word ends in *s* and its possessive ends with a double s sound, add *'s*: *St Thomas's church* and *Mavis's hat*. The one that causes most trouble is *the Jones*. Some people go to visit *the Jones*. Others visit *the Joneses*. The first group will arrive at *the Jones's house*. The second group will arrive at *the Joneses's house*. The only solution is: follow whatever your house style says. House styles vary on this point.

Only the last name in a joint relationship takes the apostrophe:

> We're going in mum and dad's car; Peter, Paul and Mary's songs; David and Clare's suitcases (where David and Clare jointly own some luggage).

But, where ownership is separate, each takes the *'s*. *David's and Clare's suitcases* means that David and Clare each have their own luggage.

It was mentioned above that we need to be careful about adding *'s* to words ending in *s*. The issue is, are we talking about a word that is a possessive (indicating ownership), or simply a descriptive term – an adjective, quite often a compound construction involving a couple of words? For example, *a glasses case*, or *an abused victims refuge* or *a visitors guide*. Here, although the words in question end in *s*, they are not possessives, but descriptors. *The case* is not owned by, or a possession of, *the glasses*, any more than *the refuge* is owned by the *victims*, or *the guide* owned by the *visitors*. What we are describing here is a case for glasses, a refuge for victims and a guide for visitors. That is the test.

> Jack's house *means* the house of Jack, *or* the house belonging to Jack.
> An old veterans home *means* a home for old veterans, *not* a home owned by old veterans.

So, if *for* can be substituted for *of* or *belonging to*, do not use the apostrophe.

There are exceptions, however, and you should consult your house style guide. *Children's book week* is always trotted out as an example.

Check your house style to detect if there is a difference between a possessive and an interval of time. Some may say we get *a moment's notice* to do *a day's work*, but in *a years time* we might get *three years jail* with hard labour if we should misbehave and if that should happen we will miss out on *four weeks leave* each year. Others will insist on the apostrophe.

None of the personal pronouns (apart from "one") takes an apostrophe to form its possessive – not even, as explained in detail in the chapter on grammar, *it*. *Ours, yours, his, hers, theirs* and *its* do not take the apostrophe.

The apostrophe also indicates omission or deletion of one or more letters from a word. *Fo'c's'le* is an extreme example. It is a nautical term sailors use instead of *forecastle*. Apostrophes can indicate a contraction, which simply means the deletion of a letter, or letters, from a word, or words (and in such a case the shortened word being joined to another), as in *can't* and *aren't* for *cannot* and *are not*. Many contracted words are used so commonly, the apostrophe has been abandoned altogether– *flu*, *phone* and *bus* are good examples instead of *'flu* (influenza), *'phone* (telephone) and *'bus* (omnibus).

Place names in Australia drop the apostrophe – **Murphys Creek**, **St Margarets school**, **Ayers Rock**. This has been the standard since 1966. Your automatic spell checker will probably tell you that you have spelled such words incorrectly, which is another reason why you should not rely on spell checkers. Other countries are more variable in their use of the apostrophe in place names, so it is wise to check.

Apostrophes are not used with words that are plurals, *1950s* and *MPs*, except to prevent confusions, such as when *dotting **i**'s and crossing **t**'s* or *minding one's **p**'s and **q**'s*. To write these without the apostrophe would be silly – *dotting **is** and crossing **ts*** or *minding one's **ps** and **qs*** makes no sense.

Question marks

Direct questions require the question mark, indirect do not. **What time is it?** or, in reported speech, **"What time is it?" he asked**, take the question mark, but, indirect speech, **He asked what time it was**, does not. Requests for information or commands do not take the question mark – **Would you get back to me on that**.

Quotation marks

Now you will be able to tell the difference between a public servant and a journalist. Journalists use double quote marks (or inverted commas) for reported, direct speech, and single quote marks for a quote within a quote. The public service does the reverse. Journalists, however, use single quote marks in headlines – it saves space. However, in the body of the story a journalist would write:

> "I heard the man call out 'Stop, or I will jump'," the detective told the court.

The quote marks always embrace the complete quotation, including the relevant punctuation marks.

> "The time has come," the walrus said.
> "Has the time come?" the walrus asked.
> The walrus said: "The time has come."

A partial quote within a quote, however, falls within the relevant punctuation marks.

> "I heard the walrus say 'The time has come'," the oyster said.

Ellipses

The ellipsis (. . .) indicates that something has been omitted from a sentence or a statement.

> There is a list of things that must be done . . . and they must all be done.

The number of points or stops is not a matter of choice. Three only make up the ellipsis, with a space before and after (unless house rules say otherwise) and **no** punctuation marks before or after, not even at the end of a sentence. The ellipsis is often used these days instead of the dash.

Exclamation marks

The exclamation mark (**!**) adds emphasis to your writing and indicates a command, shock, indignation or disbelief.

> Stop!
> You must be joking!
> "I will not!"

Subbing

The jobs and responsibilities of the subeditor are many.

In a newspaper, for example, they include: making stories fit the allocated space; pulling together several related stories into one; ensuring the structure of the stories is right; checking and correcting the spelling, punctuation and grammar; ensuring the facts are right; writing headlines and subheads; writing captions (if they have not been written by others); and checking that material is not likely to be defamatory. Someone has to do a design for the page as well (within the constraints of the space available, since the advertisements will already have been marked out).

Subs and line-up subs in radio and television have similar tasks but obviously there are differences because the delivery media involved are different. But their responsibilities are no less. Subs do a very important job and it follows they are very important people if they do their job well.

Their importance is no better illustrated than in the memo below – which "fell off the back of a truck" at work one day. The points made by the editor who wrote this memo indicate just how important subs are.

ALL EDITORIAL STAFF
Sloppy captions are again proving expensive. But also, and more importantly, affect the credibility of our paper. Poor spelling of a name disappoints a reader. The wrong name can be vastly more expensive . . .

Remember some lobby groups lie even more than politicians. Attribute their claims. If you don't and your by-line is on the story, it's your credibility that is shot. And that you may have to defend at law the proposition you have embraced. Even if you have been so gulled that you believe it, that is not of itself an adequate defence.

When putting "today", "tomorrow", etc into a story, write the date in brackets with it. And subs need to check they know what week it is. Again, too many mistakes of this kind have been happening lately.

Read the paper. Much time is being wasted by people who do not. And listen to the briefing. Subs, know what is going on . . .

There was more, but that will do. This is a serious business, carelessness can be costly, not just in terms of the balance sheet but also in terms of credibility.

In some newspapers today, complete, detailed layouts and designs are done for each page and stories are allocated to fill predetermined spaces. Reporters are told how many column centimetres their story has been allocated and they have to meet that demand. Photographers know whether the picture required will be landscape (wider than higher) or portrait (higher then wider) and shoot accordingly.

But this is not the traditional method by which pages are made. Stories are placed to a design that takes the content of the story into account. This means stories are not often written to a predetermined length; they are cut to fit a space. This is one of the tasks of the subs.

Making a story fit the space

Traditionally, reporters file their stories without knowing (at least in any detail) how or where their story will be placed on a page. Or even which page.

This means that reporters usually have no idea how much space they will get for their story. If they get any. So the subeditor will have to trim the story to make it fit, if it is longer than required. The reverse, needing more copy and having to ask the reporter to provide more, is also possible but much less common.

Hence the importance of the inverted pyramid. Stories can be cut from the bottom to fit the allocated space without the need for a complete overhaul.

But simply cutting from the bottom may not be appropriate. The subeditor in the newsroom will be aware of things that are happening that the reporter out on a job may not know. Something way down in a story may take on a particular significance because of events occurring elsewhere. The subeditor will have to rearrange the story. Rewrite it even.

The possibility that a story may be cut from the bottom means it is important that reporters do not put something vital at the end of their stories. If it is vital it should be higher up because it may disappear if space is a problem.

Subs also have to be aware that there are often important links between successive pars in a story. If the last explains the content of the second last, dropping the last to make a story fit will only confuse the reader because now the last par will not make sense on its own. Both may have to go. If so, what effect might dropping two pars have on how well the story fits the allocated space? The story may then be too short. In which case something else will have to be done to solve the length problem. Sorting these issues out is the province of the sub.

Pulling several stories together

A number of reporters could be filing on a major story. And the wire services could be covering it too. There could be a great deal of copy coming in. Each story will not necessarily get its own space. One overall story may be written from all the available sources. Subeditors do this work.

Ensuring the structure of a story is right

Reporters sometimes bury the lead to a story somewhere in the body of their copy instead of placing it where it should be – at the top. Subeditors are there to dig out such leads and rejig the story the way it ought to be.

This can happen, not necessarily because the reporter missed the point of the story, but because the sub in the newsroom knows what else is going on. The sub knows that something has occurred which demands a change to the reporter's original copy. If the story were not changed it might look quite foolish, because the reader will be aware (from other stories in the media) of what the reporter did not know when he or she filed the report.

Or, a story may need a prominent introduction to provide background for the reader. Parts of a story may have to be extracted and written into a "fact file" or a "breakout" to go with the main story. If these tasks are not handled by the reporter, a sub will have to do them.

One more reason for having subeditors.

Rewriting a story

In the main, the need to rewrite stories arises because the original author missed the point – missed what was new, or the local angle, or what was most unusual, or interesting, or controversial. Sometimes stories are just too confusing for a reader to grasp. Complexities have not been addressed in a way that makes them understandable. One of the sub's jobs then is to rewrite the story, to get the point of the story up where it should be and to sort out the logic of the pars that follow and to present a story that a reader can follow.

Sometimes journalists simply get something in their stories wrong. More than the occasional sub will tell you some reporters, even with high-profile reputations, have a great many subeditors to thank for getting their stories straight. By the same token, reporters will tell how the subs butchered their copy.

Reporters and subs can quite easily differ over what the point of a story might be and whether the story as originally submitted was satisfactory. Who wins such arguments can be a matter of personality, or authority in the newsroom, as much as any exercise of news judgment. Some reporters' copy is never touched, regardless of the problems it may contain. The subs chat about such stories and their authors quietly among themselves.

On a big news day, competition for space will be great. Stories may have to be rewritten if simply cutting them is not a solution.

Spelling, punctuation and grammar

Nothing undermines the credibility of a newspaper more than spelling, punctuation and grammar mistakes. If a paper can't get the basics of its mother tongue right, how can readers possibly believe such a paper can get its stories right?

If reporters are not good at these things, the subs are there to save the paper's reputation.

And then there are circumstances where reporters are out on a job, with only a notebook and a mobile phone. They cannot be expected to deliver everything perfectly. Covering a fast-moving story or conference of several hundred delegates may produce a nightmare for the reporter in the field.

There may be house style matters to attend to in the copy as well.

Someone will have to sort it all out if it needs sorting out.

Ensuring the facts are right

As they do with spelling, punctuation and grammar, subs make sure – as best they can – that the facts are right. The subeditor is a quality assurance mechanism. Getting the facts wrong, like getting names, spelling, grammar and punctuation wrong, undermines the credibility of a news organisation.

Subs with long experience, sitting at their screens year after year, know a great deal about what has gone on in the world, and their general knowledge is often vast. Subs are there to spot mistakes before they get on to the streets.

Getting the facts wrong may not just be an embarrassment. It may be costly. A story which incorrectly names a person could produce an action for defamation. Such cases have occurred and such cases can be expensive, as the memo at the beginning of this chapter suggests.

A sub may save a newspaper more than his or her annual salary in one night.

Writing headlines

There are different kinds of headlines. Some tell you clearly and concisely what the story is about, while others intrigue you instead.

Both are there to do the same job – to get you to read the story. Subs write headlines. Their task is to write the best headline for the story to a point size, number of lines (decks) and column width determined by the design that has been produced for the page (probably by someone else some time before). Making a headline sum up a story and "grab" the reader while making it fit the point size, number of decks and column width involved, and not taking all day or all night to do it, is quite a challenge.

Apart from what we might call the "matter of fact" vs "enigmatic" divide mentioned above, there are two broad types of headlines – those that have verbs and those that don't.

> Another victim <u>tells</u> of rape (*with a verb*)
> Indigenous Australia at 'crisis point' (*no verb*)

Please note: single quote marks only in headlines – it saves space.

Given that verbs are such powerful words, it might seem that a headline without a verb would be a poor substitute for one with a verb, and therefore that verbless headlines should be avoided. But this is not the case at all. Headlines without verbs can have force and impact; great force and impact in fact.

What is important about headlines that have verbs, is the tense of the verb. It is worth noting that while much of the copy in a newspaper story may be in the past tense, and the lead in the present perfect, the headline will be, or in most cases, should be, in the present tense.

Another reason for present tense verbs in headlines has to do with something we discussed earlier – voice.

Without wanting to be too flippant, there is a simple illustration. If our story said *The cat sat on the mat*, our headline would read, *Cat sits on mat*. It would **not** normally say, *Mat <u>sat</u> on by cat*. In other words, the active voice rather than the passive, and the present tense verb rather than the past.

There are exceptions, of course. There always are. As with a news lead, there is a case for putting the most significant first, even if that involves the use of a past tense verb. So, it can be argued that for a metropolitan newspaper *Govt condemned over road funding* (past tense verb) could be preferable to *Councillor condemns govt over road funding* (present tense). It is the object of the criticism that is important for the big paper rather than the identity (not necessarily well known, or known at all) of the individual responsible for the criticism. A suburban paper, on the other hand, would reverse the position. In such a paper the councillor involved would not be unknown. Placing emphasis on the local identity would be sensible. A headline *Councillor condemns govt over road funding* would reflect that reality.

Nevertheless, if there is a choice between past and present, taking into account the content of the story concerned, present tense verbs in headlines are preferred because they have more impact.

It has been said that a good headline is one that fits (the column width, number of decks and point size involved), but a better headline is one that works and fits. And that is a good message. Headlines that don't make immediate sense are a menace. The goal is a headline that captures attention and accurately presents the story. Catchy or humorous headlines are welcome, but they have to work too. If no one gets the joke, or if the pun is bad, the result defeats the purpose of the headline.

Helping hands

Some headlines have to work alone. Others have help. A headline for a story accompanied by a picture may well be very different from the headline for the same story if there were no picture. The picture sends all kinds of information and messages to the reader; the headline is not operating in isolation. It adds to what the reader can clearly see in the photograph or illustration. A headline without that support will have to tell its story alone. In other words, a headline for a story with an accompanying picture may work very well. But remove the picture and the same headline may be totally obscure or nonsensical.

Or in reverse, a good headline for a story without a picture may be a very dull headline if there were a photograph beside it telling the reader graphically and pictorially exactly what the words in the headline were saying. The headline, *Cat saved by fire crew*, would be fine on a story about a cat being rescued from a sticky situation if there were no pic. But the same headline beside a clear photograph of a fire fighter extracting a bedraggled cat from some predicament would be dull at best, if not silly, because it would be so obvious. An otherwise obscure headline such as *One down, eight to go*, could work with a picture of whatever the "one" was, but, by the same token, without the picture, it might not be a good choice.

Writing captions

Someone has to ensure the reader can understand what the photographs in the paper show, and someone has to explain succinctly how they relate to the stories that accompany them. Someone has to get the names of any people involved right, and in the correct order too. Reporters and photographers know what the story says and what the pictures reveal, and they write the captions. If not, it is a job for the subs. They will have to get the information.

Captions are important. One way to tell this is to send a story you are thinking of running to your lawyers for an opinion. Is there a defamation lurking somewhere in the story? Your lawyers' response will obviously deal with the content of the material you submitted but then they will ask, "What is the headline?" and then, "What does the caption say?" They may even ask what the photograph shows.

Subs, defamation and contempt

I personally do not know anyone who ever published a defamation or a contempt deliberately, without a defence or a case to support the publication of such material. Most defamations arise because no one saw them coming. If they had, they would have done something about it. Subs are the last line of defence against such problems for the journalist and publisher. Their eyes need to be everywhere.

Stories, headlines and captions are places where defamations or contempts obviously lurk. Not even the action football pic can be assumed to be free of risk. As mentioned in the chapter on Australian law there have been cases where football shorts knocked awry in a thrilling tackle have led to payouts to the player wearing the shorts concerned. One of the pics was not just used in the sports section of the paper. It was such a good shot it was used in the plug box on the front page as well! No one saw the problem. If they had, the picture would have been abandoned. A photograph of a child victim of crime or abuse, even with the face obscured, could be a problem if clothes, jewellery, school uniform – or anything, for that matter – could identify the person. To publish such a photograph could be expensive. But newsrooms can be pressure cookers when deadlines have to be met. Mistakes happen.

The news business is a pressure business. But no one else cares. Excuses are not accepted. The last pair of eyes to see a story before it goes out belongs to a sub. They are very important eyes.

Out, damned sub!

It is common in the news business for there to be tension between some reporters and some subs. The reporters claim the subs interfere and gut their stories. The subs say the reporters don't know how to write and if it wasn't for their excellent rewriting skills the reporters' bylines would never appear anywhere.

No doubt there are cases where both are right. What has to be realised in the context of a newsroom is the fact that subs get paid for doing a job. And it is simply human nature that a person should do something if he or she gets paid to do it. This quite natural response can cause subs to show they are earning their salary. Except that in the case of the sub, the old adage "if it ain't broke, don't fix it" is critical. The urge to demonstrate that a sub is neither a loafer, nor incompetent, has to be contained. Stories that do not need "fixing" should not be "fixed".

This urge to tinker with perfectly good copy does not arise in professional newsrooms. I have witnessed it in student newsrooms year after year. The sub's view invariably is: "I am here to do something, I had best get stuck into it." The result can be devastating. Reporters who had filed perfectly good stories in the first place do not recognise their work and are offended that their byline should be on the subbed version. And they are right.

The story that needs subbing should be subbed. The one that doesn't should be left alone.

House style

There is likely to be an extensive set of in-house rules designed to ensure consistency within a newsroom and within the publications it produces. While journalists are expected to write to house style, subs are expected to pick up any errors in house style and fix them before the paper goes to press.

To illustrate the point, the following are random extracts from two major news organisations' house style guides. Example one (*APN Style guide*):

> **Counsel** is singular and plural (not counsels), and it is customary to use it without an article; *Mr John Smith, counsel* (not the counsel) *for the Browns*. But *Queen's Counsel* takes an article: *Mr Smith has been made a Queen's Counsel.*
>
> Lowercase **full** when applied to any court (other than the State Full Court): *the full* High Court, Federal Court, Supreme Court.
>
> Lowercase *bench* and *full bench*.
>
> **COURT HONORIFICS**: Like witnesses, lawyers and other people in court, accused people and victims, dead or alive, are to be given honorifics. (Mr John Smith at first reference, Mr Smith at second reference.)
>
> **Never be subjective**. EVERYTHING in a court story must be attributed to someone.

House style guides may differ. Some of the illustrations above demonstrate that. But whatever the newsroom guide says is what counts, regardless of what others might say.

Try it . . . be a sub

Subediting your own work is one of the best ways to improve your writing, and to develop an understanding of what subs do and why. The following two exercises give you a chance to apply your skills as a sub, and find out what you know, and what you don't.

Unless specifically referenced, examples in this section have been prepared for illustrative purposes only and do not represent actual events or refer to actual people.

Complete the exercises before searching for the answers. That way you will learn something about your knowledge of grammar, spelling and punctuation, and you may also learn how good you are with detail.

Apply the house style rules on the previous page headed "Our newspaper house style".

"Answers", and notes explaining the changes follow the exercises.

Exercise one: Subbing pars

What, if any, changes would you make to the following? Remember, try it first without looking anything up.

a. Compared to last year the final results were much improved.
b. The company supports Mr. Stephens position on the board and recognises that him being a director of the firm provides it with much needed experience.
c. It is quite clear however that depending on your point of view the first quarters results were either very poor or quite disasterous.
d. Practicing every day and most afternoon's mean that Julies times for the 8 hundred meters are improving.
e. He said he was loathe to recomend any alternate action but some time one had to chose between ones rights and ones priveleges and this is one such occassion.
f. When your driving using your left and right hand indicators early and breaking well before intersections gives following and on coming drivers ample time to observe your intensions.

Example two (News Limited *Style*):

> Beware of contractions such as *Aussat*, which denotes an Australian satellite. Don
> write AUSSAT, as though each letter stands for a word. The same applies to *Austud*
>   Do not use full stops after contractions such *Mr, Mrs, Dr, Ald, Cr, Pty, Ltd, Cor*
> *Maj-Gen*). But always spell out *Professor* and *Point* or *Port*.
>   Avoid *e.g., i.e., n.b.*, and other abbreviations of Latin words or phrases. Spell out
> *for example* or *that is* and find another way of expressing the others.

House style guides go into great detail. They will list acceptable abbreviatior
spellings, difficult words and place names, tautologies, clichés and wor
phrases to be avoided, and much more. Each house style guide is the bible
its newsroom.

The house style guide will make clear matters such as the following:

Our newspaper house style

Numbers: 0 to 9 should be spelled out; 10 and above are written in figures; numbers
below 10,000 have no comma (thus, 3000 head of cattle but 40,000 horsemen).

Sums of money should be given as figures, not written out in words ($27,190 NOT
twenty-seven thousand one hundred and ninety dollars).

Per cent NOT %

Z: If in Australia or the United Kingdom, do not use American spellings of words
in which the "s" appears as a "z"

Times: 10am NOT 10.00 am

Dates: Monday, September 11, 2001 NOT 11 September 2001 NOR September
11th, 2001

During the **1950s** NOT During the 1950's

World War II NOT Second World War

Names: Use first name and surname at the first reference, thereafter the honorific
or title and surname. Thus: David Jones becomes Mr Jones.

Use Mr, Ms, Dr, without a full stop. Professor and Associate Professor become
Prof after the first reference. Do not refer to an academic as "the professor", nor
write "the doctor" when referring to a person with a PhD rather than a medical
qualification. "Rev" requires a given name as in, "the Rev David Jones". Thereafter,
write "Mr Jones", NOT "Rev Jones".

And so on.

It is common for student reporters to consider such detail unimportant
and not pay much, or any, attention to the demands of house style guides.
This is a serious mistake.

g. Persistant poor litaracy results among primary schoolboys are worrying the states top education burocrats.

h. Competitively-priced cars are being sort by some of our long standing customers.

i. Under the scheme seperating couples will be able to divide up their assetts, including their superanuation, their property and any savings.

j. The Treasurer said the legislation will mean tax cuts for 25% of the population.

Exercise two: Subbing a story

And here is a story to sub. It came from a "press conference" exercise.

Make the minimum number of changes necessary, and do not cut the story at all. Remember to apply house style to the story.

Australia is facing a "literacy crisis" that is having a costly effect on business, a leading academic said yesterday and warned any solutions may not take effect for another thirty years.

At a press conference held at the Centre for Language Education and Research (CLEAR), Professor Norman Blunt said that the declining standards of grammar taught in schools over the last fifty years has resulted in today's poor literacy rate which could have serious consequences for the economy and society overall.

"In this information age, communication is absolutely essential" he said, "Whenever there are breakdowns in communication, the outcomes are costly . . . the opportunity for miscommunication is potentially catastrophic."

Professor Blunt said CLEAR will be researching ways to improve the education and return higher literacy levels to the classrooms.

However, the solution is no quick fix, "It's going to take thirty years to make amends for the last thirty years," he said.

Professor Blunt said the decline began soon after the Second World War when many educational institutions came to regard grammar as secondary to other disciplines. The situation snowballed with each successive generation teaching new students with a diminishing emphasis on correct English.

"Business wants this rectified," he said, and announced that the private sector has guaranteed to support CLEAR, a research body formed by the Institute for the 21st Century that has already received bipartisan support in the Federal Parliament.

But the professor does not hold much hope for today's generation. When asked how he saw their communication skills, Professor Blunt spelt it out clearly. "Lost," he said, "L-O-S-T."

"Answers" to exercise one

a. Compared to last year . . .

> Original: Compared to last year the final results were much improved.
>
> Correction: Compared <u>with</u> last <u>year's</u>, the final results were much improved.

In this example, the writer does not intend to compare one year with another; he wants to compare one set of results with another set of results. But he ends up comparing a year with a set of results, which is nonsense.

Furthermore you compare *with* when you assess one thing against another and compare *to* when you consider similarities and/or differences. *Compared with* his record six months ago, the horse's recent performance has been poor, but *compared to* his stablemate, he is doing very well. Mistakes are made when the two are confused; unfortunately such mistakes appear regularly in the news media.

b. The company supports . . .

> Original: The company supports Mr. Stephens position on the board and recognises that him being a director of the firm provides it with much needed experience.
>
> Correction: The company supports <u>Mr Stephens'</u> position on the board and recognises that <u>his</u> being a director of the firm provides it with <u>much-needed</u> experience.

The first change is to remove the full stop following the abbreviated honorific *Mr* – this is a matter of applying house style.

Next, an apostrophe was inserted after the final *s* in *Stephens* to indicate a possessive.

Being in this case is a thing, a noun – actually a verbal noun, or a gerund – and requires the possessive pronoun *his* not the personal pronoun *him*.

Finally, *much-needed* is a compound adjective formed by an adverb that does not end in *-ly* and a past participle. It therefore takes the hyphen (as distinct from *extremely valuable experience* which would not). This is perhaps the most critical of the changes, because of the clarification of meaning. *Much-needed experience* means "vitally important experience". *Much needed experience* means "lots of the experience that is needed".

c. It is quite clear . . .

> Original: It is quite clear however that depending on your point of view the first quarters results were either very poor or quite disasterous.
>
> Correction (option one): It is quite clear, <u>however</u>, that, depending on your point of view, the first <u>quarter's</u> results were either very poor or quite <u>disastrous</u>.

Correction (option two): It is quite <u>clear, depending</u> on your point of view, the first <u>quarter's</u> results were either very poor or quite <u>disastrous</u>.

The original suffers from a deficiency of commas. This can be fixed by simply inserting commas, but three commas close together, as in option one, produces a very stilted construction. Much better to make a slightly greater change to create the more readable option two.

The possessive apostrophe is missing again, and *disastrous* is simply spelled incorrectly.

d. Practicing every day . . .

Original: Practicing every day and most afternoon's mean that Julies times for the 8 hundred meters are improving.

Correction: <u>Practising</u> every day and most <u>afternoons means Julie's</u> times for the <u>800 metres</u> are improving.

The first change is to correct a misspelling. *Practice* is a noun, but the verb is *to practise* (with an *s* not a *c*). Thus the present participle (a verb form) is *practising*, and so is the verbal noun form.

Next there is a superfluous apostrophe: *afternoons* is simply the plural of *afternoon*, not a possessive, therefore no apostrophe before the *s*.

The subject of the sentence is *practising*, which is singular, and subject verb agreement demands the verb be singular too, hence *means* not *mean*.

Now there is an apostrophe missing: the times belong to Julie, and therefore Julie requires the possessive apostrophe.

Thanks to house style, we know that *800* should be presented in figures, not words.

In Australia, *metres* refers to units of measurement, while *meters* refers to the equipment that measures things (light meter, for example).

e. He said he . . .

Original: He said he was loathe to recomend any alternate action but some time one had to chose between ones rights and ones priveleges and this is one such occassion.

Correction: He said he was <u>loath</u> to <u>recommend</u> any <u>alternative</u> action, but <u>sometimes</u> one had to <u>choose</u> between <u>one's</u> rights and <u>one's privileges</u>, and this <u>was</u> one such <u>occasion</u>.

Loath means reluctant; *loathe* means to despise; *recommend* has two *m*'s; *alternate* as an adjective means "substitute", whereas in this example the writer is talking about another choice or option, hence the adjective *alternative*.

Sometimes is one word; the infinitive is *to choose* with two "o"s; *one* is the only pronoun that takes the possessive apostrophe – *one's*. Another spelling error: *privileges* has two *i's* followed by two *e's*.

After *said*, related verbs must be in past tense; and finally, *occasion* needs only one "s".

f. When your driving . . .

> Original: When your driving using your left and right hand indicators early and breaking well before intersections gives following and on coming drivers ample time to observe your intensions.
>
> Correction: When <u>you're</u> driving, using your <u>left-</u> and <u>right-hand</u> indicators early and <u>braking</u> well before intersections gives following and <u>on-coming</u> drivers ample time to observe your <u>intentions</u>.

First, *you're* is a contraction of *you are*, while *your* is a possessive pronoun.

Next, words requiring hyphens need them even if they form part of a list where the attached word is omitted (so *left-hand and right-hand indicators* becomes *left- and right-hand indicators*).

Then *braking* was spelled incorrectly; *on-coming* needed a hyphen; and *intentions* was incorrectly spelled.

g. Persistant poor litaracy . . .

> Original: Persistant poor litaracy results among primary schoolboys are worrying the states top education burocrats.
>
> Correction: <u>Consistently</u> poor <u>literacy</u> results among <u>primary-school boys</u> are worrying the <u>state's</u> top education <u>bureaucrats</u>.

Persistent is spelled incorrectly, but, regardless, it is not the right word. If it were to be used, it would need a comma after it, or *and*, because *persistent poor* is not a compound adjective (nor is *persistently poor*). So, we might say *Persistent and poor literacy results* . . . (but that doesn't make sense), or possibly, *Persistent, poor, literacy results* . . ., but neither would seem to reflect the meaning intended here; hence *consistently poor*.

Having dealt with that, the spelling of *literacy* needs correcting. *Primary-school boys* should be hyphenated to clarify that we are talking about "boys in primary school".

Apostrophes are still causing trouble: *state's* needs the possessive apostrophe. Finally, *bureaucrats* is incorrectly spelled. Perhaps it's because of those consistently poor literacy results . . .

h. Competitively-priced cars . . .

Original: Competitively-priced cars are being sort by some of our long standing customers.
Correction: <u>Competitively priced</u> cars are being <u>sought</u> by some of our <u>long-standing</u> customers.

By now the reason for these corrections should be clear.

Competitively priced does not take a hyphen, because it is a compound adjective beginning with an *–ly* adverb.

And the spelling of *sort* is incorrect. "Sort" means to categorise items, and "sought" is the past tense of the verb "to seek".

i. Under the scheme . . .

Original: Under the scheme seperating couples will be able to divide up their assetts, including their superanuation, their property and any savings.

Correction: Under the scheme, <u>separating</u> couples will be able to <u>divide</u> their <u>assets</u>, including their <u>superannuation, property and savings</u>.

There has to be a comma after *scheme* because it's an adverbial clause beginning a sentence.

Spelling errors need to be corrected; *separating, assets* and *superannuation* were incorrectly spelled.

Divide up is a tautology. Finally, three of the last six words can be dropped, saving 12 character spaces.

j. The Treasurer said . . .

Original: The Treasurer said the legislation will mean tax cuts for 25% of the population.

Correction: The Treasurer said the legislation <u>would</u> mean tax cuts for 25 <u>per cent</u> of the population.

Remember your tenses! *Will* is incorrect; the past tense verb *would* is required after *said*.

Furthermore, *per cent* is to be spelled out as two words – house style rejects the symbol %.

"Answers" to exercise two

If we were to make just the minimum number of changes necessary and not cut the story at all, the following changes would need to be made.

The words and sections underlined in the original are those that need to be changed. Those set bold in the subbed text were changed.

Taking the story apart paragraph by paragraph we can see that five changes should be made in the first par.

First par

Original: Australia is facing a "literacy crisis" that is having a costly effect on business, a leading academic said yesterday and warned any solutions may not take effect for another thirty years.

Subbed: Australia **was** facing a "literacy crisis" that **was** having a costly effect on business, a leading academic said yesterday. **He also warned that** solutions **might** not take effect for another **30** years.

1. The present tense verb *is* is wrong. The tense of the verb in a passage of indirect speech is determined by the tense of the attribution verb that governs it. In this case that verb is *said*, which is past tense, so the opening passage should read: *Australia was facing a "literacy crisis" that was having a costly effect on business, a leading academic said yesterday.*

There are only two ways the present tense verb *is* might be used, neither of which is satisfactory. The first would be to change the tense of the attribution verb to present tense, drop the time reference *yesterday*, and say *Australia is facing a "literacy crisis" that is having a costly effect on business, a leading academic says*. This might be acceptable in radio and television but it is not normal newspaper style.

The second approach would be to retain the present tense verb *is* by using the quote as direct rather than indirect speech: *"Australia is facing a literacy crisis that is having a costly effect on business," a leading academic said yesterday*. But starting a story with a direct speech quote, unless the quote is really quite startling, is not a sensible approach to writing news and seldom appears in any news media. Except in exceptional circumstances not even radio or television adopt such an approach to starting their stories.

2. The impact of the lead is heightened considerably if it is split into two separate sentences. It will be necessary not only to link the two statements but also to ensure the second supports the first. Thus we would do the following: drop the *and*, insert a full stop, and start the new sentence with *He also said*, etc.

3. The verb *said* is past tense, which means the present *may* has to be changed to *might*. *Any* is superfluous and should be dropped. We should also, on an occasion such as this, insert *that* after *warned*. Usually subs find themselves taking out superfluous *thats* from copy, but the issue is always determined by the importance of clear, precise communication. In this case, *warned that solutions . . .* helps that process.

4. We should also recognise that newspaper style does not spell out figures after nine. So our new second par becomes: *He also warned that solutions might not take effect for another 30 years*.

Second par

> Original: <u>At a press conference</u> held at the Centre for Language Education and Research (CLEAR), <u>Professor Norman Blunt</u> said <u>that the</u> declining standards of grammar taught in schools over the last <u>fifty</u> years <u>has</u> resulted in today's poor literacy <u>rate which</u> could have serious consequences for the economy and society overall.
>
> Subbed: At a press conference (*to launch something or whatever*) the (*needs a title or a connection*) of the Centre for Language Education and Research (CLEAR), Professor Norman Blunt, said declining standards of grammar taught in schools over the last **50** years **had** resulted in poor standards of literacy in the community.
>
> **This** (*or* This situation *or* This decline *or* The decline *or* This drop in standards) could have serious consequences for the economy and society overall, **Prof Blunt said**.

5. Again there are a number of problems. Unless there is a good reason to mention it, and this story does not contain one, the fact that the statement was made at a press conference is of no relevance to the story and reference to it then becomes wasted space that could be better used. Space is a problem in newspapers, just as time is a problem in radio and television. If something is not necessary, don't include it.

6. Presumably Professor Blunt has some connection with the CLEAR organisation, but that is not explained in the story. It should be. After all, the reader will want to know. Professor Blunt has made some quite serious statements, but the story does not tell us what authority he has to make such statements. It should. Since we don't know who he is, in subbing the story we will not attempt to concoct a position for him. In a newsroom situation, by now it could be eight o'clock at night or later, which is not a good time for checking such details. Because the organisation's name is so long, the attribution is best left in its current style, even though the order is not preferred house style.

7. In this case *that* is superfluous and should be dropped.

8. The underlined *the* in *the declining standards* is also superfluous and should be dropped. If it is not necessary, it goes. Dropping these two words, which we do not need anyway, has saved eight character spaces.

9. *Fifty* should be *50*.

10. *Has* is another present tense verb governed by the past tense attribution verb *said*, and must be changed accordingly to the past tense *had*.

11. *Rate* is the wrong word. It suggests or presupposes a comparison. The rate at which something is increasing or reducing compares performance.

That is not what is meant in the story. Professor Blunt is talking about a standard or a level, not a rate. Unless the word was clearly written down in the reporter's notebook as a verbatim quote, it would have to be changed.

12. *Which* introduces a subordinate adjectival clause. Again the impact of what the speaker is saying is heightened if the clause is used as a separate sentence or par, with attribution.

Third par

Original: "In this information age, communication is absolutely essential" he said, "Whenever there are breakdowns in communication, the outcomes are costly . . . the opportunity for miscommunication is potentially catastrophic."

Subbed: "In this information age, communication is absolutely essential," he **said**.

"Whenever there are breakdowns in communication, the outcomes are costly **. . .** the opportunity for miscommunication is potentially catastrophic."

13. There are two separate statements here, not a single statement broken in mid-sentence. They should be treated as two separate sentences. Also, where *he said* is inserted, a comma is needed.

14. If the ellipsis is used at all, there should be a space before and after it.

If there had been nothing omitted from that statement (and thus no requirement for the ellipsis) it is worth considering how such a statement might have been treated. Two options arise; the first as a single sentence and the second as two sentences.

Option one: *"Whenever there are breakdowns in communication, the outcomes are costly; the opportunity for miscommunication is potentially catastrophic."* Note the use of punctuation in this version – use a semicolon because the material after it elaborates on what precedes it. Option two: *"Whenever there are breakdowns in communication, the outcomes are costly.*

"The opportunity for miscommunication is potentially catastrophic." Note the use of quote marks in this version. Because we are using a running quote (there is nothing omitted) we do not use closing quotes at the end of the first part of the statement (in this case after *costly*).

Fourth par

Original: Professor Blunt said CLEAR will be researching ways to improve the education and return higher literacy levels to the classrooms.

Subbed: **Prof** Blunt said CLEAR **would** be researching ways to improve **education** and **"return** higher literacy levels to the **classrooms"**.

15. House style says the title *Professor* should be used in full on the first occasion the word is used in a story and thereafter the accepted short form of the title, *Prof,* should be used.

16. Once again the attribution verb is *said*, so the present tense verb *will* is incorrect. The past tense of *will* is *would*, so that substitution has to be made.

17. *The* is superfluous and should be dropped.

18. The remainder of the sentence, *and return higher literacy levels to the classrooms*, sounds odd, but, if that is an accurate summary of what the professor said, we will have to leave it. Because it sounds odd, and providing it is what the professor said, one solution would be to use a partial quote. But this is only a solution if the words in inverted commas were a verbatim quote. The sub would have to check.

Fifth par

> Original: However, the solution is no quick fix, "It's going to take thirty years to make amends for the last thirty years," he said.
>
> Subbed: **However, there was no "quick fix" solution, he said.**
> "It's going to take 30 years to make amends for the last 30 years."

19. To use a comma before a complete full quote – a complete sentence of reported speech – is to fail to appreciate the role of the comma. The comma is not a pause that separates sentences. It separates parts of a sentence. Thus we again have two choices – to use a stronger pause such as a colon before the quote, or a full stop. The colon option is not often seen. But simply inserting a full stop and making two sentences out of one produces a problem. The result, if we simply put a full stop after "quick fix" (*However, the solution is no quick fix.*) sounds as if the reporter is making the statement. That is not acceptable, so we have to attribute it to Professor Blunt. And once we do that, the present tense verb *is* will have to be changed.

Sixth par

Moving on, we find more changes are needed.

> Original: Professor Blunt said the decline began soon after the Second World War when many educational institutions came to regard grammar as secondary to other disciplines. The situation snowballed with each successive generation teaching new students with a diminishing emphasis on correct English.
>
> Subbed: **Prof** Blunt said the **problem** began soon after **World War II** when **those responsible for the English curriculum in schools began to place less emphasis on the formal teaching of grammar.**
>
> **He said the downgrading of grammar** snowballed through successive generations **of teachers and students.**

20. Use the short form *Prof* instead of *Professor* (house style).

21. Decline needs explanation. What decline? Readers should not be in any doubt as to what your copy means.

22. Use *World War II* instead of *Second World War* (house style).

23. What exactly does *educational institutions* mean? Does it mean schools? Or schools and universities? Or those responsible for them? Or what was taught in them?

24. Is grammar a *discipline*? It may require discipline, but it is not normally regarded as a discrete "discipline" in an academic sense.

25. Unless we were short of space we would use single-sentence pars.

26. *Each* is superfluous.

27. *Teaching new students with a diminishing emphasis* is clumsy.

28. *New* is superfluous.

Seventh par

Original: "Business wants this rectified," he said, and <u>announced</u> that the private sector <u>has</u> guaranteed to support CLEAR, a research body <u>formed</u> by the Institute for the 21st Century that <u>has</u> already received <u>bipartisan support</u> in the Federal Parliament.

Subbed: "Business wants this rectified," **Prof Blunt** said.

He **said** the private sector **had** guaranteed support for CLEAR, a research body **created** by the Institute for the 21st Century. Both the federal government and the Opposition supported its work, he said.

29. Verbs are in wrong tenses, and need fixing.

30. The construction is clumsy, but can easily be reworked.

31. Explanatory background should be placed higher in a story than the second-last par. In the world of the inverted pyramid it is dangerous to leave important background to the end of a story. If the story should be cut from the bottom, that important background will vanish. And one might wonder whether it is CLEAR, or its effort to raise literacy standards, that has received bipartisan support in the federal parliament.

32. *Formed* is weak and lacks precision; *created* is unambiguous.

33. Are you sure that all your readers will know what "bipartisan support" means?

34. The subbed version also recognises that, in the right context, two-sentence pars do appear in newspapers.

Eighth par (final)

Original: But <u>the professor does not hold</u> much hope for <u>today's</u> generation. When asked how he saw their communication skills, <u>Professor</u> Blunt <u>spelt</u> it out clearly. "Lost," he said, "L-O-S-T."

> Subbed: But **Prof Blunt said he did not hold** much hope for the **current** genera-
> tion. When asked how he saw their communication skills, **he spelled** it out clearly:
> "Lost," he said, "L-O-S-T."

35. *The professor* is objectionable. It is like calling someone with a PhD *the doctor*. Use the title (short form, following house style) and his surname. And how do we know he does not have much hope for the current generation? Because he said so. So say that.

36. The dictionary says *spelt* and *spelled* are both acceptable. Perhaps there is a house style preference, but in this case, the sub rewriting this story prefers *spelled*.

37. Yes, the sub involved in recasting this story was aware that *generation* is singular and *their* is plural. But, he said, some contradictions in grammar are acceptable because of common usage. And he is right.

Complete subedited version

So, at last, here is the subbed version of our story in the same paragraph order as the original. A sub might change the order, but that has not been done in this example.

> Australia was facing a "literacy crisis" that was having a costly effect on business, a leading academic said yesterday. He also warned that solutions might not take effect for another 30 years.
>
> At a press conference (*to launch something or whatever*) the (*needs a title or a connection*) of the Centre for Language Education and Research (CLEAR), Professor Norman Blunt, said declining standards of grammar taught in schools over the last 50 years had resulted in poor standards of literacy in the community.
>
> This could have serious consequences for the economy and society overall, Prof Blunt said.
>
> "In this information age, communication is absolutely essential," he said.
>
> "Whenever there are breakdowns in communication, the outcomes are costly . . . the opportunity for miscommunication is potentially catastrophic."
>
> Prof Blunt said CLEAR would be researching ways to improve education and "return higher literacy levels to the classrooms".
>
> However, there was no "quick fix" solution, he said.
>
> "It's going to take 30 years to make amends for the last 30 years."
>
> Prof Blunt said the problem began soon after World War II when those respon-sible for the English curriculum in schools began to place less emphasis on the formal teaching of grammar.
>
> He said the downgrading of grammar snowballed through successive generations of teachers and students.

> "Business wants this rectified," Prof Blunt said.
>
> He said the private sector had guaranteed support for CLEAR, a research body created by the Institute for the 21st Century. Both the federal government and the Opposition supported its work, he said.
>
> But Prof Blunt said he did not hold much hope for the current generation. When asked how he saw their communication skills, he spelled it out clearly: "Lost," he said, "L-O-S-T."

How did you fare with this exercise? If you identified every problem, that is excellent. If you were able to produce acceptable solutions to every one, then you are ready to be a journalist (or a sub). Anything less means you have some work to do.

Problems and solutions

Here are some more hints about troublesome things you must get right.

The only way to go

"Only" must be treated carefully. Its precise location in a sentence can change the meaning of that sentence completely. Or produce a grammatical error. By moving the word one place at a time we get, for example:

1. *Only John went to hear his daughter sing.* None of the others went. Depending on context, this could mean that none of the other fathers went, or no one else in the family went. In an extreme case, it could mean that John was the only audience member.
2. *John only went to hear his daughter sing.* John was not interested in hearing any of the other children sing.
3. *John went only to hear his daughter sing.* He was not interested in hearing any of the other children sing.
   This construction is preferred to 2, above.
4. *John went to only hear his daughter sing.* He was not interested in watching her performance.
   The split infinitive sounds unnatural.
5. *John went to hear only his daughter sing.* He was not interested in hearing any of the other children sing.
   The construction at 3, above, is preferred to this one.
6. *John went to hear his only daughter sing.* John has a single daughter, and he went to hear her sing.
7. *John went to hear his daughter only sing.* This is confusing. Did he go to hear just his daughter or was he not interested in seeing her performance, just hearing it?

8. *John went to hear his daughter sing only*. This is not an option, unless there happens to be a song called "Only". If so, its title should be enclosed in quote marks, and it should start with an initial capital.

In these eight examples, we can ignore 7 and 8 altogether. Of the others, 1 and 6 do not present any problems, although they illustrate the point that the placement of *only* in its correct position in a sentence is vital.

Numbers 2, 3 and 5 mean the same, but the third construction, *John went only to hear his daughter sing*, is preferred. The reason is that *only* should appear as near as possible to the word or words it limits, restricts or modifies. It was the chance to hear his daughter's singing that inspired John to go, not how he went that is important in this sentence. Hence:

> John went only to hear his daughter sing.

What is tougher than "as"?

A claim that *His new car was as fast, if not faster than, his old one* could not be accepted – not because there was anything wrong with the new car, but because the English is poor.

How do we know? If we rewrite the sentence, by just changing the order of the words, we get *His new car was as fast than his old one, if not faster*. This is not English.

But we could say, *His new car was as fast as his old car, if not faster*. And so we could say, as we should have done at the outset;

> His new car was as fast as, if not faster than, his old one.

"Like"

It is not just *than* and *as* that present problems. *Like* and *as*, incorrectly used, cause plenty of problems as well. Part of the trouble arises because strict grammar and common usage do not always match.

For example, *He always caused trouble, just like his father*, is a construction you may hear, but, grammatically, it is incorrect. As it is written, the sentence is missing a word, although it can be inferred, thus: *He always caused trouble, just like his father did*, which is grammatically incorrect. You might say instead:

> He was a troublemaker, just like his father.
> *or*
> He always caused trouble just as his father did.

A quick, but unsatisfactory, solution that is sometimes given, is: *like* with nouns, *as* with verbs. And to help you remember, *Like father **like** son*, not *Like father as son*, and *As ye sow, so shall ye reap*, not *Like ye sow, so shall ye reap*.

But quick solutions are not always the best. What are we to make of: *Nothing succeeds like success*, and *She eats like a horse*, or, *He fights like the Devil*, or, *He looks like his father*? Each of these involves the use of a verb and *like*, and all are in common usage.

A more useful rule is, don't use *like* as a conjunction to introduce a clause, but do use *like* as a prepositional adverb to introduce a phrase. You may need to re-read the chapter on grammar, but as a quick reminder, prepositions introduce phrases or link words, and adverbs tell us how, where, or when an action occurred or occurs. A clause is a group of words containing a verb.

Thus we may write, *She ran **like the wind***, but not, *She ran like all the demons in Hell were chasing her*. In the first case, in *like the wind*, *like* is a preposition telling how she ran. In other words, a prepositional adverb. In the second case, *like all the demons were chasing her* is a clause (it contains the verb *were chasing*) and therefore using *like* to introduce it is grammatically wrong.

In such cases we would use the constructions *as if* or *as though* – *She ran **as if** all the demons in Hell were chasing her*. And instead of, *He looked like he could do with a good meal*, we would say, *He looked **as if** he could do with a good meal*.

Grammatically, *like* may also need to be replaced in other circumstances. Don't write:

> The concert included works like Beethoven's Fifth.

when you mean:

> The concert included works **such as** Beethoven's Fifth.

"Over" is overused

A mistake that is constantly seen is the use of *over* when what the writer meant was *more than*, as in, *Over a thousand people turned out for the rally*. Copy containing such constructions has to be corrected to: ***More than** a thousand people turned out for the rally*. And claims that something happened *over 10 years ago*, or *over 10 years after* some other event, have to be fixed as well. Such events happened ***more than** 10 years ago* or ***more than** 10 years after* something else.

Contractions can be painful

Your and *you're* are not interchangeable. Like *its* and *it's*, *your* is a possessive pronoun while *you're* is a contraction of *you are*. But the pronoun crops up consistently where it should not.

There are other examples. *Their* (possessive pronoun) and *there* (adverb) are also wrongly used instead of *they're* (contraction of *they are*).

Try to avoid "try and"

In fact, don't just **try** to avoid *try and*, make **sure** you avoid it altogether. Using *try and* instead of *try to* is a mistake that crops up regularly in the news media.

The reason is simple. It's grammatically wrong.

If you are ever in doubt, substitute *attempt* for *try*. *I will attempt and make amends* . . . makes no sense. But, *I will attempt to make amends* is perfectly appropriate – and correct English.

So, always write:

> Mr Bloggs said he would **try to** make amends for his actions.

Never:

> Mr Bloggs said he would <u>try and</u> make amends for his actions.

You should have taken more care

Similarly, there is no such construction as *should of*. And there are no such written contractions as *should've*, or *could've*, or *would've* . . . they are simply contracted sounds in quick speech.

Basic newspaper layout and design

Computer-based desktop publishing packages are very sophisticated these days. The options available and their capabilities are vast. But that can be a trap.

In producing pages for newspapers, **simple is best**. The urge to use all kinds of typefaces and colours and fancy borders, just because they are there, should be avoided. You may create a technological marvel but the readers may not love you. Indeed they may avoid you. The whole amazing result may be too much for the eye and instead of the wonder of it all appealing to the reader it may have the opposite effect.

Technology should enhance, not hinder, your efforts to communicate with your readers. There are two important issues the journalist has to keep in mind. One is readability. The other is comprehension.

The first is important because, if readers find it hard to read what you have written, they will not struggle. They will move on. And the second is important, because there is not much point in getting them to read your copy if they misunderstand it.

Your writing impacts on both. So write simply and clearly. But typography, layout and design also impact on readability and comprehension.

So it's useful to know about them too.

Typography

There are countless typefaces or fonts available today. The illustration below shows three closely related fonts, and a fourth which is not related. The first three fonts are all sans serif typefaces. The fourth is a "serif" font.

Typography	**Arial Black**
Typography	**Arial Bold**
Typography	Arial (regular or normal)
Typography	**Times New Roman**

Serif fonts or typefaces have characteristic "serifs" at the extremities of the letters which you can clearly see distinguishes them from "sans serif" fonts or type families. "Sans" is derived from Latin and French and means "without" or "the absence of", so a "sans serif" font means a typeface without serifs. And what all this means is illustrated below.

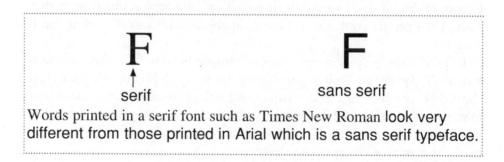

serif   sans serif

Words printed in a serif font such as Times New Roman look very different from those printed in Arial which is a sans serif typeface.

The term "Roman" as in "Times New Roman" is quite significant. It recognises the style of lettering used by the Romans in their writing and inscriptions. As it turns out, the Romans knew a thing or two. Painstakingly chipping those serifs into an inscription on a wall may have taken some effort but it was no waste of time. Serif fonts, such as Times, are widely respected for their "readability" (and I will explain why shortly).

Indeed we owe a great deal to the ancients when we consider the matter of typography.

"Italics" is another word that reflects the origins of our typefaces and printing styles. The word "italics" recognises the Italian influence on the art of typography. Italics are sloping letters, as opposed to upright letters, which makes them stand out. They have a variety of uses, such as indicating emphasis. Italics are very useful (in moderation).

There are a number of other options to make words stand out. These include, "bold face", or simply "bold", in which the letters are made darker and heavier. Bold and italic can also be combined. All of them are best used in moderation.

	Sans serif	Serif
Roman (Normal)	Typography	*Typography*
Italic	*Typography*	*Typography*
Bold	**Typography**	**Typography**
Bold italic	***Typography***	***Typography***

And of course you can change the size. As below:

Typography   Typography   Typography

Typography   Typography   Typography

So there are many options and combinations. We have to choose the best for the job.

Common newspaper fonts

Here is a selection of common typefaces you might find used for different purposes in the world of newspapers and publishing. You will see some subtle, and some not so subtle, differences.

Garamond; Times New Roman; News 701; Dutch801; Bookman; Century Schoolbook; Jansen Text; Century Gothic; Swiss 721 BT; Helvetica; DIN Medium; **DIN Bold**.

Some fonts are never seen in the news pages of newspapers. They may be seen in advertisements, but never on the news pages.

Blackadder	To be or not to be, that is the question.
Courier	To be or not to be, that is the question.
Brush Script	To be or not to be, that is the question.

Those who design newspaper styles and those who go on to produce the pages have to keep one important thing in mind – the reader. How will the reader react, at first sight, to the "look" of the paper and the "look" of a page?

If the paper as a whole looks a mess (different typefaces at every turn), or boring (nothing to attract the eye, just column after column of type), there may not be any readers. They may be "turned off" just because of the look of a publication or a page. Thus the matter of design is critical, and making the paper and its pages appealing and interesting is critical for the journalist. Once upon a time, newspapers were all just type. But there was less competition. With today's information-saturated readers, and the competition from radio, TV and internet, design has become a big issue.

Choosing fonts and typefaces

As you now know, the options are virtually endless. There are countless typefaces to choose from. But experience and research show that the bulk of them can be discounted in the world of newspapers. There are three things to juggle: the "look" of the publication and its pages; readability; and comprehension. Only a few typefaces perform well against these three criteria in the context of a newspaper. Vast numbers do not.

The first decision is relatively simple. When you select your fonts or typefaces, don't get carried away. For a newspaper, two may be enough, three is ample. If any further variety is needed, use the bold version of the ones you have selected. Desktop publishing packages these days come with a huge range of fonts, but don't be seduced by this abundance. If you are, you will produce a page that looks like a dog's breakfast. I have seen countless editions of campus newspapers that I would defy anyone to read. Every available font managed to get into the paper because it was all so much fun. The result, however, was a terrible flop. (If you are producing a magazine rather than a newspaper, you may be more flamboyant. But even here, you should be careful.)

You will need one font for your body copy (your stories) and another for your headlines. You may choose a third for what are called "pulls" or "pull quotes" (to be explained soon) or you may simply choose to use a larger, and maybe bold, version of your body copy font. Your "masthead" (the name of your publication as displayed on the front page) will almost certainly be in a different font altogether. And that's all you need.

Now the question is, which fonts to choose. And here too the answer is quite easy – at least if you want others to be able to read your paper and understand what you have written.

Despite some contrary views among designers, research conducted by Colin Wheildon in 1989–90 and published by the Australian Newspaper Advertising Bureau Ltd in *Communicating or just making pretty shapes* provides some clear answers. The research involved readability and comprehension tests to find out what worked best with readers. To understand the results, you will need some explanation of the issue of "readability".

Readability

The issue of what makes one typeface more reader-friendly than another can be illustrated quite easily and has been for years. To take a well-known example to begin, we will set the word *readability* in both "upper-case" and "lower-case" letters.

> **Upper- and lower-case letters**
>
> In the early days of typography, the letters in each font in all the various sizes were kept in "cases". The capitals (or majuscules) were stored in their cases in the upper section of a cabinet or set of drawers; the small letters (minuscules) were in the cases in the lower section. Thus capitals became known as "upper-case" letters and small letters as "lower-case".

> # READABILITY IN UPPER CASE
>
> ## readability in lower case

Now for the trick. Obscure most of the letters and see what happens.

> # DEADADILITY IN LIDDED CASE
>
> ## readahility in lower case

The upper-case words could be anything, but it is quite obvious what the lower-case words are.

Now try the opposite effect by obscuring the top of the letters.

READABILITY IN UPPER CASE

readability in lower case

The bottom of the upper-case words is meaningless again, though this time the lower-case example is not much better.

This old example demonstrates the value of lower-case lettering. Indeed, if you were to cut off the bottom half of the letters in most of your lower-case words your reader would still have no trouble reading your copy.

The example above uses a sans serif typeface – Arial. Now try it with a serif typeface – Times New Roman:

READABILITY IN UPPER CASE

readability in lower case

Lower-case wins again.

If we try the same experiment by obscuring the top of the serif letters we get:

READABILITY IN UPPER CASE

readability in lower case

Again, the bottom portion of the letters makes almost no sense at all in either upper- or lower-case.

So, the first message is, don't use capitals when you can use small letters.

The next question is, should we use a serif or a sans serif typeface? And that is a most important question if you are making a newspaper.

Take a word in both styles and have a close look at them.

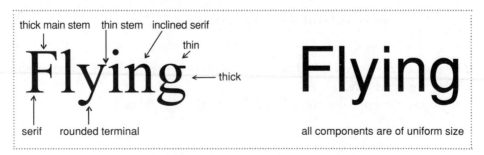

It is clear that a serif font such as the one above presents a great variety of reference points for the eye to seize upon. There are different thicknesses in most of the letters – note the way the bowls (rounded portions) of the "n" and the "g" grade from thick to thin – standard and inclined serifs, the "y" has a rounded terminal, and so on. On the other hand, there is no variety in the sans serif font; all thicknesses are uniform; and all terminals are square.

Serif vs sans serif

The eye prefers variety and serif fonts have been found to be much more readable, and produce greater comprehension, than sans serif fonts. *Communicating or just making pretty shapes* concludes: "Body type must be set in serif type if the designer intends it to be read and understood," (p. 17).

Headlines

According to Wheildon's research, the preference for serif faces in body copy does not translate so clearly to headlines, where there is little to choose between sans serif and serif (p. 22).

But he says, like Henry Ford, you can have any colour in a headline as long as it is black (p. 23). While this is an excellent rule, occasional breaches can have great impact. A red headline was used to great effect in the *Weekend Independent*, which ultimately caused the government of the day to set up a Commission of Inquiry into what lay behind the story (the drug trade in our prisons).

Type size

The size of the letters to be used is also an important matter in designing a newspaper and laying out a page. The options are infinite.

Height measurements in the publishing business are known by the term "points". Seventy-two point capital letters and figures are one inch high, which means that 1 point is 1/72 of an inch high or 0.0138 inches high.

Width measurements are in what are called "picas". There are 12 points to a pica, and thus there are 6 picas to an inch.

The following examples illustrate a range of type sizes you might encounter in a newspaper.

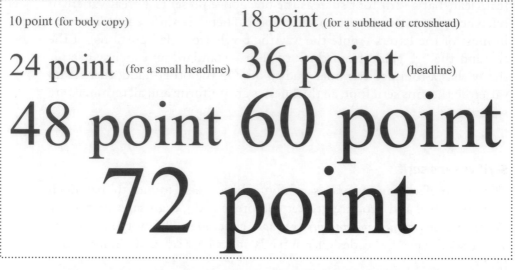

10 point (for body copy)   18 point (for a subhead or crosshead)

24 point (for a small headline) 36 point (headline)

48 point 60 point

72 point

Body text in a newspaper (depending on the typeface chosen) will normally be in the range of 9 to 11 points. Headline point sizes will vary depending on the width of the column involved. A headline across a single column will obviously have quite limited room and so the point size involved will be relatively small. Conversely, a headline spread across a whole page will allow a much larger point size to be used.

The size of the lower-case letters involved in different typefaces and the space between the letters may vary considerably, even though the typefaces involved may be designated as being of the same point size. For example:

Times New Roman, 12 point.   The time has come, the walrus said . . .
Arial, 12 point.   The time has come, the walrus said . . .
Century Schoolbook, 12 point.   The time has come, the walrus said . . .
Century Gothic, 12 point.   The time has come, the walrus said . . .

The point size height of the capital T in each of the examples above is the same – 12 points. But the size of many of the lower-case letters is considerably different, both in terms of height and width, and the spaces between some of them is also markedly different.

Since we know that serif fonts are more readable, if we were looking for a body copy typeface we might choose between the two serif fonts above. But we might also notice that we will get more words on a line, and thus on a page, if we choose Times New Roman over Century Schoolbook. And therefore we might make that choice. Many have.

Now we come to the matter of the space between the lines.

Leading

Upper-case letters in all typefaces share two characteristics. First, in any given point size they are all the same height; second, they share a common base line. For example, Times New Roman and Arial in 22 point:

ABCDEFGHIJKLM   ABCDEFGHIJKLM

But lower-case letters are quite different. Some extend above the top of others in the alphabet, and some below. The same typefaces as those above in lower-case reveal the difference.

abcdefghijklm abcdefghijklm

The middle part of the letters, the height of the letter "a", for example, is referred to as the "x height". Some letters (such as b, d, f and h) have "ascenders" which extend above the x height, usually to the same height as a capital letter, or just a fraction shorter. Some (such as g, j, p and q) have "descenders" which extend below the "baseline" on which the other letters sit. Because of the ascenders and descenders, the space between lines of text must be carefully considered or you may produce something like this – where the descenders on one line overlap the ascenders on the line below:

Am I flying
do you think?

The space between lines is referred to as "leading". The term reflects the days of linotype printing machines, when words and spaces were all produced in little rectangular blocks of lead.

When you use a modern desktop publishing package and select a font and a required point size, the program will automatically establish a default setting for the leading so that the overlap of descenders and ascenders illustrated above cannot occur. The default is based on a formula that roughly says the space between lines should be equivalent to the point size of the type involved plus 10 per cent. So setting your body text in 10 point with 11 points of leading, for example, should make for a very readable column of text.

Fortunately your desktop publishing program will default to a setting that will establish a satisfactory amount of leading for the point size of the type you are using. But remember, you can change the setting (even by tiny amounts) and you may need to do this from time to time to ensure that the bottom lines of text in your columns all line up neatly across the page.

Kerning

Just as you can adjust the amount of space between lines, so you can adjust the amount of space between letters across the page. This is called "kerning". You may kern words or lines or paragraphs "out", or you may kern them "in".

"There was movement at the station"	Normal kerning
"There was movement at the station"	Kerned out by 1 pt
"There was movement at the station"	Kerned out by 1.5 pt
"There was movement at the station"	Kerned in by 0.5 pt

Slight adjustments in kerning will not be noticed by the reader and properly used may help you overcome the unsightly and unsettling problem presented by "orphans" or "widows" (single words or short lines at the end or beginning of a column or page) in your paper.

Reading and design

It is true that the same layout page after page would soon leave the reader bored, and that has to be avoided. So we need different layouts throughout the paper. Pages have to look interesting.

However, there are some realities in the way we read and write that should not be ignored when placing stories on a page. The layout artist or designer cannot ignore the reality that, in English, when we write or read, we start at the top left and move across to the right and down, ultimately finishing at the bottom right of the page. Top-left-to-bottom-right reading and writing is what we learn in this culture from the moment our parents first show us a book.

Those who deal with this reality recognise the importance of what is called "reading gravity" (see *Communicating or just making pretty shapes*, p. 11). In other words they recognise the importance of the obvious – the top-left-to-bottom-right reading habit we all have. They also recognise the danger in laying out a page that ignores this habit.

Design aids

It is important that the "look" of a page not turn readers away. That is vital. But it is just as important that the "look" of a page should attract readers, regardless of the story involved. If the layout is appealing, they may read the story.

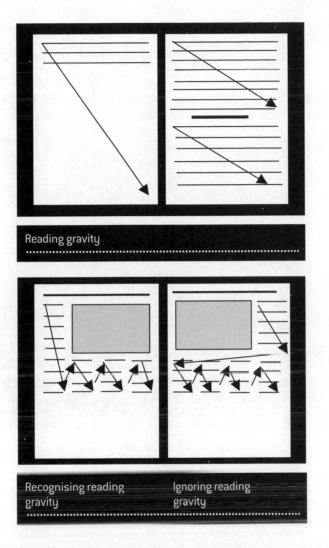

Reading gravity

Recognising reading gravity

Ignoring reading gravity

A page full of type is quite forbidding. That may have been fine in the early days of newspapers when they were few and far between and readers were hungry for news of any kind. Those days have long gone. So it is important to do more than fill pages with type.

There are a number of aids to assist the page designer to make the page attractive.

Type size

Headline type size should complement the space to be filled and should adequately support the story that follows. A skimpy headline in a too-small point size with too many words across the width of a whole page will not convince the reader that the story is important – even if the wording of the headline is really clever. A big, brassy headline in a very large point size may be equally off-putting.

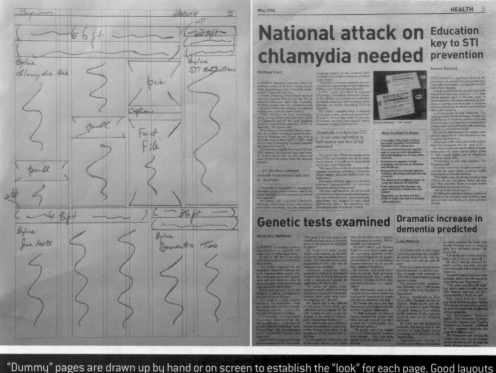

"Dummy" pages are drawn up by hand or on screen to establish the "look" for each page. Good layouts add variety to pages while respecting reading gravity.

The number of lines or "decks" occupied by a headline should be carefully considered too. A four-deck headline across a single column in 20 point type may be fine. Four decks in 60 point across two columns may not. And four decks across three columns or more in 60 point may look terrible.

Also keep in mind that there are two pages visible when a newspaper is opened. Has the design of the facing page been settled? Having two pages side by side that are the same, or clash in some way, is not a good idea. If there is a single-deck headline across the top of a left-hand page, what is on the top of the right hand page? If there is a single deck in the same typeface and same point size, will the reader read across the top of both pages? Some say no. But regardless, the "look" of the two pages will not be appealing. Newspapers use double-page spreads from time to time. If the two pages do not constitute such a spread, one of them ought to be changed.

Subheads and crossheads

Both are useful tools. Subheads change the look of the usual layout where the story comes immediately under the headline. They also provide additional support for the headline in setting up the story as one the reader should not miss. They are usually reserved for major stories. They have considerable value in providing variety in the appearance of a page.

Crossheads or crossheadings (also known as subhead or subheadings) are used within a body of text to break up large slabs of type and give the eye some relief. Large slabs of type can be forbidding. Crossheads can also flag something coming up in a story that will keep the reader interested. In other words, they can be used very effectively as a "Don't go, there is more good stuff coming up" device. Placing them within a story is a matter of choice. But the effect will need to be aesthetically pleasing. Having one in a left-hand column, nothing in the second, third and fourth, and then three in a fifth column could look very odd.

Drop caps

Again, drop caps add variety to the look of a story, help break up large blocks of copy and flag changes of scene, time or mood. They will usually be of a point size equivalent to at least three lines of text, although two-line drop caps are sometimes used. The problem with two-line drop caps is that they tend not to achieve the intended result. They are too small, and offer little in relief for the eye that is seeking some respite from a heavy column of text.

Drop caps need to be inserted judiciously. The line they start should be one that can stand being set apart from the rest. In other words, if the line should be integrally connected to, or simply an expansion of, the one above, making a point of singling it out is silly. Aesthetically it is best not to use the same letter over and over in the one story for this kind of treatment. Such repetition detracts from the "look" of the page. Well-used drop caps add a further dimension to the appeal of a story and have a useful place in the designer's kitbag.

Pulls and pull quotes

"Pulls" are extracts from the copy written by the reporter responsible for the story, and "pull quotes" are quotes from those reported in the story. These are both useful devices. They break up large slabs of text, which is desirable, and carefully chosen they highlight important material in the story. When deciding to read a story, a person skimming a newspaper page will look at a picture, read a headline and read any pulls or pull quotes that have been included. If these have been well chosen, they may ensure the skimmer will turn into a reader.

The "look" of the pulls and pull quotes has to be good. The point size and typeface used and any other design features need to be sufficiently prominent and appealing to catch the eye. So take care selecting the style to be used.

Be careful with placement as well. The words chosen must have appeared in the text **before** the pull or pull quote devices. It is most annoying to come upon a pull or a pull quote that contains information that is new and eventually appears later in the story.

Pull quotes and drop caps add variety to the text.

Breakouts

Breakouts, or side bars, are another design device that can be used to great effect. They contain information related to a story but are set apart from the main text, often defined by a border or colourful background. They fulfil a number of useful roles. They provide variety on a page that might otherwise be too text-heavy for the eye; they provide variety in the overall appearance of the page; break the story into more easily digested portions; and, significantly, provide a vehicle to present and highlight important material outside the structure of the story itself.

The impact and value of the breakout can be enhanced by changing the weight of the typeface (from normal to bold, for example), by using a different typeface altogether, or by increasing the size of the type involved.

Breakouts also offer the opportunity to include another headline on the page. This also catches the eye, and provides more relief from the heavy dose of body copy text that the story probably contains. In addition, breakouts will usually be set within a box with a border, and, providing the weight of the border is carefully selected (neither too heavy nor too light), that device will also assist in making the page appealing to the eye.

Write-ins or intro boxes

Major stories usually require some form of introduction or "write-in" to provide background or explanation.

Again, a change of point size, font, or weight (bold instead of normal), perhaps set within a border, even with a screen of colour (even grey) behind the text, may enhance the look of the page by adding some variety for the eye.

- Masthead
- Single-deck, five-column headline
- Light screen behind body copy
- Breakouts (if quoting a portion of a document, called a "tear-out")
- Caption for tear-outs
- Two-deck, single column headline
- Single-deck, four column headline
- Advertisements

Colour

A clear difference between newspapers and magazines emerges at this point. Magazines use colour everywhere. Newspapers do not (apart from photographs and advertisements). Coloured headlines and text are not used in the news pages at least. Indeed, research suggests that coloured headlines in newspapers do not improve readability or comprehension. Coloured "screens" behind breakouts can add to the appearance of a page (as long as the colour is chosen with some care). A garish purple breakout in the middle of a serious story may not be a good idea.

Coloured type in newspapers (and indeed in many other places) is also likely to turn off readers and be self-defeating. One particularly unsuitable choice can be to "reverse" text: setting white on black rather than the normal black on white.

Some colours do not work very well either. Yellow is often not a good choice on newsprint. Magazines use colour much more vividly than newspapers.

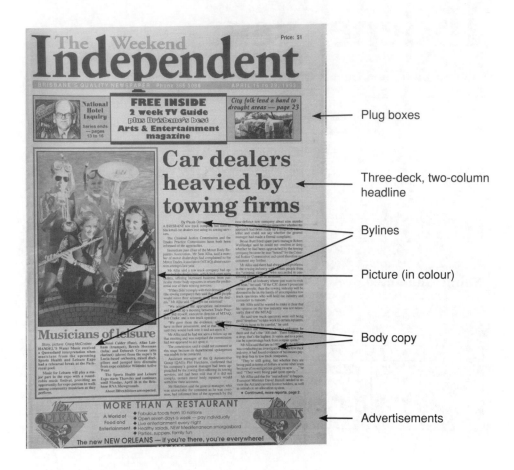

Pictures and illustrations

A newspaper page without a picture or an illustration can be hard going for the reader. Photographs and artwork are integral parts of a newspaper and provide excellent raw material for the page designer.

They have to be good, of course. Used as they are, or judiciously cropped (everything not important in the picture cut out), they will add greatly to the appeal of a page. Further variety can be obtained by running text around a subject that has been removed from its original background.

Many a story has appeared in print because someone took a wonderful photograph.

Plug boxes

Front pages may "plug" stories inside the paper using boxes with a picture, crosshead, and maybe a few words. These can be very effective at drawing readers in past the first page.

Masthead

Plug boxes

Single-deck, four-column headline

Byline

Picture with caption

Pull quote

Headline for follow-on story

Byline

White space

Despite all the suggestions offered above, the value of white space cannot be stressed too much. The eye can be overwhelmed by the amount of ink on a page whether it is all black or in various shades of dazzling colour.

White space is as much a tool of the page designer as any of the devices mentioned above. Use it to advantage. A page can look sparse (too much white space) or forbidding (not enough white space). The page designer needs to have a good "eye".

The stories may be great, but the reader may pass by if the look of the page is intimidating.

PART 3

Understanding the law

Australian law

Ignorance of the law does not excuse a person from criminal responsibility for an act that would otherwise be an offence . . .

These are the words of Queensland's Criminal Code, s 48 (1). But words to similar effect operate or prevail in all jurisdictions. Ignorance of the law is no excuse.

If it were an excuse, everyone could claim they didn't know what they did was wrong and there would be no need for courts. It would probably be a pretty wild, even dangerous place out there. Relying on what others say the law is, even those who should know, is no defence either. The matter of ignorance of the law being no excuse was most recently settled by the High Court (*Ostrowski v Palmer* (2004) HCA 30).

What this case illustrates for the journalist, as well as for people like Mr Palmer, and everyone else, is simple. You have to know the law. And there is a great deal to know.

Laws that affect you as a reporter include: common law contempt, statutory contempt, defamation, and the laws that relate to children, divorce, family matters, domestic violence, sexual assault, bail, sentencing, prisoners, rehabilitation of offenders, privacy, confidentiality, copyright, and Freedom of Information, just to mention a few. The law in each state and territory is likely to be different, and then there are some matters that are federal issues (the responsibility of the Commonwealth) and some that are state issues.

Some are based on the common law and precedent (you have to know what the decisions of the courts mean, if not the cases themselves), while some are "black letter law" and have been legislated by parliament (you can check the statutes on the internet).

Then there are the laws you need to know to ensure someone doesn't pull the wool over **your** eyes – laws that govern your rights as a member of the public (since there are no special privileges for journalists) – laws that govern access to courts, and access to court records, for example.

How does the law affect journalists?

Some years ago a newspaper covering the opening day of a trial in the local courthouse reported that on the morning of the trial there had been a strong police presence outside the building and some additional security inside the building. Which was accurate and true.

The story appeared and subsequently the newspaper was fined $20,000 for contempt.

Why?

If you are going to be a reporter you need to know.

A reporter got the first letter of a judge's name wrong. The paper won a defamation action brought by another judge (whose surname was the same as that of the incorrect spelling) but lost when the decision was appealed.

Then there were the picture editors so impressed by the graphic expressions on the faces of a couple of footballers in mid-tackle that they failed to notice the shorts of one of the tacklers had been knocked considerably askew. It has happened more than once. The papers had to pay up. How come?

There are many more cases, but the message should be clear by now. Knowing what the law says, and requires, is vital for the journalist. The new reporter may not be expected to know, but someone in the newsroom has to know.

At the very least, they have to know when it is time to call in the lawyers.

Origins of our legal system

In days long gone God played a critical role in determining the innocence or guilt of a person or in settling a dispute.

The theory was that God would not allow an innocent person to be punished for something he or she did not do. And by the same token, God would not allow the guilty to get off.

So, issues were settled in a number of interesting ways. Trial by battle – God would see to it that whoever won was either innocent, or in the right. Trial by ordeal. If you survived you were innocent. If you didn't you were clearly guilty. Trial by morsel. Given an ounce of dry bread and an ounce of cheese to swallow, an offender might manage to get it down (innocent) or choke (guilty).

Witch swimming was popular at one time and this practice also relied on the omnipotence of the Almighty to determine guilt or innocence.

A woman alleged to be a witch would be trussed up tightly and tossed into a body of water (which had previously been blessed by a priest or man of the cloth). If the blessed water accepted the no-doubt terrified and probably struggling soul, i.e. she started to drown, it meant she was innocent! And hopefully those nearby would get her out before it was too late.

If, however, she floated, and the blessed water did not take her in, clearly God knew she was a witch and she would therefore be retrieved from the water and taken off to a handy stake and burned to death.

In his detailed critiques of our legal system (*Trial by voodoo* and *The Cartel*), Evan Whitton details the matters outlined above and discusses the circumstances in which the British legal system and that of the rest of Europe diverged after 1215.

The Europeans chose the inquisitorial path. Trained magistrates and judges would investigate a matter in an endeavour to discover the truth.

The British chose the adversarial path. There would be a small group of citizens (called a jury) who would determine the guilt or innocence of anyone charged with committing a crime, after hearing arguments for and against them. The arguments would usually, but not necessarily, be presented by those conversant with the law, who would operate as adversaries, much as they might in a trial by battle – except they would use oratory rather than weapons to secure a decision in their favour.

The Australian legal system is derived from the British system. But there are many parts of the world in which the jury system as we know it does not operate. Our "adversarial" system, in which opposing legal teams try to convince a jury the accused is innocent or guilty, does not operate in lots of countries. In many countries magistrates and judges conduct investigations, and the proceedings in court, and hear the cases too. Anyone who watched the cases of Schapelle Corby and "the Bali Nine" being heard in Indonesia will have seen the difference between their system and ours. The most obvious difference on the TV news at night was the absence of a jury.

Much of the legal terminology we use today has its origins in the quite distant past.

Terms

"Courts" is a reference to the days when the monarch settled disputes.

The "bench" was simply a table a judge or magistrate would set up in a community when he held "court".

The judge would also place a rail in front of his bench to provide a bit of space between him and those who came to have matters settled. Those who brought matters before him (they were always men) did so from this rail, or "bar".

Advocates with persuasive skills of oratory could be hired to speak on behalf of those who wanted to bring a case, or those accused of committing some wrong. These advocates did so from "the bar", and thus became known as "barristers".

The "barristers" in turn paid others to find or solicit business for them, and these individuals became known as "solicitors".

The system remains largely the same to this day. Solicitors brief barristers on behalf of clients. Barristers are those who have been admitted to "the bar" and thus are recognised as sufficiently qualified in the law to appear before those who have been appointed to "the bench", i.e. the judges.

Criminal cases, civil cases and the role of the jury

Much of the work of our courts involves the hearing of criminal cases (in which the State prosecutes those it alleges have broken the law) and civil disputes in which citizens or organisations seek to have grievances against each other settled.

While our court processes are determined by our adherence to an adversarial system, there are occasions when we opt for the inquisitorial model. Royal Commissions and Commissions of Inquiry (of which there have been any number in recent years) are examples of the inquisitorial model. A staff of investigators works closely with, and under the direction of, the Commissioner/s to investigate the matter involved. The Commissioner often questions witnesses directly. But this system does not operate within our courts.

Under our system, the police conduct their investigations quite separately from the courts. Situations vary, but typically these days the police provide a brief to a prosecuting agency (which does not have any investigatory role, such as the Office of Public Prosecutions) which decides whether to go to trial. Judges have no part in any of these processes.

In more serious criminal matters, juries will be involved. At a criminal trial, the prosecution seeks to convince a jury, not a judge, that the accused is guilty. The accused, or his or her legal counsel, will seek to convince the jury of his or her innocence. It is the members of the jury who decide whether an accused is guilty or innocent. When necessary, the judge involved will determine what the law says or requires on any matter, and advise the jury accordingly. The judge also determines any sentence that might result. Whether this process leads to the uncovering of the truth of the matter in question may never be known. In the end it is incidental. The process we have adopted is about advocacy; which argument wins over the jury. Such is the nature of the adversarial system.

If an offender pleads guilty, there is no need for a jury and the penalty will be determined by a judge after hearing both sides of the story involved. In the case of minor offences, magistrates sitting alone hear cases and fix penalties.

Civil matters may involve juries or may be determined by a magistrate or judge alone (depending on the seriousness of the issue or on the value of whatever it is that is at the centre of the dispute).

The British model

Some of the features of the British legal system, apart from its adversarial rather than inquisitorial nature, that set it apart from others, include: trial by jury; the common law; and the rules of evidence.

Trial by jury

While minor infringements of the law (and minor disputes between citizens) can be settled by magistrates sitting alone, serious offences (indictable offences) are heard before a judge and jury. Juries may be involved in civil cases too. Or they may not. A judge sitting alone may hear civil cases

Juries in criminal trials comprise 12 citizens chosen at random from the community at large. Computers randomly select names from the electoral roll. Those selected eventually turn up at the court and are lined up on one side of the courtroom. Marbles with numbers on them are drawn from a cylinder, the numbers are called, and those individuals with the corresponding numbers set off to walk to the jury box and if they do so without being challenged, they are "empanelled" (selected as jury members).

Important aspects of the jury system include:
- Jurors decide the guilt or innocence of an accused party . . . they decide the facts of the matter. Did the accused do what the prosecution alleged, or not?
- When necessary the judge will determine what the law says, and advise the jury accordingly.
- In court, jurors simply listen. They take no part in the processes of questioning witnesses.
- Jury deliberations are private.

- Juries give no reasons for their decisions.
- Jury deliberations are not open to examination. Very little is known about what goes on in jury rooms (including whether juries are influenced or not by media coverage of matters brought before them).
- Some jurisdictions require unanimous verdicts (agreement amongst all, usually 12, jurors), while others accept majority decisions (11–1, or 10–2).
- The standard of proof required in a criminal trial is "beyond reasonable doubt", while in a civil case it is "on the balance of probability", that it was more likely the argument put by one side happened rather than that of the other side. "Beyond reasonable doubt" is regarded as a higher standard of proof than "on the balance of probability".

Should you ever wonder what "beyond reasonable doubt" means you may go on wondering, at least until the day you are picked for a jury. Then you will have to decide – for yourself, by yourself. The judge will not be able to help you. That has been clearly established in law. New trials have been ordered by appeal courts in cases where judges have sought to advise jurors on the meaning of "reasonable doubt".

The common law and the hierarchy of authority

The law is made in two ways. One, via legislation passed by parliament (statute law) and two, by judges adjudicating on matters brought before them (including the interpretation of laws passed by parliaments).

It is vital for everyone in a society that the law be applied consistently, not arbitrarily nor capriciously. So decisions made by judges need to be consistent. This means that when a court makes a decision in relation to a matter, or a matter of law, that decision becomes binding – at least until that interpretation is changed or overturned by a court of equal or higher standing in the hierarchy.

Unless and until decisions and interpretations are changed or overturned, the courts are required, in cases of a similar nature, to follow the precedent that has already been settled, if one has.

The law that emerges from decisions made by courts is known as case law, or common law. The common law is an aspect of the legal landscape that is traditionally seen as part of the British legal tradition.

That reality is recognised in dictionary meanings. According to the *Macquarie Dictionary*, common law is the system of law originating in England as distinct from the civil or Roman law and the ecclesiastical or canon law; the unwritten law, especially of England, based on custom or court decision, as distinct from statute law.

The standing or position of courts in the hierarchy looks like this:

High Court of Australia

↑

Appeal Court / Full Court (states and territories)

↑

Supreme Court (states and territories)

↑

District or County Court

↑

Magistrates or Local Court

The diagram shows that decisions of magistrates can be appealed to the District or County Court. Decisions of District or County Courts can be reviewed by state Supreme Courts (or Appeal Courts or Full Courts) and finally, decisions at this level can be taken to the High Court. The High Court may not necessarily "grant leave" for an appeal if it believes there are no grounds for such an appeal to be considered.

It is important in journalism to appreciate the significance of case law (or the common law). In some areas of reporting, such as covering courts, case law (common law) is very influential in determining what can be reported, and when. The consequences of not knowing the case law involved, or ignoring it, can be quite serious. There will be more on this later.

Rules of evidence

There are a couple of issues regarded as fundamental to the operation of our criminal justice system that introduce some tensions into the circumstances surrounding the delivery of justice. The first is the notion of justice itself. Justice has a number of faces. There is the justice that the individual accused of a crime expects to get. There is the justice that the community, whose rules or standards have been violated, expects. And there is justice for the victim of whatever crime may have been committed.

The accused, naturally, expects to get a fair trial. The community agrees. But it also expects to be able to audit the process; it expects the process to be open and transparent. The victim expects the perpetrator will be dealt with appropriately (according to the law established by the community) and punished for his or her action in offending against that law.

Journalists find themselves in the middle of some competing expectations here. On the one hand, a person accused of a crime is innocent until **proven** guilty. On the other, justice must not only be done, it must be **seen** to be done; courts should not operate in secret.

Unfortunately, the interests of the community in relation to the delivery of justice often run second to other interests. Many in the legal tangle that surrounds the justice system do not appreciate, or prefer not to appreciate, that journalists who cover that process are the eyes and ears of the community. Many in that tangle seem to regard the processes of the courts as their private affair and resent, at times even obstruct, journalists in their work.

Journalists are often seen as nuisances. Not only may the courts pay no heed to their needs (to be able to hear or get accurate details and information), but along with others who operate within the system, may regard journalists as nosy stickybeaks rather than individuals performing an important function for the community. It is well established that unless specifically barred, the community has a right to know what is going on and a right, normally, to be present in court. For all kinds of practical reasons few people can attend. Journalists, as best they can, cover the courts for them.

There are a few issues which can clearly come into conflict. The law says an accused's right to a fair trial and to be regarded as innocent until proven guilty can override the community's right to know everything that goes on in a trial. The law may also set out to protect some people (victims for example, but others as well) from suffering more distress as a result of the trial process than they have already suffered from the crime itself. And so on. Somewhere in the middle of all this one finds the journalist.

Certain rules of evidence operate in our courts. They are not without their critics. It is claimed they are necessary to ensure that an accused person gets a fair trial; that anyone before the courts will be regarded as innocent until proven guilty. These rules include such things as: the accused's right to silence; the exclusion of similar facts; exclusion of hearsay; exclusion of evidence illegally or dubiously gained; and the judge's discretion.

These matters may not trouble most journalists unless they are reporting courts but they are matters that have their roots in the British legal tradition and may set those who follow that tradition apart from others. While they are very significant matters, we will deal with them only briefly since they are not likely to impinge too much on the daily affairs of journalists unless they are reporting courts.

The accused's right to silence

An accused person does not have to give evidence at his or her trial (but may choose to do so). An accused person does not have to submit to cross examination or to questioning about the matter before the court. This is a significant difference between our system and those in many other countries.

Furthermore, a decision not to give evidence cannot be taken as counting against an accused. Further rules apply should a person choose to give evidence, but we will leave them for another day.

Exclusion of similar facts

A person appearing before a court can be dealt with only in connection with those matters before the court. That a person has committed a similar crime in the past, or any other crime, or has a propensity to commit criminal acts, are not matters that can be placed before a jury.

They may be raised after the jury has deliberated and when the judge is passing sentence. But not until then. It is said that jurors are sometimes surprised, when they open their newspaper at the end of a trial, to discover for the first time, the serious criminal history of the person on whom they passed judgment the previous day. But that is the way it is.

The judge's discretion

Presiding judges have a discretion not to admit into evidence information or material that may have a serious impact on an accused person, but add little to the case being made against him/her. Evidence that is "highly prejudicial" but only "slightly probative" (tending to prove) may be ruled as inadmissible.

Furthermore, the jury will not hear any arguments raised by the prosecution or defence to have material allowed or disallowed. If they are not to hear certain material, it makes no sense that they should be allowed to hear arguments in favour or against such a proposition. So the jury will leave the courtroom until a decision is made by the presiding judge.

But reporters covering the trial should **not** take the opportunity of the jury being out to make a phone call or slip out for a cup of coffee. They should instead carefully take down every word of the arguments being presented to the judge. I will explain the reason in due course.

Exclusion of "hearsay"

What someone is alleged to have said to another is not admissible as evidence in a court. It is known as "hearsay". Courts will not accept second- or third-hand accounts of conversations that may (or may not) have taken place. They will want to hear directly from those involved in the conversation and will normally go to some lengths to achieve this.

Exclusion of evidence illegally or dubiously obtained

During one trial in recent years it was revealed that the authorities had made a tape recording of a telephone conversation. The recording was a key piece of evidence against the accused. But when it was revealed in court that those who had made the recording had represented themselves as technicians from a phone company (to gain access to the building to place their "bug"), the tape was determined to be inadmissible and the case collapsed.

A distinction can be drawn here between evidence that is "illegally" or "dubiously" obtained and that which might be "fortuitously" obtained.

Police who stumble fortuitously on some evidence while undertaking other investigations can seek the approval of a court (at least in some jurisdictions) to have that evidence accepted should it be required.

Summary

Supporters of these rules argue that it is better for 10 guilty people to go free than for one innocent person to be wrongly convicted. Others disagree, claiming that the balance is too heavily weighted in favour of the guilty getting off. They also point out that the system has not prevented innocent people being wrongly convicted. There are plenty of examples of terrible miscarriages of justice having occurred. The arguments for and against will not be canvassed here but it should be pointed out the matters raised above about the way our system works mean these rules are not without their critics.

Federal, state and territory law

When they arrived in the Great South Land, later Australia, the British established not just one colony, but ultimately six separate colonies. These colonies became separate, self-governing entities. They had their own customs arrangements at their border crossings (and arrangements to deal with smugglers), separate defence forces, and were not beholden in any way to the whims or wishes of any of the others.

In 1901, after a referendum, the people in the various colonies agreed to federate – to create a single nation with a national government, one that would look after "national" things (defence, foreign affairs, immigration, and a great deal more), and the states (the former colonies) would be responsible for other more parochial things such as policing, schools and education, hospitals, railways, plus a whole lot more.

There would eventually be two territories as well (the Northern Territory and the Australian Capital Territory), which although self-governing are still not completely autonomous entities – as was demonstrated very clearly in the case of the euthanasia legislation passed by the Northern Territory parliament, and the recognition of same-sex unions in the ACT. Both were overridden by the federal parliament.

This organisation of political power and responsibility means there may be eight (six states and two territories) or possibly nine (with the Commonwealth included) sets of laws in existence throughout the country covering matters of relevance to journalists.

And in turn this means that if a journalist moves across state borders, or his or her publication does, it may be necessary for the journalist to get to know a whole new set of laws.

Two further points should be made. If there is a conflict between the law in a state and federal legislation, the federal law prevails. This is why the federal Attorney-General's threat in 2004 to introduce national defamation law (under the powers of the national *Corporations Act 2001*, a power that was voluntarily handed over to the Commonwealth by the states) caused the states to agree to establishing uniform defamation law.

If they had not, and the Commonwealth had passed its proposed legislation, it would have overridden the existing laws in the various states.

Secondly, where there is no statute law, the common law, or case law established via hierarchical precedent by the courts, operates. Where there is statute law, law passed by a parliament, it prevails over case law.

The law and the journalist

There are two areas of law in particular that impact very seriously on what journalists may publish. One is defamation (damaging someone's reputation) and the other is one we have briefly touched on above: interfering with a person's right to a fair trial (known as "contempt"). These two matters will be given detailed treatment in separate chapters. For the moment I will deal with other legal issues that concern the journalist.

Privacy

There is federal legislation that deals with matters of privacy and sets out how those who are entrusted with private information should treat it. While the law recognises the right of citizens to protect their private affairs, it also recognises the right of a community to know about things that might affect the running of an ordered society. Thus it recognises the existence of a public interest, and also that this public interest can be served by the media acting as a "watchdog" on behalf of the community. The media is basically exempt from the provisions of this privacy legislation if they can demonstrate they have established and follow a code of conduct covering matters of personal privacy. If they do not comply, or if they breach their code, the law can be brought to bear on them.

Confidences

Breaching a confidence is not just an ethical issue, it is a legal issue as well. Court records contain no shortage of case law on the matter. To breach a confidence is to break the law, although in exceptional circumstances a public interest test may excuse such breaches in connection with crimes or misdeeds or where public safety, for example, is involved.

Confidentiality is a sensitive issue for journalists. The law, however, operates a splendid double standard in regard to the issue of confidentiality. While it generally demands that confidences be kept, it extends no right to journalists to maintain confidentiality over matter given to them and, indeed, requires that they breach any confidential undertaking they may have given to another if required to do so by a court. In other words, a journalist who refuses to tell a court the source of some confidential information, or details of such confidential information, is breaking the law for **not** breaching the confidence.

In the last 17 years four journalists in Australia have been jailed for refusing to reveal the identity of their sources. Two more were taken to the courtroom door quite recently by federal authorities who finally decided not to proceed.

Should you have to give evidence in a case in which the source of some information you published might be sought, take a toothbrush with you. You may be, probably will be, admonished by the judge for not providing the information and perhaps given a little time to consider your position. But as a journalist you have a professional obligation not to reveal your source/s, and so you may be sent to jail.

Recording conversations

The law relating to the use of recording devices differs around the country. In some states (such as Queensland) it is legal to record a private conversation without the other party or parties being aware of such recording, providing the person making the recording is party to the conversation. New South Wales law requires that parties to a conversation agree before it can be lawfully recorded.

Publishing matter gained from such conversations may also be prohibited, although in Queensland and Victoria for instance, while publication is generally prohibited, such publication on the grounds of public interest is recognised. In Queensland, there is another requirement – as long as the publication is not more than "reasonably necessary". This means you should not suddenly increase your newspaper print run by an extra 100,000 copies or organise a national hook-up of radio stations to broadcast what was on your tape.

Recording telephone conversations without permission of the other party or parties is a breach of federal law (*Telecommunications (Interception) Act*).

Trespass

Being on premises without permission or invitation is a breach of the law. Gaining access to a property or premises via deceit or subterfuge is not acceptable either. The law (as well as ethical conduct) frowns on such practices. But, since a person standing on public land may be able to see beyond the immediate boundary line of a private property, taking a photograph of a private property or private premises from public property is neither a trespass nor a breach of any privacy law.

It is lawful to enter property, to seek to contact someone for instance, unless such entry is clearly not welcomed or denied (by signs or locks). But having entered you may remain on the property only for as long as the owner or occupier agrees. If you do not leave when asked to do so, you will be trespassing.

Copyright

As a journalist, copyright may affect you directly – in two ways. First of all, as a journalist you may wish to reproduce the work of others, and secondly, as a writer you may wish to control the reproduction of your work by others, or you may wish to control the circumstances in which any reproduction of your work might occur.

Here we are talking about "intellectual property". Intellectual property exists in many forms. There are obvious ones such as patents, architectural drawings, designs, trademarks, and the like, but also a poem, a painting, even a sketch or a statistical table can qualify. All of these are regarded as intellectual property and are protected by the law one way or another. We have patent law and trademark law, for example. Designs can be registered and may not be used by others without permission. And so on.

There are two federal statutes in Australia that deal with the issue of copyright and which you should know: the *Copyright Act 1968* and the *Copyright Amendment (Moral Rights) Act 2000*. First, we need to establish what copyright is and what it protects.

In a nutshell, copyright law protects the right of the individual to the ownership of the output of one's creative effort – even if others do not believe the effort was worthwhile or produced anything of value. At the very heart of copyright law is the requirement that this creative effort be original. But, in addition to that, there are other demands – that the work, or the thing, be the product of some intellectual process, requiring the application of skill or labour.

Copyright exists in a work for the life of the author plus 70 years. It used to be 50 years, but has been extended to 70.

It is important to recognise that what we are talking about here is intellectual property. We are not talking about ideas. In the same way that you cannot patent an idea, you cannot copyright an idea. Anyone can claim to have had a good idea, and that they had it before anyone else. But how are we to know? So, unless the idea has been translated into some observable form, it cannot be copyrighted. This means if you have worked out the plot for a fantastic movie, don't tell anyone before you have translated the idea into something that can be copyrighted – a draft of a script, or a story board. Otherwise, if you find yourself going to the movies and, horror of horrors, seeing your idea/s "stolen" by someone else, you will just have to find solace in weeping. You will not have any claim against the people who made the movie.

In addition to having the right to publish their work, change it, adapt it or present it, creators, via the copyright law, have the right to copy their work. Others do not, unless the creator is happy about that by assigning (including selling) that right to someone else, or unless the copying is done under certain conditions. These conditions are governed by what is called "fair dealing". "Fair dealing" requires that the material be dealt with fairly, which is to say that it not be used excessively nor without acknowledgment. "Acknowledgment" means recognising the creator's action in producing the work. Even with acknowledgment, simply using someone's work to attract a readership or audience is not fair dealing. Copyright for such purposes would have to be assigned by the author. "Fair dealing" when reproducing unassigned material requires the additional factors of research or study; criticism or review; or reporting news.

Additionally, you may use short extracts or quotes without permission, as long as you acknowledge the source and they are not considered a "substantial" part of the copyright material. Defining a "substantial" part is tricky; even a very small part of the original may be considered "substantial" if it is important, essential or distinctive to the original work.

News cannot be copyrighted, but the form in which the news is presented can be protected. Thus, it is not an infringement of copyright to listen to another radio station's news bulletin, take notes of the content and rebroadcast it in a different format. The original broadcaster may squeal about plagiarism but a claim for breach of copyright would be unlikely to succeed.

Journalists need to observe the rules when using other people's work in their publications.

Moral rights

This is an area of the law that may affect you as a creator. A creator's "moral rights" in a work means that even after assigning the copyright in a work (including selling that right) to another, a creator is still entitled to have the integrity of the work protected.

Moral rights are basically twofold. One is the right to have authorship in a work recognised and the second is the right to object to any mutilation or distortion of a work damaging to a creator's reputation. Australia claims to have been in the vanguard of the legislative push to introduce moral rights legislation.

For the journalist, a moral rights regime means it is not acceptable, for example, to slaughter a contributor's work. Editing for reasonable considerations of space and the demands of accuracy, the law, spelling, punctuation and grammar are fine, but hacking up the work of another, just because the author has been, or will be, paid for it, is not fine. So freelance journalists should be clear about the rules if they enter into any agreement with a publisher, in case that agreement somehow assigns away their moral rights' protection.

Although matters relating to breach of copyright are more likely to be sorted out in the civil courts, it should not be forgotten that offending against the law of copyright is a criminal offence.

Freedom of information

By now it will come as no surprise to find that, as with most other things we have discussed in this chapter, there is no single set of laws across the nation that governs access to documents held by government agencies. There are in fact nine sets of FOI laws in Australia . . . one for each of the states and territories and one for the Commonwealth.

If you are thinking of making an FOI application, there are two things you should do at the outset. First of all, go to the legislation in the jurisdiction concerned and check to see whether what you are seeking is likely to be covered by an exemption. If the agency involved, or the kind of material you are seeking, turns out to be exempt from the provisions of the Act, you will not be able to get access to such material. The Act will specify the kinds of things, or agencies, that are exempt. You will find a list of exemptions or exempt bodies either in a section in the Act itself, or in a "schedule" attached to the Act.

If it appears there is no exemption, the next thing to do is to be sure you know what the Act says about the matter of cost. Getting the material you are seeking may come at a price, and you need to know that. The legislation will set out the application process to be followed and this will alert you to the matter of cost. If costs are involved, the Act will probably say that on receipt of your application, the agency will give you an estimate of the costs involved in searching for and collecting the documents or material you have applied for. However, there may be circumstances where you can claim an exemption from the charges and you need to know that as well.

The Act will certainly say somewhere that documents held on the personal affairs of citizens cannot be accessed by others . . . that such documents are exempt, in other words. However, personal documents can be accessed by the person to whom they apply. And usually there is no cost involved in accessing your own records. So, while you may not access documents held on another, an individual may be happy to access them him/herself and then provide them to you. Many of the outrageous and terrible stories I have published in recent years about the abuse of children in care have come about through the process just described. The unfortunate victims accessed their records and made them available.

If access is granted to what you are seeking, you may find you may not get all of it. Some of it may be withheld completely, or some of it may be blanked out. There will be a schedule setting out the sections of the Act under which such material was exempted or withheld. Check it all carefully. If the material is sensitive – and if you as a reporter are looking for it, it will probably be regarded as very sensitive – check that no one has been over-zealous with the black pen, and ended up illegally withholding material. It has happened.

If you are denied access, or denied access to some of it, you may appeal. The Act will set out the appeal process and the timelines involved. The timelines in relation to the application and appeal processes are important. You should be sure you stick to them. Then you can insist the agency involved sticks to them too. The Act will set all this out quite clearly. If it is in the Act it is the law. Public officials have to obey the law too. So, you need to know what the law says.

Seeking material through FOI will not produce results overnight. If appeals are involved it may take months, or years, or never, and the wait will try your patience. But there is no other way. Don't be put off.

Contempt

Common law contempt

Now we begin to deal with matters that all journalists must know, whether they are court reporters or not. To begin, there is the issue of contempt of court, and here the landscape can be quite dangerous. There are landmines just under the surface and more than the odd pitfall into which the unwary may easily stumble.

Much of the law dealing with contempt of court in Australia is judge-made law . . . case law. The central issue involved is the expectation that a person accused of a crime should be able to get a fair trial. To go one step further, the expectation is that anything that interferes with a fair trial can be a serious attack on the delivery of justice or a contempt of the court. Indeed it goes further than that. Anything that may be seen as having **a tendency** to interfere with the delivery of justice may be regarded as a threat to the delivery of justice. And the law does not look kindly on anyone who would seek to interfere with the course of justice. Thus the law is inclined to frown on those who would deliberately, **or inadvertently**, interfere with an accused person's right to a fair trial. The unwary journalist may just be one of those.

As mentioned earlier, some years ago a newspaper reported the opening day of a trial in the local courthouse. The story quite accurately noted that outside the courthouse that morning there had been an unusually heavy police presence and some extra security was obvious in the courtroom itself. It then went on to report the case that unfolded in the court that day. The story appeared as written in the paper the next morning. However, as a result, the trial was abandoned and the paper was fined a large sum of money.

The issues here highlight the conflict between an individual's right to a fair trial and the community's right to know. In this case it was determined that the public right to know (about the extra police and security) was subservient to the individual's right to a fair trial. So what did the paper do that it ought not to have done in the eyes of the law?

Many people believe that juries are locked up each night and live in some sort of cocoon or vacuum for the duration of the trial concerned. But this is not the case. Juries can be locked up (once their deliberations start for instance) but for the most part they go home each night. They are cautioned to take no notice of anything they might see or hear about the trial they are witnessing (apart from what they hear in court), but if they were to read a story in the newspaper over breakfast (from which it could be inferred that the person on trial might be someone who was dangerous), could that leave, or have a tendency to leave, some kind of impression about the person in a juror's mind? An impression that might count against him? In this case it was clearly thought this was so and thus the trial was aborted.

The case law says that anything that might have "a tendency" to interfere with a fair trial is a contempt. And so it was not necessary to show that any of the jurors had been influenced by what the paper had quite accurately reported but only to observe that such a story might have a tendency to influence a juror.

There is another side to this matter. Journalists have to be aware that from time to time there are people who would like to see a trial aborted and may deliberately do things to snare an unwary reporter into writing something to secure such an outcome. It has happened.

A trial does not necessarily have to be under way for a contempt to occur. The law also frowns on material that might influence a **potential** juror. The important considerations for the journalist are: has "the course of justice" begun to run, or is "the course of justice" over. In practical terms, this means has anyone been arrested in connection with a crime, or is the court process over? If no one has been arrested (or charged) for an offence, no one is in danger of having their right to a fair trial interfered with. If the case is over, nothing reported in the media can have any influence on the case – it is finished, so there can be no contempt. There can be something else, however, that journalists must take into consideration before rushing to publish something about somebody which they could not when that person was before the courts. This something is called defamation.

Defamation will be covered in the next chapter, but it is appropriate to say a few words about it now. The laws of contempt discussed in this chapter protect people's right to a fair trial. Anything that might interfere with that can be a serious problem for journalists. Defamation laws protect people's reputation: their good name – assuming they have one, of course. Wrongly harming or damaging a person's reputation can be a serious problem too. What all this means is this: while it may be possible to publish all kinds of material before the "course of justice" has commenced or after it has concluded and not commit a contempt, what you publish could be defamatory. And someone may sue you. So, even when there is no "course of justice" running, you still need to be careful about the things you publish.

Contempt: some key cases

There is just a handful of cases the journalist needs to know to cover the major issues involved in what is called "sub judice" (literally, "under a judge") contempt.

Packer v. Peacock (1912) 13 CLR 577

This case arose when some newspapers in Melbourne published stories about a certain Dr Peacock who was accused (thus the course of justice was running) of murdering a woman. It was claimed the articles were prejudicial to the interests of the accused. In its judgment the High Court said the lawfulness of the publication of material carried in the newspapers depended " . . . upon whether the publication [was] likely to interfere with a fair trial of the charge against the accused person". The court also said: "Comment adverse to him upon the facts is certainly not admissible."

In essence the court took the view that the articles concerned either created an impression, or left little doubt, that Dr Peacock had done the deed . . . and could therefore influence a juror. The stories were found to be contemptuous. In other words, the ruling made it clear that convicting a person for a crime was a job for a jury, not a newspaper.

Significantly, the court said:

> . . . it is, in our opinion, lawful for any person to publish information as to the bare facts relating to such a matter [a crime]. By 'bare facts' we mean (but not as an exclusive definition) extrinsic ascertained facts to which any eyewitness could bear testimony, such as the finding of a body and its condition, the place in which it was found . . . by whom . . . the arrest of a person accused, and so on.

What this means is, **beyond what might be said in front of a jury at trial**, all that may be reported about a crime **while the course of justice is running**, are "the bare extrinsic facts". Thus, once someone has been charged (in effect, once someone has been arrested), reporters should not publish anything that might prejudice a fair trial. So interviews with witnesses, reports of their own investigations or the investigations of others, and the like, will have to wait until the course of justice stops running.

Once a **trial has commenced**, the media may publish whatever the jury hears (unless there is an order banning publication) . . . and what a jury might hear will often go much further than the "bare extrinsic facts". Once the trial is over (and the course of justice is over), the media may then publish what the jury did not hear – unless there is an order banning publication.

Two significant points emerge from the *Packer v. Peacock* case. The first is whether a publication is **likely** to interfere with someone's fair trial. The issue is not whether a publication **did** interfere with a fair trial, but whether it might have a tendency to do so. The second point is, until the case is heard in court, the ruling about reporting only "the bare extrinsic facts" applies.

It may now be almost a century since the case of *Packer v. Peacock* came before the court. But no matter. That is the point about case law (judge-made law, common law) or indeed statute law. Until it is overturned in the case of judge-made law or amended or replaced in the case of statute law, it is the law. *Packer v. Peacock* is as relevant today as it was in 1912.

Packer v. Peacock is about a criminal matter, a murder. But what about a civil matter? Do the same rules apply once a civil proceeding starts?

The *Sunday Times* case: *A-G v. Times Newspapers Ltd* (1974) AC 273

For the journalist, civil cases can be different from criminal cases. Some civil cases are held before a jury, some are not. The point here is that judges (unlike juries, it appears) will not be swayed by anything they read, see or hear in the media. And we can be grateful for that. It would be unthinkable for a judge to admit that he or she could be influenced by what might be in the paper or on the radio or TV. So nothing published about a civil matter being heard by a judge will have a tendency to influence a judge. But what if the case were to be heard before a jury? The law is not so confident about juries not being influenced by media reports.

The *Sunday Times* in London conducted an investigation into the matter of what was known about the drug thalidomide at the time it was being prescribed to help pregnant women deal with morning sickness. It was eventually revealed by an Australian doctor (who later became involved in a scandal of his own) that thalidomide was responsible for causing terrible deformities among babies born to mothers who had taken the drug. Some of the victims had commenced legal action against the company that produced thalidomide and the case had dragged on for years (although no trial had yet commenced). When the company became aware the *Sunday Times* article was set to appear, it sought an injunction to prohibit publication. The injunction was granted (A-G v. Times Newspapers (1973)). The Lords said an article which could influence jurors, or witnesses, or the public against the company was "intrinsically objectionable". Despite the different circumstances that prevail in cases heard by, or to be heard by a judge, and those heard by, or to be heard by, a jury (judges are not influenced by the media . . . juries may be, it is suspected) the authors of *Media Law in Australia* noted that "where a jury trial is pending, the greatest caution is needed" (p. 105).

Courts in Australia have generally taken a relaxed attitude to the reporting of civil trials. But the advice above cannot be ignored. Whether a jury may be involved in a case is a matter that may not be determined until quite late in the process.

The Luna Park case: *A-G (NSW) v. Mirror Newspapers* [1980] 1 NSLR 374

A fire in a ghost train in a Sydney amusement park was responsible for the deaths of some of those taking the ride. Ultimately the matter came before a coroner. A newspaper published an article in which an attendant at the park (who was to give evidence before the coroner) was critical of some of the evidence already given. That paper was fined for contempt. It was held that the attendant might be inclined, when giving evidence to the coroner, to stick to the version he had already given the paper; and that other witnesses might feel intimidated if their evidence could be subjected to public attack.

Thus interviewing witnesses for a story, even in the case of a coronial inquiry, let alone a trial, is likely to be contemptuous.

The BLF case: *Victoria v. Australian Building Construction Employees' and Builders Labourers' Federation* [1982] HCA 31; (1982) 152 CLR 25

We have dealt with situations involving criminal trials, civil trials and coronial inquests. There is one more environment we need to consider where material relevant to a trial might be reported.

At the time a Royal Commission was being held into the practices of the Builders Labourers' Federation, a case was mounted in the Federal Court to have the union deregistered. The union claimed the Royal Commission would be in contempt of the Federal Court if it continued its investigation. The High Court, however, rejected this view on the grounds that there was sufficient separation between the two matters for both to proceed.

This issue of separation was also highlighted in two other significant cases – the *Bread Manufacturers* case and the *Rigby* case.

The Bread Manufacturers case: *Ex Parte Bread Manufacturers Ltd; Re Truth and Sportsman Ltd* (1937) 37 SR (NSW)

This case involved a bread carter who was suing Bread Manufacturers Ltd for defamation. A newspaper began running a series of articles suggesting the same company was acting as a cartel, keeping bread prices artificially high and putting pressure on smaller operators.

The paper was cited for contempt on the grounds that the articles could have influenced a jury in the defamation case. However, the judge hearing the contempt matter said the discussion of public affairs could not be "suspended" just because such discussion, "as an incidental but not intended by-product", might cause some disadvantage to a litigant at the time.

The Rigby case: *John Fairfax & Sons Pty Ltd v. McRae* [1955] HCA 12; (1955) 93 CLR 351

In the *Bread Manufacturers* case it was recognised that the paper had been unaware of the defamation action that had been commenced. However, in the *Rigby* case, the newspaper had been aware that Rigby had been charged with certain offences.

Its story revolved around a statutory declaration he had made asserting police violence against him, and a letter his solicitors had written to the Premier calling for an investigation into the police service. The High Court said the *Herald*'s article was not contemptuous as there had been continuing controversy about the police force and its administration, the lawyers' claim that Rigby had been falsely charged had to be seen in the context of some wider concern about the police, and the police violence complained of post-dated the matters over which Rigby had been charged.

Summary

What the *BLF*, *Bread Manufacturers* and *Rigby* cases mean is this: whether an article you publish will be determined to be in contempt or not will depend on how directly, or tangentially, your article related to a matter before the courts (and not necessarily at the trial stage) and whether the story might interfere with someone's right to a fair trial. If the article can be seen to be directly connected, and thus possibly prejudicial, you may have a problem on your hands. If it can be argued that there is no direct link, your lawyers will probably have a look at the *Bread Manufacturers* and *Rigby* judgments for some assistance with your argument.

Are juries swayed by the media anyway?

Despite the reality that an untold number of cases have been heard in the British legal environment over hundreds of years, little effort has been made to discover whether juries are, in fact, influenced by the media. Of itself this seems quite remarkable, given the time and effort put into researching other issues that bother us as a society. And there is another confounding element in this matter. The United States does not have the same restrictions on its media that exist in the United Kingdom and Australia, and other places that cling to the British system. Could it be, then, that Americans don't get a fair trial when they face the courts? That is the serious question that must arise from the differences between the two environments.

We have almost no knowledge of what goes on in jury rooms. Indeed in Queensland, as a consequence of what happened in a most celebrated (and disturbing) case of strange things happening in a jury room (see *Joh's Jury*, ABC TV), the authorities moved to pull an even tighter veil of secrecy around jury deliberations. Given the disturbing nature of what took place, it might have been thought that more light rather than less was needed on juries' deliberations. But in Queensland the light has been all-but turned off. It is now probable that a media organisation would commit an offence against the *Jury Act* if it were to re-publish the widely disseminated material the jurors divulged about what went on during the *Joh's Jury* deliberations.

What can be published when?

Pre-arrest

If the course of justice has not begun to run, nobody's fair trial can be jeopardised. As far as the law is concerned, juror's memories apparently do not kick in until someone has been charged with an offence. Indeed the cautious approach sees the point at which a person is arrested as the time at which the *Packer v. Peacock* decision begins to take effect. Prior to arrest, the media may report what they like, at least in terms of "contempt". You can't be in contempt of court if there is no court action under way . . . unless it could be shown that you set out to deliberately derail a potential court action. However, remember that defamation is another matter altogether, and publishing defamatory material about someone following the commission of a crime and prior to arrest could see an action brought against you. So exercise normal care in that regard.

Indeed all manner of prejudicial, not to mention defamatory, material may be published at this time without the prospect of contempt or defamation proceedings being instituted against you – providing the authorities ask you to publish it, or provide it to you for publication. The police may seek **your** cooperation in an effort to gain **public** cooperation and assistance to find an offender. Identikit drawings and security camera pictures and detailed descriptions of suspects police might be seeking "to assist" their inquiries may be published. If the pictures look like someone else, and in the end bear no resemblance to the offender whatsoever, it will not be a problem, if, as a journalist, you were asked by the appropriate authorities to assist. You will not have to worry if they got it wrong and the material resembles someone else.

Police recently released very detailed descriptions of some individuals and their car after a girl complained she had been the victim of an attempted abduction. Had there been men out there who fitted those descriptions they would have been instantly recognisable, given the detail that was published about them. So detailed were the descriptions it would have been a particularly interesting time for anyone who matched the information provided by the girl. They would have needed a good alibi. Some days later the girl said she had made it all up. Any unfortunate who had fitted her bogus description might then have taken to carrying a placard saying "It wasn't me!" but that is all they would have been able to do. The media, in assisting the community to find an offender, at the request of the authorities, is not liable for the accuracy of the information provided by those authorities, or its unintended consequences. But if the material does not come with official approval, that is an entirely different matter.

According to the law, a potential juror who might see identikit pictures or security camera footage or hear detailed descriptions of individuals being sought in connection with crimes prior to an arrest, is either able to erase the material from his or her memory if selected for a jury, or is capable of ignoring it. Once an arrest is made, neither of those things, it seems, is possible. Hence the *Packer v. Peacock* decision.

Arrest/charges

Apart from what might be said in a court, once someone has been arrested, the prudent will publish only the "bare extrinsic facts" that any witness to the crime might have ascertained. So private investigations by the newsroom sleuth into what happened, interviews with victims or witnesses, speculation about the guilt **or innocence** of anyone charged, and so on, that go beyond the "bare extrinsic facts" are likely to be seen as contemptuous. To be precise, the point at which legal proceedings commence is when a person is charged, but this moment may not be easily ascertained and so, for practical purposes, the point of arrest should be taken as the beginning of the sub judice period.

There is nothing to prevent you publishing material in which a person charged claims he or she is innocent. That will not interfere with their quest for justice. But let **them** do it. Do not do it for them, for your suggesting that someone is innocent is seen by the courts no differently from your suggesting they are guilty.

The first steps in the trial process may involve arrest, or the issuing of a warrant for a person to be arrested, or the issuing of a summons for a person to appear to answer a charge. If an arrest is made, the individual will be charged with an offence that he or she did something (or omitted to do something) that breached the law. Depending on the seriousness of the offence the person may be released by the police, given watch-house bail or held in custody until the earliest opportunity to appear before a magistrate. The magistrate might deal with the matter at that time (should the offender admit the offence), or might set a date for the person to reappear before the court for the matter to be dealt with. The magistrate may also determine whether to grant bail (if the person had been detained by the police in custody) or continue bail (if that had been granted by the police).

Such appearances are usually brief, and what is said can usually be reported. However, reporters have to be aware that the magistrate may order that something not be published (issue a suppression order) and there could be a range of issues (in the case of sexual offences, for instance) that might prevent the publication of the identity of the person charged. There could also be matters raised in connection with bail that may not be published.

By the time an individual appears before a magistrate (which should occur as soon as practicable after arrest) the legal process has clearly begun and the sub judice rules apply. At this stage the matter of bail, or continued bail, will be raised. This is an interesting stage in the proceedings. The police may object to the granting of bail and in doing so may raise matters about the alleged offender that go beyond the basic facts of whatever it was that caused him or her to be arrested. For example, the person might have a history of offending, a serious criminal record and/or a history of skipping bail. You will need to know what the rules about publishing such material are in your jurisdiction. You may or may not be able to publish.

The magistrate will decide whether to grant bail or not and will determine a date when the person has to appear before the court again. This will allow the defendant time to organise a defence and arrange legal representation and the police to prepare a case for the prosecution. These things may be settled by the time of the next appearance, but they may not. If not, the magistrate will set another date for the matter to return to court. Magistrates do not necessarily accept that these appearances can go on forever and have been known to dismiss cases because the prosecution of them had taken too long. Assuming this does not happen, a hearing known as a committal or "an examination of witnesses", which is the next stage in the process, will be held.

Committal

This is a hearing held before a magistrate, who will determine if there is sufficient evidence for a jury to make a decision as to the guilt or innocence of the accused. The magistrate will not determine either way. He or she will simply determine if there is evidence sufficient for a jury to be able to make up its mind. If so, the alleged offender will be committed to stand trial at a later date. If not, the case against the person will be dismissed and the matter closed.

In some cases (but rarely) a person charged with an offence may seek to go straight to trial without going through the committal process.

Committal hearings and the evidence presented (unless specifically prohibited) may be reported even though what is presented may be one-sided. The defence case is not put at this stage, although the defence may question witnesses. Journalists should also be aware that magistrates may order that something not be published (issue a suppression order) or may close the court (if matters relating to a sexual offence, for instance, emerge).

Assuming the magistrate is satisfied there is sufficient evidence for a jury to make up its mind, the matter will go to trial.

Trial

Matters that go to trial are the subject of what is called "an indictment". An indictment sets out the detail of the law that was broken and how it is alleged that this was done.

At trial the accused will be asked to plead – guilty or not guilty – of the matter/s contained in the indictment. If the plea is guilty the judge may deal with the matter immediately. All that has to be done is for him or her to determine the penalty to be imposed. There will be a summary of the case, the prosecution will outline the circumstances, and the defence will make a submission about matters that might be in the accused person's favour and might be considered as mitigating in the circumstances involved. There may be character references which speak well of the defendant and these can be raised. The judge will sum up the case and decide a penalty.

Journalists need to be aware that there are such things as *Penalties and Sentences Acts* and these set out matters that a judge has to consider in establishing a penalty (see the section on penalties and sentencing). As well, the dual issues of precedent and consistency apply. What kind of sentences have been determined in similar cases in the past? If one offender before Judge A gets 10 years and another before judge B gets 12 months, and the circumstances are roughly identical, there might be some disquiet in the community. So sentences handed down in similar cases may be considered as well. The judge will then pronounce the penalty and the court will rise. It could all be over in half an hour.

If the plea is "not guilty", the matter (as an indictable offence) will go before a jury. A jury will then be selected and sworn in.

The rules about reporting jury trials are clear. Reports must be "fair and accurate".

Fairness and accuracy

It has long been settled that unless there is good reason to the contrary the courts should be open to the public. (It has also long been settled that there **can** be good reason to close the courts to the public.) The notion of open courts is central to the notion of open justice. Therefore, unless there is good reason, the press may report to the community at large what goes on in our courts. But such reports of proceedings must be "fair and accurate".

A trial may last several days, or weeks, and sometimes months. The case against the defendant is presented first and this of itself may take quite some time. A single witness may be questioned by the prosecutor for an entire day's proceedings, or more. This necessarily means that a reporter writing a story about what happened may be able to present material from only one side of the case. It also means that to be "fair", whenever the defence presents its case, that has to be reported too.

The two stories do not have to be of the same length and do not have to appear on the same page. But the treatment has to seen as "fair" – by a fair-minded person. Thus coverage of one side of a case across four columns under a huge headline on page three and coverage of the other side in just three pars of five-point type tucked away at the back of the Business section on page 53, is unlikely to be considered "fair" reporting.

Accuracy speaks for itself: reporters have to get it right. Honest mistakes are not acceptable. Reporters, unlike other mortals, are not allowed to make mistakes. But achieving accuracy is not necessarily an easy task. Magistrates, judges and lawyers may, or more likely may not, care two bits about you, nor the demand that you cover cases fairly and accurately. They will care if you don't, but up to that point whether you can hear their submissions, their exchanges, what witnesses tell the court, and so on, may not bother them one skerrick. Lawyers and court staff may assist you with the spelling of names and so on, or they may not.

An interesting thing about the court process is the double standard that can be applied to you as a reporter. While some will be extraordinarily helpful, others involved in the process will do as little as possible to assist you, but will be absolutely furious, and may want you dealt with, if you should get anything wrong.

From time to time statements are made about how important it is that the courts be open to the public (and therefore the press who report them on behalf of the public) but little or nothing may be done to encourage the "fair and accurate" reporting that is demanded, by providing reporters with basic assistance to do their jobs. The situation is highlighted by the advice sometimes handed out to those who do report the courts: you have to "get to know" the people involved. That may involve a straightforward, courteous, professional relationship, or it may require an obsequious, cap-in-hand, forelock-tugging relationship – which is what some people in the system demand. And that is outrageous.

Whatever the hurdles, the legal demand exists: your reports must be fair and accurate.

If you are not reporting what took place in court, the demands of *Packer v. Peacock* apply.

Open court

With some exceptions, whatever is heard in "open court" may be reported. "Open court" means in the presence of the jury. If the jury leaves the court-room (while the prosecution and defence argue points of law for instance, or the judge hears submissions about evidence that should or should not be presented), such material cannot be reported while the trial is in progress (i.e. while the course of justice is running). To do so would be a contempt, and causing a jury trial to be aborted is not a good idea. If the jury is not to hear something in the courtroom, they clearly ought not to be able to read it in a newspaper or hear it on the radio or TV.

I said earlier that as a reporter, taking the opportunity to leave the court-room when a jury is out is not a good idea. For although the matters heard in the absence of the jury **cannot** be reported at that time, there is no reason why they cannot be reported once the course of justice has been run. If nobody's fair trial can be prejudiced, reporting what the jury did not hear cannot be a detriment to the person accused at the time. They will have been acquitted or dealt with.

A significant example occurred when a former police commissioner went to trial over matters uncovered by a Royal Commission into corruption in the state concerned. *The Courier-Mail*'s reporter, Jason Gagliardi, faithfully recorded the exchanges that took place between counsel and the judge in relation to the admissibility of certain evidence. The judge determined that quite a deal of evidence was not admissible and it was not placed before the jury (the issue is dealt with in the section on judge's discretion, above). In bringing this material to public attention after the trial was over, the reporter and the paper performed a great service by informing people about the ways of the law. Despite the judge's rulings and a suggestion that there was not enough evidence to convict him, the individual was found guilty and sentenced to a term in jail. However, at the time some people were greatly surprised to discover the amount and content of material relating to the case that the jury did not hear. Others said the judge exercised appropriate caution in not allowing certain evidence to be admitted. There was thus little likelihood of an appeal succeeding on the grounds the judge had erred in what he had allowed the jury to hear. Nevertheless, the message is clear. When the jury is out, keep writing.

I have heard of individuals on the bench rebuking reporters for continuing to make notes while a jury in a trial was out of the courtroom. The fact is, judges may not like it, but reporters may make notes of whatever they like in a courtroom. It is what they publish that is the issue.

Off the record

Unlike the rest of us, judges have the power to say that something that was said was not said. Thus, in court, the appropriateness of a question from counsel to a witness might be challenged. Reporters should be aware that if the objection is sustained, it will be "struck from the record" and the jury will be told to ignore it. Reporters have to do likewise. It didn't happen. Judges and magistrates can also issue suppression orders prohibiting publication of material presented in court. An order banning publication of something means what it says. Publishing is banned.

When does the course of justice end?

A question that arises, of course, is when precisely is the course of justice over? The quick answer might be, when the trial is over, because if there were an appeal, it would be heard by an appeal court judge, not a jury. As we already know, judges are not held to be influenced by what is said in the media.

However, the course of justice may **not** be over at that stage. The trial may be over, but what if the jury could not make up its mind – a hung jury? In such a situation, there is no verdict and it will be a matter for the prosecuting authority (Director of Public Prosecutions Office, for example) to decide whether to go to trial again. Sometimes they do, sometimes they don't. And there could be an appeal.

Appeal

Guilty verdicts and sentences may be appealed. Acquittals may not. In other words, a person convicted of a crime may institute an appeal on various grounds:

- that the verdict was wrong in law (the judge misdirected the jury as to what the law meant or how it should be applied, for instance) or
- the judge permitted evidence to be heard that ought not to have been placed before the jury or
- certain material was withheld from the defence or
- the sentence handed down was too harsh.

The Crown (the State) may appeal that the sentence was too light. Obviously, given that it prosecuted the case, the Crown will not appeal a guilty verdict.

Now in reaching a decision, an appeal court will **not** be influenced by anything published about the case in the media. Nevertheless, as indicated above, an appeal court may decide that the verdict was not sound, and may quash a guilty verdict entirely. It happens. The celebrated cases of former political figure Pauline Hanson and former Queensland Chief Magistrate Di Fingleton are two that come to mind. So there may be a retrial, in which case the course of justice is, indeed, not yet over. If that is the case and a second trial held, the question then becomes: could anything published after the first trial have a tendency to be prejudicial to the interests of the accused at the second trial?

It is likely there would be some lapse of time before the second trial could begin, but that is a matter that will be determined more by the court's schedule and workload rather than the need for the prosecution and defence to organise their cases. They have already done that once and should be ready to start again quite quickly.

There is a fixed period in which an appeal may be lodged – usually a matter of a few weeks. Clearly if an appeal were to be lodged, the course of justice will **not** have been completely run. A date for such an appeal hearing could be months away. Then, if that decision were to go against the accused, and there were grounds, the High Court of Australia might agree to hear a further appeal. More months could go by. The appeal process may put some "distance" between the publication of a story at the end of a trial and the commencement of a second trial (if that should be granted). And that "distance" may limit the possibility of any prejudice arising. But in such a case, the course of justice has not run its full course and will not have until the second trial is over.

There is one more circumstance in which the end of a trial may not be the end of the course of justice. What if the jury cannot agree – what is known as a "hung" jury? In such a case the jury will be discharged, and the trial aborted. The Crown may decide to go ahead with a second trial. The course of justice is thus still running.

If there is a second trial, do not then report that there had been an earlier trial and the jury could not make up its mind. Such a statement might have some influence on a juror or potential juror. And there is also the chance that a person convicted or acquitted of an offence, or offences, may face other charges and another trial sometime in the future.

It is generally believed that, since appeal court judges will not be influenced by what appears in the media, once a trial is over the media can publish material they could not publish while the trial was in progress. But there is a chance, as we have seen, this may not be so.

Defamation

We have not yet covered the matter of defamation, but at the stage where an appeal may be lodged, and until it is heard, care should be exercised as to what is published about someone convicted of a crime. A person who has been convicted may not have much of a reputation to protect, and what might be published about such a person may **not** constitute a serious defamation risk. But what if the individual were eventually to have the conviction quashed by an appeal court? That person's reputation would still be intact, and as we shall see, in a defamation sense that could be a serious matter.

Statutory contempt

The constraints on journalists that flow from common law contempt decisions apply equally throughout the land and affect journalists and publishers alike, regardless of what state or territory they may be in. But these constraints are not all there is to know. Apart from the case law we have covered, there are other kinds of contempt that are spelled out in legislation. These are called statutory contempt.

Anything which might undermine the authority of the law or bring it into disrepute may be treated as a contempt. Ignoring an order of a court, scandalising a court, behaving badly in court or showing "disrespect" or "contempt" for a court, can be dealt with as a contempt. Unlike other offences, these can be dealt with on the spot. Immediately. A magistrate or judge can thus become victim, witness, prosecutor, judge and jury all at once and deal with you "summarily".

> ### Guilty until proven innocent
>
> Unlike all other cases in which you may be dealt with by the courts (apart from one, defamation), in the matter of contempt of court, common law or statutory, you will be assumed to be **guilty** and have to plead your innocence. Not the other way round.

There are any number of statutes that deal with the treatment of matters before the courts. And the journalist has to know about these. The details may differ quite markedly from state to state and territory to territory. Journalists have to know their statutory contempt law as well as the demands of the common law.

This is an area then where no single set of "rules" or guidelines apply. After all, there are six states and two territories in Australia and there is federal law as well. And each may differ from all the others. The headings below indicate those areas where journalists may find themselves needing to know their local statutory contempt law. It will be up to each individual to check on what applies in that locality.

The court environment

Cameras and recorders

Generally speaking there are laws which prohibit the use of recorders and cameras in court and in the court precinct, including corridors. The use of such equipment may be approved in certain situations (ceremonial occasions for instance) but in general the prohibition on such equipment means reporters who cover courts need to be able to take good verbatim notes.

Non-publication orders

The operation and procedures of each of the courts will be governed by a relevant statute – the *Justices Act* (magistrates court), the *District Court Act* or *County Court Act*, the *Supreme Court Act*, for instance. Such Acts will specify, for example, the authority of the courts to allow or prohibit publication of matters brought before them. Non-publication orders, or suppression orders as they are usually known by journalists, mean exactly what their name suggests. Publication of material covered by such orders is an offence against the Act concerned and anyone who does publish such material can be dealt with.

Disobeying a lawful order of a court may also be mentioned separately in the statutes as a criminal offence. The penalties in that case could be even higher. If there is a Criminal Code or Crimes Act that applies in your jurisdiction, check it. Otherwise the possibility could be mentioned under a separate Act.

Coroners courts

In the main, coroners investigate unexplained or suspicious deaths and coroners have the authority to prohibit publication of information that comes before them. In some cases the legislation does not specify the grounds on which publication can be suppressed. Details vary, so the local *Coroners Act* or equivalent will have to be examined. In some jurisdictions, the statutes limit the publication of information concerning suicides. Reporters have to know what the limits might be.

Adoption of children

Documents, records and proceedings generally are not accessible and material may not be published anyway.

Bail

When an individual is arrested, he or she may be detained in a police watchhouse until that person can be taken before a magistrate, or given "watchhouse bail" by the police, released and required to attend a specified court hearing. At that appearance, the matter of the offence will be brought to the attention of a magistrate. Depending on the circumstances, the magistrate may deal with the matter immediately, or may give the defendant a chance to get legal assistance. In such a case, a date will be set when the matter must come before the court again, and the magistrate will determine whether to grant or continue bail. Both sides, the police (or prosecutor) and the defendant (or defence counsel), will have an opportunity to put a case to the magistrate for or against the granting of bail. The prosecution may oppose bail and in doing so may outline information about the accused that might indicate the person could be a serious risk to the community, or that the person had a history of offending . . . or a history of absconding.

The magistrate may place a non-publication order on such matter, or publishing such matter may be prohibited by the relevant *Bail Act*. You will have to know. If there is no ban, the matter can be reported, whether a potential juror is listening or not.

Depending on the jurisdiction and the offence concerned (such as murder), magistrates may not have the power to grant bail. Only the Supreme Court, for instance, might have such authority. Magistrates dealing with such cases in the preliminary stages of the process understandably become irritated when they read in the paper or hear on the radio that they "refused" to grant someone bail. The magistrate may not have had the power to do so, and you cannot say somebody refused to do something if he or she did not have the power to do it in the first place.

Identifying victims/parties

There will certainly be laws to prevent or limit the identification of complainants or victims in certain cases – those of a sexual nature, for instance, or parties generally in domestic matters (divorce, child custody and maintenance matters, and domestic violence), or matters relating to child offenders and witnesses. These laws may even mean that the identity of **offenders** may not be revealed since that information, combined with other information, may be sufficient to reveal the identity of a victim or a child.

Reporters should keep in mind that simply omitting a person's name or masking a photograph may not be considered sufficient to conceal the person's identity. A photograph which masks a person's face but reveals hair colour and style, jewellery, clothing, other people, a place, which together or separately might identify an individual, could be in breach of the law.

Children

Statutes will almost certainly prohibit the publication of matters relating to the identity of children as offenders, witnesses, or victims. Children's courts are also normally closed courts, unless special permission is granted otherwise. Unless a matter involving a child is serious enough to come before a higher court (murder for example), publishing anything about a case involving a child will likely be banned altogether.

The age at which a child becomes an adult is also something reporters need to know. For example, according to the law, children become adults at a younger age in Queensland than in the other states. In terms of the criminal law, a 17-year-old is an **adult** in Queensland (the *Juvenile Justice Act*), whereas a 17-year-old in the other states is a child. Ironically, if that same 17-year-old were at risk of some kind of harm, under Queensland's *Child Protection Act*, he or she would be a **child**, not an adult. The ramifications of this ridiculous situation for the media are obvious and serious. To reveal the identity of such a person if he or she were charged with a criminal offence would not be an issue, since he or she would be an adult for the purposes of the criminal law. But to reveal his or her identity as a person at risk of harm, or as a victim of abuse, or in care as a ward of the state, for instance, could incur a fine for a news organisation of tens of thousands of dollars. The reporter personally could also face a very steep fine.

Reporters also need to know what happens when someone who committed an offence as a child is subsequently dealt with as an adult. Getting that timeframe wrong can also result in an offence against the law. And the fines in these cases can be very steep.

Matrimonial matters

Once upon a time the divorce courts produced an endless stream of copy for certain newspapers. Not any more. It is now recognised that the breakdown of a relationship between two people is a private affair and thus the annulments of marriage, and consequent property settlements and any matters relating to the custody of children involved are also private matters. Family law is a federal matter and the *Family Law Act* prohibits identification of parties involved in such proceedings and settlements.

Domestic violence

The law relating to domestic violence or anyone seeking a domestic violence order against another may prohibit publication of anything that might identify anyone involved – apart from a police officer who might have been called on to intervene. The prohibition could include the identity of the victim spouse, the accused spouse, children and witnesses. Publication may be permitted by a court or in certain circumstances. Check for your version of the Act, such as the *Domestic and Family Violence Protection Act 1989* (Qld).

Sex offences

Different rules apply in different jurisdictions, but in general the identification of victims (complainants) of sexual assaults (rape, attempted rape, sexual assault and so on) is prohibited. Identification of others involved – the accused, witnesses, family members, in fact anyone or anything which may identify the victim – are also swept up in this prohibition. You need to know the detail of specific legislation, since the rules are not uniform across the states and territories and prohibition may not apply to all matters of a sex-related nature. For example, the identification of a prominent swimming coach in connection with a sex-related matter gained nationwide attention some years ago. Because the matter involved was not a "prescribed sexual offence" under the law in the state concerned, identification was not an issue.

The law as it relates to each jurisdiction has to be known, because in some cases publication of the identity of an accused may not be prohibited, whereas in others it may be, at least until after the committal stage.

Rehabilitation of offenders

In some circumstances a person who pays his or her debt to society and does not re-offend may be protected from having their past revisited in the media (and elsewhere for that matter). For example the *Criminal Law (Rehabilitation of Offenders Act)* in one state says, in summary, that;

> where an offender was convicted on indictment and ten years have elapsed or, where an offender was convicted other than on indictment and five years have elapsed and, in either case, had no later convictions recorded [anywhere], publication of those criminal convictions is prohibited where: a non-custodial sentence was imposed or, less than 30 months imprisonment imposed or, the offender was dealt with as a child, unless the person agrees to publication.

If you were not aware of this prohibition it might be quite easy to make a mistake.

Prisoners

Interviewing prisoners or even obtaining documents or recordings made by them may be prohibited. It is in some jurisdictions. Entering or attempting to enter a prison without permission, or more likely, assuming a false identity to do so, may also be offences. Check. They are in some jurisdictions. Photographing or attempting to photograph a prisoner, or a prison, or part of one, is another area where a breach of the law may be involved. Even publishing a photograph of a prison may be an offence. Whether the authorities would pursue such a matter these days is doubtful. Anyone interested in having a reasonably close look at the local jail or correctional centre need not wait for a newspaper to publish a picture. Google Earth provides very good overhead shots of such establishments from all around the globe.

Mental health matters

The identity of those who appear before bodies such as Mental Health Courts or Tribunals are likely to be protected. And identifying offenders who have been released from prison after receiving treatment for their condition is also likely to be an issue. The *Mental Health Act*, or an equivalent, should be one of the statutes you examine.

Jurors

This issue has been touched on briefly already. Laws relating to jurors vary from jurisdiction to jurisdiction. Revealing the content of jury room deliberations or votes taken, attempting to contact jurors, or revealing the identity of jurors, or nominating the cases concerned, may land the eager but misinformed reporter in hot water.

Jurors who reveal their identity themselves and approach reporters, rather than the other way round, may be a different matter. Check the *Jury Act* (or equivalent).

Penalties and sentencing

From time to time public outrage erupts over a sentence handed down in a court. This does not usually happen because the outraged feel the sentence was too harsh. You may have to write a story on the issue. It is as well that you should know a few things about sentencing so that you might see the issue in some sort of context.

The community expects that the law should operate and be applied consistently. One of the manifestations of this is referred to as the "rule of law". The Chief Justice of the High Court, Mr Justice Murray Gleeson, has put it this way:

> . . . The first two of the three aspects of the rule of law . . . regularity as opposed to arbitrariness or unconfined discretion, and equal subjection of all, the governors as well as the governed, to law, also reflect a view of the nature of law. Judgments in the High Court of Australia contain numerous assertions of practical conclusions said to be required by the principle of the rule of law. They include the following: . . . that citizens are equal before the law; and that the criminal law should operate uniformly in circumstances which are not materially different . . .

And New South Wales Chief Justice Jim Spigelman, has said:

> . . . A State cannot claim to be operating under the rule of law unless laws are administered fairly, rationally, predictably, consistently and impartially. Improper external influences, including inducements and pressures, are inconsistent with each of these objectives . . .
> . . . Improper influence, whether political pressure or bias or corruption, distorts all of these objectives.

And if you come across examples of someone being treated more favourably, or less favourably, by the law, you have the basis in the quotes above, for a good story. Sadly, it happens.

One aspect of the requirement that the law should be applied consistently, is the requirement that the law should deal with offenders consistently; that one person should not be jailed, for instance, for ten years and another get off with a good behaviour bond for committing much the same crime.

So when you go to court you may see the judge spend a little time considering the appropriate penalty to be applied in the case concerned. He or she may even hear the views of those at the bar table – the prosecution and the defence. They may raise examples of what happened in similar cases in the past. In addition, a matter that may have to be considered is whether the accused pleaded guilty. If so, the law may require that a guilty plea, and when it arose, be considered in the sentencing process. It may not stipulate that a lesser sentence should flow from a guilty plea, but it may require that such a matter be taken into account.

The judge may also order that a conviction not be recorded and it is useful to know what that means. Having a criminal record can be a bit of a burden. Some professions, such as the law, may be closed to someone with a criminal record. Some might find this ironic. But getting employment in some fields may not be easy for those with a criminal record. Judges therefore may determine, in the interests of encouraging an offender to stay out of trouble and not having to deal with obstacles such as those mentioned above, that a conviction not be recorded.

In effect this means that the only record of the conviction concerned will be held in the court itself, for reasons of possible appeal, or in the event that the offender should come to the notice of the court again, and so on. Publicly, however, there is no record of such a conviction, and apart from mentioning that no conviction was recorded at the time the sentence was pronounced, it is not something to be dredged up at some time in the future. Reporters should not do so.

In determining whether to record a conviction the judge or magistrate will be guided by the *Penalties and Sentences Act* (or its equivalent) that operates in the jurisdiction concerned. Such an Act may say, as indeed one does, that when considering whether to record a conviction a court should have regard to, for example, "all the circumstances of the case including **the nature of the offence, the age and character of the offender, the impact that recording a conviction might have on the offender's social and economic well being or his or her chances of finding employment**".

The point of the various matters raised above may mean that outrage and criticism of a sentence may not be well founded. On the other hand, of course, it may. And if that is the case, one of the jobs of the reporter is to report that outrage and criticism. But you do have to know the landscape in which a bushfire may be raging. Have a look at the *Penalties and Sentences Act* or its equivalent that operates in your patch. It is likely to be instructive, and could keep you out of trouble too.

Defamation

There are two areas of law where the normal rules, that a person should be innocent until proven guilty, do not apply. One is contempt, which was covered in the last chapter. The other is defamation. In the case of defamation you are assumed to be guilty and have to prove your innocence.

Just as contempt law attempts to balance an individual's right to a fair trial with the community's right to know what is going on, so defamation sets out to juggle some very important rights and competing interests – this time the right of individuals to their reputations versus the fundamentally important issues of freedom of speech, freedom of the press, and the public's right to know.

Defamation law in Australia was changed significantly on January 1, 2006. On that day, similar (not necessarily identical) sets of rules prevailed throughout most of Australia for the very first time. Until then, there were eight sets of rules – one for each of the six states and the two territories.

Much has been said over the years about the need for uniform defamation law in Australia and thus some things have been said in favour of the new regime that came into force at the beginning of 2006. Some not so favourable comments have been made as well, because there are losers in this matter too. But uniform defamation law is in force, so there is no point complaining. At the time of going to press there was little activity to indicate how well the new legislation was working. Time will tell.

Before we consider what the new uniform statute law says, we need to look at a few other things. First of all we need to understand very clearly what it is we are doing when as reporters we put pen to paper, or fingers to keyboards.

What is defamation?

There are three things necessary for a defamation to occur. The first is **publication**, the second is the content of that publication must have carried a **defamatory imputation** (or imputations), and the third is **identification**.

Publication

Every reporter who has ever written a story that has been printed or broadcast (or been read by a mate) has been involved in publishing. Publishing, or the act of publication, is making something known to another, or making it available to be known to another. It is obvious enough.

But there is a most important reality that is attached to any act of publishing and reporters have to appreciate it. The ink cannot be washed off the page. What is published cannot be unpublished. That reality was wonderfully put in the Rubyiat of Omar Khayam and the words should never be forgotten:

> The moving finger writes and having writ
> Moves on.
> Nor all your piety nor wit,
> Shall call it back to cancel half a line
> Nor all your tears wash out a word of it.

No amount of apology, anguish, tearing of hair or renting of clothes can ever unpublish anything once it has been published. The only way that might be done has so far not been achieved. It would require reversing the rotation of the earth around the sun, going back to the point where the decision to publish was made, and reversing that decision . . . and thus not publishing whatever it was that was published. Unless that can be done, anything published stays published. It is just a natural law.

Of course, there are those who believe their positions of authority mean they can ignore such realities. This is the kind of situation where, as a reporter, it is vital you understand and know the law so that you can keep a check on the powerful who, from time to time, attempt to exceed the authority we have vested in them. As a reporter you are not just in the courts to inform the public of what is happening there, you are there on our behalf to keep an eye on the magistrates and judges and the officials as well. By publishing your stories you also assist the community generally, by revealing to those who might break the law what can happen to them, but you are there for more than that. You are there to keep an eye on things. There are plenty of instances where the courts have gone off the rails.

Since no amount of tears will wash out a word of anything you publish, the act of publishing, like marriage, has to be taken seriously and not entered into lightly. Although of course it is much easier to get out of a marriage than it is to get out of publishing something you might wish you had not.

As is the case in contempt, your intention in the area of defamation is not an issue. You may not have intended a contempt or to publish something defamatory about someone, but that is no defence. It may ultimately be a mitigating factor in terms of damages, however, it will not excuse you from, or protect you against, a claim.

And furthermore, you will not be able to defend yourself against what you said, you will have to defend yourself against what the aggrieved party says you said.

That needs to be remembered.

Publishing a defamation

There is one small point about publishing a defamation . . . a very small point for the journalist, but it has to be mentioned. To publish a defamation requires that the defamatory material must come to the attention of someone other than the aggrieved party. In other words, you may say what you like about a person if that individual is the only one who knows what you said. You cannot damage someone's reputation by reflecting on it to that person alone. Defamation requires the matter be made available by the publisher to a third party. If the aggrieved party makes the matter available to others, you are not responsible for his or her action.

Defamatory imputation

The issue that will arise if someone is aggrieved by something you said or wrote is whether that material carried a "defamatory imputation" or, possibly, a number of "defamatory imputations".

The new uniform *Defamation Act* does not spell out what a defamatory imputation is. But the matter is well settled. Anything that might **disparage a person's reputation** or **cause ordinary decent folk in the community in general to think less of a person**, or hold a person up to **ridicule or contempt** or likely to cause others to **shun and avoid** an individual is defamatory of him or her.

That is the essence of the matter.

There are any number of cases where people's reputations have been found to have been "disparaged", while a good example of someone being held up to ridicule or contempt involved the publication of a photograph of a footballer naked in the locker room. And the most famous "shun and avoid" case was that of a woman who was portrayed in a movie as having been the victim of a rape.

Identification

A person who claims to have been defamed will have to be able to establish that he or she can be identified in connection with the offending material. If they are unable to establish that connection, the action should not succeed.

However, it is not necessary to name people to identify them. An address, a position, a description, could be enough.

Which raises a famous case that provides a useful lesson for the aspiring journalist – the case of Artemus Jones (*Hulton v. Jones* [1910] AC 20).

A **fictitious** "Artemus Jones" appeared in a humorous story in a British newspaper. Artemus was a married man and a church-goer, but he was frolicking abroad, according to the story, and generally enjoying himself. However, there was a real Artemus Jones living not far from where the story appeared. Although he did not quite fit the description of the man in the story, some witnesses said they thought the article referred to him. He sued and won.

There are a couple of morals in the Artemus Jones story. The first is your intentions do not matter. And the second is beware of fictitious characters in your stories. If they have surnames, in particular, check your bank balance.

In other words, if you are writing a story about a victim of some outrage and the person does not want to be identified, give him or her a first name only, put it in inverted commas, at least at the first mention, and it may not hurt to say it is not that person's real name as well.

Members of the public often wonder why it is that journalists, in their court reports in particular, go to a lot of bother reporting unimportant details about people. Who cares how many names they have, or their age, or occupation, or what suburb they live in, or even the name of the street they live in? Why do they write all that stuff? The simple answer is defamation. The journalist has to identify the individual concerned precisely lest someone else with the same name should claim that they have been wrongly reported as being a murderer or rapist or whatever.

There is a very serious message here for the new reporter covering courts in particular, but not just courts. You have to get all the details mentioned above, and they have to be accurate. Hearing them read out in court will not be enough. Someone you call Graham Sean Somebody might really be Graeme Shaun Somebody and if you were to write a story that identified the wrong person, you might find a defamation writ not far behind. So you need to see the name and the other details mentioned above written down. Taking someone's word for a spelling over the telephone is a dangerous practice. Serious matters are at stake.

Remember too, when dealing with common names for people, even their street address may not differentiate between individuals. How many John Smiths might there be on a major road that traverses several suburbs? That is why name, suburb, age and occupation are important. Unless you confine the identity of a person to that person, you may find someone else of the same name will claim you have defamed him or her.

Who cannot be defamed?

The list of those who cannot be defamed is not large. The dead cannot be defamed, but it is quite possible to defame a living person when talking about the dead. A suggestion that someone recently departed had constantly associated with undesirables, or enjoyed the company of loose women may not be appreciated by members of the company boards on which he had served, nor by his wife, for example. You may not be sued by the man's estate (because they cannot sue), but his wife, alive and well, may be a different matter.

The suggestion that groups and organisations cannot be defamed is true – up to a point. The issue of identification is important here too, because while a person may be affronted by what someone says about a group to which he or she belongs, the person may not be able to sue. The person may not have been identified. Someone may say something very uncomplimentary about the political party you have served faithfully for 20 years. But, despite your outrage, you are unlikely to have grounds for a defamation action. If the group is small enough, however, and you are identifiable, that could be a different matter.

Members of the board of a public company, for instance, rely on their reputations to secure funds from shareholders and the public generally. They may be successful in an action if they believe those reputations have been damaged. It has happened. The new Act says corporations established for profit with 10 employees or more cannot sue. Nor can public bodies (government entities for instance). But corporations with less than 10 employees, not-for-profit organisations (charities for instance), and individuals (who may be associated with larger corporations) are not barred from taking defamation action.

It should also be remembered that whilst public bodies and some corporations no longer have rights of action for defamation they may have other rights available to them, such as claims for negligent misstatement, injurious falsehood and breaches of the *Trade Practices Act*.

Living individuals, however, can certainly be defamed.

How?

You do not need to write or say something to publish a defamation. Mime, street theatre, a painting, smoke signals for that matter are all capable of conveying meaning and are thus capable of conveying a defamatory meaning – a defamatory imputation.

Fortunately, cartoonists, comics and comedians have escaped most actions for defamation and while their work may satirise, it is not necessarily seen as defamatory. A cartoon, like a skit on stage or a comedy line in a revue, is an exaggeration, an over-the-top bit of fun if you like. Nevertheless it is possible to cross the line and there could be defamatory imputations behind what may appear on the surface to be just good fun.

Definitions and meanings

While we need to know what the statute (the *Defamation Act*) says, we also need to know what judges have said (case law). The case law is important because it has established some of the definitions, or meanings, that set the ground rules involved in the world of defamation. And there are some important lessons in the case law for journalists.

The meaning of words

This is a landscape littered with traps for the unwary. For it is not the meaning of the words you intended when you said or wrote something that matters. Your intentions, your intended meanings, do not matter a jot. Words have literal meanings, but they may have other meanings too. And such meanings may be the ones that could cause you a defamation problem.

Not only is it necessary for you to exercise care in respect of the literal meaning of words used for the purposes of a story, it is also important to be wary of inadvertently conveying an innuendo. An innuendo may simply be an inference or it may require the proof of some extrinsic or outside fact. The following are three simple examples of the various forms of defamatory meaning:

> Literal meaning: Mrs Smith is frequently beaten by her husband.
> Innuendo: Mr Smith's wife is frequently observed to be battered and bruised.
> True innuendo: Mr Smith's wife has been observed to be residing at the hostel situated on the corner of Smith and Brown Streets.

In the third instance a true innuendo meaning arises if some or all of the readers of the report are aware that the address referred to is a women's shelter.

And who is the arbiter? The law says ordinary decent folk in the community taken in general or the right-thinking man. So if ordinary decent folk could be expected to detect in what you had written a meaning other than the one you intended, you could be in trouble.

Thus it might not be a good idea to describe a woman fitness fanatic who walks 10 kilometres a day around her local streets as a "street walker".

And while the "ordinary decent folk taken in general" test may exclude a particular section of the community who might object to something you wrote, it is as well to remember that specialist knowledge can allow for a defamatory imputation to be detected in your writing. So innocently suggesting that a woman walked the streets in such and such a suburb might be a problem if the streets of that suburb were known by locals as the regular beat of the city's prostitutes.

Defences

There are situations and circumstances where publishing defamatory matter will not present a problem for the journalist. These are areas where the public interest is seen to overwhelm the private interest of an individual who may be defamed. In some situations the person making the defamatory statements is granted protection from prosecution, or put another way, is said to enjoy either absolute or qualified privilege. Then there is the issue of truth. We will deal with them in turn.

Absolute privilege

Statements made in, and documents read into the record or tabled in or published by, our parliaments and courts and Royal Commissions are afforded absolute privilege.

Some people complain from time to time about parliament being a "coward's castle" because a Member has said something about them in parliament they claim to be defamatory. Usually such people go on to challenge the politician to say whatever it was outside the chamber. Were the Member to do so, he or she might very easily get a writ alleging defamation. But, if they confine their remarks to speaking in the parliament, they are protected by absolute privilege. The view is that, in the best interests of the community and for the good of society generally, members of parliament must be able to raise matters of concern without being inhibited by the fear of being sued.

The same views apply to the running of our courts. Witnesses who give testimony in court are likely to say things about an accused person, or anyone else for that matter, that may well carry defamatory imputations. If they were not protected from defamation action, they would be unlikely to give their evidence freely and the courts would become a farce. Absolute privilege provides them with protection.

Qualified privilege

Qualified privilege exists in two important circumstances for journalists.

The first is the area in which journalists report on matters covered by absolute privilege. Absolute privilege protects those who utter defamatory matter in the parliaments and courts. But if such people were to restate their remarks outside the parliaments or courts, they would have no protection. So, the question arises: assuming those who make such statements are unlikely to repeat their remarks publicly, and assuming that their defamatory remarks concern matters of public importance and interest, how could the public become aware of them?

The answer is qualified privilege. Those who report the proceedings of parliaments and the courts "accurately and fairly" are afforded qualified privilege. In other words, if the possibly defamatory material uttered in the parliament or a court is reported "accurately and fairly", the reporter is protected against an action for defamation. Again, the issue of qualified privilege acknowledges that the public interest may overwhelm an individual's private interest.

This qualified privilege may be extended to cover local government councils and even public meetings – provided the matter involved is in the public interest, the reporter acts "reasonably", is not actuated by malice and so far as the circumstances will permit, both sides of the story are published. Reporters need to know where the limits have been set, and that is why they need to have read the *Defamation Act*. Given that the current defamation regime is new, there is little about the law that has so far been tested in, or brought before, the courts. In such a situation, consulting a lawyer for advice is likely to be a good idea.

The second circumstance in which qualified privilege resides is one that provides much less comfort for the journalist.

Here is a scenario. You are working in an organisation and become aware that another member of staff is stealing widgets and sneaking them home every day in his or her lunchbox. You think this is dishonest and even a breach of the law. You go to your supervisor and explain what is going on. Such a report is bound to be defamatory (it is hard to imagine suggesting someone is a thief could enhance their reputation). So you have quite seriously defamed a workmate. Providing you were not actuated by malice or ill-will and you act "reasonably" (i.e. did not make the whole thing up), you would be covered by qualified privilege. Qualified privilege operates in a circumstance where you have a duty to report (you become aware that the organisation is being ripped off by an employee) and you report it to your supervisor, who has a duty to hear your report. That is one of the things about being a supervisor. You are given responsibilities to ensure the good, honest running of the company.

The issue here is one of reciprocity. And this is where the problem lies for journalists. As a checkout assistant you have a duty to report the theft outlined above. Your supervisor has a reciprocal duty to receive it. Thus, providing you act "reasonably" and you are not motivated by malice, etc., qualified privilege will protect you. But the courts have been loath to find equivalent circumstances exist in the case of the media. Despite the significance of the media and journalism as a "fourth estate", and the watchdog role they perform, the courts have taken a very limited view of the claim that there is any duty on the part of the media to report anything, and any duty on the part of the community to receive what the media report. Hence, outside those areas where statutory protection may have been legislated, there has been scant recognition of a claim for protection for journalists under a qualified privilege defence.

Regardless, there is a defence of qualified privilege contained in the new Act. But to mount a defence under this section requires that the publisher must have acted "reasonably" in gathering and presenting the story. The tests for "reasonableness" are so unreasonable and broad that it is unlikely anyone would contemplate such a defence. We will have to wait and see.

Truth

Under the new uniform defamation law, "truth" or "substantial truth" or "contextual truth" are defences you may claim. In a philosophical sense there are always arguments about what constitutes "truth" – my view of the "truth" and someone else's may differ. But in the context of defamation law, if you can **demonstrate** that what you have said is the case, that there are facts or evidence to reveal it, then you may be able to establish a defence of "truth".

But it is very likely that anyone complaining about your story will claim there is not just one defamatory imputation that can be deduced from your publication. They may claim there are many such imputations. In some jurisdictions in the past, dealing with claims that a story contained multiple defamatory imputations has been a most serious issue for publishers. The new law says a defence can be based on the "substantial" truth of what you said or wrote, or that what you wrote was "substantially true".

It might be true, but can you prove it?

So you published a story and received a defamation writ. Your defence is "truth". No question about it. The story is true. But can you prove it? More to the point, can you prove it under the rules of evidence (see the chapter on Australian law)?

You may have 10 or 20 or 100 sources for your story, which is pretty good, but what if none of them will stand up in court and tell the court what they told you? And if the court should ask you who your sources were (and you will be asked), and you refuse (which you will), the court may not believe your story about what you said your sources told you. The judge may also get cross, advise you that you will be in contempt if you continue to refuse to answer questions about the identity of your sources, and give you a few minutes to think about it. By now you are looking at a jail sentence. Even if you don't get sent to jail, your defence against the defamation action may be looking more than a little shaky. Proving truth is not necessarily an easy matter.

Substantial truth

The new Act says at section 26: "It is a defence to the publication of defamatory matter if the defendant proves that the defamatory imputations carried by the matter of which the plaintiff complains are substantially true."

There is no definition given of what "substantially" means. And we may have to wait until some cases are determined to find out. On the surface it would appear to mean that a defendant does not have to prove the truth in relation to every defamatory imputation claimed by a plaintiff (as has been the case in certain jurisdictions in the past) but that, taken in general, the material published was true.

Contextual truth

This is a concept that bears some similarities to what was previously contained in the old New South Wales statute. In order to rely upon the defence of "contextual truth" under section 26 of the new Act, a reporter has to be able to prove that quite apart from the defamatory imputations complained of by the plaintiff, there are one or more other imputations contained in the story (contextual imputations), which can be proven to be substantially true. It must then be established that no further harm has been caused to the plaintiff's reputation by virtue of the substantial truth of the contextual imputations.

Or to put it another way, if a publisher published a story alleging that a person was a tax evader and had a conviction for car theft, a defence of "contextual truth" may be successfully argued if the publisher can prove the conviction for car theft even though he may be unable to substantiate the allegation pertaining to tax evasion. The person's reputation is not further harmed by virtue of the fact that he is proven to have a criminal conviction for car theft. It could be claimed that in the context of those things that were shown to be true, the one that was shown not to be true could not damage the plaintiff's reputation any further, since there wasn't much to damage.

Honest opinion

This defence bears some similarities to the former defence of "fair comment". What it means is, regardless of how mistaken your comments might be, you will have a defence against defamation if you can show:

- the opinion was honestly held at the time of publication
- it was not borne out of malice or ill-will (you were not trying to get back at someone for something, for instance)
- the comments were on a matter of public interest (not just some personal tittle-tat, scuttlebutt or salacious gossip) and
- the opinion was based on material that was either:
    a.   substantially true; or
    b.   was published on an occasion of either absolute or qualified privilege; or
    c.   was published on an occasion that attracted the protection of section 28 (defence for publication of public documents) or section 29 (defence of fair report of proceedings of public concern).

This last point is one of two reasons reporters need to keep comment and opinions out of their news stories.

To write a defamatory comment in a **news story** is to present such material as a fact, not comment or opinion. And that is a very different matter altogether. So it is important to separate the two. News stories are news stories and opinions are opinions. It is not just a good idea to make the separation quite clear, it is essential.

It would also be sensible to put a headline such as "Comment" on the opinion piece. Then there can be no doubt about which is which. The other reason why reporters should keep their comments out of news stories is, the reader wants the story and the views of others, not the views of the reporter, thank you very much. If the reporter wants to provide the reader with the benefit of his or her wisdom, he or she should do it somewhere else. The readers can read it there if they want to, but don't entangle it in a story with other people's comments and opinions.

Public document

Matter contained in "public documents" (or "fair" summaries of them) may be published without attracting an action for defamation provided that it is a fair report, that is done honestly for the information of the public or for the advancement of education. Broadly, "public documents" cover documents and records published by parliaments, governments and the courts.

Fair report

The Act says it is a defence against an action if the defendant can prove the matter complained of "was, or was contained in, a fair report of any proceedings of public concern". There is a long list of what constitutes such an environment, but, again, in broad terms, "proceedings of public concern" embrace those occurring in parliaments, courts, public inquiries, shareholders meetings and public meetings held on a matter of public interest, including election rallies and meetings. A "fair report" in the usual context of journalism is taken to mean one which accurately presents any differing points of view that may have been canvassed during such a meeting or proceeding. As with the defence of publication of public documents, this defence is defeated if it is proven that the defamatory matter was not published honestly for the information of the public or the advancement of education.

Political matter

In a case involving reporting of a matter dealing with issues of politics or government, the law recognises that the news media do have some responsibility to inform the public about what is going on in a democracy such as ours. The important point is that the matter has to do with politics or government. The case that established this point is known as the Lange case (*Lange v. Australian Broadcasting Corporation* (1997) 189 CLR 520).

Former New Zealand Prime Minister David Lange sued the Australian Broadcasting Corporation over a *Four Corners* program. In determining an appeal, the High Court overturned an earlier judgment that had substantially liberalised the defamation landscape in relation to the reporting of political matters. The original judgment had increased the scope of the common law definition of qualified privilege (reciprocal duty to report and receive information) to the role the media play in a democracy in informing citizens about issues of politics and government they are entitled to know.

By virtue of the High Court's subsequent decision, in order to rely upon the "political matter" defence, media organisations have to prove three things.

(1) They have the onus of proving that at the time of publication, reasonable grounds existed for believing the truth of any imputations that are found to arise.

(2) Those who were the subject of any imputations must, prior to publication, have been given a reasonable opportunity to respond to the allegations made against them.

(3) It must be shown that all proper steps were taken to verify the truth and accuracy of the story.

For all practical purposes, hope that you will not have to rely on the *Lange* decision to mount a defence against a defamation claim.

Innocent dissemination and triviality

"Innocent dissemination" and "triviality" are both seen as defences against an action for defamation. These mean: the newsagent who throws a newspaper onto the driveway of a subscriber to a newspaper which contains defamatory material can claim a defence as an "innocent disseminator"; and if a court should regard the defamatory imputations claimed by a plaintiff to be of no consequence in connection with that person's reputation or standing in the community, a defence of "triviality" may succeed. No real surprises there.

Other features of the new defamation law

Cap on damages

Under the new defamation law regime, the maximum amount of damages that can be awarded has been set at $250,000 (to be adjusted in line with the value of our money over time. A dollar today may not be worth as much in ten years time, thanks to inflation). This is a major change. In the past, defamation payouts involving much greater sums were awarded. In addition, exemplary damages (to make an example of) and punitive damages (to punish a defendant) now cannot be awarded.

Offer of amends

The new legislation also outlines procedures that may be followed so that aggrieved parties and publishers may settle matters out of court. These arrangements may involve the publication of an apology, payment of compensation for costs incurred, and the like. Significantly the law says that, should the matter go to court, an apology cannot be regarded as an admission of guilt. In the past publishers were reluctant to offer apologies because to do so might have been seen as an admission of guilt and major damages might have been awarded against them.

Time limit

The new Act sets a limit of a year after publication for a plaintiff to commence a defamation action. This limit may be extended by a court by an additional two years. The requirement in the new regime substantially reduces the timeframe for an action to be commenced in some jurisdictions, which formerly allowed for actions to be commenced up to six years following publication.

The "newspaper rule"

As a general rule, the court will normally not require a media organisation (not just newspapers) to reveal documents that expose the identity of their sources in a defamation action during pretrial proceedings. This, however, is not a hard and fast rule and each case will depend on its circumstances. It certainly does not protect journalists from having to reveal their sources at trial.

Myths, misconceptions and mistakes

Over the years I have heard students come up with all manner of strange ideas about defamation. Where and how these arose is a mystery, but they need to be dealt with in case anyone should take them to heart.

1. **This is a student publication. We are still learning, so we cannot be expected to know everything about the law**. Everyone in the court may feel sorry for you. But you should have waited until you had finished learning and then started publishing. As pointed out earlier, ignorance of the law is no excuse, not even for earnest student reporters.

2. **It's the publisher who gets sued, not the reporter**. Sadly this is not so. In fact, virtually everyone in the chain can be sued. Your employer may cover you, so you may not have to pay. Let us hope that is the arrangement, but it might be a good idea to check. The same issue arises in the matter of contempt. As recently as 2006, in both Melbourne and Adelaide, executives as well as the news organisation involved were fined over matters of contempt.

3. **I can publish. My source is impeccable**. Is there any other kind? While your source may be beyond reproach, that is not the issue. The issue is, can you or your source prove what was said? And further, is your impeccable source prepared to go into the witness box? Your telling the court your version of what was said will, most likely, not be good enough. And if your impeccable source does not want to be identified, would you breach that confidence and reveal the person's identity to the court? Of course not. Which will put you in an interesting position because the court will start getting angry with you.

4. **I can publish, because my source is the Lord Mayor**. If you look at the list of defences above, you will not find one headed "Eminence Excuse" or "Famous Name Exemption". If you cannot claim one of the defences that are listed above, it matters not a jot who your source is. Famous, important, or powerful will not make any difference. It wasn't a defamation matter, but a newspaper was fined a very large sum of money for reporting the words of a state premier. It was a contempt matter and the premier was also fined many thousands of dollars. The same risk applies in the area of defamation. Don't drop your guard just because you are quoting a bigshot.

5. **Spring cleans are good. You can throw out all the old stuff you never use**. Don't throw out anything for at least three years, particularly your notebooks and any tape recordings of interviews you conducted, or witness statements if you happen to have any. You should keep them for three years. Just in case.

6. **It's okay, I can publish because it's in the public interest**. It may well be in the public interest, but is it true, or substantially true? That will be the test. If it is true, you won't need to worry about the issue of public interest. Truth alone is a defence. There is no defence of "Public Interest".

7. **It's deadline. We have to go with it**. Deadlines are not a defence either. If there is any doubt, leave it out.

8. **I didn't say it "was", I said it was "alleged"**. The suggestion that you can get around the problem of defamation by saying something was an allegation, will not save you. In fact it could make it worse. To report an allegation without some effort to check may not be well regarded if the matter goes to trial. But remember, this is a different set of circumstances from a report of a court proceeding. In such a situation all the things that emerge in connection with an offence being argued in court are allegations or claims until they are admitted (defendant pleads guilty) or the jury brings in a guilty verdict. Refer to them as such. Don't turn unproven allegations into facts in a court report – at least not before the jury decides.

One last word

Defamations are published all the time. There are some obvious reasons – there is a watertight defence; it was a court report or a report on Question Time in parliament; given what else might emerge during the discovery process, they will never sue; it's worth the risk.

But the fact remains that most defamations that cause problems occur because no one saw the problem in the first place. If they had they would have done something about it.

And, of course, often it is impossible to say if something is defamatory until the jury decides.

Knowing your rights

Unless you know what the law says you may get into hot water, as has been discussed in the previous pages. But you also need to know what the law says for another reason – to protect your rights as a citizen, and as a reporter.

Sadly, you cannot assume that those you deal with will always play by the rules, and unless you know what the law says they may well attempt to pull the wool over your eyes. Some people are inclined to extend their authority if they can get away with it. Given the chance, they may attempt to bluff or bluster you in an effort to hinder or prevent your legitimate work. Or they may make a genuine mistake, though this is much less likely in my experience.

The following, then, may assist you. If necessary, you may have to point out some, or all, of the following to anyone who might fit the description above. Remember, statute law overwhelms case law, so you will have to know whether there are particular pieces of legislation that may override the following. It is imperative that you know the law.

"Publicity is the soul of justice"

The judgment in the case of *Scott v. Scott* (1913) AC 417 is one you should carve into your memory. The case itself was a little tawdry, but the judgment is a gem for the journalist and for the community at large, for it wrote into law the notion that unless there are compelling reasons to the contrary (including statute law), justice must not only be done, **it must be seen to be done**.

There was a divorce case and the detail became, we might say, a bit tacky. The detail of the case, however, doesn't matter. What matters is that after the case, the woman involved sent a transcript of the proceedings of the hearings to her former in-laws to reveal that she was not the one responsible for the breakdown of their son's marriage. She was charged with contempt, since the judge had determined the proceedings should be held in private.

The Lords were not impressed with the decision to hear the case in private and made it clear that unless the ends of justice required it, courts should be held in public, or to put it another way, courts should not be held in secret. Lord Shaw famously quoted the words of the 18th century jurist and philosopher Jeremy Bentham (of Benthamism – the greatest good for the greatest number – fame) who said:

> Where there is no publicity there is no justice. Publicity is the very soul of justice. It is the very spur to exertion and the surest of all guards against improbity.

I recommend that you commit that extract to memory. And the case reference too. It is the law. And some day you may need to remind someone what the law says. Unless there is a statute somewhere (and there are) that overrides the above, do not be afraid to raise it. Judges and magistrates and those who oversee the administration of the courts have to obey the law too.

If the day should arrive when it becomes necessary for you to remind someone (because they will surely know) of *Scott v. Scott*, you might also remind, or inform, them of a couple of other judgments. These are also worth committing to memory – I am eternally grateful to the person who originally drew them to my attention.

In the first, *Mahliklili Dhalamani v. The King* (1942) AC 583 at 590, the Privy Council said:

> Prima facie, the failure to hold the whole of the proceedings in public must amount to such a disregard of the forms of justice as to lead to substantial and grave injustice.

In the second, *R v. Sussex JJ Exparte McCarthy* (1924) 1. K. B. 256 at 259, Lord Hewatt CJ said: ". . . justice should not only be done, but manifestly and undoubtedly be seen to be done".

It is to be hoped that the above will be sufficient.

The public interest

The courts have looked at the matter of the public interest, and the words of Morris LJ (*Ellis v. Home Office* (1953) 2 QB 135; 1953 All ER 149) are instructive. He said:

> One feature of the public interest is that justice should always be done and should be seen to be done.

Another observation about the "public interest" from the bench in London, *Artists Ltd v. Littler* (1969) 2 QB 375, said:

> Whenever a matter is to affect people at large, so that they may be legitimately interested in, or concerned at, what is going on, or what may happen to them or others; then it is a matter of public interest on which everyone is entitled to make fair comment.

Both the above are worth remembering. You may need to remind some people that there is such a thing as the public interest and it cannot be dismissed or ignored.

If that is what the judges have said, what do the statutes say?

The statutes, wherever you are, may have something to say on the matter of open courts. You'd better check. For example, section 70 of the *Justices Act* in Queensland provides the following:

> The room or place in which justices sit to hear and determine any complaint upon which a conviction or order may be made, [i.e. a magistrates court] shall be determined an open and public court, to which all persons may have access . . .
> . . . provided nevertheless that in any case in which, in the opinion of the justices, the interests of **public morality** [emphasis added] require that all or any persons should be excluded from the Court, the justices may exclude such persons accordingly . . .

In this case, the scope of the grounds on which the public (and thus journalists) may be excluded, i.e. public morality, is not great. Is there anything that might be heard in court today, or anywhere else for that matter, that would offend against current notions of public morality? And thus if a hearing were to be held in camera, as a journalist you would want to know why, and how the reason fitted within the law.

Section 71 of the Queensland *Justices Act* is also illustrative. It says, in essence, that the place where examinations of witnesses (committal hearings) are held shall **not** be an "open court" and nobody may attend such hearings without the magistrate's permission, except that this may occur only if the magistrate believes the ends of justice will be served by **excluding** members of the public.

If such proceedings were to be closed, as a journalist you would want to know why. The law is well established that courts should not be held in secret (unless there is an overwhelming reason). Nor is it acceptable that some people should have to face the courts publicly, while others be granted anonymity.

Publicity about the things that go on in courts is important for another reason. Such publicity, or the potential for publicity, may have an important influence on members of the community generally. It may help to keep them from being tempted to break the law. Thus the media play an important role in the functioning of a law-abiding society. And this is another reason why the hurdles placed before reporters in covering courts are so objectionable.

Accessing court records

Higher courts

Transcripts of proceedings

Accessing records of District (or County) or Supreme Court hearings should not be difficult. Court reporters record the proceedings (which are also taped) and transcripts of cases generally become available within a matter of hours or days of a case being heard. Decisions, however, can be reserved and a judge may take some time to deliver a finding. Judges can also take some time in checking the paperwork before it becomes available.

Transcripts are not likely to be any use to the reporter covering the courts day to day. They will not be ready in time. But they can be very useful for those doing stories with a longer timeframe. Copies of transcripts can cost a lot of money and the copying process will take more time. But when there is a complicated story to cover, or a need for careful scrutiny and examination of the record, there is no alternative. On the other hand, reporters (or the public) are usually allowed to peruse such documents at the relevant office where they are held without charge, and to take notes as they read.

Files

Records of documents related to cases heard in District (County) and Supreme Courts can be accessed too. Such records may include writs, details of claims, submissions made by the parties, judgments, and so on. There will almost certainly be a fee, unless you are a recognised court reporter. If that is the case, one of your jobs may be to check what writs have been issued each day and this material may be provided for you to look at without charge.

Records of cases heard in chambers (not in public before a jury) can also be accessed at the relevant court registries.

Procedures vary, but to obtain District (County) or Supreme Court records you may need to complete a request form. You will need to give as much detail as you can about the case (who the parties were, judge's name perhaps, date, etc.) and you may be asked to give a reason for seeking such records. It goes without saying, that you must be sure to give an accurate answer. If you are researching a story, say so. Don't hedge or give the impression you are there on behalf of one of the parties.

When the file is delivered, you may read it and make notes. Make good notes. If you have to go back you will have to pay another fee.

Magistrates (or local) courts

Transcripts and files

Obtaining documents, transcripts and files at the Magistrates or Local Court level can be quite another matter. Again, different rules apply in different jurisdictions and journalists tell different stories of their experiences. Access may not be easy and certainly not automatic. You will need to check what the law says about getting access to documents at the Magistrates or Local Court level. Obtaining court documents from these sources may be difficult . . . or impossible.

Problems accessing files – an example

A reporter attended a court proceeding in which he was interested. Other members of the public also attended. At the end of the proceeding, the presiding magistrate made a most important decision. It meant that a nonsense, but convenient, view of the law had for years been peddled by no end of legal, quasi-legal and political figures in the state concerned.

The decision was something of a bombshell. Given that the matter was gravely important for the proper administration of justice in the jurisdiction involved, the reporter sought access to the record of the proceeding in question.

At this point your need to know the law cannot be stressed too much. If you know it, you may be able to deal with people who try to circumvent it. Again, as in this case, a piece of statute law will be taken to illustrate the point – section 154 of Queensland's *Justices Act*:

> When in any proceeding before justices an order is made, or the justices commit the defendant to be tried or for sentence, or discharge the defendant, the person having custody of the record of the proceeding shall upon (a) the application in writing of any person who, in his opinion, has a sufficient interest in the proceeding or in securing a copy of the record thereof or of part of such record applied for; and (b) payment of the amount of the prescribed fee, supply to the applicant a copy of the complaint . . ., the depositions taken . . ., any order . . ., any documentary exhibit other than a photograph, or . . . a copy of such of them as the applicant applies for.

This section means, if the person in charge of the record being sought considers the person applying for it to have "a sufficient interest" in such a record, it should be provided – except in the case of a photograph – and depending on the payment of the required fee. Of course, the issue of whether journalists have "sufficient interest" in matters before the courts is one that has not always been determined in their favour.

In this case an application was made for access to the transcript of the hearing concerned, and the application was rejected.

Given what had happened at the hearing and the extraordinary turnaround this case represented for the state's legal community, a second request was made. It quoted some of the case law discussed above and again sought access to the record of proceedings. What happened next came as something of a shock.

The court official who responded said the **entire** proceeding had been subject to a suppression order and access was denied.

There are two points to be made here. The first is the entire proceedings had **not** been suppressed . . . at one point a name had been suppressed, but at the end of the hearing even this suppression had been lifted. The second point is one that journalists should remember. A suppression order does not prevent anyone present from knowing what was suppressed. For example, those in court at the time will hear such information quite clearly. A suppression order means that the information that has been suppressed should not be published – and if anyone should publish, that person would be in contempt of the court. A suppression order does **not** mean you cannot access the record. What it means is, if you do access the record and publish what is suppressed, you will be in trouble.

A reply was sent pointing out that the proceedings had not been suppressed and access was sought to the record once again.

The response to this letter was deeply troubling. It said:

> In response to your further request in respect of the above matter I wish to advise I have personally contacted the presiding magistrate who has confirmed that a suppression order was in force for the entirety of the proceedings and further to the best of his recollection the [proceeding] was conducted under the provision of section 70 of the Justices Act which precludes any entitlement to copies of record under Section 154 of the Justices Act.

This was serious nonsense . . . and even more disturbingly, a magistrate had now been drawn into the matter. The facts were that the entire proceedings were **not** covered by a suppression order, and they had **not** been conducted in camera under section 70 of the *Justices Act*. As well as the reporter, several members of the public had attended the proceedings . . . although at one time the court had been closed for a short while.

These matters were raised with the court bureaucracy, who responded by saying there was no reason to suggest the court official, in denying access to the documents, had acted in anything but good faith and no good purpose would be served by investigating the matter.

By this stage, of course, the reporter had obtained a copy of the transcript elsewhere and was able to write his stories "fairly and accurately". But the case illustrates the point that your efforts to write a story may not be appreciated and considerable effort may be made to frustrate you.

Words mean what they say

At law it is established that English words mean what they say . . . or words mean what they mean. If that helps. But, of course, it is only reasonable that such an axiom apply. If it were otherwise, we would never know where we stood with the law.

So to go back to the case above, the word "sufficient" is significant because on its definition a bureaucrat may determine whether the public may access the record of a matter before a court. In determining what words mean, or what they say, dictionary definitions are relevant and appropriate. And thus we find that, in the *Macquarie Dictionary*, "sufficient" means "enough" or "adequate".

The journalist seeking access to a court record is not doing so for some private purpose. He or she is doing so to prepare a report for the public at large. And the right of the public to know what goes on in our courts, and the role of the media in informing that public, have been recognised by the courts. Thus, it can be argued, the reporter writing a story for publication has "sufficient" or "enough" or "adequate" interest because his interest is the "public interest".

It is recognised that people who appear before magistrates and plead their innocence are not necessarily guilty. A jury may determine that one day. But to say that no records of magistrates court proceedings may be made public is to deny the existence of a public interest in what happens in that court. And that is nonsense. But you may well confront it some day.

Sooner rather than later, I suspect.

Open courts . . . open government?

If the courts belong to the public, and not to the judges and the bureaucrats who operate them, what about the government? Do politicians and bureaucrats own the government, or do we, the public? After all, we choose these people to represent us in making decisions about how our affairs should be run, and we pay their salaries. Yet governments and bureaucrats sometimes (even often) see themselves as operating beyond the reach or scrutiny of the those who elect them or pay their wages.

Just as the courts have established that, unless there is good reason, the public has a right to know what goes on in our courtrooms, they have also determined that, unless there is a good reason, we have a right to know what goes on in the government. Of course, as noted above, a good deal of statute law (FOI legislation) exists which overwhelms this notion . . . but not entirely.

There is an important case in this regard that you should commit to memory, for it establishes some important principles about the public's right to know and what constitutes the public interest.

The case is *The Commonwealth of Australia v. John Fairfax and Sons Ltd* (1980) 147 CLR 39. And it is the law.

A book was to be published which contained, in part, the content of some cables sent between the Department of Foreign Affairs in Canberra and the Australian embassy in Jakarta. The *Sydney Morning Herald* planned to publish extracts from the book. The government sought an injunction to prevent such publication on the grounds that the material was "classified" and "confidential", its disclosure might harm Australia's relations with other countries, and the planned publication had not been approved or authorised.

Mr Justice Mason's judgment is worth remembering. In part he said:

> It may be a sufficient detriment to the citizen that disclosure of information relating to his affairs will expose his actions to public discussion and criticism. But it can scarcely be a relevant detriment to the government that publication of material concerning its actions will merely expose it to public discussion and criticism.
>
> **It is unacceptable in our democratic society that there should be a restraint on the publication of information relating to government when the only vice of that information is that it enables the public to discuss, review and criticize government action.** [emphasis added]

Mr Justice Mason spoke with the authority of the High Court. His decision is law. It means that unless there is an overwhelming matter of public importance at stake (for example, national security), the government cannot claim that the public which it represents cannot know what it is doing on the basis of "confidentiality". I had better stress again that FOI laws (statutes) may reduce the impact of Judge Mason's decision.

Problems accessing files – another example

Some time after a Royal Commission had been held into a most serious issue, a reporter sought access to the transcripts of the public hearings of that inquiry. Permission was eventually granted and the reporter was allowed to peruse the material.

Some time later he mentioned what he had done to a person who also had an interest in the matter and had sought access to the documents. His request, however, was denied . . . on the grounds that the documents were "confidential". The person was a little confused and contacted the reporter (who had already seen the material and copied some of it). The reporter suggested he have a look at the case of *The Commonwealth of Australia v. John Fairfax and Sons Ltd* (1980). The decision denying access to the documents was reversed immediately.

Recording devices

This issue has already been touched on. But in terms of knowing your rights, it should be raised again.

There are situations (such as courts) where you may not be able to record material, but for the most part people are happy to have their interviews recorded. You should always ask – in case someone is not happy. But people are generally aware that recordings provide a backup check in the interests of accuracy and everyone involved wants the story reported accurately.

Not everyone you may come across in your career will necessarily be happy about being reported – and certainly not recorded. There is a world out there in which some people are not playing by the rules of the rest of society.

You need to be careful when dealing with people in this category. Can you be certain, if you talk with them, that they won't deny what they told you and reject what you wrote in your story? If someone is operating on the edges of, or outside, the rules, can you really expect they will stick by what they told you if that should become uncomfortable? Then it is your word against theirs. This is not the best of situations for you to be in. (It is not just the dodgy who are a worry in this context. A senior public official agreed to be interviewed by a reporter but declined to be recorded. When the story appeared he denied he had said what the reporter had written.)

But what if you could verify your story?

Some jurisdictions protect the reporter in such circumstances. Some do not. For example, the law in one state says it is an offence to record a private conversation unless the person making the recording is party to the conversation. This means it is an offence to record a private conversation others might be having, but **not** if you are involved as a party to the conversation. That is the first point. This means that you can protect yourself if someone should deny your story. Making such recordings would only be done in exceptional circumstances . . . but exceptional circumstances arise.

The law in question then goes on to deal with the issue of what you might do with your recording. The Act says, in effect, that it is an offence to communicate or publish to another anything contained in a recording of such a conversation or any statement prepared from such a recording. The penalty for doing so could be two years in jail.

However, the law recognises that there are other considerations; it removes the ban on publication if such publication is not more than is "reasonably necessary" and in "the public interest".

If such a situation should apply to you, this means that your story will have to be more than just some private tittle-tat and you should not double your print run just because you have a big story on your hands. But, if you comply, you have a defence for publishing.

In other jurisdictions, recording conversations without everyone involved knowing a recording is being made is unlawful. The effect this has on good reporting can be considerable. Your story can be denied and you cannot defend yourself . . . because there is no record.

You need to know what the law says in your situation. The rules that apply are different from state to state.

PART 4

Research skills

Research and finding things

Using the internet

In the main, computers are able to do the remarkable tasks they do and perform extraordinarily complex calculations just because they are able to do something very simple. Computers can tell the difference between a 0 and 1, or they can tell when something is "on" and when it is "off", or they can detect the presence or absence of an electrical impulse.

Just knowing the difference between a one and a nought, or "on" or "off" is all it takes to make your computer so terribly smart.

Computers make sense, via codes called programs, of squillions of 1s and 0s (or "ons" and "offs", impulses or no impulses).

They are also very good at recognising combinations of these things. And this is where Boolean algebra, or Boolean logic, becomes important for those who use computers to find things or conduct research.

George Boole was a 19th century mathematician who was interested in the algebraic relationships that arise when combinations of data or cases are considered.

For example: We have *this*. Quite separately we also have *that*.

So what happens, Boole pondered, when we consider *this* AND *that* together? What happens when we consider this OR that? Or *this* but NOT *that*? And so on.

So, if you give your computer directions on how to search for information **based on Boolean logic** (i.e. find ***this*** in combination with ***that*** but not with ***those***, etc.) you may get useful results – instead of being swamped by garbage.

The common Boolean terms that computers respond to include AND, OR, NOT, ADJ (adjacent), and WITH. Try them.

Search engines

Boolean logic is very useful. It forms the operational basis for what we know today as search engines . . . computer programs that find information for us (combinations of 0s and 1s, for example).

Search engines operate on the basis of defaults which they "insert" between the words you put into their search field. Most now default to AND. In the early days of search engines, lots of them had an OR default. This was not very helpful for the searcher. The more words you entered in the search field, thinking that this might refine your search, the more OR alternatives the search engine looked for. Instead of refining your search, additional words expanded it. A search engine with an AND default, on the other hand, allows you to start narrowing down your search straightaway. But even that is not necessarily enough.

Here are some examples. For some reason, you need to know the range of temperatures that occur on the planet Mercury. A Google search for the word *mercury* or *Mercury* will produce the same results since the search engine is not case sensitive. But it will be a useless search. You will get all the hits Google can find for Mercury the planet, Mercury the Greek god, Mercury outboard motors and the liquid metal you find in thermometers. The result, last time I tried it, was an overwhelming 183 million hits.

So you enter *temperature Mercury* in the search field. Now you get about 13.5 million hits, which is an improvement, but not much. If, however, you enclose your request within inverted commas, *"temperature of Mercury"*, you are no longer searching for hits that contain *temperature* AND *Mercury* but the specific string of words, *"temperature of Mercury"* and you get just 500-odd hits. Now you have a useful range of sources to consider. You will have eliminated Greek gods and outboard motors, but you may still have information about the liquid metal getting in the way. If so, search again on *"temperature of Mercury"* AND *planet*. Now we're talking.

If you are using computer databases or search engines learn how to use Boolean logic and inverted commas to refine your searches. And learn which engines will allow you to do so.

Who wrote it and when?

Search engines, whether driven by clever digital "crawlers" or "spiders" finding information in accessible documents, or by human beings, are, nevertheless, not very discriminating. They locate garbage as well as pearls; they find material produced by reputable authors and they find junk produced by who knows. They are also not very good at housework. Sites and materials that haven't been updated for ages still come up on their hit lists. Before finishing this chapter, I did a Google search for the "top 10 search engines". It produced an avalanche of hits. Number four on the hit list opened up a site that ranked the top ten engines based on some criteria, which I have forgotten, because I noticed some of the engines had run out of gas donkeys' years ago! The site involved had not been updated since 2002. It was four years old, but it still came in fourth from the top on page one of Google's list of X million hits.

There is a message here. You have to be alive, awake and alert to use a search engine. Check out the date of the material you find, providing there is a date to find. Just because it comes up at the top of the search engine hit list does not mean the stuff isn't older than you are.

Another search for sites that claimed to list the "top ten search engines" produced some interesting results. One in particular was very thorough in reviewing the engines involved, and in justifying its grading of them. But the article was two years old. Do we want two-year-old material if we want to know which are the best search engines? More disturbingly, what if we hadn't checked when the article was written?

So there are two essentials that have to be met when using search engines and sources on the net. The first is to ask, who wrote the stuff, and the second, when was it written? Then, with those questions answered, you may decide it is useful, or you may decide it is junk. There is much more junk on the net than there are treasures.

Which engine to fire up . . . or fire?

In case you thought there was only Google, be assured there are many more engines out there. Google may be the biggest and currently the most popular, but there is no shortage of competitors. One way to find out which search engine might be the best, or the best for you, is to ask several of them to do a search for you and compare the results. Or you could use your current favourite to search for reviews of search engines, and see what the web-heads say. Australia has some local engines and you should keep an eye out in case others pop up in the future. Anzwers (anzwers.com.au, now with Yahoo) has been around for a long while. It handles Boolean discriminators very well.

A search for *Murray River flood plain* on Anzwers produced 208,000 hits. *"Murray River flood plain"* (enclosed in inverted commas) reduced the number of hits to 244. The same searches on Ansearch produced 20 and 13 hits respectively. If those 20 or 13 hits give you what you are looking for, the small number is clearly better. But you may not find what you are looking for in such a small list. A search engine that lacks the power to search widely may not be much help.

A useful thing to do, if you have never done it before, is to open up a site that explains the search engine landscape for you – a site such as searchenginewatch.com. Read it and read the links that explain what you want to know. Then you can check out its rankings of the best tools to use. Other sites will give you rankings too, some of them based on surveys and samples and focus group responses. By the time you have done a little research you will be better able to deal with these search tools and better able to understand how they might work for you. Sites that explain how search engines work will help explain why you get different results in both volume and priority from different engines. Search engines can be such valuable tools. It is worth learning to use them well.

The invisible web

Despite its capacity and reputation, it is said that Google indexes only about 9 billion of the estimated 200 billion World Wide Web pages – or about 5 per cent of the total. Only 5 per cent. The rest is in the "invisible web" not accessible to the crawlers that digitally trawl the net looking for material to index. If Google is the biggest, that means there is a great deal of material that is not being picked up by search engines.

It is possible to access at least some of the invisible web by deciding not to search for words in documents, but to search for the owners or creators of documents instead. Once you find them it may be possible to search for documents.

So, if you are doing a story on land degradation, for instance, instead of thinking "desalination" as a possible topic to explore, think of who might "own" issues surrounding desalination. A Department of the Environment almost certainly would. Perhaps there are river commissions, agricultural research bodies, peak farmer lobby groups, conservation groups, and so on, who would have an interest in, and documents on, salinity and its effects. Find them and go to work on what they have available. You might get better results this way than simply calling up Google and entering "salinity" in the search field.

An excellent site that provides a large index of bodies and organisations likely to be of interest to the journalist and lists them under clear and useful headings is www.journoz.com. The site was created by, and is maintained and updated by, Belinda Weaver, at the University of Queensland. Belinda also has a blog which carries some good ideas for journalists looking for a story.

Sites to have at your fingertips

There are some sites and tools you must have at your fingertips. Bookmark them (or put them in your "favourites" list) or download them if they come as software. You could start with:

- a local search engine (Anzwers perhaps)
- a couple of internationally recognised search engines (including Google)
- specialist sites created for journalists (such as www.journoz.com)
- your state or territory parliament site (in particular the link to Hansard)
- the link that will take you directly to your state or territory Acts and Sub-ordinate Legislation index (through your parliament or via the Office of Parliamentary Counsel site or equivalent)
- the Commonwealth parliament (www.aph.gov.au) and the federal Hansard link
- the (federal) government online directory (www.gold.gov.au), which provides a directory of officials on the federal payroll and the bodies they work for
- the Australian Bureau of Statistics (www.abs.gov.au)
- a unit converter (for converting weights and measures)
- a link to a site that offers up-to-date currency conversions
- the Bureau of Meteorology (www.bom.gov.au)
- Telephone directories (www.whitepages.com.au and www. yellowpages. com.au as a minimum).

Other links you should have handy will depend on what you cover or what your interests might be.

Old-fangled v. new-fangled research

Wearing out your shoe leather (or rubber or some plastic alternative) in the interests of getting a story is no bad thing. In fact it's probably a good thing. Because not everything is on the internet.

One of the most valuable resources cannot be got online, even though it will be on a computer – the computer in the office of the state or federal Electoral Commission. They used to use microfiche transparencies to store their records so you had best know how to use a microfiche reader just in case they are still in service, or the computer has crashed.

These records are not online. You will have to use the wearing-out-of-rubber-and-shoe-leather research technique for this task.

Electoral rolls

In Australia everyone entitled to vote is supposed to do so. Voting in local, state and federal elections is compulsory. It is one of the great contradictions of a democracy. The citizen has no choice. If you do not vote and do not have an acceptable excuse you can be punished.

Therefore, everyone over the age of 18 is supposed to be on the electoral rolls. There are some exceptions, but not many. And unless you have an acceptable reason, the address of every voter is listed too. The rolls are open to public inspection. They have to be lest someone should attempt to rig them. That has happened of course.

One of the most famous cases concerns The Esplanade on Bribie Island, Queensland. It appears that at one election in recent memory voters living on both sides of that road were sent electioneering material by a candidate. The mail-out was based on the addresses of voters contained on the local electoral roll. The problem was, when the matter came to light, that the only things living on the western side of The Esplanade were fish and crabs. The western side of The Esplanade was, and is, in fact, Pumicestone Passage, the narrow strait that separates Bribie from the mainland. It appears that several kilometres of The Esplanade were inhabited by people who did not exist. Whether they voted, or who voted for them, is unknown, but if they did vote, there may have been enough of them to make a difference to the count.

The rolls are updated twice a year and if a voter changes address, he or she is supposed to advise the Commonwealth Electoral Commission. There is only one set of rolls and they are used for all three elections – local, state and national.

Copies of the rolls are held at the office of the Commonwealth Electoral Commission in each federal electorate or division and at the headquarters of both the state and federal electoral commissions in the capital cities. They can be viewed during normal business hours. They are alphabetic and contain the names and most of the addresses of everyone who has applied to become a voter and who is entitled to vote.

Names are removed when voters die or become incapable or are ineligible for some other (limited) reason.

The electoral rolls are an important source of information, although it must be said, many people are not registered, or the details are out of date – despite the efforts of staff to ensure they are complete and up to date. The electoral rolls have been critical in the context of many a story written by journalists and were certainly vital in several I have written over the years, in particular stories about the abuse of children in the care of the State and the Churches.

The example that follows is a story about using the electoral rolls to find critical information. The story was published on the internet in 2000 and became a "twin" for "The search for Kate" (about the hunt for a large flat rock somewhere in south east Queensland, see the chapter on fundamentals of reporting).

by Bruce Grundy

The Federal Division of Ryan electoral office was in Station Road, Indooroop-illy, just down the way from the multi-storey shopping centre that fills an entire block off Moggill Road and just up the way from another famous local landmark – the life-size fibreglass horse on the footpath outside Horseland, the riding equip-ment shop it promoted during trading hours each day. He had come to know the horse quite well. There was almost always a vacant parking space not far from the grey, and that was a consolation. He was always calling there and didn't need a long walk from the car. The man behind the desk at the electoral office said he should be on the payroll – he was their best customer by far. Which was no surprise. Over the last year or so he had searched hundreds of names on the microfiche transparencies there, more often than not without success. Many of the people he was looking for were not model citizens, least of all model voters. He had found that, for whatever reason, a lot of people were clearly not voting in state or national elections. But it was the place he always started and sometimes the rolls came up trumps.

It was because of this place that he had finally found "Y" – the code-named girl who had been handcuffed overnight to a tennis court fence in a youth detention centre. Stories he and others had written about the abuse of children in care finally forced a Royal Commission into the matter and the handcuffing had been the subject of a special open session of that Inquiry. The names of those who had been handcuffed had been suppressed and in its report the Inquiry had simply referred to the three as "X", "Y" and "Z". "Z" had been released back to the wings after an hour but "X" and "Y" were kept handcuffed to a fence and a stormwater grating (where the inmates believed the snakes lived) until after 9 and 10 o'clock the following morning.

He had missed the hearings into the handcuffing – which he regretted – but that was history. The incident still intrigued him. The Royal Commissioners said it was all too long ago for any criminal charges to be laid and the time limit for charges under the Children's Services Act had also long passed. So there were no charges. The reason given for handcuffing the children, a fear that their rowdy behaviour might spark a riot, was rejected by the Commissioners. But they offered no explanation for the action.

The question remained: why was it done? Handcuffing a boy to a stormwater drain and a small girl to a tennis court fence overnight was bad enough, but there was something else that had angered him.

He had phoned the Bureau of Meteorology and asked what the minimum tem-perature had been on the day in question. As one who had spent his childhood in the bush, he was well aware that the coldest part of the night is usually about dawn. Since the three had been handcuffed about 9pm on 26 September, he asked what the minimum was on the morning of the 27th. At Amberley airbase not far away it had been 2.9 degrees C, the Bureau said. He later discovered the Royal Commission had been told, and apparently accepted, it was 18 degrees. But that was the minimum on the morning of the 26th – the morning before the handcuffing, when, presumably, the residents, including Y and Z were all tucked up in bed in their rooms! The witness had simply presented data to a Royal Commission for the wrong day. Spending a night outside handcuffed to a tennis court fence or a stormwater drain when the temperature was 18 degrees would be one thing. But 2.9 degrees? Torture would be an appropriate word.

What was really behind the handcuffing, he wondered. And where to next? Children's Courts are closed courts in Australia and the names of those sent to institutions are simply not available. But he knew the name of a little not-even-teenage kid who had been sent to that place at the time. The boy should never have been put there, and died in tragic circumstances shortly after his release. That rankled too. He called the still-distressed parents and within hours found himself in touch with two people who not only had some first-hand knowledge of the institution, but who also had some documents. He was always interested in documents and soon after, over a cup of coffee in a modest suburban dining room, he went through a set. The man and woman with him had suffered terribly. The story of what had happened to their little boy and what the State had done to him was appalling. They were happy for the reporter to look at their files. The files contained all kinds of interesting material but at that moment the most interesting was the name of the girl who had been handcuffed to the tennis court fence. She was no longer "Y". She had a real name. He committed it to memory but there was no need. His hosts gave him all their precious documents to photocopy. But photocopying could wait. He collected the files, thanked his hosts and set off for the horse in Station Road.

The trip to the electoral office was more a matter of ritual. The likelihood of finding the girl's name on the roll he reckoned at about a squillion to one. But it was always the place to start.

His luck was in and he found a vacant space to park the car just up Station Road from the horse and just across the street from the office of the Member for Indooroopilly. He always found a certain irony in getting a park just there. The member had once been Attorney-General and had tried to find out why a former government had shredded all the evidence taken by an inquiry into the institution where the handcuffing had occurred. Two barristers had examined the documents involved in the shredding matter and in their report they had recommended a full and open public inquiry into the matter. They said there was prima facie evidence that public officials had committed numerous offences against the criminal law. Despite the seriousness of the findings of the two barristers, nothing was done.

Just inside the electoral office door was the familiar garish orange chair he had sat in so many times, an office table, a microfiche reader and little boxes with flip-up lids, one plastic for Queensland names, one metal for the rest of Australia, and an exercise book in which people accessing the rolls were supposed to register their names and the dates and times they did so. He never filled in the register because he had no desire to tell the world at large he had been calling there so much. He opened the Queensland box, flicked through the alphabet and found the transparency that would, or would not, contain the name of the code-named girl. He switched the reader on and slid the transparency sideways under the lens of the machine. The names and addresses of voters whizzed across the screen. As he neared his target he scanned the names more slowly. And then stopped.

He could not believe what he was seeing. There it was. There she was. There was the name he had seen in the dining room of the man and woman who had lost their little boy. And the address too. Eureka. That was a bonus. People with a good reason could have their address withheld from the rolls. He had seen a few large blank spaces on the screen at various times that indicated a missing address. But not this time. No blank spaces this time. The squillion to one shot had paid off.

The address was about an hour's drive away in one of those little villages you miss if you blink. He decided to get there about half past five. The woman (by now, all these years later) might work and there was no point arriving any earlier. He had a couple of hours to kill and the time dragged. He collected some things he thought might come in handy – copies of the magazines he had written about the abuse of children in care in Queensland – at the wretched Neerkol orphanage near Rockhampton, run, sadistically, by of all people, the Sisters of Mercy, and the hell-hole known as Nazareth House at Wynnum, superintended by a group of nuns called The Poor Sisters of Nazareth, and copies of other stories he had written, or had supervised, on the outrages that had occurred in places like Silky Oaks, Westbrook and John Oxley. And then he set off.

The trip was uneventful and finding one house among fifty was not all that hard. He arrived as planned and gathered up a handful of his magazines and papers from the back seat. As he approached the front steps of the house he could see a young woman in the kitchen talking on a walk-about phone. He waited until the call was over and knocked. A woman in her twenties came out. The reporter introduced himself and asked if the woman he was looking for lived there. No, came the cautious reply. Her name was on the electoral rolls at this address, he suggested. Oh yes, the young woman said, but she hadn't seen her for ages. Maybe, he thought. But she did know who he was talking about. He explained who he was and showed the woman his magazines and stories. He was anxious to find this person, he said, because she might be interested in talking with him. Sorry, the young woman said, she hadn't seen her for months. She was pregnant, the young woman said. Not too many months, he thought. The reporter went through his magazines and papers and his interest in children-in-care spiel again. She sometimes saw her, the woman volunteered, and she would tell her of his visit if she should ever see her again, the young woman said. Another run through the magazines and stories and spiel. I will, if I see her, the woman said, I will tell her you called. By now, the magazines and the spiel had run their race. There was no point going through all that again. The woman had said all she was going to say. He took a chance and gave her his card, made some pleasant small talk about living in such a lovely place and when that was exhausted thanked the woman and left. The card was a gamble. It might alarm the woman he was seeking, or it might not. But there was no alternative. He was very disappointed. To have come so far and so close. But not nearly close enough.

After a thirty-second tour of the village, which covered all its major attractions, he set off for home. Where to go next? He called his wife on the mobile to say he would collect her in an hour and that his trip had been "a dog" – a waste of time. It had been a good try but hadn't paid off. He switched off the phone and put it down on the seat beside him. Where to go next? The phone rang. It would be his wife with a message to get something at the shop. "Hellooo," he said. "Is that you Bruce?" a voice he did not recognise said. "Yes," he replied. "It's me," the voice said. "You came looking for me."

It was an unfortunate moment. The car was now X kilometres from the nearest mobile phone tower. But however far it was, X was the point where the mobile service ran out. The voice on the end of the phone suddenly vanished to be replaced by the infuriating sound of silence. No, NO, NO, he cursed. Jesus Christ. NO. As he wheeled the Falcon around on the narrow bitumen strip he realised the voice might have been calling from Perth or Oodnadatta – or Rome or Timbucktoo. The woman back at the house he had just left had had plenty of time to call anywhere on the globe. And the mobile phone service chose that moment to die on him. Thank you very much God, he hissed. He had long ago decided if there was a God, which he doubted, he/she had never been a journalist. Still he knew that the woman back at the house had contacted the woman he was looking for and he would go back to that house and take it up with her. Torture would not be out of the question if that was what it would take to get her to talk.

A couple of kilometres back down the road the phone rang again. "Hello," he said, again. And again the voice said, "It's me. Where are you?" "I'm heading back to the house I just left," he said. "Fine," said the voice. "I'm in the phone box at the end of the street. I'll meet you at the house."

Perhaps there was a God, he conceded. But one with a very twisted mind. Probably had been a journalist in that case after all. He parked outside the house and found two young women, an older woman and several children waiting for him in the front yard. The two younger women were sisters, the older woman their mother and the children brothers, sisters, cousins and grandchildren.

It was an extraordinary meeting. As he had driven out of the street a short time earlier, cursing his rotten luck, the woman he was trying to find was driving into that very street – with her mother and her children on a very irregular visit to see her sister. They lived fifty kilometres apart and visited only occasionally to keep up family ties. Today was one of those irregular visits.

Three hours later the reporter again set course for home. He would be a little late picking up his wife. But he had the story behind the handcuffing and a great deal more.

That was how it happened. Thanks to the electoral rolls. Of course, there was a great deal of luck involved. But you make your own luck.

Finding this woman and discovering her story unwrapped another layer in a saga that became known, because of an earlier variation that had occurred overseas, as Shreddergate. It was an elaborate affair involving the destruction of documents that managed to prevent the public of Queensland finding out what had been going on in a juvenile detention centre in the state capital, Brisbane, for more then 10 years. It was the detention centre where the girl known simply as Y had been sent.

The electoral rolls also played a vital part in finding some of the other victims of the institution concerned. Their stories were not about handcuffing. Their stories were about rape. And pack rape.

A summary of one of the cases in particular is contained in Volume Two of the House of Representatives Legal and Constitutional Affairs Committee of Inquiry into Crime in the Community (2005). The cover of that report is a montage of headlines from the *Weekend Independent*.

It is true to say that without the electoral rolls, the extent of the John Oxley Shreddergate cover-up may never have been unravelled.

Some day, without doubt, you will need to use the electoral rolls. When you do, here are some tips.

1. Unless you have seen the name you are seeking authoritatively written down, do not assume you know how to spell it. Brown might be Browne, McKay might be Mackay, Shelley might be Shellie, or, just as likely, short for Michelle. How many ways are there to spell what sounds like Sean?

2. Do not assume the first (or Christian) name you have been given is in fact the first name of the person you are seeking. I know this only too well: the name I have been known by all my life is not my first name.

3. The name of the street on the rolls may not be spelled correctly. There may be an alternative spelling.

4. Do not assume that everyone who should be enrolled is enrolled. Searching old rolls from the archives may, or may not, produce any results either.

5. Do not assume everyone who changes their address advises the authorities of the change. The listed address could be years out of date.

6. Because you cannot find the name of a woman you have been given does not mean she is not enrolled. Women who marry still frequently adopt their husband's surname. When that happens, the electoral roll also uses their new name. And changes of name, like births, deaths and marriages, cannot be searched unless you are a family member with a very good reason. Being a reporter chasing a story is not one of them.

There are software packages available that contain, in reverse format, data you find on the electoral rolls and the telephone's White Pages. With these tools it is possible to enter an address and find out who lives where, or a phone number and discover the name of the subscriber (if it is not a silent number). But such reverse searching tools are not free, and the cost may be prohibitive for an individual.

Documents, documents, documents

People telling you things is great; people giving you documents is better. Getting documents yourself is another approach. But it can be a difficult path.

Freedom of information

Unless you work for an organisation that can afford the costs, Freedom of Information legislation may not be of much use to you. What began as an excellent idea to enhance accountability and achieve better government has turned into a farce in most cases. The costs of pursuing an FOI claim can be huge, and certainly prohibitive for the student, or the freelance reporter.

There is one way FOI may work for you. The other ways will almost certainly cost too much. If your story is about a person and his or her interaction with some agency of government, the person can apply for all the files held on him or her. Even criminal records can be accessed. Usually there are no fees involved in such requests. The person can then give you access to the material when it arrives, or allow you to see it if the copying costs are too great.

Before making any FOI application, check the legislation that prevails in your situation and follow it. It will set out the application process and the timelines involved. It will also reveal what appeal processes may be considered if the application is rejected. Significantly, it will tell you what exemptions exist. In other words it will tell you what kinds of information you will **not** be able to access through FOI. In most cases the exemptions are considerable.

Knowing the legislation and its requirements is important. Applications have to be in writing. If the person you are seeking information about does not have the skills to write the letter, you may write the letter on their behalf and get them to sign it. Some form of identification may have to be sent to verify their identity.

Should you have any reason for concern that the request might not be greeted with joy at the other end, and might "go astray", send a copy at the same time to a related agency. It is usually required in the legislation that if a request goes to the wrong place, it should be re-directed to its rightful destination. Some years ago a particularly sensitive application was made to a state government agency. The weeks passed but there was no acknowledgment that the request had been received. Some days after the appropriate period for acknowledgment had passed, an enquiry was made as to the fate of the application. "We never received it," the agency said. However, when the request was posted, an identical letter was sent to another agency. This body occupied a building not far from the one that housed the intended recipient. When asked if they had received the request, the second agency happily replied in the affirmative. A letter pointing out the delivery failure was then sent to the person responsible for the overall administration of the FOI regime in the state concerned. The applicant had several hundred pages of quite shocking documents within three days.

Knowing the legislation is also important because some, or all, of your request may be rejected. You may have grounds for an appeal. It may now be useful to know what kinds of appeals have succeeded in the past. Such determinations may be contained in specific publications of the FOI agency itself, or in its reports to the parliament. In one particular case, a request was partially successful, except that the names of several public officials who had been responsible for some quite serious things had been blanked out in the documents provided. But blanking out the names of people on the public payroll had already been examined in an earlier FOI adjudication and such action had been rejected as unacceptable. An appeal was lodged and the names of the individuals were provided.

Public officials are quite capable of doing the wrong thing, particularly if it might save the skin of someone important. The victim of a rape was provided with a most important document but, contrary to the requirements of the law, it had been all but totally blanked out. Such breaches occur from time to time and have to be met head-on.

Should you work for a major organisation you are almost certain to find there is someone on the staff who is the resident FOI expert. If, on the other hand, you are on your own, you must check the legislation; otherwise you will waste a great deal of time.

Other sources of documents

Higher court files and records can normally be accessed by filling in a form at the court registry and paying the fee ... but you will have to know some details about the case/s to complete the form sufficiently for the staff to locate what you want. Magistrates (or local) court records are not usually available and you may have to make a special application (and a convincing case) to get them. This is covered in the chapter on knowing your rights. Transcripts of cases that occur in the higher courts should be accessible. Copying fees will apply, but you may be allowed to peruse the transcript in the office at no charge.

Organisations known as Information Service Providers can link you to a great deal of information held by governments and government agencies around the country (land titles records, company documents of various kinds required to be lodged by the Australian Securities and Investments Commission, contaminated sites records perhaps, and much more). Fees will apply, but you can pay by credit card and the search can be done from home via your computer. Otherwise you will have to go to the agency directly.

The Commonwealth and State Electoral Commissions have a great deal of useful information about electorates and voting details from recent elections. They also produce reports on financial contributions made to political parties, which can make interesting reading.

The parliament may require members to provide information about their pecuniary interests (what they own or control) and you may be able to access the register. The parliament may also produce a report on members' pecuniary interests.

The Australian Stock Exchange (www.asx.com.au) carries a great deal of information required of those public companies listed with it. Company announcements that are required to ensure the market is informed can be a very useful source of information for the journalist.

Of course a great deal of material is not publicly available. Privacy rules apply. But there is much that can be obtained . . . if you make the effort to obtain it.

Facts and figures

People attach great importance to knowing "the facts". And figures have a special significance for many. But they are also easy to misread, to misunderstand and to manipulate. That's why you sometimes hear the phrase "lies, damned lies and statistics" (first coined by Benjamin Disraeli, Prime Minister of England in the late 1800s).

This chapter sets out particular areas where journalists need to take extra care. It is easy to stumble if you are not careful. Knowing about percentage errors, means, averages, medians, modes and standard deviations, for instance, could be vital if you are to report meaningfully. Understanding polls might also be critical. A knowledge of spreadsheets will allow you to read other people's and help you construct your own.

This chapter can't show you everything you need to know, any more than the chapter on grammar gave you a complete course in English grammar. What follows are examples of situations where mistakes all too easily arise, with explanations of how to avoid those mistakes.

Percentage error

A change in the rate of inflation from 2% to 3% is not a 1% rise in inflation. It is a 50% rise. A rise from 2% to 3% is a one percentage point change. And a percentage change to a base figure to produce a new figure cannot be reversed back to the original base by applying an equal percentage change to the new figure in the opposite direction. But people often think it can.

If there were 100 traffic accidents in a police district two years ago and there had been a 50% increase since, a reporter might write that the number of accidents in the area had risen dramatically to 150. And that would be fine. But if the reporter were to say the number of accidents in the area had risen dramatically with the latest figures showing there had been 150 accidents in the area, while two years ago there had been 50% fewer accidents, that would not be fine. The error would be huge. Instead of 100 accidents two years ago, the reporter's maths would produce the very misleading result of 75.

Similarly, if unemployment were to rise by 2% during a given period to a point where 87,720 people were out of work, that would mean that at the beginning of the period 86,000 people were out of work ($86,000 \times 0.02 = 1720$, and $86,000 + 1720 = 87,720$, giving the overall total for the period of 87,720). If, at the end of the following period, unemployment fell by 2%, you might think that there had been no change. But, on the contrary, it would mean 85,966 people would then be out of work, an overall improvement in the number of jobless of 34. (That's because $87,720 \times 0.02 = 1754$ and $87,720 - 1754 = 85,966$). Not a lot perhaps, but the sums have to be right. Some readers and viewers will know, and credibility is at stake. Regardless, you should get it right to start with.

Another example: A corporation makes a profit of $40 million at the beginning of one financial year. It makes a 14% loss that year, then a 14% improvement the next financial year. But is still close to $2 million short of where it was two years ago.

The message is, take care with percentage shifts. Going up is not the same as coming down, and vice versa. And a change of one percentage point is not the same as a change of 1%. In fact, the term "percentage point" exists so that you can avoid confusion. Use it wisely.

Being mean can be pretty average

Research tells you that the average maximum temperature across the year in Utopia, a place currently in the news, is a comfortable 18°C. That sounds excellent. But while averages can be useful, they have their limitations.

Averages (or "means") by themselves fail to explain the range of data involved (from the biggest to the smallest, or the highest to the lowest, etc.), and the frequency with which the average or mean might occur. These might be important matters. They frequently are. Making the observation that such and such is an average could be, in reality, quite misleading.

Indeed, in the case of Utopia, it is. As it turns out, the country is mainly high mountains in the north and deserts in the west. This means that in both places the winter temperatures are very low, and in the desert, summer temperatures are very high. For most of the inhabitants the balmy 18°C day is rare indeed. It is more often either minus 5 or plus 40 in the shade. So although the averages tell us something, it is not actually something useful in this case. We need to know a bit more, such as the range involved in producing an average or mean. And it might also be good to know, as in the case of Utopia, how often the mean occurs.

The number, or spread, of occurrences can be critical information. If the average weekly income in Utopia is $875 per week, that may sound okay. But how many actually get it? If there are 200 people taking home a squillion dollars each, every day, and several million taking home very little every month, the average weekly income may well be $875. But, if you knew the detail, you might not want to sell up and emigrate there.

Averages can be mean. Give your readers useful rather than misleading information. In this case, as in most cases, it is important to know how the mean was reached. A bland average often says very little – or hides a great deal.

In a case such as this, the median (the value of the middle case) or the mode (the value most frequently represented), would be more useful than the mean alone.

Raising the standard (deviation)

A group of 40 students sat for an examination. There were 20 questions. The top student got 18 answers right, the worst just 3. By adding the results for the class and dividing that figure by the number who sat the exam, it was calculated that the mean performance for the group was 12 questions correctly answered. The teacher might be satisfied that the average result for the class was at least better than 50%. Indeed it was 60%.

But what if a whole bunch of students got 17 questions right and another whole bunch got just 4 right. It might be good for the teacher to know that. The average (12) appears to be okay, but in fact many in the group appear not to be "getting" the subject at all. What the teacher might like to know is, how did the class perform against the mean? What was the average variation across the group from the mean for the group? Or what was the average deviation from the mean across the class? Knowing the deviation from the mean that arose in the case of that examination might be very helpful for the teacher. It might also be helpful for the students.

Of course the group might have performed differently. The mean might have been 12, but what if the highest score had been 15 and the lowest 9? In this case the dispersal of results around the mean is very different from the earlier group and the average variation from the mean is also very different and says very different things about this group compared with the earlier class we looked at.

The standard deviation from the mean, more often called simply the standard deviation, that can be deduced from a set of results is a useful piece of information. It tells us something useful about the group that the raw figures of themselves do not necessarily reveal, particularly when the number of cases involved is large. The size of the sample and the number of results overwhelms the picture, as it were. But the standard deviation clears away the blur and a much clearer picture of the group's results emerges.

The worst thing about calculating a standard deviation for the newcomer is the formula involved. It looks particularly daunting for something that is actually quite simple. All we want to know is the average of the variations that occurred across the group from the mean. To get that we need to do the following: take each result and subtract the mean from it to get the variation from the mean in each case, add those results and divide by the number of cases. Simple. Well, almost. Subtracting the mean from those results that are less than the mean will produce a negative figure, and so if we were to simply add the results, the positives and negatives would cancel each other out rather than produce a total. To overcome this problem we square the difference from the mean in each case, since squaring a negative number produces a positive. Then we add the squared results (to be divided by the number of cases), and because we squared those results we then have to apply the opposite process and take the square root of the variance involved in the cases we are considering to reduce that figure to a base number. Divide by the number of cases, and presto, the standard deviation.

The daunting bit probably arises because of the maths symbols involved but $\sqrt{}$ is simply the square root sign, Σ means "add" or "take the sum of" and the ^{2} symbol indicates "to the power of 2" or "square the preceding number". Thus the standard deviation formula is:

$$\sqrt{\frac{(\Sigma x_N - M)^2}{N \text{ (or } N-1)}}$$

Where X is the value of each case, N the number of cases and M the mean of the cases. Another way of presenting the formula would be:

$$\sqrt{\frac{(x_1 - M)^2 + (x_2 - M)^2 + (x_3 - M)^2 \ldots (x_N - M)^2}{N \text{ (or } N-1)}}$$

The formula differs slightly if a sample rather than a population is being considered, but we will not go into that.

Something most students will be familiar with is the bell curve that may be applied to their class results. Unless a group is aberrant in some way or very small, it is usual to find that there are a few who do particularly well in a test, a few who do not do particularly well and a large number who cluster around the mean. In such a situation plotting the results on a graph showing how many achieved each result from the highest to the lowest would look something like this.

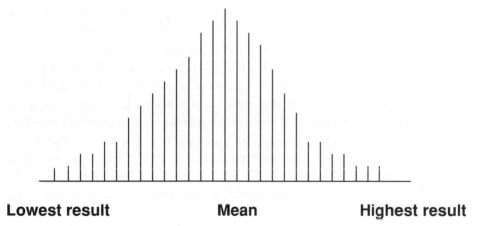

Lowest result   **Mean**   **Highest result**

If you should draw an outline around the top points of the graph you will see the familiar shape of a bell emerge. In a case such as this, a normal distribution, where the bulk of the group cluster around the mean, it will be found that about two thirds (actually about 68%) of the class will fall within one standard deviation of the mean and 95% within two standard deviations of the mean. If the standard deviation is large, the bell will necessarily be quite flat, and if the standard deviation is small, the bell will be rather slim in the middle at least.

So, finally, when presented with a set of numbers it is desirable to know a few things – how many cases, the mean, the highest/lowest, best/worst, etc., a frequency distribution for the various results involved, or at least the standard deviation involved in the results, and any comparison with previous or other results. A good result this time may be something to trumpet, but if it is aberrant, to trumpet it without mentioning the overall picture could be quite misleading.

With all the information mentioned above a reporter should be able to produce a decent story. Just to say, in the case of the first example above, that the average result for the class was 12 out of 20 (60%) does not tell the whole story at all, particularly when we know that quite a few failed dismally.

Problems with polls

Asking a handful of people in the street a few questions about some topical issue is one way to produce a quick story (which might be an attractive option for a student reporter facing an imminent deadline) but the story cannot be represented as any measure of public opinion. It was not based on a survey, even if that is what the story claims. Unfortunately there are lots of nonsense surveys and polls popping up in the media these days and, indeed, the news media mostly perform quite badly when they present stories based on public opinion surveys and polls.

If you are going to attempt to do a survey or conduct a poll you have to get a few things right. And getting them right might be quite difficult, unless you hand the whole thing over to a professional organisation.

The most important thing you have to get right is the sample (i.e. the people you question), both in terms of the number of respondents involved and how representative they might be of the population concerned. A sample that is too small or unrepresentative of the target population is worthless. Depending on who you are surveying, is the age breakdown in the target population important and if so, is it represented in the sample? If it is supposed to represent the views of some broad community, does the sample reflect the gender balance in the target community? Perhaps there are special issues that have to be addressed. Is the education profile of the community reflected in the sample? Or religious affiliation? How is the sample to be chosen? Is it random? Asking questions of random shoppers in a major shopping centre at lunchtime, for instance, does not necessarily produce a sample that is representative of a community. There are almost certainly people in that community who never shop at lunch-time. Perhaps asking questions at a variety of times might produce a better result, but some people never shop. At all. They will be excluded from your sample.

By now the prospect of turning in something meaningful may be looking a little daunting. Then there is the matter of questions. Getting the wording right is important. Questions that are unclear or offer a choice of so many responses that they are impossible to collate are clearly unsatisfactory. Perhaps the questions are "loaded". Even the order in which questions are asked may produce a skewed result. Organisations that conduct polls and surveys test the questions before they start.

Kinds of samples

There are different kinds of samples and different ways of choosing them, not to mention different levels of probability that your sample will accurately represent the population you are surveying. If you know your population is 23,000 adults, say, and you choose to question just five people about their voting intentions or preferred choice of toothpaste, the chance of those five accurately representing the voting intentions or the toothpaste buying habits of that population at large will be very remote. If instead you chose to question 5000 of the population, or 15,000, the chances that those samples would produce accurate results would be substantially increased. But interviewing 15,000 people or even 5000 is quite a task. The question is, how many should you choose? That will depend on what level of accuracy you want to achieve, or what level of inaccuracy (or error) you are prepared to accept. Clearly, in the interests of efficiency and economy, you will want to interview as few as you need to, to get a decent result. How many is that?

For a quick answer to this question, how many is enough, you can go to the internet and use a random sample calculator. I found one at custominsight.com <http://www.custominsight. com/articles/random-sample-calculator.asp>.

> It may come as a surprise to know that the television ratings in Australia are produced by sampling the viewing habits of just a few hundred people. This shows how important sampling can be. It also shows how important it is to get the sample right. Advertisers spend millions of dollars advertising their products based on what the ratings survey tells them.

The calculator will ask you for the information discussed above. How many are there in the population involved, and what level of accuracy do you want? Just enter these figures in the search fields, and press the button. Lo, the answer, according to the site you are using, appears.

Confidence levels and sampling errors

If you wanted your sample to represent or reflect the population accurately, you would have to choose the whole population as your sample. Anything less and you could not be sure your sample would be 100% accurate. You could not be confident that a smaller sample did not under- or over-represent something in the population involved. Because surveying the whole population is normally impossible or not practical, we choose samples and try to get them to reflect the test population as accurately as possible.

Picking a sample that would give us acceptable or satisfactory results 50% of the time would hardly be useful, because our results would be wrong as often as they would be right. At 60%, 8 out of 20 sample groups would not be satisfactory.

However, if we were to consider that a sample that was acceptable 19 times out of 20 was satisfactory (since 20 out of 20 is not realistic) then we would settle on a "confidence level" of 95% (19 out of 20). If we said 18 times out of 20 was okay, then our "confidence level" would be 90%. If, on the other hand we insisted on a 99 per cent confidence level, we would be happy 19.8 times out of 20. But clearly our sample size would vary in each case. The higher the confidence level expected the bigger the sample required. Confidence level is a matter of choice. But clearly something in the order of 95 per cent is appropriate if results are to be meaningful.

So in choosing a sample, we acknowledge that such a sample may not be 100% accurate in reflecting the population at large. We have to acknowledge the existence of a "sampling error" when we choose a sample. This does not mean "mistake". It means the degree of certainty with which a similar result would have been produced by asking a sample of the same size the same questions at the same time – or the degree of certainty that the sample represents the population being surveyed. Sampling errors are "plus or minus" figures. A sampling error of 3% means plus or minus (±)3%. At a confidence level of 95%, a 3% sampling error means that in 19 out of 20 cases our sample would be within 3% of accurately representing the population involved.

This is why knowing the sampling error in a poll or survey is so important. In the case of an election, for instance, where voters are fairly evenly divided in their support for two opposing candidates (Labor vs Liberal perhaps), a sampling error of ±3% is substantial. A swing of 5% in an election is a landslide result and our survey has a 6% margin of error (three percentage points either way). So when producing stories about voting intentions it is important to know, if a claim is made that one candidate has a lead of say 2% over an opponent, what the sampling error is. The claim may not stack up. A sampling error of ±3% would not allow for such a claim to be made because the sample was not accurate enough for such a prediction to be made.

Sampling error reflects the luck of the draw. By definition, no two samples will necessarily be the same, and none that might be chosen might absolutely mirror the population from which it was drawn. But properly selected, they and the results they produce can be very accurate.

Properly selecting a random sample requires that everyone in the population has an equal chance of being selected in the sample. If that can't happen, the sample isn't random. Telephone polls, for instance, throw up a number of problems. Not everyone in the population concerned may have a telephone, or at least a number that can be accessed. Not everyone has his or her number listed. Thus not everyone has an equal chance of being selected. Some households may have two phones, and thus have more than an equal chance of being selected. What happens then? Not everyone will be home when the phone rings. What happens then? Some who are home will not want to take the call because they are busy or sick of being surveyed. What happens then? Some who do agree to take part will balk at some of the questions. Some may not be prepared to give answers that fit the questionnaire format. Some may tell lies.

Accuracy and errors

If you play Two-Up you would know that if you flip a coin there is a 50/50 chance it will come down heads. Or tails. And if you played long enough you would also know that if you always gambled on the same outcome, heads or tails, and did not try to predict the outcome by chancing your bet, you would probably not lose any, or very much, money. You would not win any or very much either, because, if you played long enough, the number of times the coins came down heads would be the same, or about the same, as the number of times they came down tails – half the number of times each.

Using the coin flipper at www.random.org we flipped the coin just 100 times. Here are the results, one by one (t = tails, h = heads):

```
 1  2  3  4  5  6  7  8  9 10 11 12 13 14 15 16 17 18 19 20 21 22 23 24 25 26 27 28 29 30 31 32 33

 t  t  h  h  t  t  t  h  t  t  h  h  t  h  t  h  t  t  h  t  t  t  h  t  t  t  t  t  h  h  h  h  h  h


34 35 36 37 38 39 40 41 42 43 44 45 46 47 48 49 50 51 52 53 54 55 56 57 58 59 60 61 62 63 64

 h  t  h  t  t  t  h  h  h  h  t  t  t  t  h  t  t  t  h  h  h  h  h  h  h  h  t  t  h  h  t  t  t


65 66 67 68 69 70 71 72 73 74 75 76 77 78 79 80 81 82 83 84 85 86 87 88 89 90 91 92 93 94 95

 t  t  h  h  h  h  h  h  h  h  h  t  h  t  h  h  h  t  t  t  t  h  h  t  h  t  h  t  h  t  h  t  t  t


96 97 98 99 100

 t  h  t  t  h
```

From 100 flips we recorded 52 tails and 48 heads – a result that was two tails more and two heads less than the theoretical outcome of 50/50 each.

So our result was within ±2 of the theoretical result. Since we flipped 100 times, our error was therefore ±2 out of 100, or ±2%. The chances of our tossing exactly 50 heads and 50 tails are not great, but they are infinitely greater than the chance that we might toss 100 heads in a row or 100 tails. We can say, however, there is a good chance (it happens to be about 70%) that we will toss between 45 and 55 heads or tails (±5%) in every 100 throws.

Now it is easy to see from the above that predicting such an outcome across 100 flips from, say, half a dozen or even 10 flips might be a bit courageous. In fact if you closed your eyes and chose a sample from the results of our exercise above that happened to lie between the 67th and 76th tosses you would have got a very poor result in terms of a 50/50 outcome. You would have all heads or mostly heads. So a small sample can be very inaccurate. But the values of sampling can be demonstrated with even small samples.

Instead of taking a consecutive sample such as the one just mentioned, we might choose a completely random sample.

At www.randomizer.org/form.htm you will find another random numbers generator (something like the one you can access at the Lotto agency when you buy a ticket and don't want to fill out a coupon yourself), and without getting into the argument about the value of hardware- vs software-based generators, we asked for 10 sets of random numbers between 0 and 100.

For example, the first set we were given was: 65, 10, 95, 7, 37, 68, 49, 22, 31, and 64.

These were then matched against the corresponding flip numbers above and we discovered that our first sample was: t t t t t h t t h t – 8 tails and 2 heads. Not a very good predictor of what to expect if you flipped a coin 100 times. The results for the remaining nine randomly generated samples were more encouraging:

4 tails, 6 heads; **3 tails, 7 heads**; 3 tails 7 heads; **5 tails, 5 heads**; 3 tails, 7 heads; **5 tails, 5 heads**; 4 tails, 6 heads; **6 tails, 4 heads**; 5 tails, 5 heads.

In three out of the 10 cases, the randomly generated samples of just 10 flips correctly indicated the theoretical outcome that might be achieved with 100 tosses of the coins (i.e. 5 heads and 5 tails from the sample, or a 50/50 split in 100 tosses), in two cases the samples were one head too many and one tail too few (10%) and in three cases (7 of one and 3 of the other) the error was 20%.

Now these are tiny samples from a very small population. But the results, given such small numbers, are instructive. We got pretty close to the correct result on most occasions using small samples from a small population. So let us try something else.

If we should consider the numbers from 1 to 1000, we would know that half of them would be odd and half even. The question then might be, how accurately might a sample reflect that reality? Let's start with a small random sample of 20 numbers, just 2% of the population of 1000. Thanks to www.randomizer.org, our first 20-number sample turned up these figures:

424, 487, 133, 929, 852, 233, 27, 67, 624, 744, 16, 466, 100, 88, 831, 860, 849, 612, 623, 373. So the result was 10 odd numbers and 10 even numbers. Thus our random sample of 10 numbers accurately reflected the odd/even breakdown involved in 1000 consecutive numbers (half odd and half even). Which was a good start. but we might just have been very lucky.

So let's do it again. In fact let's do it several times. And the results? Without reproducing the actual numbers, this is what we got for each of four additional requests: 12 even, 8 odd; **6 even**, **14 odd**; 7 even, 13 odd; **11 even**, **9 odd**. Thus, apart from one case again, and despite the small sample (20 out of 1000), we still managed to get fairly close to the target of 10 even and 10 odd.

Increasing our sample size to 60 (6% of the population being surveyed) produced the following results by drawing five separate samples: 31 even, 29 odd; **25 even**, **35 odd**; 33 even, 27 odd; **32 even**, **28 odd**; 29 even, 31 odd. The worst result produced an error margin of ±8.3%, but the margin for the other four cases ranged from ±5% to ±1.65% – from a sample of just 6%.

As indicated earlier, mathematicians and statisticians tell us if you tossed 100 coins, you would have 680 chances out of 1000 (68%) of getting between 45 and 55 heads for each 100 throws. They also tell us in the case of a dichotomous question (only two possible options available, such as heads or tails, male or female, yes or no), that at a confidence level of 95% (19 out of 20 cases) we need to sample only 384 respondents to achieve a result that would be within 5% either way of the true value that might be arrived at by examining each case in the population concerned (i.e. the true or perfect result).

Let us assume the population is equally divided between males and females. In fact, in Australia, at the last count there were 99 males for every 100 females (women live longer). But for the purposes of this exercise, let us assume a neat 50/50 split.

Let us call odd numbers male and even numbers female, and for argument's sake for the moment, let us choose a sample of 384 from a total of 10,000, or a sample of 3.84% of the population in question.

To get a theoretically perfect result from such a sample we need a split of 192 evens (females) and 192 odds (males). We took six samples of 384 each (just to see how the samples might vary). The results we achieved for each sample were: 189 even, 195 odd (a margin of ±0.7%); 197 even, 187 odd (±1.3%); 197 even, 187 odd (±1.3%); 176 even, 208 odd (±4.15%); 210 even, 174 odd (±4.7%); and 212 even, 172 odd (±5.2%)

All the samples above (with one slight exception . . . which is why we say 19 out of 20 times) from just 3.84% of a total population of 10,000 satisfied the statistical outcome expected.

A sampling error of ±5 per cent is, of course, nowhere near good enough for many polls and surveys, not to mention scientific test results. So bigger samples are needed, although dramatically increasing the size of the sample does not necessarily produce a dramatic increase in the accuracy of the results.

If we take the case mentioned at the beginning of this section, a population of 23,000 people, and decide we will accept a 5% level of error, the calculator at custominsight.com says that a sample of 269 will provide a result that will offer a confidence level of accuracy of 90%, 378 will lift the accuracy confidence level to 95%, and a sample of 645 will provide an accuracy confidence level of 99%. That is probably as good as you will get. But with a starting point of 378 respondents to get 90%, it clearly shows that just interviewing a few, or a few dozen, or even a few score of people in the street is not going to give you results you can rely on.

Suppose in the case above you reduce your population by a factor of 10 (to produce a population of 2300). Despite the reduction, you need almost as many in your sample as you did originally with 10 times more. To use the custominsight.com calculator, your samples (for 90%, 95% and 99% confidence levels) would need to be 243, 329 and 515.

However, should you **increase** your original population size 10 times (from 23,000 to 230,000) the sample size changes by only a fraction; from 269 to 272 (at 90% confidence level), from 378 to 384 (95%), and from 645 to 662 (99%).

Now if you increase your population size a further 10 times (from 230,000 to 2,300,000), the sample size does not change at all. Even if you increase the population another tenfold (to 23,000,000), the sample size still remains what it was when the population was 230,000. This should help explain why it is possible to survey the TV viewing habits of 150 million Americans with a sample size of just over a thousand homes.

So, organising your own survey is probably not a good idea. But reporting other people's surveys, which is a more sensible approach, also calls for some discipline on the part of the reporter. This is an area in which the news media frequently transgress. Polls are reported without mentioning the necessary details described above. If the readers do not know how a poll was conducted, why should they place any value on the results obtained? That is one issue, and it is a major issue. But there is another. The media, including the news media, regularly conduct polls and present the findings as if they were meaningful. Given the methodology used in many cases (viewers or listeners invited to phone or SMS this number or that) and given the opportunity these polls present for manipulation by individuals in the audience (by arranging for the swamping of one of the phone number options), it is clear any connection between such polls and reality may be broad or coincidental at best, or misleading and useless at worst. There is one further overwhelming reason why such polls are dubious. The respondents select themselves.

Reporting polls properly

Anyone producing a poll story has to allow some room on the page for foot-notes or a "fact file" giving details of authorship and the methodology used in the poll. Here is a list of things readers are entitled to know if they are to place any credibility on the information contained in the story.

Who conducted the poll?

There are professional market research and polling companies who conduct polls regularly. They have professional reputations to protect and the answers they provide are relied upon by other organisations. Reputable companies do not get into "cooking" results for their clients. There is no point. The client wants to know what is really happening in the market place, even if the news is bad. Giving a client good news when it should have been a bad report will soon destroy a market researcher's reputation. In other words, the client will say the message they got from the poll or the market research was inaccurate, and the word will quickly spread.

Readers are also entitled to know if the people who conducted the poll on which a story is based can be relied on to deliver meaningful information.

Who paid the bill?

Is the poll what it seems? Was it done for the news organisation present-ing the story? Or someone else? Who commissioned it? The reader is enti-tled to know, in case the story might come with a little bit of baggage attached. Alarm bells might start ringing if there is no mention of who paid the bill. Why were they not identified? Did they not want to be identified, perhaps?

Any story without this information attached should be treated with suspicion.

Who was polled/questioned?

This is vital information and must be included since it will reveal whether the claims made in the story have any potential validity. A story forecasting the outcome of an election based on the voting intentions of a group of X hundred respondents could be fine, depending on who they were. But if they were all over the age of fifty and if voting were compulsory for everyone over the age of 18, then the poll would be totally unrepresentative.

How were they chosen?

Was this a random sample or a specialised sample? Choosing a random sample from a community is very different from just conveniently choosing shoppers in that community, albeit randomly, at lunchtime. Who knows how many of them might have been visitors to the shopping centre? And what about the opinions of those who never shop at that time of day, or at that place? The reader needs to know.

If it was a special sample, football fans perhaps, how were they chosen? The views of fans at a particular match may in no way represent the views of supporters generally. Football fans tend to have allegiances that are welded-on. They may be "one-eyed" or biased. This may render completely invalid any generalisation that the opinions of supporters of one or two clubs might represent the views of football fans generally.

When was the survey conducted?

Timing could be a significant issue. For instance, responses to a survey about financial matters could be very different just before or just after a budget announcing tax increases or tax relief. A poll taken before some significant event could be quite meaningless after the event.

The reader should know. Some polls are taken over time, perhaps a week. Again the reader has to be told, in case something happened during that week that might cause the reader to have reservations about the information contained in the story.

What questions were asked?

Getting the questions right so as not to introduce a bias into the impartiality of the survey is most important. Obviously leading questions have to be avoided. But even the order in which questions are asked could be an issue. Some questions may also disturb respondents who may not wish to answer, thus reducing the sample size and impacting on the validity of the poll, or respondents may answer less than frankly because they could regard the question as intrusive. So the reader needs to know what questions were asked.

What was the sampling error involved?

Again this information is necessary if the reader is to be convinced the survey and the story based on it have any merit. Not to reveal a sampling error might raise some questions. Oversight, or deliberate omission? Either way, the absence of such information does nothing for the story. Include the sampling error.

Are there any relevant comparisons?

Presenting a bland poll result can be like presenting a bland average. It doesn't tell all the story. Perhaps there have been other polls published on the issue recently. Perhaps the matter was looked into a year ago, or maybe every year for the last several years. What did they show and how do their results compare? This kind of information will make a better story.

At least in the case of newspapers, there are some requirements that are supposed to be met when reporting polls. The Australian Press Council (which among other things adjudicates on complaints brought to it against newspaper members) has produced a list of things that should be mentioned when polls and surveys are reported. Some might say the list does not go far enough, and the list is not always followed, but here it is.

"The Press Council believes that reports should as far as possible include the following details:

1. The identity of the sponsor (if any) of the survey.
2. The exact wording of the question(s) asked.
3. A definition of the population from which the sample was drawn.
4. The sample size and method of sampling.
5. Which results were based on only part of the sample: e.g. men or women; adherents of particular political parties; and the base number from which percentages were derived.
6. Name of the organisation that carried out the survey.
   Additionally, the following information may also be included:
7. How and where the interviews were carried out: in person, in homes, by telephone, by mail, in the street, or whatever.
8. Date when the interviews were carried out.
9. Who carried out the poll, e.g. trained interviewers, telephonists, reporters etc."

Try it . . . use a spreadsheet to calculate data

A document falls off the back of a truck. You open it. It's a spreadsheet.

Do you know what it means? Could you interrogate it? Could you make sense of it? And write a story from it?

Whatever programs you use, if you have a professional package, as well as a word processor it almost certainly includes a spreadsheet package. If you use the Microsoft Office suite, these are called Word and Excel. You should learn how to use the spreadsheet. It is very helpful.

In this section, I'll talk about Excel, because it's the one I'm most familiar with, but all spreadsheets allow you to do an extraordinary range of calculations that could take forever if you did them manually, even with a calculator. And they also allow you to manipulate or re-configure data for your own convenience.

Some of the things spreadsheets can do for you include:

- tell you how many entries you have on a spreadsheet that you have to deal with (how many cases there are)
- tell you how many there are of a particular kind (figures or letters)
- add groups of data or chosen portions of a data set
- find the maximum entry, the minimum, and the mean (average) for whole groups or portions of data
- determine a standard deviation
- calculate how many cases are greater or lesser than a chosen base figure.

While this section is no substitute for a training course, it will introduce you to the basic tools you might use to advantage as a journalist.

Excel operates on the basis of cell addresses. Each cell is located in a row and a column and thus has an "address" – much like the coordinates on a map or the x, y axis references on a simple graph.

It performs instant calculations and when you have an answer it will remind you what the calculation was that produced that answer. This can be very useful a week later.

Exercise

A spreadsheet, which is not designed to be taken as representing any reality, is available at [www.cambridge.edu.au/grundy]. If you open the document and complete the exercise that follows, it may help you gain at least some basic understanding of how to use Excel.

To find out what is in a cell, place your cursor in the title top cell of each column and double click. The column opens out to reveal all the wording of the column heading. For example, place your cursor over the "O" in "Offence" in column D and double left click. The wording opens out to reveal "Offence: Break and Enter". Do the same for Column G.

If you need to expand a column, click your cursor onto the title row of the columns, where it says A B C etc. then move the mouse over the right-hand extremity. An up-down, left-right arrow should appear, and you may increase the width of the column by dragging it to the right. Now you should be able to see the data.

For the sake of the exercise, your fictional spreadsheet was prepared by the North Region Commander of the state's police force, Inspector Smith. He was appointed to the job in 2000 and at the end of 2005 wanted to get some idea of what was happening in relation to some of the crime that was occurring. The entries on the spreadsheet in bold indicate raw data, those in normal type are his calculations from that data.

His spreadsheet shows changes in the incidence of break-and-enters and motor vehicle theft dealt with by officers in the 30 police stations under his control during the years 2000–2005. It also shows the change that took place in staff numbers over that period.

Column	Data
A	the identifying number of each of his 30 stations
B	the number of officers in each station handling break-and-enter and motor vehicle cases in 2000
C	the number he had working on those cases in each station in 2005
D	the number of break-and-enter offences handled by each station in 2000
E	the number of break-and-enters in 2005
F	the figures for motor vehicle theft in 2000
G	the motor vehicle theft figures for 2005

Now for some calculations. Clearly Insp Smith would want to know the total number of officers he had working on such cases in each of the years under review.

Calculating totals

Go to the very bottom of column B and click in the last cell (containing the figure 197). Immediately you will see (in the calculation field at the top of your screen next to the = sign above column D), the calculation used to obtain that total, i.e. =SUM(B3:B32). This instruction simply means "add the entries in column B from rows 3 to 32". If you click in the last entry in row C, the calculation to produce a figure for the total number of staff in 2005 appears in the calculation field, i.e. =SUM(C3:C32).

> To add figures in rows across the page rather than in columns down the page, the calculation would still involve =SUM(beginning cell address: end cell address). For example, if the first cell were B3 and the last K3, the calculation would be: =SUM(B3:K3).

Totals for the other columns of interest, D, E, G and H, can be obtained using similar calculation instructions for each of the columns involved.

Calculating percentage increases

Insp Smith then wanted to know what these raw figures revealed. For instance, compared with the base year of 2000, he wondered by how much had the incidence of these offences increased? In other words, based on the 2000 figures, by what percentage had the incidence of these offences increased across the 30 stations in his command?

He produced the result for each of them in a flash. Click on the cell at the top of column F on the internet spreadsheet (the figure of 28.74). The calculation involved opens up in the calculation display field as: (E3-D3)/E3*100.

This is a simple calculation of the percentage increase that has occurred over the period 2000–2005, using the figure for 2000 as the base number. In other words: the latest figure minus the original figure as a percentage of the original figure; or put another way, the latest figure minus the original figure divided by the original figure multiplied by 100; or the difference between the two figures expressed as a decimal fraction of the original figure. A simple percentage change in other words.

Now place the cursor over the small black square on the bottom right-hand corner of the heavy outline around cell F3. The large cross cursor becomes a small cross. When the cursor changes, click, hold and drag to the bottom of the data. A calculation similar to that which produced the result in cell F3 is carried out all the way down the column. To do this with a calculator would involve 30 separate calculations (and in a big spreadsheet, hundreds).

Now Insp Smith can see how the incidence of break-and-enters has changed over the years 2000–2005 in each of his police station areas and that, in total, there has been a 58 per cent increase in the number of such offences over those years.

He can perform the same calculation for motor vehicle thefts. Go to cell I3, click and drag. This reveals the percentage change for each station and that there has been a 62 per cent increase in such offences during the period under review.

Calculating averages

Insp Smith might like to know how many of his stations recorded a result higher than the overall average for the region. On a one-page spreadsheet he could probably tell by having a close look. But there is a better way (particularly if the spreadsheet is large).

Go to the top of column J. If you click on cell J3, you will find the following calculation displayed in the calculation field window: =COUNTIF(F3:F32,">58.5"). This calculation simply asks, in the entries in the column from F3 to F32, what is the frequency with which scores higher than 58.5 appear? And the answer is 18. In other words, 18 of Insp Smith's stations are above the mean for the group and 12 are at or below it, in relation to the offence of break-and-enter. That may be of interest to him.

He can perform the same calculation in relation to motor vehicle thefts. Go to cell J4. The calculation appears in the window and reveals the number of times a figure greater than 62 (the overall average increase in car theft offences in the region) appears in column I.

Other calculations

Now if Insp Smith were aware that over the whole state the increase in such offences was 48 per cent for break-and-enters and 53 per cent for car thefts, he could do a quick calculation to find how many of his stations were above or below the state average. Click on cells J9 and J10 and check the calculations in the field window. Slightly more than two thirds of his stations are above the state average in relation to the increase in break-and-enter offences and slightly more than half exceed the state average for the increase in car theft.

Insp Smith might also want to know what change had taken place in the number of incidents being investigated by his station staff in 2000 compared with 2005. To do so he would add the number of break-and-enters and car thefts recorded by each station in 2000 and divide this result by the number of staff in each station at the time. And he would do the same for 2005. If you click and drag on cells K3 and L3 you will see the results – which would no doubt be useful for the Inspector.

If these were real figures, it would also be possible to write an interesting story from them.

Some common calculations

Sum

To add a group of figures, use: =SUM(start cell address:end cell address)

Maximum

To identify the highest in any group of figures, use: =MAX(start cell address:end cell address).

Minimum

To identify the lowest in any group of figures, use: =MIN(start cell address:end cell address).

Mean

To find a mean, use: =AVERAGE(start cell address:end cell address).

Standard deviation

To calculate a standard deviation (the average deviation of each item from the mean), use: =STDEV(start cell address:end cell address).

Less or more than

To discover how many entries in a column were less than a certain figure (say 9), use: =COUNTIF(start cell address:end cell address,"<9").

For more than, use: =COUNTIF(start cell address:end cell address,">9").

Empty cells

It is important to know whether empty cells are regarded as 0's or are ignored during a calculation. For instance, if three entries in a column were 14, 0, and 10, the average would be 8 (24 divided by 3). But if the entries were seen as 14, blank and 10, the average would be 12 (24 divided by 2). Excel will ignore empty cells. If you want them to represent zero, enter 0.

Number of this or that

If a column contained names rather than numbers, you could determine, for instance, how many widgets (as distinct from gadgets, wingwongs and thingamies) were recorded via the following: =COUNTIF(start cell address:end cell address,"widget").

Extending your capabilities

There are a number of helpful books and internet sites available should you wish to improve your spreadsheet skills in any particular package.

Some of the more advanced features require optional software to be loaded as an extra, or "plug in". Many of these are free, but they may not have been loaded on to your computer when the package was installed.

Should you wish to do correlations (for instance, what correlation might there be between the incidence of break-and-enter robberies and car theft – on the basis that those who commit such robberies often steal their transport and getaway vehicles), you would need to check if the necessary software has been loaded to your computer.

Questions and interviews

There is a difference between asking questions and conducting an interview. Asking questions is what reporters do all the time. They don't necessarily do interviews all the time. We will deal with questions first.

Questions

A reporter in the middle of a breaking news event, either on the spot where it is happening, or in the office on the telephone, will be busy enough just asking questions and looking for more people to question. He or she will not be fussy about how the questions are asked. It will not matter, for instance, in what order the questions are asked. What will be important is, were they asked? And who was asked? There will be no time, or need, for fancy footwork. Just get the information.

At their core the questions in such a situation will be those we have encountered already – who, what, where, when, why and how, in various ways.

What happened? Who was there? Who was responsible? When was it? Where? How did it happen? Any reason why?

And then, perhaps:

> Has it happened before? When was that? What happened on that occasion? Who was involved?
>
>   What happens next? When will that be? Why then?

Questions that ask **who**, **when** and **where** usually produce short responses – names, times and places. Unless the names introduce an extra dimension to the story, answers to these questions may be brief.

The **what**, **how** and **why** questions are the ones that are likely to produce more extensive copy. They are questions that usually cannot be answered in a word or even a few words. These are the questions the reporter always has on stand-by when chasing a story.

Questions starting with "could" have a place in the reporter's kitbag. But to produce a good result, you will probably need to combine them with **how** or **why**.

> Q: "Could the situation have been prevented?"   A: "I guess so."
>
> Q: "**How?**"   A: "Well . . . "
>
> Q: "Could the situation have been prevented?"   A: "Probably not."
>
> Q: "**Why?**" *or* "**Why not?**"   A: "Because . . . "

As you see, the first response gives you very little; it is the second that might get you some copy.

If you asked, "How could the situation have been prevented?", you are assuming it could have been prevented. The answer might be: "Who said it could have been prevented?" and now you are being questioned. It is to be hoped that you have a good answer.

"Is", "Are", "Was" and "Were" should also be in your kitbag of question-starters, but once again **how**, **what**, **why** and **why not** should be at the ready. They may produce some results.

> Q: "Are you happy with this result?"   A: "No, not really."
>
> Q: "**What** are you going to do about it then?"
>
> Q: "Are you happy with this result?"   A: "Yes, quite happy."
>
> Q: "It doesn't seem particularly good. **Why** are you happy with it?"

Now you might get a useful response, even if your talent (the person you are asking questions) should disagree with you.

This situation could have been handled another way, but it is fraught with danger for the inexperienced. Let us go back a little. What if the exchange went like this?

Q: "Are you happy with this result?"   A: "Yes, quite happy."
Q: "But it is a very poor result."   A: "Is it? Why do you say that?"

Now the reporter has to be on the ball, because the roles have been reversed. The question-asker has become the question-answerer; the reporter has become the interviewee. It is better to finish an exchange with a question rather than with a statement. You have more chance of retaining control.

Preparing for interviews

Good interviewing takes some care and preparation. The following points should get you off to a good start. They are not in priority order.

Know who your audience is

Is the story for the general news pages, the business section, travel, lifestyle, sport? Some people could be interviewed for all of the above. Unless you know who you are writing for, you might do the wrong interview!

Know whether you are writing news or a feature

If you are doing the interview for a news story you will get to the heart of the matter pretty quickly and not beat around the bush. If the story is for a feature you will be interested in a great deal more: appearance, features, mannerisms, personality, clothes, grooming perhaps, memorabilia in the office, background, hobbies . . . In fact there is no limit to the things that might give you the insight you are seeking and make your feature a "must-read".

Know the news

You have to be informed. If you go to interview someone and are unaware of what has been happening in the news, you may be caught out and left to feel very foolish.

It is taken for granted that as a journalist you will be up to speed with what is going on in the world. If that is a bother, perhaps you should choose another path.

Do some research

There was a time when research was quite difficult and time-consuming. The only resource that was available in a practical sense was the office library and its collection of cuttings.

Now there is the internet, and there is no excuse. It is a challenge these days to find someone who does **not** have at least a couple of entries on the internet. Going into an interview ignorant of your subject (unless the individual is really **completely** unknown) is as bad as not knowing the news of the day.

If the person you are to interview has no background that you can uncover, you should be candid about your ignorance. If the individual does have a career or a track record that you should have called up but didn't, candour is less desirable.

In these days of the internet, failing to research your subject is not professional. So, be professional. Do some research.

Prepare a structure or a strategy

Unless you are either very confident or very experienced, you should prepare a plan for an interview. If you expect the interview to be easy, you will just need a structure of what you want to ask. If you expect the interview to be difficult, you will do well to produce a strategy. A strategy is more than a plan. To build a strategy you not only need to think clearly about the things you want to cover, but you also have to think about the answers you might get, and consider how you might respond. You will be well prepared, regardless of which way the answers go, and you will be able to enter into the interview with confidence.

Contrary to popular belief it is not a good idea to write out a list of questions. Prepare a list of points. A few words each at the most. A list of questions will be too long and take up too much room in your notebook, you will read them rather than speak naturally, and you will concentrate too much on them and not enough on the answers you are getting to your questions.

And you should have a dedicated notebook. Not just scraps or sheets of paper. More on that later.

A list of points can be referred to quickly if you need to check how you are going. Of course, you will have to rely on your professional ability to construct articulate questions, since they will not be written down. But that's part of becoming a professional; the sooner you are capable of being articulate the better. Don't waffle. Force yourself to ask questions that are clear and unambiguous. If you start to "umm" and "ahh", check yourself. Tell yourself you can do better, and do it. It is a matter of discipline and practice.

Arrange the points in a sensible, logical order, the way you think the interview should go. Be aware that it may not go that way, but having a structure prepared beforehand will still produce a coherent result and notes that you will be able to access easily when you come to write the story.

If we are talking about a strategy, rather than just a structure, you will have a roadmap in front of you. You can refer to it quickly and easily thus keeping the interview on the track you want it to take instead of being sidetracked by your subject.

Make yourself a notebook

The chances are at this stage in your career you will not have shorthand. If you do, so much the better, but it is unlikely. So you will have to use longhand, or your own "shorthand", to make notes.

Don't assume that an audio recorder is a substitute for a notebook. By all means have one and use it if your talent (interviewee) is happy about that, but finding quotes when you want them, with the clock ticking ever faster, can be a nightmare. At least with a notebook you can skim through the pages quickly and find what you want. Remember too, there are places where recorders are not allowed. You can't take recorders to court for example. One day you will be sent to court, or someone will object to being recorded, so you might as well get used to making notes.

There is a further issue. If some legal problem should arise from your story, you will need to have all your notes. Notebooks are important and you should keep them for at least three years. Legal matters can drag on.

For telephone and face-to-face interviews for newspapers, here is my advice. Buy a notebook that is big enough for a longhand writer, but not so big that it is clumsy. Don't get a shorthand notebook ruled down the middle. It will be too small. A notebook about 18 cm wide by 22.5 cm high (7 inches × 9 inches) is about right. It should be lined, and spiral bound on the left – not at the top. Get a sharp handyman's blade, buy one if necessary, fold the heavy front and back covers out of the way, and with a straight edge, cut the pages horizontally about 6 or 7 cm from the bottom all the way from the spiral binding to the right-hand edge.

Now you have a notebook with a section at the top (three quarters of the page) for your notes, and a section at the bottom for the points you want to cover. Both are in the one place, not on separate sheets of paper which will be difficult to manage if you don't have a table for the interview. Quite often you will have no more than your knee (if you are lucky).

The point about cutting the pages so that the points are on the bottom and your notes at the top will become clear when you do your first interview. You will soon fill the first page with notes. When you turn it to reveal a fresh

A well-designed notebook makes organising interview notes much easier

page, the points you made will still be in front of you at the bottom of the page and you can quickly glance at them if you need to.

Divide the bottom section into three columns. Write your points clearly in the first two columns. You may need to write a little smaller than usual. Leave the third column blank so that you can quickly add a point during the interview if something crops up that you had not considered. Relying on your memory to recall the matter before the end of the interview could be foolish.

If you need more space for points, turn the bottom section of your page. You can write on the back of it and on the front of the following page and the two opened out should give you enough space for any interview. This way all your points will be in front of you all the time, you will have space to add more if need be, and you will still have plenty of room for your notes.

During the interview, as your notes get near the bottom of your shortened page and the need to turn to a fresh page approaches, use your free hand to push the page slightly upward. Because you are using a spiral bound notebook, the top of the page will skew upwards just a little. You will be able to get a finger of your free hand under it and be able to turn it easily when the time comes. Struggling with a page that refuses to turn, and having to turn 10 or 20 instead is something you do not need when you are concentrating on what your subject is saying and writing it down at the same time.

You will use many more pages of the top section of your notebook than the bottom of course, but that is a small price to pay for a very good system at a time when you may need all the help you can get.

Be sure to write the name of the person you are interviewing and the date at the top of the first page. That could be important if a legal matter should arise.

Reporters working for radio and television need only worry about making a list of points. Make them big enough so you can see at a glance what they say. You will not have to worry about your note-taking skills. All your answers will be on tape (or digital stick).

Learn shorthand or make your own

Shorthand is a really valuable tool. If you choose to learn it, Teeline is the simplest.

Good shorthand is the only thing that will allow you to keep up with a speaker. When you have to make notes longhand, keeping up with a speaker isn't easy. But even for you, help is at hand.

Those of you who use mobile phones which predict or second-guess the words you are writing will know how seldom you need to change the predicted text … even though the 26 letters of the alphabet are reduced to combinations of just 9. It is extraordinary how often a combination of those nine keys produces one obvious intelligible word. In a similar way this also indicates that you can shorten words quite substantially and still be able to read them accurately. As well, it has been shown that readers can still quite easily decipher words that are very badly spelled.

Try it. Leave out vowels for instance.

> "Shorthand": Whn I cm t Aus I ws 14 & I lvd n lvpl in Syd fr th fst 3 yrs I ws hr.
> Longhand: When I came to Australia I was 14 and I lived in Liverpool in Sydney for the first 3 years I was here.

The "shorthand" version above contains 43 characters and the longhand 81 … almost double.

You will need to practise, but next to having shorthand there is really no other way.

At the interview

Get the details up front

It is wise to check name, title and position, address, and so on, early in the process. Get the spelling right.

One wrong letter in a name cost an Australian newspaper a considerable amount of money. And another had to pay up because a reporter called

Police Sergeant Bloggs, Detective Sergeant Bloggs. That is how easy it is to get a defamation writ.

And it is embarrassing if you have to call back from the office because you forgot to ask an important question.

Listening is just as important as asking

The reason your structure should be a list of points, not questions, and the reason for making your own special notebook so you can refer quickly to your points is to give you every opportunity to concentrate on what is being said to you. **You must listen** to the answers to your questions.

Answers may be incomplete; they may be evasive; they may not have dealt with your questions at all; and most importantly, they may raise fresh matters you had not considered.

If the interviewee does raise something new, you have two choices. The first is to deal with it straightaway. The second is to quickly add it to your list of points. This is often the better choice, because dealing with it straightaway may interrupt the flow of the interview, or interfere with your strategy.

Remember, not everyone you will interview will be thrilled to see you. Which is why your strategy will be important. It may not be a good idea to deal with a new issue before you have finished with one you have already started. But if that is your decision, making a mental note that you have another matter to deal with is often not good enough. You may forget altogether, or just as bad, you may remember there was something you had to cover, but 15 minutes later, you can't recall what it was. You will almost certainly remember in the car on the way back to the office.

In newspaper reporting, unlike radio and television reporting, your performance as an interviewer will not be on public display. You will do many of your interviews over the phone. You may be able to conceal a poorly conducted interview from the rest of the newsroom, and the world, as long as the answers you got covered the subject matter of the interview somehow. But that is not the end of the matter. The person you spoke with will have a view of how you handled yourself and will no doubt chatter to those around. Word spreads, particularly from prominent people. And you will deal with that kind of person quite a lot in your job. It is thus a folly to think it is okay to fumble your way through an interview. Besides, practising the process and improving your skill will pay off one day when you are given a tough assignment.

In radio and television your performance is on public display. You will have to sound professional. You may be standing and have nowhere for your notebook except to hold it in your hand. The other may be holding a microphone. Referring to your notebook will have to be done quickly, otherwise your talent may become distracted or feel you are not paying attention. Unless it is a quick or minor story, one thing you must do is **prepare** for the interview.

Clarify what is not clear

Listening is vital, for a range of reasons. One of them is so that you are aware of, and can clarify, answers that are not clear. You may think it impolite to ask someone to explain again what they have just explained, but if it is not clear to you on the spot, it is hardly likely to become clear by the time you get back to the office, or after you put the phone down.

Calling back may be a bit embarrassing.

So, one way to deal with such a situation is to be upfront about it.

> Can I be clear about that? What you are saying is . . . *(summarise what you think you have been told)*?

If you are right, well and good. If you are wrong, you will be put right. There is no point at the end of an interview having a book full of notes that you do not understand. You will not be able to write a useful story from them.

Go beyond clarification, seek justification too

Your readers, or some of them, will expect more than just a recital of guff from your interview. If the individual wants only to inform, let them put out a press release.

Interviews are for getting more than just a person's position on a matter. Interviews are for getting the arguments that support that position.

You may need to know the counter arguments. You will probably need to be well informed. You will certainly need to be up with the news. But that has been covered already. Be prepared. Ask the questions that need to be asked.

Don't leave your mind behind

As you listen to what you are being told, keep your mind in gear. Does this add up? Does it make sense? If not, or if there is some doubt, you should query such remarks or comments. Again, there is no point having a notebook full of stuff (or guff) that will make you look foolish when you come to write your story.

During an interview your brain has to be quite active. You have to listen to what is being said. You have to write it down, legibly enough so you can write a story from it, including some direct quotes. You have to be ready with the next, or a follow-up question. And you have to evaluate what you are being told. You need to do all of this at once. Concentrating on just one, or a couple of them, will not do. If you are worrying about the next question and miss the content of the current answer, you have a problem.

Conducting a good interview is much more than asking some questions.

Beware the fallacy of "eye contact"

There is a suggestion you will come across in books on interviewing that you should "maintain eye contact" with your subject. This message is regularly pressed on those starting out in radio and television. In my experience, however, it is quite silly. Try it sometime. Too much eye contact will cause great discomfort in most people. Look at your subject by all means, but don't focus your eyes on his or hers. If you do, you will probably not get much of an interview. Your subject will be very distracted.

As a newspaper reporter with a notebook, you will be making notes during the interview so you will be looking where you are writing for much of the time. You need to look up regularly so the interviewee is aware that you are interested . . . and listening. But watch out for "eye contact".

Playing dumb is one thing; being dumb is another

There will be occasions when, despite your best efforts, you will not know much about the subject of the interview or perhaps the person you are interviewing. On other occasions you may be very well informed. It will be part of your strategy whether you reveal or conceal that knowledge during the interview.

Sometimes it is a good idea to let your talent know that you are well informed and up to speed, and on other occasions it is just as good to keep that to yourself . . . until you need it, at least.

The point is, just because you are well informed on something, or even a bit of an expert, does not mean that you should flaunt that in front of your talent to show off. "Showing off" is something you find from time to time among journalists, as in any other profession. The smart ones, on the other hand, are more cautious . . . sometimes they are up to speed and knowledgable, sometimes not. There is a difference between knowing it all and being a "know-all". You may get better results at times by withholding your knowledge unless you need to produce it.

Beware "double-barrel" and "scattergun" questions

Trying too hard, or trying to impress by showing how much they know, can lead interviewers into error. If there are two sides, or more, to a story or argument, they may be led into asking questions that cover too much. These are known as double-barrelled or scattergun questions.

A double-barrelled question looks like this:

> Q: Lord Mayor, is the council going to increase water rates or introduce restrictions to cut water consumption?

This is what a scattergun question looks like:

> Q: Lord Mayor, the Council wants people to stop using so much water and has banned sprinklers. Wouldn't it be better to increase the price of water, which would mean some people will use much less but some will pay the extra, and at least the city won't turn into a desert, and maybe increase fines for out-of-hours use so that budget revenues will at least be maintained? Surely the loss of income normally generated by excess water charges, because no one is using excess water, will impact seriously on the bottom line this year?
> A: The loss of revenue . . .

If you ask a double-barrelled question or fire a scattergun, you will almost certainly not get answers to all the matters raised. Usually, only the last point will be dealt with.

A strategy for this interview, for example, might have involved something like this:

> Q: Lord Mayor, because the Council has banned sprinklers, how much revenue will be lost on excess water charges?
> A: The amount . . .
>
> Q: If the drought continues – and that seems likely given that the autumn/winter dry season is almost here – are you concerned the city will turn into a "desert"?
> A: Well of course . . .
>
> Q: Would it not have been better to simply increase the price of water and the fines for illegal use? (*Your background thinking includes. Some would be prepared to pay, some would not, thus preserving at least something of the "look" of the city, while saving water, and not affecting revenue so drastically.*)
> A: It might seem that way, but . . .
>
> Q: How many households have installed tanks?
> A: Approximately . . .
>
> Q: How many households are there where tanks are not an option?
> A: That's a harder question . . .
>   *And so on.*

The above would have to be reduced to point form, but at least a serious attempt has been made to organise the interview into a sensible structure.

Remember too, that not everyone you interview will give you straight and open answers. They may be evasive, sharp and short, and even dismissive of you. If you toss up double-barrelled or scattergun questions to such a person, you will be mauled, figuratively speaking.

That is another reason why you must have your mind in gear. Sometimes you will have to deal with challenging and unhelpful people.

Don't become the subject of the interview

There is a whole industry out there based on teaching people how to handle the media: how to handle an interview, how to put the best "spin" on a situation and how to avoid answering questions. These sessions are often conducted by journalists or former journalists. Two of the "skills" participants learn in simulated interview settings are how to turn the interview on the interviewer, and how to stay "on message" regardless of the question.

An example of the first case is the high-profile interviewer who pointed out to former British Prime Minister Margaret Thatcher that "some people" were critical of the way she did things. Mrs Thatcher wanted to know who these people were. It's a common scenario. Be careful about asking "some people say" questions. You might be asked to justify your claim. If you were, could you?

You may also have to deal with people who will answer only their own questions, not yours. This is called staying "on message". Politicians do it; those with a crisis management situation to deal with (and a PR team in the background) do it all the time.

A recent example occurred during an interview about a scandal involving an Australian organisation paying illegal "kickbacks" to Saddam Hussein's government as part of a United Nations "food for oil" program. The Opposition spokesman on foreign affairs was asked if his party would have performed any better in relation to the scandal had it been in power. The spokesman simply continued his attack on what the government had done and made no attempt to answer the question. Time was up and he got away with it.

Don't ignore hypothetical and even "silly" questions

Some things are always worth a try. If they don't work, it's no loss. If they do, good.

The first is the hypothetical question . . . the one that starts with "If". "If you don't get the support you need, what then?" The response may well be: "That's a hypothetical question and I'm not getting into hypotheticals." But not always. So don't be concerned if it doesn't work, or worry that someone might snigger at you for asking such a dud question. Dud questions sometimes come off.

And the "silly" question, the so-obvious question that no one asks lest they be thought a fool, may not be as silly as it seems. I recall a whole press conference once almost breaking up with mirth when an earnest reporter asked a very senior political figure about a policy that was seen to be very out-of-date and discredited. It was surely a silly question and produced a ripple of mirth among the questioner's colleagues. But the smiles quickly evaporated when the answer emerged. In fact it became a major story.

You have to be strong and not easily affected by the reaction of others if you ask hypothetical or "silly" questions. But there is nothing wrong with a bit of self-confidence and self-assurance if you know what you are doing. You will need both when dealing with some of the folk you will be sent to interview.

Silence can be golden

Sometimes, if you don't respond immediately after an answer, the interviewee will keep talking. Not always, and then it will be a case of who cracks first, you or your talent. But silence is not expected in a formal situation like an interview. Indeed, most people are uncomfortable with silences of more than a few seconds. If you indicate, by saying nothing, that you are waiting for more, you may get it. And "it" may be good.

Saying nothing will usually be interpreted as indicating that you heard what was said, but you are not convinced that is the real story, or all of the story, so you are waiting to hear more. Of course, silence may not bring it out, in which case you will have to start probing for it.

Other advice for interviewers

Are you ready for the hard questions?

Taking part in chatty interviews with lovely people can be really quite nice, of course. And quite easy. But are you ready for the day you have to ask the hard question? Are you? It is something worth thinking about.

All your life so far you have been popular: lots of friends, always treated others with care and respect, particularly those more senior, and that is the way you like it. Now you have to go and talk with whoever about some controversy or scam and the time has come when the interview will not necessarily be happy and chatty.

Some people are even terrified of the telephone and hate calling strangers for interviews. Such strangers often have mean secretaries who aren't at all sweet and lovely – some are really scary – and so on. If you are in this "shy" category, you need to find a way to become more assertive. Journalism is not necessarily the ideal vocation for the shrinking violet.

And it could get worse. You could be asked some day to talk to the family of a local 16-year-old killed in a car accident on the way home from her school "formal", or some equally distressing incident. Such tasks are known in the business as "death knocks". If you are not comfortable with this, check your professional code of ethics. It may allow you to decline such assignments.

You may think that people will object to your approach at such a difficult time. Some will, to be sure, but others will not. They will be concerned that others not go through what they have suffered and will be prepared or anxious to tell their story in case it should help someone else. For some, telling a reporter about an incident or the danger involved in some activity, or whatever, can be a release and a relief. Others will find your approach confronting and distressing.

In either case you will need all the tact and sensitivity you can muster to deal with the task, because it will not be easy. You will need a few human relations skills. It is as well to think about these things beforehand. You will be better prepared and perhaps sufficiently confident to do the job whenever it arises. One thing is certain, the day of the tough assignment and the hard question will surely come.

Be sure everyone knows the rules

Is the interview on the record? Is the subject aware that you are a reporter writing a story for publication? This will often be obvious. You phoned, announced who you were and sought an appointment. But there are times when you will be talking with bystanders or witnesses to some incident and unless you tell them, they will not know who you are. They may be surprised and angry to find they have been quoted in a story in the newspaper next day. Unless there are special "public interest" circumstances, people should know who and what you are.

Check what the terms "on the record", "off the record" and "background" mean in your newsroom. Interpretations of these terms can vary and you should not be in any doubt. Remember too, that agreeing to these kinds of arrangements with your sources can produce problems. If you are told something by a source, but it is not for publication, and then you are told it separately by someone else, and publish it, your first source may well be unhappy and may not accept your story about the second source. As well, "off the record" sources may be "flying a kite" or using you to "run a message" they are not prepared to own. See the section on sources in chapter 1. Being used in such a way is not really your role.

Children – proceed with caution

Interviewing children can throw up more than a few problems. Children do make news, quite a lot in fact – acts of bravery, or achievement at school or sport are regulars. Your code of ethics may have something to say on the matter of interviewing them. You should check. There may be a newsroom policy too.

Do you need a parent's permission? One parent or two? Internal family relationships can be a minefield at times. And if the matter should be serious, physical or sexual abuse, for instance, are you likely to get permission from the parents anyway? One or other or both may be involved. It happens. These are all matters that need to be addressed case by case and you should address them in the newsroom.

Is there another side to the story?

This matter is covered separately in the section on "sources" in chapter 1, but good practice, being professional, fairness, and the law all require that when there is one, you actively seek the other side of the story. Depending on the story, it may not be a pleasant experience, but it has to be done. No room for shrinking violets here.

PART 5

Being professional in journalism

Ethics and choices

Reporting what goes on in the world is not necessarily a straightforward, uncomplicated activity. Not everything that happens day to day is simple. Nor are the things that happen necessarily black and white. They may well be quite complex – all manner of shades of grey. Reporting them can be a challenge, given the inevitable limits that exist on time and space. Choosing what to cover is the first issue. Choosing from that what to present is the next. All kinds of things may be left out, sometimes inadvertently, usually deliberately. What should be left out and what should be left in present serious, real and difficult choices at times for the journalist.

Nevertheless, despite the difficulties, journalism is a business in which decisions have to be made, and made smartly. A reporter or an editor might have 10 hours to deadline, which may not feel like much, or he or she might have only 10 minutes. In radio news, deadlines come around every hour. There is no time for long debates about what should or should not be done. This is never an excuse if anything goes wrong. It is just the reality of what happens. So, there is pressure in the business and those who can keep their cool while others around are losing theirs are valuable people to have in a newsroom. Quick decisions are good; quick decisions that are also the right decisions are better.

"Getting it right" in journalism is a multi-faceted task, for right means many things. It does not just mean: "Is it accurate?". It also means: "Is it legal? Is it honest? Is it fair? Is it skewed? Is it what it seems? Is it just convenient?"

Each of these questions has to be answered in the business of reporting all the time. They have to do with what it means to be a professional.

Ethical issues

Is it legal?

Is it legal? Does it break or offend against the law? There are the laws of defamation and contempt of court, and laws that may limit or prohibit the reporting of all kinds of material – a matter of a criminal record perhaps, or the identity of a child offender, or a child victim, or a sex offender or victim, or any number of other possibilities. And those are all serious matters.

You must consider the legality of your reporting of the story. But just because a story does not offend against the law, or it was obtained lawfully, does not mean there is nothing else to worry about. Just because a story is legal does not mean that should be the end of the matter. There are other considerations.

Is it honest?

It is against the law to steal someone else's things, but it is not necessarily against the law to steal someone else's work. Of course copyright and intellectual property rights are protected at law, and to steal someone's trademark or copy their design may infringe the law. Stealing a story (the intellectual property of another) is also a breach of the law.

Stealing a page or a passage from someone's book, or pinching their story without attributing the material to the original author, is called plagiarism, but we should not split hairs – it is theft.

Plagiarism is not just taking another person's words and using them as if they were your own. Taking anything without attributing it to its rightful owner is plagiarism (theft). A reporter once produced a truly remarkable photograph to accompany a story he had written. It made an enormously powerful statement in support of the story. The picture was so telling it was used, not only with the story, but also in the plug box on the front page of the paper.

Only after the paper was printed did the truth emerge. The photograph belonged to someone else. This caused embarrassment for the paper, not to mention some problems for the reporter.

Stealing is dishonest, and so is invention. To make up a story, to make up quotes, to invent a source, to add something extra for the sake of effect, are all dishonest. Such inventions have no place in journalism.

Is it fair?

It may be legal and there may be no question of dishonesty involved but publishing a story about, or a photograph of, a person in a vulnerable position or an emotionally distressed state may simply not be fair.

A source may lack sufficient experience or sophistication to understand the consequences that may flow from a story. To reveal the identity of such a source (and publishing stories without sources can produce major credibility problems for a news organisation) may leave the source open to all kinds of reactions. Their job may be on the line. There could be retribution from workmates or harassment of some kind. It might be a great story, but was the person really aware of what might happen? Did anyone spell out the dangers to the source?

To publish knowing that these issues were not canvassed with a person is unfair and irresponsible. Such matters have to be canvassed and sources have to be aware of what may lie ahead.

The research literature on the fate of whistleblowers is full of stories of people who faced terrible retribution for doing the honest and community-minded thing. Governments and public officials are just as severe as private organisations in their treatment of those who blow the whistle. Almost without exception whistleblowers' lives are changed forever from the moment they go public. The journalist has to be sure the whistleblower knows what he or she is doing.

The issue of fairness also arises in the case of the grief-stricken or those in an emotionally distressed state. Someone has died, is missing, or has received bad news. Sorrow, anger, fear perhaps, abound. These can be difficult times for the journalist. There is often an assumption that the last thing people in such situations want is a journalist knocking at the door. That may well be the case, but not necessarily.

Victims of tragedies or loss may want their story told. They may take the position that media coverage gives them a chance to warn others of the danger of whatever happened to them. In this way, they may feel that some good can come out of their suffering.

Negotiating these environments can be difficult, requiring tact, courtesy and decency. Depending on the circumstances, publishing something may not be acceptable. It may be a dreadful invasion on a very private matter. But this is not always the case. There can be equally serious public interest stakes involved, even in private grief. The murder of a couple of dozen individuals in Melbourne during the underworld war there in recent years is a good example. Journalists were not necessarily welcome, but murder in the streets is a serious matter and there is a clear public interest test that can be applied in such a case. The same test may determine that other private matters should **not** be covered. To cover them would be unfair, rather than illegal or dishonest.

Additional considerations with children

Dealing with children also brings up some difficult issues. Children are often the sources of news stories – they do interesting and even amazing things. Some suggest that talking with children should be "off-limits" to journalists, but this is nonsense. Kids are talented, brave, kind, sick, good, bad and everything else adults are. Their stories of achievement and success are heartwarming and uplifting and should be told. Their stories of abuse and harm are no less important and should also be told.

But if something bad is happening to a child and a parent is involved, as they not infrequently are, the child is no less a victim. Thus the guideline that children should be interviewed only with a parent's consent cannot be taken as a binding rule. In most cases, of course, it is appropriate. But a child who is a victim should not be denied a voice. Having to seek permission from a parent who may be involved in hurting their child is clearly a nonsense.

Publishing interviews with, or comments from, children must also pass another commonsense test. It is said that "out of the mouths of babes and sucklings come all manner of things", and this is entirely true. All kinds of things might emerge from a conversation with a child and reporting them could be entirely unfair on the child or some other person.

Finally, the law in some places may prohibit journalists reporting on child victims of harm or family breakdown without the approval of some public official. The penalties for doing so could be harsh. Whether such laws were drafted to protect the interests of the child or those who are, or should have been, looking after the child is something that lends itself to speculation. But such laws exist. As a reporter you should check what the law dealing with publishing and child protection in your jurisdiction says. You may be startled.

Is it skewed?

To emphasise or pay particular attention to one aspect of a story while ignoring other aspects is to skew a story.

In cricket, it is a legitimate part of the game. Except that they skew balls, not stories. Members of the fielding side vigorously polish the ball whenever it comes their way. But they polish only one side of it. You see them on the TV rubbing the ball on their trousers before returning it to the bowler, who also gives it a rub on his trousers just for good measure. In the right conditions and when bowled at speed, the aerodynamics involved with the half-polished ball can cause it to swing or veer violently to one side of the pitch or the other just as the batsman is about to play his stroke. Cricketers know this. Slow bowlers do something else. They expertly spin the ball as it leaves their grip. When it bites into the pitch on landing, it can veer sharply to the left or right.

Stories too can be spun or swung if one side is given special attention at the expense of the other side, or other sides. Good spin bowlers conceal their intention to spin the ball one way or the other as long as they can, and the spin on stories can be camouflaged as well. Who is quoted, what questions were asked, which answers highlighted, and so on, are all capable of skewing a story. Choosing an unflattering picture, or a flattering one, may achieve the same result.

It can be difficult for a reader to detect a skewed story. The major players may know, but how do they inform the reader? Complain? Write a letter? Put out a press release? Who will carry their complaint?

Stories can be given the ultimate skew by not covering them at all. Justification for making a decision not to cover a story is easy. Sorry, but we can't cover everything. We don't have the space. The story goes unreported. The lack of information, or knowledge, thus available to the community introduces a distortion into their perception of the world around them. Not to tell the public something is an enormous exercise of power. The problem is, journalists can't cover everything. Which is why what they do cover, and what they ignore, is so important.

Beware how you polish the ball.

Is it what it seems?

This is an area of journalism that has caused a good deal of anguish and distress in recent years. The classic examples are the manipulated photographs that have been published, thanks to the tricks computer technology has made possible. "Enhancing", distorting or manufacturing an image is now so easy a five-year-old could do it. It is a fraud of course, and quite dishonest. But it happens.

And you don't need a clever software package to conjure up a trick. A recent travel section in a newspaper ran a story on San Francisco accompanied by a picture looking down one of the famous terraced streets of the city towards the bay. There, a few hundred metres out from the shore was escape-proof Alcatraz, the infamous island prison of days gone by. Had Alcatraz been as close to the shore as the picture suggested, the authorities may well have had to deal with many more escapes from that escape-proof prison. The island is quite a distance from the city, but in the travel story pic it was just a stone's throw away.

The effect was probably not achieved via computer manipulation or anything of that nature. A decent telephoto lens on a camera in the right position will not only pull in a distant background to the point where the photographer could almost touch it, but it can make a row of parking meters or telegraph poles look like a picket fence. A wide-angle lens produces the opposite effect; pushes things further out; makes them bigger or wider than they are.

The American journalist who lost the Pulitzer Prize she had won for a story about a boy who was a drug addict lost it because the story was not what it seemed. The boy didn't exist. He was a composite. He represented a collection of individuals, not, as the story suggested, a particular boy. The story misled readers.

Stories may not be what they seem in other ways. Audiences assume, because they are led to assume, that the stories they get each day are "objective" – that they don't come with some "baggage" that advantages the interests of someone in the newsroom. Running stories that embrace a conflict of interest without declaring it, or taking advantage of one's access to the news media (which other people don't have) to push a personal barrow is a serious abuse of trust.

Some newsrooms have policies on journalists accepting "freebies", others do not. The "freebie" business is alive and well in some industries in particular, yet one seldom sees any mention of it in the media. Why might that be?

Is it just convenient?

Getting a quote from a source today but not running it until some time later, can be a serious ethical breach if the story's dynamics have changed considerably. The appropriate course is to contact the source again and ask, in the light of developments, if their views are the same as they were, and if not, how they have changed. This produces extra work of course, but quoting a source responding to questions that are several days out of date does nothing for the reputation of the newsroom. The claim that, "Well, you said it, so too bad", is just not professional.

Other conveniences exist. The stereotype is an example. Putting people into handy boxes when they may not fit, or creating labels to cover them and their activities are media shorthands that may be convenient but inaccurate or inappropriate. And recycling the same sources over and over because they can be relied upon to always come up with a punchy "grab" is another.

Journalism is a serious business and it deserves to be treated that way.

News selection

Despite all the ethical questions raised above that are important and deserving of careful attention, the journalist, nevertheless, has other considerations to weigh up.

In whose interest?

The matter of the public interest is not to be taken lightly. Stories in the public interest are usually controversial, and in almost every story with even the slightest touch of controversy to it, somebody's private interest will be affected, probably adversely. Pulling (i.e. not publishing) stories because of who might be affected is to wield considerable power. How such power is used, or abused, is a matter of great concern for readers and audiences. If the ethical questions of legality, honesty, fairness, balance, accuracy, and convenience can be dealt with, then the chips should fall wherever they fall.

This view of journalism infuriates many people. But we are not, and should not be the arbiters of what is good, bad or indifferent. When the *Weekend Independent* began to lift the lid on the drug trade in our jails, the cry went up deploring the story and some pressure emerged to have the investigation dropped. After all, drugs helped the prisoners better cope with their lives. They were calmer, and quieter, in general much happier, we were told. We were being very irresponsible. Never mind that people were being bashed, banks robbed and parents working themselves to the bone to pay for drug debts incurred in secure custody.

At one time it was said that prostitution was a victimless crime, so why did the media go on reporting stories about people breaking a silly law? Except that at the time, the "victimless crimes" of prostitution and illegal gambling were actually being franchised by the police. A good rule of thumb is, if it is against the law, report it. If the law is bad or silly, it should be changed. It is not for journalists to decide which are good laws and which are bad. Report it all and let others do something, or nothing, about it.

The right story in the right place

Journalism is all about selection and choices. The claim one hears from time to time on the radio when a newsreader says, "Here is the news", is nonsense. There is no such thing as "the news". It would be more accurate for the newsreader to say, "Here is our news".

The fact is, presenting a news story in its final form involves an absolute host of decisions. For example:
- out of all the stories that might be done, why choose this one instead of that one
- and assign the task of getting the story to this reporter and not that one
- who then contacts these people but not those
- and asks these questions but not those, in this order rather than that
- from which we take these bits and throw those away
- and put the ones we keep in that order rather than some other possibility

- and then arrange the whole thing into this kind of hierarchy (lead story on front page with a big headline) rather than that (last story before the final ad break) (or as a brief at the bottom of page 24), and so on.

These processes go on constantly in newsrooms. Media observers call it "gatekeeping" and those who do it "gatekeepers".

"Gatekeeping" is a good analogy. Farmers and graziers do it all the time when they draft their cattle and sheep. As the animals go through a race, the person working the gate opens it this way or that and the livestock are sorted into different pens. Some are in, the rest are out. And that is what happens in newsrooms. But the process is complicated, as numerous newsroom studies have revealed. Decisions are based on any number of possible influences, and value judgments made on the basis of any number of possible criteria. These might include:

- professional values, those things that people in the business generally regard as significant (political upheaval, disasters, tragedies, big sporting events, for instance)
- organisational values, those that a media group might regard as important
- newsroom values, those that might reflect the preferences of a particular editor
- individual values, the preferences of those on the newsroom floor, the chief of staff, the subs and the reporters on the job.

There are other factors. The audience or readership will be influential. A financial paper and provincial daily will probably treat the same story very differently. Which is only common sense, of course, but nevertheless, the kind of outlet involved determines news content too.

The medium itself is highly influential. Television, for instance, must have pictures. No pictures might well mean no story, regardless of how significant someone else might consider the story to be.

And what drives the operation anyway, in most cases? The answer is a commercially viable balance sheet. Ratings and circulation figures are vitally important. The evidence for this is stark. The number of newspapers that have closed in the last 30 years is bleak testament to the significance of circulation figures.

News bulletin transcripts and stories

The stories and transcripts that follow (from television, radio, a newspaper and an online site) reveal evidence of many of the matters already discussed in this book – forms of attribution, use of tenses and the significance of house style, to mention just a few. But they also say a great deal about the business of journalism itself.

The most obvious point is how different the coverage revealed in the stories and transcripts is between the outlets. All of them covered the same event, but they all made different choices in delivering their stories. Even when they used the same bits of information, they placed them in different spots, and in different contexts, in their coverage. These observations are quite central to the issue of what is involved in the business of journalism and are illustrated in the material that follows.

Television News Bulletin (6pm 26 May 2006)

Channel 9 Brisbane

Studio: A platoon of army commandos rolled into Dili in armoured vehicles getting a warm welcome from relieved locals.

They're now patrolling the streets and rebel fighters have begun to surrender.

Reporter: For the second time in almost seven years Australian troops are back in the heart of the East Timorese capital and the people are jubilant once more.

Actuality: "Really great, really great. We're really, really grateful for Australia."

Reporter: It was a show of force by soldiers in armoured personnel carriers. These men, the first of many, who will secure the city.

This time yesterday just a hundred metres from here there were fierce gun battles between government troops and the rebels.

But now it's clear the Australian troops are the ones in control.

Our Special Forces started calling on local military bases this morning . . . a friendly welcome as they set the ground rules for our peace making effort.

A short time later the East Timorese leadership ordered their troops to return to their barracks . . . but one local unit was suddenly called back to action as gunfire broke out and terrified locals began to flee.

At the UN Headquarters a small group of policemen in civilian clothes came to surrender and hand over their concealed hand guns.

There's been a tragic demonstration of the need for urgent military action. The bodies of a mother and her five children have been found inside a home which was set on fire yesterday.

On the waterfront this morning the navy transport "Kanimbla" was approaching port as the frigate "Adelaide" stood at anchor. Overhead an air force Hercules flew in more troops and supplies.

The full deployment should be complete by tomorrow afternoon. Also arriving, Mick Mumford, the man who is spearheading this latest Australian military expedition.

Actuality: "We will defend ourselves with the appropriate level of force."

Reporter: Gathered at the airport hundreds of East Timorese hoping they can escape the country. One is the wife of a policeman, one of the twelve who was massacred by their own soldiers yesterday.

Actuality: "They killed him. I don't know why."

Reporter: UN officials were outraged. They tried to head off the attack by local soldiers who suspected the police were part of the rebel uprising.

Actuality: "We have ordered it . . . make a strong protest to their local commander."

Reporter: A UN security guard was shot in the leg during the attack and he has been flown out for medical treatment.

Actuality: "Were you surprised by what happened?" "Yes, of course, we were surprised . . . but that's our job."

Reporter: During the last four weeks of chaos, many headed for this school run by Catholic nuns. Now 13 thousand people are camped in the grounds and the sisters worry how they can keep caring for so many people.

Actuality: "When you are keeping a lot of people in a small place like this, there is disease . . ."

Reporter: For our soldiers, hard work ahead, keeping apart the rivals, disarming rebels and ultimately trying once again to lay the foundation for a lasting peace.

Studio: Prime Minister Howard has criticised Timorese leaders saying they should have foreseen the troubles in the army.

Despite the arrival of our troops, plenty of Australians in Dili are taking no chances and are heading home.

Reporter: As more troops prepare to fly into Dili, hundreds of Australians, many of them women and children, are getting out.

Some have been evacuated on RAAF transport planes, clearly shaken by what they'd seen and heard.

Actuality: "It was going on around us, machine guns going off, so, yeah, just wanted to get out for my child, I'm having a little baby. It was time to get out."

Reporter: They worry about those they left behind.

Actuality: "We have a lot of friends over there. It's very tough to have to leave them in a very difficult situation."

Reporter: But there's also relief at the arrival of Australian forces.

Actuality: "When the locals heard the Australian troops were coming, they were ecstatic, they were really happy."

Reporter: The Prime Minister says our full complement of soldiers will remain in East Timor for as long as it takes.

Actuality: "It's a very foolish, short-sighted thing to pull them out before their job is completed and these tasks always last longer than you expect."

Reporter: Meanwhile, Mr Howard today had a blunt message for the East Timor government. He said divisions in the country's army were plain to see months ago. Yet the situation was allowed to spiral out of control.

Actuality: "There's no point beating about the bush, the country is not being well governed."

Television News Bulletin (7pm 26 May 2006)

ABC Brisbane

Studio: Australian troops are on patrol in East Timor tonight and more soldiers are on the way.

By the end of the weekend all 13 hundred combat troops will be in place.

Although the streets of the capital Dili are calmer, the young nation still faces an uncertain future.

No one knows exactly how many were killed in this week's fighting, but at least nine policemen died and six bodies were found in a burnt-out house.

Reporter: Australian troops touched down in force and quickly moved to secure Dili's airport.

Their commander says they'll shoot if they have to.

Actuality: "It's certainly our hope though, that anyone who is currently in conflict will go back to their containments, go back to their barracks, go back to their places of duty."

Reporter: And this is what they could be up against . . . whether they're rebels, vengeful police or armed civilians, is hard to tell. But today they advanced towards Dili's main UN compound which reported an attack.

East Timorese soldiers responded by taking up positions in the area. There was some shooting. But no real fight.

Late today Australian troops secured the UN premises.

When Australian troops were here in 1999, it was pretty clear who the militia were. Now they face the same obstacle faced by East Timorese locals . . . working out who is who and who they are loyal to . . . and working out whether they want to just be friends . . . or kill you.

Yesterday's Timorese army attack on disarmed police killed nine and injured almost 30, after a UN negotiation went badly wrong.

Actuality: "And I regret very much again that promises was not kept by few individuals who are on the scene."

Reporter: Today Australian troops moved in to secure the police station where the attack occurred.

This local woman says she is happy with her new neighbours, but still afraid because much of Dili remains unsafe . . . as six women and children found out last night . . . killed when their house was torched on the city's edge.

Actuality: "I think yesterday we saw the worst day in the history of this small country and we're all very hopeful things will get a lot better very soon, very dramatically."

Reporter: But disunity on the ground is now reflected at the top.

East Timor's prime minister Mari Alkatiri has dismissed claims by the president's supporters that Xanana Gusmão now has exclusive control of the country's security forces.

Studio: Operation Astute is now in top gear. The defence force now says Australian combat troops should be in East Timor by tomorrow, one day ahead of schedule.

John Howard has vented his anger at the East Timorese government, demanding leaders smarten up their acts to prevent a repeat of this week's deadly revolt.

Reporter: Soldiers weighed down with packs, body armour and weapons, C130's fuelling up to push on with the round-the-clock airlift, Darwin was abuzz with activity today as the East Timor build-up pressed ahead with all speed.

Deputy defence chief Ken Gillespie flew in from his hazardous overnight mission in Dili securing approval for the terms of Australia's intervention from East Timor's president and prime minister.

Defence chief Angus Houston expects the 13 hundred troops to be in place 24 hours ahead of schedule.

Actuality: "All the combat elements will be in by the end of tomorrow."

Reporter: In addition, four Blackhawk helicopters are in Dili, the frigate HMAS Adelaide is in Dili harbour, the transport Kanimbla is off East Timor's south coast, its sister ship the Manoura is due in Dili tomorrow, and the landing ship Tobruk is due on Monday.

The first task is to get the East Timorese soldiers accused of firing on unarmed police and the breakaway troops led by Alfredo Reinado to retire from their battle stations.

Actuality: "We will use whatever level of force is required to see that they are disarmed."

Actuality: "What we need to do is go in there with plenty of combat power, demonstrate that we have a very good capability and cause these groups to retire to their barracks."

Reporter: Some defence analysts, including the government's own Strategic Policy Institute have pointed to the pressures of Australia's military responsibilities in the so-called Arc of Instability.

Radio News Bulletin (7pm 26 May 2006)

ABC Brisbane

Studio: About 450 Australian soldiers are on patrol in East Timor tonight and more troops are on the way. By the end of the weekend all 13 hundred combat troops will be in place.

Although the streets of Dili are calmer, the country still faces an uncertain future.

At least nine policemen and several civilians have been killed in the wave of violence this week.

Reporter: The bodies of a woman and at least four children were found in the charred ruins of a house in Komora, a few kilometres west of Dili. It's understood she was the sister-in-law of the Interior Minister Rogerio Lobato who was responsible for the country's police force. Another four houses nearby were also torched in yesterday's violence.

Australian troops have now begun scouting through the capital Dili in a bid to restore law and order to the strife-torn region.

Studio: The head of the defence force, Air Chief Marshal Angus Houston, says the primary aim is clear.

Actuality: "What we need to do is go in there with plenty of combat power, demonstrate that we have a very good capability and cause these groups to retire to their barracks."

Studio: More evacuees have arrived in Darwin tonight aboard a defence force aircraft.

Reporter: Twenty-three evacuees have arrived on the latest flight from Dili. Most of them were Australians working in the East Timorese capital. Some are foreign nationals either booked into hotels or flying off to other destinations. Darwin resident [. . .] says the East Timorese people are feeling better now that the Australian troops have arrived in the country.

Actuality: "The situation is a lot calmer than it was yesterday. Things seem to have calmed down a lot on the streets, there are people on the streets again, there's still a lot of gunfire up in the hills but it seems the Australian troops secured the airport and too, the Australian mission, but not the whole city yet."

Reporter: More evacuees are expected tonight.

Studio: And Japan is withdrawing its aid workers from East Timor because of the security concerns there.

Reporter: Japan's International Cooperation Agency, JICA, has told the ABC it will fly its 29 aid workers out of Dili tonight. They'll be taken to the Indonesian capital Jakarta while assessments continue of the security situation. Japan is telling travellers not to visit East Timor and says around 60 of its citizens who normally live in the country should consider leaving as soon as possible. The government says it is closely monitoring the situation to see what assistance it can offer.

Metropolitan newspaper front page story (27 May 2006)

Sydney Morning Herald

By Mark Forbes and Tom Allard

East Timor's military has armed the militias ripping the country apart, presenting a major challenge to the Australia-led international intervention, the Foreign Minister, José Ramos Horta, has revealed.

In a surprise move last night, more than 50 United States marines arrived at Dili International Airport. Until now, there had been no mention of US involvement in the military intervention.

As East Timor's President, Xanana Gusmao, accused the government of losing control, Dr Ramos Horta told the Herald last night that some army elements had given "weapons to civilians, in the most irresponsible manner. This is very dangerous. Disarming them is difficult."

He said the Timorese army had been ordered back to its barracks and told to halt all fighting. "That will eliminate one of the sources of the problems."

The revelations came as Australian troops intervened to halt fears of an attack on the United Nations compound by rebel soldiers in the heart of Dili.

After a bloody massacre on Thursday – in which a mother and her five children were among those slaughtered – Australian armoured personnel carriers were guarding the compound, with UN officials concerned more assaults could be launched against them. Blackhawk helicopters circled overhead with snipers dangling out their doors.

Australian troops are trying to secure key locations around the capital, including the nearby police headquarters. Almost 1800 ADF personnel are involved in the East Timor operation, including the 1300 troops on deployment plus 500 supporting staff, some in Darwin and others in ships off Dili.

Fighting between rebel forces and loyalist troops continued despite the Australian deployment. Rebels even invited the Herald to accompany them as they attacked government targets. The death toll from the past 48 hours has climbed to more than 18, with confirmation that 12 police were slaughtered by government troops in an attack on the police headquarters on Thursday. The bodies of a woman – related to the Police Minister – and her five children were discovered in a Dili house that was torched by a rampaging mob just hours before Australian troops arrived on Thursday. The mother, her body blackened, was clutching her four-year-old daughter.

Last night it was unclear who was in control of the military: the Prime Minister, Mari Alkatiri, rejected Mr Gusmao's announcement he was assuming "all control" of the country's security forces, claiming the move was unconstitutional. Mr Gusmao's Australian wife, Kirsty Sword, told the ABC that Timor's armed forces did not appear to be taking orders from anyone. "I think Xanana just feels very strongly that clearly the Government is unable to control the situation. It's unclear exactly under whose control the armed forces are operating.

"They seem to be targeting the families, now, of police officers down in Dili. That's the latest information we've received. It's hard to believe these could be orders given from above and so it would appear that the armed forces are actually acting arbitrarily."

The Prime Minister, John Howard, who joined in the condemnation, blamed the unrest on the Timor government. He said there was a "significant governance problem inside East Timor and he hoped this week's events were a wake-up call for the country's leaders.

"There's no point beating about the bush," he said. "The country has not been well governed and I do hope that the sobering experience for those in elected positions of having to call in help from outside will induce the appropriate behaviours inside the country."

The Foreign Affairs Minister, Alexander Downer, said there was "no doubt" there was an element of disagreement between Mr Gusmao and Dr Alkatiri.

"It's a politically fractured situation," he said. However, he said the East Timorese Government was operating as normal. "The Prime Minister is still very much the prime minister," he said.

About 450 Australian troops were in Dili by noon yesterday, including a commando company from the 4th Battalion and four Blackhawk helicopters. The Chief of Defence Force, Air Chief Marshal Angus Houston, said the capital was "much calmer", though the situation remained "unstable and dangerous".

Before the troops made their presence known and secured the UN compound there were skirmishes between military police and a small team of rebel soldiers. The rag-tag ensemble of loyalists – some were barefoot – ran up and down the street intermittently spraying fire at their adversaries.

There were clear signs of militias working in concert with the loyalist military police; several men brandishing weapons were wearing jeans.

Locals were pleased by Australia's arrival. "It's all very good to see the Australians," said Carlos Suarez, from the suburb of Caicoli, where the violence took place.

Lieutenant Colonel Mick Slater, the commander of the Australian forces, said he did not want to disarm the warring parties but get them to return to barracks.

ABC Online (7pm 26 May 2006)

The East Timorese Government has confirmed reports that a woman and at least four children were killed in Dili yesterday.

Several houses in Dili were torched yesterday; one of them was home to a family with four or five children.

The charred bodies of a woman and children were found in the ruins, but it is not clear if they died in the fire or were killed before.

One government official said he saw photos suggesting they were killed in a machete attack first.

It is understood they were relatives of the Interior Minister Rogerio Lobato, who controls East Timor's police force, and may have been targeted by anti-government forces.

Extreme violence

Chief of the Australian Defence Force has revealed that violence in Dili was so extreme yesterday that a plane carrying his deputy was ordered to turn back from East Timor.

Air Chief Marshal Angus Houston says the arrival of Australian troops helped calm the situation in Dili, but earlier it was too dangerous for the Vice Chief of the Defence Force to land.

"What I did was I turned the aircraft around and gave them direction to go with the force that was coming in a little later on, so I guess that indicates the level of my concern," he said.

Related video

The full deployment of all 1,300 troops committed to East Timor has been accelerated as a result of increasing violence.

[Real Broadband] [Real Dialup] [Win Broadband] [Win Dialup]

The leader of the rebel military faction in East Timor says Australian troops deployed to the country have nothing to fear from those he commands.

[Real Broadband] [Real Dialup] [Win Broadband] [Win Dialup]

Related audio

There have been conflicting reports over who is in control of armed forces in East Timor. It is also unclear how many people were killed in a battle outside the main police station yesterday.

[RealMedia 28k+] [WinMedia 28k+] [MP3]

East Timorese Prime Minister Mari Alkatiri has dismissed claims from supporters of the President that Xanana Gusmao had assumed exclusive control of security forces.

[RealMedia 28k+] [WinMedia 28k+] [MP3]

Kirsty Sword, wife of East Timorese President Xanana Gusmao, says her husband has lost faith in the Government of Mari Alkatiri and has taken control of all military, including international forces.

[RealMedia 28k+] [WinMedia 28k+] [MP3]

ABC correspondent Anne Barker says comments by Mari Alkatiri and Xanana Gusmao suggest there is a split in the East Timor Government.

The author gratefully acknowledges the assistance of the Australian Broadcasting Corporation, Mark Forbes and Tom Allard (*The Sydney Morning Herald*) and Channel Nine, Brisbane, for permission to reproduce the transcripts of the stories above.

Bibliography

Armstrong, M., M. Blakeney & R. Watterson 1983, *Media law in Australia: a manual*, Melbourne: Oxford University Press. (p. 105 cited)

Audit Bureau of Circulations 2006, Report, Jan–June, Sydney: ABC. (pp. 10–54 cited)

Australian Government Publishing Service 1994, *Style manual for authors, editors and printers* (5th edn.), Canberra: AGPS. (pp. xi & 3 cited)

Australian Press Council 2001, 'Reporting guidelines: Opinion polls', General Press Release No. 246 (iv) July 2001, viewed 10 Oct 2006, http://www.presscouncil.org.au/pcsite/activities/guides/gpr246_4.html

Australian Provincial Newspapers 1997, *APN style guide*, Rockhampton: *The Morning Bulletin*. (p. 9 cited)

Blundell, W. 1988, *The art and craft of feature writing*, New York: Penguin Books.

Carlyon, L. 2001, *Gallipoli*. Sydney: Pan Macmillan Australia Ltd. (pp. 3, 4 & 6 cited)

Chase, M. 2004, 'High tech trial in fight against drugs, bombs and weapons', *The Independent Monthly* (May p. 3) Brisbane: The University of Queensland.

Courtenay, B. 1989, *The power of one*, Ringwood: Penguin Books. (pp. 1 & 4 cited)

Darling, C. 2003, 'The royal order of adjectives' in Ellen Beck & Dawn Taylor *Parts of speech review*, English works site, viewed 10 Oct 2006, http://depts.gallaudet.edu/englishworks/grammar/partsofspeech.html#adjectives quoting http://webster.commnet.edu/graqmmar/adjectives.htm

Doneman, P. 1995, 'Drugs in jail', *The Weekend Independent* (May 19, p. 1) Brisbane: The University of Queensland.

Drum, S. 2005, 'The Choir', *Writing for the reader*, Brisbane: The University of Queensland.

Ellerman, Z. 2005, 'Murrii court', *Writing for the reader*, Brisbane: The University of Queensland.

Gascoigne, C. 1994, 'Security firms fail the test', *The Weekend Independent* (September 30, p. 1) Brisbane: The University of Queensland.

Gleeson, M. 2001, *Courts and the Rule of Law*, Rule of Law Series, University of Melbourne, November 7.

Gowers, E. 1973, *The complete plain words* (2nd edn), Harmondsworth: Penguin Books. (p. 219 cited)

Grundy, B. 1998, 'Sin, sweat and sorrow', *Inside Queensland*, vol. 1, no. 2, Brisbane: Wamboin Pty Ltd. (pp. 23–26)

Grundy, B. 2001, 'Centre inmate, 14, pack-raped', *The Courier-Mail* (November 3, p. 3) Brisbane.

Grundy, B. 2001, 'Painful recollection of a wretched crime', *The Courier-Mail* (November 3, p. 14) Brisbane.

Henningham, J. 1988, *Looking at television news*, Melbourne: Longman Cheshire. (pp. 154–155 cited)

Kohn, H. & D. Weir 1975, 'Tania's world', *The best of Rolling Stone: 25 years of journalism on the edge*, New York: Doubleday. (p. 174 cited)

London, J. 2005, 'Bird flu drugs hit the internet', *The Independent Monthly* (October, p. 1) Brisbane: The University of Queensland.

Macafee, M. 2003, 'Vietnam voices', *Writing for the reader*, Brisbane: The University of Queensland.

Macquarie Dictionary 1991, 2005 (2nd & 4th edns) Sydney: Macquarie Library.

Mengler, C. 1996, *Report of the Commission of Inquiry into drugs in Queensland custodial correctional centres*, Brisbane: Queensland Government.

Morris, A. (QC) & E. Howard 1996, *Report of an investigation into allegations by Mr Kevin Lindeberg and allegations by Mr Gordon Harris and Mr John Reynolds*, Brisbane: Queensland Government.

Naess, O. 2005, 'I saw the red roses', *Writing for the reader*, Brisbane: The University of Queensland.

Needham, K. 2003, *Sydney Morning Herald* (March 1, p. 3) Sydney: John Fairfax and Sons.

News Limited 2001, *Style: a guide for journalists*, Surry Hills: Nationwide News Pty Ltd. (p. 40)

Niesche, C. 2000, 'The Kirribilli cat ducks out for a bite', *The Australian* (March 4, p. 1) Sydney: News Ltd.

Nye, W. 1881 'Suggestions for School of Journalism', reprinted in *The Penguin book of columnists*, C. Silvester (ed) 1997, London: Penguin Books. (p. 3 cited)

Paus, K. 2005, 'Byron for beginners', *Writing for the reader*, Brisbane: The University of Queensland.

Quinn, S. & V. Filak (eds) 2005, *Convergent Journalism*, Oxford: Focal Press (pp. 218–221 cited).

Robinson, G. 2004, 'Movies present opposing views of journalism', *The Independent Monthly* (February, p. 16) Brisbane: The University of Queensland.

Rochfort, S. 2001, 'First day of school given a run-through to head off tantrums and tears', *Sydney Morning Herald* (October 26, p. 3) Sydney: John Fairfax and Sons.

Silvester, C. (ed) 1997, *The Penguin Book of Columnists*, London: Penguin Books.

Spigelman, J.J. 2003, 'The rule of law in the Asian region', Address to the International Legal Services Advisory Council Conference, March 20, Sydney.

Wheildon, C. 1990, *Communicating or just making pretty shapes*, Sydney: Newspaper Advertising Bureau of Australia.

White, S. 1996, *Reporting in Australia* (2nd ed), South Yarra: Macmillan. (p. 268 cited)

Whitton, E. 1987, *Amazing scenes*, The Fairfax Library: Sydney. (pp. 8, 17 & 23 cited)

Whitton, E. 1994, *Trial by voodoo*, Milsons Point: Random House. (pp. 9–12 cited)

Whitton, E. 1998, *The cartel: lawyers and their nine magic tricks*, Glebe: Herwick Pty Ltd. (p. 12 cited)

Wilkinson, M. 2001, 'PM enlists emus, kangaroos to save Jackie Kelly's hide', *Sydney Morning Herald* (October 25, p. 1) Sydney: John Fairfax and Sons.

Wolfe, T. 1975, *The new journalism*. London: Pan Books. (pp. 25–26, 35, 46–47)

Further reading

Avieson, J. 1980, *Applied journalism in Australia*, Waurn Ponds: Deakin University.

Baugh, S. 2005 (3rd edn), *Essentials of English grammar*, New York: McGraw-Hill.

Conley, D. & S. Lamble 2006 (3rd edn), *The daily miracle*, Melbourne: Oxford University Press.

Fogg, C. 2005, *Release the hounds*, Crows Nest: Allen and Unwin.

Gregory, P. 2005, *Court reporting in Australia*, Melbourne: Cambridge University Press.

Jervis, R. 1985, *News sense*, Adelaide: Adelaide Newspapers.

—— 1988, *More news sense*, Adelaide: Adelaide Newspapers.

Pearson, M. 2004, *The journalist's guide to media law: dealing with legal and ethical issues*, Crows Nest: Allen and Unwin.

Phillips, G. & M. Lindgren 2006, *Australian broadcast journalism*, Melbourne: Oxford University Press.

Quinn, S. & V. Filak (eds) 2005, *Convergent journalism*, Oxford: Focal Press.

Strunk W. (Jnr) & E. B. White 1979, *The elements of style*, New York: Macmillan.

Tanner, S. (ed) 2002, *Journalism investigation and research*, Frenchs Forest: Pearson Education Australia.

Tanner, S., G. Phillips, C. Smyth & S. Tapsall 2005, *Journalism ethics at work*, Frenchs Forest: Pearson Education Australia.

Tapsall, S. & C. Varley (eds) 2001, *Journalism: theory in practice*, Melbourne: Oxford University Press.

Weaver, B. 2003, *Catch the wave*, Melbourne: RMIT Publishing.

White, S. 1996 (2nd edn), *Reporting in Australia*, South Yarra: Macmillan Education Australia.

Index